THE
ITALIAN-AMERICAN
COOKBOOK

THE ITALIAN-AMERICAN COOKBOOK

A Feast of Food from a Great American Cooking Tradition

JOHN MARIANI AND GALINA MARIANI
ILLUSTRATIONS BY LAURA TEDESCHI

THE HARVARD COMMON PRESS
BOSTON, MASSACHUSETTS

The Harvard Common Press
535 Albany Street
Boston, Massachusetts 02118

Printed in the United States of America

Printed on acid-free paper

Library of Congress Cataloging-in-Publication Data

Mariani, John. F.
The Italian-American cookbook : a feast of food from a great American cooking
tradition / John Mariani and Galina Mariani ;
illustrations by Laura Tedeschi.
p. cm.
Includes index.
ISBN 1-55832-165-9 (hc : alk. paper) — ISBN 1-55832-166-7 (pbk. : alk. paper)
1. Cookery, Italian. 2. Cookery, American. I. Mariani, Galina. II. Title.

TX723.M3282 2000
641.5945—dc21
00-033475

Special bulk-order discounts are available on this and other Harvard Common Press
books. Companies and organizations may purchase books for premiums or resale, or may
arrange a custom edition, by contacting the Marketing Director at the address above.

10 9 8 7 6 5 4 3 2 1

COVER AND BOOK DESIGN BY KATHLEEN HERLIHY-PAOLI WITH JOANNA YARDLEY,
INKSTONE DESIGN

12/00

TO MISHA AND CHRISTOPHER

CONTENTS

PREFACE

❧

The turning of a century offers a convenient vantage point for reflecting on just what makes people eat what and the way they do. And when the closing century is the twentieth, which brought such unimagined changes in every aspect of human civilization, there seems every reason to think about and commemorate the extraordinary ways that a gastronomy has changed, mutated, adapted, and evolved.

This book, then, is both an exploration of and a delectable introduction to a cuisine that is easily the most diverse, the most popular, and the most evolved of any that arrived on these shores during the great waves of immigration in the late nineteenth century. It treats the full panoply of Italian-American cooking, from fried calamari served in seaside fish houses to pasta showered with white truffles presented at deluxe dining rooms from New York to San Francisco. What began in the kitchens of immigrants, where grandmothers, mothers, and aunts sought to feed their families according to sacrosanct tradition but with the ingredients they found on this side of Ellis Island, grew into a genre all its own.

Our book is a loving look at a hundred years of a continually evolving cuisine, one that in another hundred years may seem quite different but will surely be based on the best traditions of the Italian immigrant experience, whether those immigrants came from the poorest neighborhood of Naples or an aristocrat's vineyard in Tuscany. Without recognizing this continual evolution, there seems little reason to write this book in the first place.

Initially we were reluctant to undertake a project that appeared to us to be at the very least outdated, and at best merely another Italian cookbook recycling the same old material. We have also been frequent critics of the mediocrity of so many Italian-American restaurants that cut corners, use inferior ingredients, and never evolve beyond the clichés of a genre that had become cloyed with "red sauce" and fried foods.

Our familiarity with the wonderful diversity of regional foods in Italy, always based on the freshest seasonal ingredients, has soured us on much of what passes as Italian-American cookery, even though some of the "classic" items in the Italian-American repertoire, from *mozzarella in carozza* to cheesecake, have always been among our favorites. We could easily name Italian-American restaurants where you can get one or two terrific dishes, some with their own regional American twist to them. We also believe that the very finest Italian restaurants in the United States—those that have built on the best concepts of Italian cuisine—rank with the best in Italy itself.

And we are certainly enthralled by many dishes made by Italian-American home cooks, whose specialties, often made only for feast days, are among our most cherished culinary memories. As detailed in the introduction to this book, Italian immigrant cooking evolved rapidly from what was basically a poor people's food, predominantly southern Italian in origin, to become its own genre, which was usually inexpensive, high in calories, and huge in portion size. When so-called northern Italian restaurants became popular in the 1970s and '80s, the ingredients and techniques used gave rise to a new appreciation of what was possible.

But it was with the amazing wave of first-rate Italian ingredients, such as balsamic vinegar and extra-virgin olive oil, which began filtering down to the markets of every major city and suburb that a radically new style of Italian-American cookery took hold.

As Neil Simon once observed, "There are two laws in the universe: The Law of Gravity, and Everybody Likes Italian Food." Italian dishes are now found on 75 percent of American restaurant menus, with 51 percent of Americans claiming to eat Italian food often. According to the National Restaurant Association, there are now more than 15,000 table-service Italian establishments in the country (compared to 17,000 Chinese and 10,775 Mexican), along with 3,154 limited-service Italian eateries, which combine to generate sales of nearly $9 billion annually.

More important, every section of the United States offers its own style of Italian food. In New Orleans they add a Creole accent; in the West there is a California buzz to everything from Wolfgang Puck's "Jewish pizza" to San Francisco's Chicken Tetrazzini. In St. Louis "toasted" ravioli is a regional favorite. In 1964 in Buffalo, New York, Teresa Bellissimo created Buffalo Chicken Wings for her famished sons (which they were not allowed to eat until midnight, because it was Friday, when good Catholics don't eat meat). In Philadelphia, Pat Olivieri created the Philly Cheese Steak around 1930, and Marzetti's restaurant in St. Louis came up with a form of Sloppy Joe called Johnny Marzetti.

In addition, the influx of serious Italian restaurants—like San Domenico in New York City, Valentino in Santa Monica, and Tony's in Houston—has played an important part in bringing refined *cucina Italiana* to the world's attention.

What we began to realize was that the "old" Italian-American cooking has been transformed by the availability of better ingredients and more serious cooks. Modern Italian cuisine has become a part of America's gastronomy as it has in France, England, Germany, even Japan and Hong Kong, where you're just as likely to find pasta primavera and saltimbocca as in New York or Los Angeles.

We realized the truth of the adage that there really are no bad dishes, just bad cooks, and in writing *The Italian-American Cookbook* our goal has been to revisit the old-fashioned Italian-American dishes, including those that seemed to have become tired clichés, and to make them the best we could, using good ingredients and modern techniques while at the same time respecting the traditions of the dish. At the same time, we set out to gather the best recipes from the finest chefs who are using Italian ingredients and culinary ideas to wondrous advantage. Many of these chefs are not of Italian extraction at all; others are recently arrived immigrants from Italy who are giving more and more diversity to the genre. It would be hard to find an haute cuisine French restaurant here or abroad where ravioli (albeit stuffed with foie gras and black truffles) is not a standard item on the menu. American chefs today use balsamic vinegar and extra-virgin olive with far more frequency than they do red wine vinegar, butter, or other vegetable oils.

This book, then, attempts to take in the whole panoply of Italian-American cooking, from the white truffle risottos to the ubiquitous *tiramisù*. By drawing on recipes and reminiscences of friends, relatives, restaurateurs, bakers, and pastry-makers, the book presents more than 250 recipes—the very best of their kind.

Our goal is to show just how far Italian-American cooking has come and how it continues to evolve each year, not only getting closer to the original sources in Italy but incorporating the best American ideas and products into the mix, so that one can speak of the new Italian-American cuisine as one of the major food cultures of the world.

ACKNOWLEDGMENTS

This book began when Harvard Common Press publisher Bruce Shaw came up with the idea of doing a serious look at Italian-American cooking, and we are very grateful for the opportunity to be the ones to do it.

To our agent, Heide Lange, our continuing thanks for her support and enthusiasm, and to our editor, Dan Rosenberg, whose support from day one carried us along blissfully through the weeks and months of writing and recipe testing, and to Pam Hoenig for seeing the book to fruition. For zealously ferreting out so many fine photographs for this book, Sunshine Erickson deserves enormous credit, as does our copy editor, Katherine Ness, for her work.

For information, recipes, and friendship we thank Ingrid and Fabrizio Aielli, Andrea Apuzzo, Alberto Baffoni, Paul Bartolotta, Lidia and Joseph Bastianich, Mario Batali, Brian Bellanca, Fern Berman, Dominic Biancardi, Pam Blanton, Daniel Boulud, Edward Brivio, the Capatanini family, Lucio Caputo, Kimberly Charles, Arrigo Cipriani, Anna and Tony Cortese, Joe Cosenza, Alan Davidson, Emily Dello Russo, Lynn DiMenna, Todd English, Odette Fada, Nora Fine, Larry Forgione, Jessica Genova, George Germon, Laurent Gras, David Greco, Denise Harrigan, Frank Iacobellis, Verity Liljedahl, Michael Lomonaco, Sirio and Egi Maccioni, Laura Maioglio, Augusto Marchini, Robert Mariani, Tony and Marisa May, the Miglucci family, Robert Mondavi, Paul Murphy, Tom Passavant, Tessie Patterson, Bill Pepe, Wolfgang Puck, Joseph Scelsa, Arthur Schwartz, Barbara Seldin, Piero Selvaggio, Marilyn Sofia, Jane and Michael Stern, Melissa Stevens, Tony Vallone, and Brian Whittmer.

And most of all we thank our parents, Renee and Al Mariani, and Lana and George Stepanoff-Dargery, for all they taught us about food and life.

INTRODUCTION

TOWARD AN UNDERSTANDING
OF THE NEW ITALIAN-AMERICAN CUISINE

"Italian-American" may be an easily understood hyphenate, but the term "Italian-American food" is far fuzzier as a convenient descriptor of a gastronomy that draws from myriad influences on both side of the Atlantic.

While most countries' cuisines are the result of centuries of adapting to the influences of other, sometimes invasive, food cultures, Italian-American food was born in the early twentieth century and has evolved, decade by decade, to the point where it is a legitimate genre all its own, one that has had a remarkable influence on other food cultures—even to the point of altering the way people in Italy itself now eat.

Walk down the Champs Elysées in Paris, along Knightsbridge Road in London, or through the Ginza in Tokyo, and you'll find restaurants whose menus closely copy Italian-American models. Even in Milan, pizzerias have English names like Paper Moon, and only after *tiramisù*, which originated at El Toulà restaurant in Treviso, became wildly popular in the United States did it find its way onto menus in Rome, Florence, and Naples.

Rare is the contemporary Michelin-starred French chef who does not dot his menus with ravioli and cannelloni, while cooking with olive oil and *aceto balsamico* as much as he does with butter and red wine vinegar. Rarer still is the "California grill" in the United States that does not list pastas and pizzas among its offerings. Dishes like Osso Buco (page 275) are as common on American menus these days as they are on Italian-American.

This is a far cry from the time when Italian-American food was considered rather crude stuff riddled with garlic, drowned in "red sauce," accompanied by "dago red" wine. As Waverly Root noted of garlic in his encyclopedia, *Food*, "Garlic has been the vehicle in the United States of a self-reversing snobbery. Before I left America to live in Europe in 1927, you were looked down upon if you ate garlic, a food fit only for ditchdiggers; when I returned in 1940, you were looked down upon if you didn't eat it." The pizza—

now with "gourmet toppings"—was once regarded as nothing more than cheap, filling snack food or something you ordered on Friday night before going out somewhere else.

The iconography of Italian-American restaurant decor was set by Hollywood in film after film where the tablecloths were always checkered, bottles of Chianti hung from the ceiling or doubled as candle holders, the waiters spoke widda big-ga eye-tal-yun accent, and the plates always contained spaghetti and meatballs.

Most Italian-American restaurant owners played to those clichés because Americans—their customers—seemed to adore them. How this all began and how Italian-American food became so distinct from the regional cooking of Italy, and eventually such a powerful force in international gastronomy, says much about the Italian immigrants' ability both to adapt and to capitalize on the possibilities American society offered.

The story begins, of course, within the wider context of the Mediterranean basin, for Italy's position in that region and its own natural resources have always made it ripe for trade and conquest. The Greek and North African influences on the food culture of southern Italy, particularly Sicily, were tremendous from the very beginning of the region's history, and after Rome's conquest of what was then the known Western world, Italy drew to it an amazing diversity of foods and culinary ideas from Gaul, Britain, Germany, Iberia, and Byzantium while at the same time exporting Roman foods, wines, and manners.

With the fall of the Roman Empire, Italy was divided into three large regions. The north was dominated by the German rulers of the Holy Roman Empire, the middle by the papacy, and the south by a succession of Norman, German, French, and Aragonese rulers; all brought strong culinary influences to bear on those regions. And while the common people chronically suffered from terrible food shortages, Italy itself remained fertile and fecund.

By the end of the Crusades, Europeans' appetite for Eastern spices had grown insatiable. Much of the supply came from the Middle East through Venice, one of the powerful new city-states that had thrown off foreign domination.

In the wake of Marco Polo's travels to the East (1271–1295), the voyages of other Genoese explorers like Ugolino and Vadino Vivaldo, Lanzarote Mallocello, and, most famously, Cristoforo Colombo, the Venetian Alvise da Cadamosto, the Florentine

Amerigo Vespucci, and Portuguese like Ferdinand Magellan, Diogo Cão, Pero de Covilha, and Vasco da Gama were undertaken to find a route to the wealth of spices to be found in the Orient. It is now quite clear that one of the most important, and certainly the most immediate, results of Columbus's "discovery" of the New World was how it revolutionized the way the rest of the world would eat. Before Columbus and other explorers brought back tomatoes, potatoes, corn, chocolate, and peppers, such foods were unknown in Europe, Africa, and Asia. Within a century of their import from the Americas, those food cultures were transformed. As Raymond Sokolov has written in *Why We Eat What We Eat* (1991), "The ostensibly traditional foods of billions of living people are the mute documents of a process set in motion by Columbus."

In turn, coffee and sugar were exported to the Americas, where they were grown in vast plantations whose European owners, backed by the ships and guns of European powers, not only served to enslave and wipe out entire New World civilizations but also altered the balance of those powers in a series of wars entirely economic in origin.

During those centuries of European empire building and colonization, Italy did not even exist as a national entity but only as numerous city-states. The Italian royal courts, particularly that of the Florentine Medicis, became the tastemakers of their day. When Caterina de Medici moved to France upon marrying Henri II in 1533, she brought with her fifty chefs, waiters, and household personnel who helped introduce a new refinement to the French court's cooking; she also brought the two sexes together in one dining room, which had hitherto been segregated.

Yet these city-states were themselves ripe for colonization by Spain, France, and the Austro-Hungarian Empire, each of which brought their own culinary touches to the local regional fare. Culinary scholars still debate whether Vienna's Wienerschnitzel or Milan's *costoletta alla milanese* came first, and it was the Spanish who brought peppers to southern Italy. The domination of Italy by foreign powers continued well into the nineteenth century, and it was not until the unification of Italy in 1861 that one could even begin to speak of an "Italian cuisine," though by then its regional food culture was perhaps richer and more varied than any in Europe. After Unification and the subsequent

Neil Simon once wrote, "There are two laws in the universe: The Law of Gravity, and, Everybody Likes Italian Food."

industrialization, the general outlines of what might be characterized as indigenous Italian cookery began to emerge as more and more Italians gained access to ingredients that were once available only in specific regions. The first mention in print of *spaghetti* (actually *vermicelli*) with tomato sauce appeared in 1839, in a book on Neapolitan home cooking, and it was not until 1875 that the canning of tomatoes from southern Italy had any marked effect on the consumption of tomatoes in the rest of Italy.

Prior to the Unification there had been cookbooks detailing what people ate in Italy, but these were almost exclusively written by and for aristocrats' or wealthy families' cooks. There had been Roman authors like Apicius, a gourmet in the reign of Tiberius, who wrote down recipes, but the first attempt at a true cookbook on Italian cuisine did not appear until 1475, when the librarian of the Vatican, Bartolomeo Sacchi, published *Platina de Honestate Voluptate et Valetudine Vulgare* (*Concerning Honest Pleasure and Physical Well-Being*) in Cremona. Sacchi, later known simply as "Platina," drew mainly from Roman sources for his recipes and advocated a less contrived, more healthful kind of cooking than the extravagant cuisines of the Renaissance courts. Platina's work was widely disseminated, and it appeared in a French edition in 1505. In 1570 Bartolomeo Scappi published *Cuoco Secreto di Papa Pio Quinto* (*Cooking Secrets of Pope Pius V*), which detailed the food and service in the court of Pope Pius V and earned an international reputation for its dissertations on table service. It also included the first picture of a new invention—the fork.

But there was little in print that could be made use of by the Italian home cook—who in any case had no need for a cookbook because he or she probably could not read or write. The publication of Pellegrino Artusi's *La Scienza in Cucina e l'Arte di Mangiar Bene* (*The Science of Cookery and the Art of Eating Well*) in 1891—thirty years after the Unification—had an importance that went beyond the novelty of its being the first cookbook to bring together many of the strains of Italian cookery in one volume. Artusi's book, written in formal Italian, also had the effect of spreading the Italian language among a developing class of people who were learning to read and write Italian, though they might still speak their local dialect at home.

Artusi's work did not delve deeply into regional Italian cookery, nor did he show much interest in the humblest of foods prepared by the majority of Italians of his day, who were extremely poor and who had to make something palatable from very meager resources. His understandable pride in the food of his own region (Tuscany) favored the cooking of the north, but he did not pretend that he was setting down a strict, pro forma "classical" recipe for a dish, as did Auguste Escoffier in his text on French classic cuisine, *Le Guide Culinaire* (1903), which was itself preceded by Carême's standards-setting *L'Art de la Cuisine au XIXe Siecle* (1833).

France's gastronomy had certainly developed along similar provincial lines to Italy's, though the country itself was far more unified early on than was Italy. And France developed a more sophisticated gastronomy both at home and in the new taverns, bistros, brasseries, and restaurants that blossomed after the revolution of 1789, when the chefs and cooks of the aristocratic homes, finding themselves without patronage, opened the new eating establishments for the burgeoning French bourgeoisie.

THE WAY WEST

While roadside *osterie* and *taverne* had long existed in Italy, it was really not until the twentieth century that full-fledged restaurants appeared in the larger cities. Nor was there a population large enough to support more than a few, for few Italians had the means to eat out. Not unreasonably, Italians also regarded the food at restaurants as inferior to what could be made at home, and the true repository of regional cooking is still to this day in the homes. Even in the poorest of Italian villages, the people take enormous pride in their indigenous cooking, and dishes made one way in one town may be made quite differently in another.

But it was poverty, shackled to an oppressive system of land ownership, that forced the *contadini*—the term used in southern Italy for "peasant"—to leave a land still rich in natural resources. The landlord system made it impossible for the *contadini* ever to rise above a subsistence level, no matter how hard they worked. Peasants seeking to buy their own small plot of land were forced to borrow money from those same landlords at outrageous interest rates of up to 50 percent. The *contadini* endured such abuses for centuries, until the prospect of emigration to America became a reality in the

late nineteenth century. Emigrating from Abruzzi to New York in 1910, Pascal D'Angelo wrote in his autobiography that in the past a peasant had to turn over four-fifths of whatever he grew to his landlord—who made his tenant pay for the manure and seeds to work the plot: "This was possible up to a short while ago. But today such a thing is absolutely impossible since no peasant would agree to it unless his head were not functioning normally. And what is it that saves the man and keeps him from being ground under the hard power of necessity? The New World! Previously, there was no escape; but now there is."

Ironically, much of the industrialization of Italian agriculture in the early twentieth century was the result of landowners being forced to buy machinery in order to replace the cheap labor of the *contadini* who had emigrated. And Benito Mussolini's exhortations to Italians to increase the size of their families were the result of so many of them having left for America.

From the years 1890 to 1910 more than 5 million Italians emigrated to the United States, 4 million of them from southern Italy—Campanians, Calabrians, Abruzzesi, Pugliesi, and Sicilians. In fact, between 1880 and 1920 one out of every four immigrants was a Sicilian. Ninety-seven percent of them came through New York's Ellis Island and settled quickly in the East Coast cities, while many others went on to New Orleans. By the 1920s there were more Italians living in New York than in Florence. The living and working conditions of those decades of momentous immigration were difficult in the extreme, in a climate of furious bigotry against the newcomers. The manipulation of people who did not speak English was easy and effective, so it should not be surprising to learn that fully half of the Italian immigrants returned to their native country, some almost immediately, some to fight for the motherland in World War I, others only after they had made enough money in America to do so. The tragedy of the southern Italian *contadini* was that they had come from a strictly agricultural background yet found themselves in an urban ghetto upon arriving in the New World, living under wretched conditions in tenement neighborhoods where they had little opportunity even to learn to speak English.

But the immigrants who stayed bore sons and daughters who went to school, learned English, and created a new hybrid—the Italian-American—who joined German-, Irish-, Polish-, Swedish-, and Jewish-Americans in the great melting pot.

While the immigrants of the eastern cities inched their way toward respectability, the possibilities for advancement in the West, specifically California, were much brighter for the many northern Italians who settled there. By 1905 there were approximately 60,000 Italians in San Francisco, and the fertile farmland of Napa, Sonoma, Mendocino, and other counties was far closer to what the Italians imagined America could offer them. Others readily found jobs in the fishing industry of the Pacific Coast and some were soon able to afford their own boats.

No chronicler of those years ever suggested that the Italians were not resourceful or hardworking. They were perfectly willing to enter into any business or industry that would hire them, whether it was moving furniture, quarrying limestone and marble, repairing shoes, working as seamstresses and tailors, or opening little groceries.

At first these food shops catered exclusively to other Italians within their neighborhoods, and there was good trade in importing canned and bottled goods from Italy. "[Southern Italians'] nostalgia for the food of their homeland paralleled their nostalgia for their patron saints," wrote gastronomic chronicler Massimo Alberini. "They sent to Italy for cases of macaroni, and they managed to provide reasonable substitutes for missing ingredients." Photos, posters, and food labels of the time show cans of imported tomatoes right alongside boxes of macaroni made in the United States and cans of Carnation evaporated milk. By the 1930s there were eight major macaroni plants operating in Brooklyn and Queens. The grocers made their own salami and sausages, bakers reproduced the shapes and styles of Italian regional breads, and though the mozzarella could not be made from water buffalo's milk as in the Old Country, they learned to make cheeses from American cow's milk. Mexican chile peppers replaced Calabrese *peperoncini*, and wines were made from Zinfandel grapes shipped in from California, where a thriving wine industry developed, largely run by families with names like Sebastiani, Foppiano, Rossi, Martini, Pedroncelli, Mondavi, and Gallo. (Curiously, few Italian immigrants in New York made wine commercially, although the Hudson Valley Wine Company was established in 1907 by a retired Wall Street banker named Alexander Bolognesi.)

The immigrants clung fast to their culinary roots, and turn-of-the-century social workers would report of Italian families "not yet Americanized, still eating Italian food." Even far from the eastern cities, in small communities where Italians settled, their diet closely resembled that in the Old Country. In her book *We Are What We Eat: Ethnic Food and the Making of Americans*, Donna R. Gabaccia describes how, in a ten-block Italian-American neighborhood called Greenbush in Madison, Wisconsin, the daily diet included polenta, vegetable soups, wild greens, eel, dried codfish, offal, baby lamb, *cassatta* cake, and Italian cookies. The men made their own wines, which they called *marsala*.

The Italian immigrants everywhere ate fairly well and quite nutritiously, while spending less than a quarter of their income on food, whereas back in Italy they had been spending up to 75 percent. My grandmother, who was born in the United States in 1887 to parents who arrived here from a small town in Campania in 1883, spoke of how her father would have a veal chop every morning before going off to work as a plasterer, and no one ever went to bed hungry. Still, despite the cheap price of bread in New York, they wasted not a crumb, wrapping a big round crusty loaf in a damp cloth to keep it from drying out from day to day until it was finished. (Of course, being of a generation that was already feeling more American than Italian, my grandmother yearned for the white loaf bread she saw American children eating and disdained the coarser whole-wheat bread she had at home.)

FEEDING THE AMERICANI

Of course, none of the immigrants had any experience eating in or running a restaurant, nor was there usually any excess money to spend on such frivolities as dining out. They were, however, well aware that Americans did love to eat out and saw that American chophouses, German *rathskellers*, Jewish delicatessens, and Irish taverns were enormously popular. They had also heard of the grand dining palaces like Delmonico's in New York; the original restaurant was opened by an Italian-Swiss sea captain back in 1831 and had set the standard for deluxe dining in America. Such places glowed with gaslight, rich mahogany and crystal, gleaming mirrors, fine silverware, and crisp white tablecloths. Waiters wore dark jackets and aprons, and there were fine

wines from California and New York State, some with Italian names on their labels.

None of this was lost on the immigrants, many of whom found employment as cooks and waiters in those restaurants. At palatial restaurants like Delmonico's, Rector's, and Louis Sherry's, the chef might be French or German, but the kitchen crew was largely Italian. In fact, the kitchen staff at the elegant St. Regis Hotel in New York, opened in 1906, was composed entirely of Italians. By the last quarter of the nineteenth century, Italian dishes in the international style were also to be found on the menus at such restaurants—*The Epicurean*, a comprehensive cookbook written by chef Charles Ranhofer in 1893, included recipes for gnocchi, polenta, ravioli, risotto, and "Macaroni, Neapolitan Style," made with tomato and larded beef, quite obviously drawn from Pellegrino Artusi's cookbook published two years earlier.

It was inevitable, then, that the Italian-Americans would open their own eateries. At first they were small family businesses, where mamma was the cook, pappa the dining-room host, and the children the waiters. They operated within the Italian sections of eastern cities like New York, Boston, New Haven, and Providence, as well as in San Francisco, where full-scale restaurants in the Italian North End, such as Fior d'Italia and Scolari's, were up and running by 1910. In 1930 a restaurant called Lucca opened there, advertising "All You Can Eat for Fifty Cents," which included antipasto, soup, spaghetti or ravioli, meat, something called "fried cream," and a tray of pastries and ice cream.

With very few exceptions, almost all Italian-style restaurants in the East were opened by southern Italians who based their menus not on any Old Country restaurant models but on their own family food. For this reason the Italian-American restaurant was not a replication of any in Italy but a whole new kind of eating place. You would as soon find platters of pork chops with vinegar and sirloin steaks as you would spaghetti and meatballs, most of them lavished in garlic-rich "red sauce," which became a synonym for long-cooked tomato sauce and synonymous with the Italian-American restaurant itself. Dishes that would once have been considered a feast-day extravagance, like veal, swordfish, lasagna, and cheesecake, were everyday items on the new Italian-American menus. Portions were larger, there was plenty of meat and sausages, and everyone ordered rich desserts like spumoni ice

cream, zabaglione, and cannoli. Dinner ended with a drip-pot of espresso, served with lemon peel (which originally was added to take away the bitterness of the inferior coffee used, but later became a fixture at Italian-American restaurants).

New dishes were adapted and elaborated on from old ideas. One will not find terms like "veal *Sorrentino*," "clams *alla Posilippo*," and "fillet of sole *alla Livornese*," on any menu in Italy, yet they have become standard items at every old-fashioned Italian-American restaurant. In most cases such dishes were named by cooks commemorating their home towns. In others they were created in honor of famous Italians, as in "turkey alla Tetrazzini," named after the reigning Italian diva of the early twentieth century, Luisa Tetrazzini. Even though few Italians had ever heard of a dish called "fettuccine Alfredo," recipes for it began appearing in American cookbooks after Hollywood movie stars Douglas Fairbanks and Mary Pickford raved about the dish served at Alfredo di Lelio's restaurant in Rome, where they spent their honeymoon. So famous did the dish become in this country that "Alfredo" became synonymous with a sauce made with heavy cream and Parmesan cheese, even though the original contained no cream at all.

It is amazing how quickly such dishes were adapted as standards on Italian-American menus, so much so that one 1939 New York restaurant guide remarked that the city was "full of Italian restaurants—good, bad, and indifferent—all serving the same courses of minestrone, spaghetti, ravioli, scaloppine and tortoni."

Like their menus, the decor of Italian-American restaurants did not vary much from the clichés of red-checkered tablecloths, stucco walls, and murals of the Bay of Naples. What began as small storefronts expanded and expanded, until Italian-American restaurants of the 1930s grew to enormous size. Multitiered, with a warren of private and banquet dining rooms, decked out with facsimiles of baroque Italian sculpture, paintings of the owner's father and mother, and photos of famous customers, the Italian-American restaurant became a place where everyone came for a good time, plenty of food, cheap prices, and maybe some music by a strolling accordion player.

In New Orleans, where thousands of Sicilians settled, the menus were pretty much the same as in the northeastern cities, though the influence of well-entrenched French and Creole culinary traditions added a good deal of butter to the Italian-American recipes, so that a local favorite—spaghetti bordelaise—is basically spaghetti with garlic and oil to which butter has been added, which has nothing to do with a traditional French bordelaise sauce made with shallots and red wine. Local seafood was featured far more than anywhere else in the United States. In San Francisco, Italian-American restaurants became oddly associated with Bohemians—not the immigrants from Bohemia but the unconventional artists and writers who found such inexpensive restaurants and coffee-houses amenable meeting spots.

Italian-Americans certainly didn't invent the steakhouse, which had been popular since beef became readily available in the United States after 1870 when refrigerated railway cars made that possible, but they did create a sub-genre in New York, where steaks and lobsters were served alongside spaghetti, plates of tomatoes and mozzarella cheese, and generous slices of cheesecake. The Palm restaurant in New York, originally a speakeasy opened in 1926 by Pio Bozzi and John Ganzi, set the no-nonsense style of such Italian-American steakhouses, whose decor and brash style of service have been copied ever since around the United States. (Incidentally the name "Palm" was a mistake: The restaurant was supposed to be called "Parma," but a clerk registering the name didn't quite understand the owner's accent, and so Palm it became.) The Palm's menu is built mainly around steaks and lobsters, but to this day the restaurant still offers five Italian-American veal dishes, linguine with clam sauce, spaghetti with garlic and oil, *rigatoni bolognese*, *penne pomodoro*, and *broccoli rabe*.

And then there was the novelty called "pizza," whose success is, without question, more an Italian-American than an Italian phenomenon. Before the days of the great immigration, pizza was a food enjoyed exclusively by the poor people of Naples, who folded over the dough and ate it as a kind of sandwich. Its fame remained wholly localized, even after a successful promotional stunt by a *pizzaiolo* named Raffaele Esposito, who commemorated the visit to Naples in 1889 of the new Queen of Italy by naming a pizza after her. Pizza *alla Margherita*, made in the three colors of the new Italian national flag—red tomatoes, white mozzarella, and green basil—became suddenly fashionable among Neapolitans, and the idea came to America via the Neapolitans who settled in the eastern cities.

The first known pizzeria to open here was G. Lombardi's, established in 1905 on Spring Street in New York's Little Italy.

From there its popularity grew rapidly, at first in and then beyond the Italian-American neighborhoods. Given the low cost of the ingredients, Italian-American pizzas grew larger than the Neapolitan original, and the toppings grew quickly in number, often with a regional American twist, like the white clam pizza created at Pepe's Pizza, which opened in New Haven in 1925. "Chicago-style deep-dish" pizza, cooked in a black iron skillet, was the creation of Ike Sewell of Pizzeria Uno in 1943. The thickness of the dough and the lavish use of disparate ingredients typified the midwestern idea that making a dish larger is always better.

Americans regarded the pizza as fast food—some called it junk food—right along with hamburgers, hot dogs, and French fries. Friday night became "pizza night," first among Italian-Americans whose Catholicism prohibited them from eating meat on that day, and later, as toppings grew heavier and more regional, among Americans of any background. Back in Italy the appreciation of this humble food item was still largely confined to Naples until well after World War II, and the 1953 hit "That's Amore," sung by Italian-American crooner Dean Martin, made much more sense here than in Italy.

Nevertheless, even among Italian-Americans, pizzerias were considered to be the low end of the restaurant chain, and many owners of pizzerias considered it a rise in class to later open a full-fledged restaurant that did not serve pizza.

The appearance of true restaurants—*ristoranti*—above the pizzeria and trattoria level was indicative of the acknowledgment of both Italian-American cooking and the rise in social status of Italian-American entrepreneurs. In New York a few Italian-run restaurants grew to be among the most fashionable of their time. Barbetta, opened by Sebastiano Maioglio in 1906 on West 39th Street and moved in 1925 to West 46th Street, was one of the fine-dining Italian restaurants of the era, set in an elegant townhouse; to this day Barbetta caters to famous musicians, opera singers, and Broadway stars. Its menu has always included an array of Piemontese specialties like *fonduta* and *agnolotti*, and the restaurant has always served imported Italian wines.

The apotheosis of the big-hearted, carnival-like Italian-American restaurant of the first half of the twentieth century was Mamma Leone's, which originally opened in 1906 in a little room above a wine cellar at the back of the Metropolitan Opera

THE GREATEST MOVIES EVER MADE FEATURING ITALIAN FOOD

Big Night—*Every scene, set in an Italian restaurant in New Jersey in the 1950s.*

Moonstruck—*The family dinners.*

The Godfather—*The recipe for tomato sauce with red wine.*

The Godfather, Part III—*How to make gnocchi.*

Breaking Away—*A midwestern father complains about eating so much "eeni food"— fettuccine, linguine, tortellini. . .*

Goodfellas—*Slicing garlic with a razor blade.*

Lady and the Tramp—*Tony feeds the dogs spaghetti and meatballs.*

Summertime—*Katherine Hepburn courted by Rossano Brazzi over dinner.*

Little Rascals—*Making spaghetti for Miss Crabtree.*

Perhaps the quintessential movie scene that shows the romantic appeal of Italian-American food is from Walt Disney's Lady and the Tramp, in which the hero and heroine are serenaded to the tune of "Bella Notte" by the owner and the chef of an Italian restaurant.

and moved to much larger premises on West 48th Street in 1914, playing host to everyone from Will Rogers to George M. Cohan. At Mamma Leone's Mamma was always there, dressed in black, overseeing every aspect of her domain. The nude statues were scandalous, the baroque dining rooms—more like feed halls—full of color, light, and noise. You sat down with your family and were presented with big baskets of Italian bread and a huge wedge of cheese. Platters of celery and olives followed, then garlic bread, massive portions of lasagna, gnocchi, meatballs and macaroni, juicy pork chops, fillets, veal steaming with marinara sauce and melted cheese, and crispy fried calamari. There was music in the air, streamers, party hats, and waiters who spoke in singsong broken English, laughed heartily at everything the Americans joked about, and promised the ladies there were no calories in the cheesecake.

Mamma Leone's was one of the first theme restaurants, and its theme was an Italian-American fantasy that had absolutely no basis in reality back in the Old Country, where the majority of Italians were still economically deprived of the pleasure of going out to dinner. For most Americans, the experience of dining at an Italian restaurant like Mamma Leone's was one of the cheaper

Many of the stereotypes about Italian-American restaurants were epitomized in the gargantuan Mamma Leone's restaurant in New York, with its carnival-like atmosphere and its menu of sacrosanct Italian-American dishes.

forms of entertainment available in a country that was still pulling itself out of the Depression.

By the late 1930s Italian-American food was well established around the United States, but it never did receive the same respect accorded French "cuisine" of the same period, even though the ingredients used in French kitchens were no better or worse than those used in Italian kitchens, and the likelihood of a French meal being cooked by an Italian back in the kitchen was very high. An Italian-American restaurateur would have to be suicidal to charge the same price for veal scaloppine as a French restaurateur did, even if the latter served half the amount of veal as the Italian-American.

Back in Italy *ristoranti* were still of minor importance and were designed more for tourists than for locals. The grand hotels of Italian cities featured what became known as "continental cuisine," an amalgam of French and Italian favorites dressed up to look "fancy." This was the kind of food likely to be encountered on the Italian cruise ships, where cooking and service did have a higher degree of finesse than in the trattorias in Italy or the Italian-American restaurants in the United States.

Many of those cooks, maître d's, and waiters on the Italian liners jumped ship to remain in America, where they easily found work at restaurants of every stripe. Cooks from Abruzzi were particularly well regarded, and many opened their own restaurants. Others went to work at the Italian Pavilion at the 1939 New York World's Fair, which offered many Americans their first glimpse of refined Italian food and service. The setting was a simulation of the Italian ocean liner M. V. *Victoria*, and one could feast on all manner of dishes not found on the typical Italian-American menus of the day—saltimbocca, *agnolotti*, and *fonduta* with shavings of white Alba truffles, all complemented by fine wines like Barbera and Barolo poured by genteel Italian waiters who could have been Hollywood movie stars.

The New York World's Fair was an eye-opener, not just for Italian food but for all those nations' foods represented, and out of it grew the most famous French restaurant of the day, Le Pavillon, which set the standards for French dining rooms for the rest of the century, and set the high prices one came to expect at such dining rooms, even while Italian restaurants were expected to be inexpensive.

ALLA CASA

Meanwhile, in Italian-American homes, the traditional foods were still being consumed with enormous relish. As historian Arthur Schlesinger, Jr., has noted, after a single generation in this country, the sons and daughters of immigrant families shook off almost all their traditions, including their ancestors' language and dialects, except for the culinary ones. In most Italian-American families pasta might be served two or three times a week; tomato sauce was served over chicken, meat, and seafood; Sunday dinner was a family affair where the table was set with the old dishes from an ancestor's region; and feast days like Christmas and Easter featured a wealth of traditional dishes.

In my own family the approval of the marriage between my father and mother depended heavily on whether the prospective bride could reproduce her future mother-in-law's Abruzzese dishes. Later on, our Sunday meals were a combination of those dishes right along with American foods: We'd likely begin with breadsticks and prosciutto, then lasagna, move on to roast beef with Yorkshire pudding, and end with anything from cheesecake to pecan pie. Wine was not something my father and his friends drank regularly; Scotch for cocktails and beer for dinner was more the rule.

When we did go out to dinner, it was invariably to an Italian-American restaurant in the Bronx or Manhattan, where the menus were typical.

Certainly after World War II Italian-Americans had ample

The despicable association some restaurants have tried to make between Italians and Italian mobsters has long been part of American advertising, not least in the names of the nationwide chains Godfather's Pizza and Little Caesars Pizza. One Chicago company mounted an ad for its Italian restaurant with a photo of Italian gangsters, reading "Bring the mob." Worst of all was a restaurant in New York called Monzù, whose full-page ads pictured what was obviously meant to be a gunned-down mobster lying on the tile floor of a barber shop, the copy reading, "Italian food to die for."

The license such restaurants take in playing off the association of Italian mobsters with the Italian community as a whole is an appalling affront to an entire ethnic group and one that perpetuates vile stereotypes that every Italian has suffered from.

resources to cook whatever they felt like eating, and portions were far larger than any served back in the Old Country. Indeed, one of the hallmarks of Italian-American cooking is what one TV ad for Italian food called "*abbondanza!*"—an abundance almost unknown by the immigrants. One of the dishes that symbolizes just how far Italian-American food had progressed was lobster *alla fra diavolo*, which would have been an unimaginable luxury back in the Old Country as well as to the first generation of immigrants. Here was a dish whose name meant "brother devil," owing to the spicy, chile pepper–spiked tomato sauce that the lobster was cooked in. The American lobster, a species unavailable in European waters, would be an extravagance unthinkable in Italy; in America it was a still an extravagance, but one that could be indulged several times a year, and it became a fixture on Italian-American restaurant menus.

Italian-Americans ate well at home and grew taller and larger as a result, leaving many Americans to assume that Italians in the Old Country were short and fat—a misapprehension corrected by looking through photos of the thin, impoverished immigrants who got off the boat at Ellis Island. The image of the big, fat, roly-poly Italian-American was perpetuated as an ethnic stereotype, sometimes meanly, sometimes lovingly, the latter in the Walt Disney animated feature *Lady and the Tramp* (1955) when a rotund, mistachioed Italian-American restaurateur serves two stray dogs spaghetti and meatballs while serenading them with the beautiful song "Bella Notte."

The movies have always portrayed Italian-Americans with an obtuse ignorance of how stereotypical those portrayals are, setting so many scenes of so many gangster movies in Italian-American restaurants that Americans have come to connect Italian-American restaurants with the romantic, if threatening, heroes of films like *Scarface*, *Al Capone*, and *The Godfather*, which did nothing to change the image of Italian food in the United States. The bloody gunning down of Mafia dons in or outside of Italian-American restaurants reinforced such stereotyping to the point where such places became tourist sites (as well as tourist traps). Some restaurateurs even took to dressing up like gangsters as portrayed in movies, and decorated their dining rooms with photos of cinematic Mafiosi, while midwestern pizza chains dared name their eateries—with complete impunity—Godfather's Pizza and Little Caesars.

When Americans cooked Italian-American food at home, it almost invariably came out of a can or a box. It was actually a Frenchman named Alphonse Biardot who first put spaghetti in a can under the Franco-American label in 1887 (later purchased by Campbell Soup Co.). Chef Boyardee canned spaghetti (originally called the more difficult to pronounce "Chef Boiardi" after its creator Hector Boiardi, an immigrant from Piacenza), introduced in the 1950s, grew in popularity right along with the new TV dinners and other frozen foods. The first frozen pizza, produced by Celentano Brothers, appeared in 1957 and spurred a huge industry in frozen Italian foods.

By the 1950s Italian-American cookbooks had become available, including a remarkably good paperback entitled *The Italian Cookbook,* published by the Culinary Arts Institute of Chicago, whose staff lacked any Italian-American names but whose consultant was one Marion Granato, owner of Granato's Pizzeria Restaurant in Chicago. In its preface the authors make a statement quite advanced for its day: "The bases of the most colorful Italian dishes are tomatoes, garlic and olive oil. Yet, foods in Italy are as diversified as they are traditional. It is not at all unusual to find an Italian who likes neither tomato sauce nor garlic—he probably has his spaghetti with butter and cheese sauce and prefers Melon and Prosciutto to an ordinary antipasto course."

Italian-American recipes were printed in the women's magazines like *Ladies' Home Journal* and *Good Housekeeping,* although there were no significant Italian cooking shows of any kind until well into the 1980s, despite the success of Julia Child's *French Chef* series in the 1960s.

WHEN MACARONI BECAME PASTA

The "gourmet era" that began in the 1960s—led, of course, by the well-entrenched promoters of French cuisine—did have its effect on Italian food, initially more so here than in Italy. At first, recently arrived Italian restaurateurs, many of them coming off the last of the Italian ocean liners of the era, captured Americans' attention by advertising something called "northern Italian" cooking, which was usually little more than the addition of a few regional dishes from Tuscany or Umbria to the old standard menu of Italian-American classics. There were more cream sauces (despite the rarity of such in northern Italian cooking), a somewhat lighter touch with garlic, oregano, and tomato, and an emphasis on the supposed superiority of freshly made "pasta"—a word that replaced "macaroni" and "spaghetti" in an effort to distinguish this new Italian-American style from the old. This was supposed to reflect a more refined style of Italian cuisine, somewhat closer to French and therefore worth paying more for.

It hardly mattered that most of the Italians who ran such restaurants were the same ones who had run the old spaghetti houses or who had come over from Sicily, Abruzzo, and Campania rather than from northern regions like Liguria, Tuscany, and the Veneto. The style of the new restaurants was what was important: The red-checkered tablecloths and stucco were replaced with white linen and artfully mottled walls. Chianti-bottle candle holders gave way to Venetian glass sconces, and red waiters' jackets to black tuxedos. There was a good deal of tableside service—the mixing of pasta with sauce, deboning of fish, and whipping of zabaglione. And prices shot up beyond what any Italian-American could have imagined a decade earlier. The $5.95 bowl of spaghetti was replaced with the $15 plate of fettuccine, and the platter of thin veal chops at $12.95 was traded in for a single massive veal chop at $29. The carafe of unnamed red wine referred to by many customers as "dago red" was dumped in favor of bottles of estate wines from Tuscany and Piedmont, decanted over a candle.

There was much show biz in all this, but there was also a definite rise in the quality of Italian-American food. As Americans got used to paying more for such dishes, the quality of ingredients improved and there was more reason to use the best olive oil, the best balsamic vinegar, the best tomatoes from Marzano, the most delicate prosciutto di Parma (allowed into the United

TOUJOURS, LES FRANÇAIS!

So condescending toward Italian food is France's famous Larousse Gastronomique cooking bible that its entire section on pasta comprises less than two pages. Its directions for cooking pasta say only to "plunge the pasta into a large quantity of boiling water" and to "drain the pasta completely when it is cooked." In its two pages on Italy, Larousse notes, "Choose any ordinary Italian dish and it is the replica of one that was once enjoyed by gourmands of ancient Rome," which completely ignores the historic fact that tomatoes, potatoes, corn, and peppers did not reach Italy until a thousand years after the fall of the Roman Empire.

States by the FDA only as of the 1980s), the most fragrant fresh porcini mushrooms, and the first white truffles of the season. This last item became such an event of the fall season that prices of up to $75 for a portion of risotto with a shaving of the gems from Alba were insignificant to those who wanted to be the first to eat them or impress their friends with them.

The earliest Italian cooking show on American TV was called Cooking with the Bontempis. It was shown live, requiring Pino Bontempi to sing Italian arias (badly) while his wife finished off the cooking in the kitchen.

New Italian-American "classics" were created, like pasta alla primavera (page 157), made up on a whim one evening by the owner of New York's very French Le Cirque, Tuscan-born Sirio Maccioni. The mention of this dish in the *New York Times* made it an enormous hit, and every Italian-American restaurant, and many of other sorts, had to have it on their menu. Eventually pasta alla primavera found its way into the frozen food section of the supermarket, along with fettuccine Alfredo, sole Florentine, and chicken parmigiana. Breaded veal scaloppine topped with chopped radicchio, endive, and tomato became an overnight cliché on menus under various names like "veal *giardiniera*," while *tiramisù* became ubiquitous in the 1980s and 1990s.

As those decades wore on, the dazzling style of those initial "northern Italian" dining rooms gave way to a much more refined regional style of restaurant run by owners who actually came from the regions they promoted. In New York one can now dine on the distinctive foods of Liguria, Tuscany, Abruzzo, Piedmont, Rome, Sicily, and Calabria, while in Dallas and Houston there are two Sardinian restaurants. A few restaurants, like San Domenico in New York, Spiaggia in Chicago, and Valentino in Santa Monica, though not specifically regional, have elevated the food and service of Italian food in this country to the point where they are quite literally copied by chefs in Italy itself. Valentino, in particular, seems to symbolize just how far Italian-American food has come, for while owner Piero Selvaggio rigorously oversees a kitchen dedicated to the highest principles and traditions of Italian cuisine, there is a definite Californian and American style to everything served there. This is evident in dishes like sweet corn risotto, a pasta stuffed with Sonoma County goat's cheese, and service of Hudson Valley duck foie gras with hundred-year-old balsamic vinegar. The extra-virgin olive oil may well be from California too, and the wine list has just as many great Chardonnays and Zinfandels as it does Barbarescos

and Barolos from Piedmont. Valentino was a pioneer of this style of Italian-American food, which has found expression throughout the country. Nor can one ignore the contributions of Austrian-born California chef Wolfgang Puck, whose "gourmet pizzas," such as the "Jewish pizza" topped with smoked salmon, sour cream, and caviar (page 378), have completely changed the way Americans regard that former fast food. At his celebrity-rich Hollywood restaurant Spago, Puck put his classical French training to good use, producing a new genre called "Cal-Ital" cuisine, which relied on the best California produce and his dazzling sense of style to create dishes like saffron fettuccine with Maine lobster, tomatoes, and spinach, and butternut squash risotto with sautéed Louisiana shrimp, mascarpone, and sage.

Curiously enough, a retro-chic that has attached itself to the more old-fashioned style of Italian-American restaurants, complete with red checkered tablecloths and vats of red sauce cooking on the stove. One of the first, called Carmine's, opened in 1991 on New York's Upper West Side, fitted out to look like one of those turn-of-the-century Little Italy restaurants everyone assumed had become passé. Yet Carmine's gimmicky success engendered imitators in every major American city, so that old-fashioned pork chops with vinegar peppers, manicotti, clams Posillipo, and cheesecake are all back in favor. The difference and it is a significant one—is that such dishes are now being made with much finer ingredients, from good olive oil to first-rate imported pastas.

Though once at the bottom of most publishers' lists, Italian cookbooks started to appear among the best-sellers. In fact, so many Italian cookbooks came out in the 1990s that a separate category had to be created for some of the cookbook awards. Many of these beautifully produced volumes capitalized on the new style of Italian-American cooking; others were as authoritative as any written in Italy, by authors like Giuliano Bugialli, Marcella Hazan, Anna Teresa Callen, and quite a few non-Italians. Some of the best cookbooks on regional Italian food have been written by Arthur Schwartz (Naples), Colman Andrews (Liguria), Matt Kramer (Piedmont), and Clifford Wright (Sicily)—all passionately devoted to investigating the roots and traditions of the foods of the Old Country. Then, in the mid-'90s, there was a rash of books reviving interest in the old-fashioned Italian-American food before World War II. At least one—the despicable *Mafia Cookbook*—traded

on the worst stereotypes of a restricted and minuscule segment of Italian-American society.

The authority of the best cookbooks has influenced much of what is within the pages of this book. In *The Italian-American Cookbook*, we have tried to gather together all the strains of traditional Italian-American food and to show how they can rank among the most delicious foods in the world. We have been amazed to see how Italian-American food has evolved to the point where it is not just the favorite ethnic cuisine of all Americans but it actually sets the standards for Italian-style food in the rest of the world.

Not for a moment are we suggesting that the new Italian-American cuisine is superior to the great traditional regional cooking in Italy or to the immigrant food that established the genre in the first place. It is simply a different kind of food based on a gastronomy that, like America itself, has accepted many outside and internal influences, some of which have as much to do with fashion as they do with good taste.

There is a great deal of snobbery in food these days. We hope that this book will go a long way toward explaining how and why Italian-American food developed along the lines it did, from a peasant immigrant cookery to an adaptive one that has become far more than one might ever have imagined. We have tried to show that "toasted" ravioli from St. Louis can be as delectable as Indian *samosas* or Russian *pelmeni*; that a carpaccio of seafood is a natural extension of the original beef carpaccio served at Harry's Bar in Venice; that a Chinese-American chef like Ming Tsai, born in Ohio, can marry Italian and Asian flavors in impressive harmony; and that a simple plate of good spaghetti with golden olive oil and a little sautéed garlic can be among the most wonderful dishes in any food culture.

—JOHN MARIANI

INGREDIENTS

As we emphasize again and again in this book, nothing good can come from inferior ingredients. This is true of every cuisine in the world but has particular meaning in Italian cookery because so many of the dishes are so simple and so much based on seasonal ingredients. Without the best-quality ingredients, the dish is bound to taste less than wonderful. While it may seem odd to name a plate of sliced mozzarella, basil, and tomato *Insalata Caprese* (page 118) when such a simple amalgam of ingredients could be made almost anywhere, it is with justifiable pride that Capri gives its name to the dish, because in season the basil and tomatoes, along with the mozzarella of the region, are at their best in and around Capri and the Amalfi coast.

A brief look at the ingredients used in Italian cooking, and at their counterparts in American markets, is crucial in understanding why, so often, the same dish here never tastes quite the way it does in Italy. Thank heavens that the availability of first-rate imported Italian ingredients—from extra-virgin olive oil to prosciutto—has blurred these distinctions so that now some of the finest Italian food in the world is to be found on American shores, in both restaurant and home kitchens.

Nevertheless, American ingredients are very much a part of the traditions and flavors of Italian-American cuisine: A great American-raised veal chop puts to shame most of what you would find in Italy, and there are olive oils coming out of California today that would be a match for the finest from Tuscany. In this cookbook we recommend using the best ingredients available, no matter where they come from, in order to produce the best results. (A source list for all such ingredients is given at the end of the book.)

ANCHOVIES

Though Italians eat them in every possible form—fresh, salted, marinated in oil—in the United States anchovies are most commonly found salted or marinated in oil and sold in cans or

bottles. (Fresh anchovies may be found occasionally at international seafood markets.) The salted variety—the best now coming in from Sicily—come with the bones still in, but they are preferable to the canned, filleted variety. The salted anchovies should be rinsed, the bone structure pulled out, and the anchovy separated into two fillets.

While anchovies undoubtedly have a very strong taste, good ones are not all that "fishy," and, when fresh, can be enjoyed simply grilled with olive oil and lemon. The salted and marinated anchovies have a remarkable ability to add a subtle depth of flavor to many dishes even when they are not discernible in the dish (see our Osso Buco recipe, page 275). Many people who don't like anchovies would be surprised how often they've eaten them in Italian dishes without knowing it.

Once you open a can or bottle of anchovies, use them fairly soon, although the oil does act as a preservative. Store them in the refrigerator.

BASIL

Fresh basil, now readily available year-round in American markets, is essential to making Italian tomato sauces, pesto (see page 128), and many other dishes. Dried basil is nearly worthless, acrid and counterproductive. Fresh basil has the smell of summer in it, and the best basil is grown in summer.

The best part of a basil sprig comes from the smallest, youngest shoots at the top of the plant. They are more fragrant and have a lovely peppery quality, but are never bitter. In the market look for basil that has a tender but not flaccid leaf. The leaves should be shiny, the young ones at the top a lighter green. Cutting out the main stem in the center of the basil leaf is not really reasonable, though some cooks believe it will make it less bitter.

It is possible to freeze basil by first rinsing the leaves and removing the stems, then drying them with paper towels and sealing them in a sealable plastic bag. They may darken in color, but they will retain a good deal of flavor. An alternative is to preserve the fresh leaves in olive oil, but there is a remote possibility of botulism poisoning, so we do not recommend it.

BEEF

American beef, to our minds, is the best and most flavorful in the world, the result of animals that are well fattened and carcasses that are left to age for weeks in order to achieve a real beefy flavor. The top grade—USDA Prime—though somewhat compromised over the past decade, has consistent fat marbling inside the meat (not on the outside) that gives it enormous flavor. The aging provides tenderness, although a well-aged piece of steak should not be mushy. Other grades—Choice and Select—are not in the same league with Prime, but they are still fattier and more aged than European beef.

In Europe beef is aged very little, if at all. Europeans prefer the fresh taste of the meat, and even the highly praised *Val di Chiana* beef of Italy hasn't the flavor of American beef. But a massive Bistecca alla Fiorentina (page 259) is a delicious and popular meal in northern Italy.

Cuts of meat also differ in Europe, but within the pages of this book we have of course used American butchers' terminology for the most readily available cuts.

BREAD

"Italian bread" in this country is usually just a larger, fatter version of a French bread loaf, though, inexplicably, sesame seeds are often added to the top before baking. We've rarely seen sesame seeds on breads in Italy, though in the south—where most Italian immigrants came from—one finds this now and again.

In Italy there are scores of different breads of every shape and size, many made only on feast days. But the fact is that, as in France, very few Italians make their own bread at home, preferring to buy it, as they have for hundreds of years, from the local baker. For this reason, with the exception of focaccia and pizza, we decided not to give any bread recipes in this book. Those who seek such guidance will be eminently rewarded by seeking out Carol Field's *The Italian Baker* (1985); her preface notes that there are 35,000 bakers in Italy, 90 percent of them artisanal bakers who maintain those traditions of special regional breads, and she makes scant mention of anyone making bread at home.

BREADCRUMBS

Italians use breadcrumbs in the same ways most other European and American food cultures do—mainly to coat a piece of food that is to be fried or sautéed—but they also use them as a substitute for grated cheese. This used to be more the case when poor Italians could not afford to use cheese, but the economy measure became so much a part of their cooking that it persists to this day as a delectable way of adding flavor and texture to a dish that is placed under the broiler or baked in an oven. See page 239 for directions on making homemade breadcrumbs. Flavored breadcrumbs, such as are found in American groceries, are all but unknown in Italy.

BROTH

It may surprise some to learn that Italians often used bouillon cubes, called *dadi* (DAH-dee), but the cubes sold in Italy are far superior to those found here, where extra seasonings are often added. If you're ever in Italy, pick up a box or two and see what we mean.

Of course, cubes are no substitute for a well-made or even canned broth, although they may bolster the flavor of a weak broth. We have always used College Inn brand with success, although admittedly it is quite salty. They also make an unsalted version, but we prefer either to dilute the salted kind with a little water or to add some of our own homemade broth.

Beef broth is another thing, and since so few recipes call for it, we think it's perfectly all right to use canned broth.

CAPERS

M ost capers (*capperi*: KAH-peh-ree) that you'll find in U.S. markets are bottled in vinegar and have a pronounced sour taste, that bears scant resemblance to the delightfully complex taste of fresh capers or those packed in salt (which must be rinsed before using). The best capers come from the islands of Pantelleria and Salina and can be somewhat expensive. But one does not use capers liberally, and a few add an ineffable flavor to those dishes that require them.

CHEESES

T he variety and availability of Italian cheeses were for so long so limited that it's not difficult to understand why people used them mostly for grating onto dishes. Today this situation has changed radically: A well-stocked grocery will carry a good variety of domestic and imported Italian cheeses, and in an Italian neighborhood you'll find literally dozens of options, ranging from buffalo mozzarella to excellent *caciocavallo*. You can also easily order good Italian cheeses from notable groceries like those listed at the end of the book, and checking the Internet will reveal a world of cheese you may not have been aware of.

Here is a description of the principal types.

ASIAGO (ah-see-AH-goh). A cow's milk cheese from the Veneto, with a resemblance to Danish cheeses like Havarti. It has a semi-soft texture and a mild flavor, and when aged it may be used as a grating cheese.

BEL PAESE (bell pye-AY-zeh). A brand-name cheese (it means "beautiful country") from Lombardy, invented in 1929 by the well-known Galbani company. It is a pleasant cheese, mild and without much character, nice to serve as a snack on crackers or with Italian bread.

CACIOCAVALLO (kah-choh-kah-VAH-loh). The name of this buffalo's or cow's milk cheese means "horse cheese," supposedly because its shape resembles saddle-bags thrown over a horse's back. Originally from

GOAT'S CHEESE

G oat's cheese—called caprino (*kah-PREE-noh*) in Italian—is of minor importance in Italy, but in the United States it has become a popular cheese, found in ravioli, on top of pizza, and in salads, and also eaten fresh. We've found that far too many of the imported goat's cheeses, mainly from France, do not arrive in very good condition here. So if you're going to use goat's cheese, pick an American producer like Laura Chenel of California.

27

Campania, this ancient cheese, aged three months or more, is perfectly good to eat with a nice country bread, though the more aged varieties are intended for grating. *Butirro* is a Calabrian version made with a center of butter.

FONTINA (fohn-TEE-nah). A semi-firm cow's milk cheese with a lovely grassy, fruity flavor. Unfortunately the name Fontina is applied by Italian and non-Italian producers to a lot of inferior cheeses, like Fontinella and Fontal. The best come from the Val d'Aosta and have a stenciled image of a mountain with the word "Fontina" on it.

GORGONZOLA (gohr-gohn-ZOH-lah). Most people know Gorgonzola by its domestic variety, which resembles Roquefort with its mottled blue-green veins. Domestic examples can range from pleasantly pungent with a nice rich creaminess to harshly acrid and salty. Imported Gorgonzola is a very different cheese, made in the town outside of Milan that gives it its name. Once Gorgonzola developed its noble mold naturally, but today it comes through an injection of *Penicillium gorgonzola*. The Italian varieties may be either "sweet" (*dolce*) or "sharp" (*naturale* or *piccante*); the former is not actually sweet but has a dreamy fresh cream flavor and a nice touch of the blue to it; the latter is a formidable cheese with an assertive punch, and, when well aged, is not a cheese for the timid.

If you come across a Gorgonzola that seems to be dripping moisture, avoid it; the liquid indicates that it may have been frozen. Neither should Gorgonzola be too crumbly and dry.

Gorgonzola melts well on certain vegetables, like asparagus, and works well as a pasta sauce. Eaten on its own, perhaps with a ripe pear, it cries out for a sweet wine like Moscato d'Asti, Picolit, or Marsala.

GRANA PADANO (GRAH-nah pah-DAH-noh). If you can't abide spending so much money on a true Parmigiano-Reggiano (see below) to be grated on a pasta dish, consider *grana padano*, which is made in the same area as Parmigiano-Reggiano and is produced in much the same way, except that it is not aged as long (six months versus a minimum of fourteen). It is ideal for such a purpose, and the better varieties, which are not much exported, unfortunately, are good as eating cheeses too.

MASCARPONE (mah-skahr-POH-neh). I suspect most Americans who have ever heard of mascarpone know it only because they've enjoyed or made Tiramisù (page 391), for which it is the crucial ingredient. Mascarpone is a cow's milk cheese that is almost closer to butter than cheese, and almost a dead ringer for cream cheese. It has a very high butterfat content, 70 to 75 percent, which is why it's used in desserts like *tiramisù* and cheesecakes. But it can be used as you might otherwise use butter in Italian cookery, perhaps as a gloss over pasta before the sauce goes on, or as an accompaniment to fresh fruit like ripe pears or apple tart.

MONTASIO (mohn-TAH-zee-oh). Way up in northern Italy—the alpine Friuli–Venezia Giulia—this raw cow's milk cheese has been made by the local monastery since the thirteenth century. It is fairly mild, similar to Asiago, and makes a good stuffing for ravioli.

MOZZARELLA (moh-t'zah-REH-lah). Unquestionably the most recognizable of all Italian-style cheeses, mozzarella originated in southern Italy as a buffalo's milk cheese with a subtle piquancy that distinguished it from other fresh, slightly rubbery cheeses. On its retreat from southern Italy, the German army systematically destroyed nearly every water buffalo in the country (the herds were restocked over a long period of time with animals from India), and for a time cow's milk was used to make mozzarella.

Mozzarella was easily made from cow's milk by the Italian immigrants in the United States, and it remains to this day a delicious fresh cheese, in both fresh and dry versions, often better than imported *mozzarella di bufala* that has taken a day or two longer than it should to reach our markets. At its best and freshest *mozzarella di bufala* is a superb, slightly tangy cheese, but domestic mozzarella— at least that made on the premises by Italian grocers—is excellent.

The packaged, plastic-wrapped mozzarella bought in supermarkets is adequate for melting over pizza or lasagna, though a freshly made, but dry, mozzarella will be better still. The very fresh mozzarella you see floating in water in Italian groceries has too much moisture to work as a topping for pizza and lasagna, but eaten fresh on its own, with some prosciutto, figs, or tomatoes, and good olive oil, it is one of the greatest of all simple foods.

Fresh mozzarella is made either salted or unsalted; the latter is a better choice, for you can always add salt at the table. If you've ever had a morsel of mozzarella straight from its warm bath of water and whey, you'll know that the texture of the cheese is softer and the creaminess concentrated. It is, therefore, always a nice idea to place

fresh mozzarella in a bowl of hot (not boiling) water to relax the texture and bring out the flavors before serving.

PARMIGIANO-REGGIANO (pahr-mee-JAH-noh reh-jee-AH-noh). Indisputably the greatest of Italian cheeses, in this country Parmigiano-Reggiano is too often regarded only as the cheese you grate over pasta and other dishes. It can certainly serve in this capacity, especially if you're using the cheese close to the rind after eating the rest of it on its own, but at the price charged for Parmigiano-Reggiano, it is probably a better idea to use the cheaper *grana padana* (see above) or a good Pecorino (see below).

Parmigiano-Reggiano is the protected (trademarked) name of the firm cow's milk cheese produced in the region around Parma under very strict regulations. There are records of Parmigiano cheesemaking in the earliest Christian era, and by the thirteenth century the cheese made in this region was widely known and appreciated. Today the production is limited by law to specific regions within the zone in the middle of the Enza River valley between Parma and Reggio-Emilia. The cheese must be aged for at least fourteen months, but it usually ages far longer (at three years it is called *stravecchio*—"very old"—and takes on a particular flavor that is an acquired taste). The huge sixty-six-pound rounds are stamped with the official seal and the date the cheese was made.

Fortunately Parmigiano-Reggiano is readily available in the United States today, although imitators with similar names like "*Reggianato*" are also on the market. Domestic "Parmesan" cheese bears no resemblance whatever to a true Parmigiano-Reggiano, which has a superb butter-nut flavor, a gorgeous aroma, and a crumbly texture. It is never cut with a straight-edged, sharp knife, which compromises the texture, but with a special little leaf-shaped knife with a knob on the end that allows the cheese to break off like chunks of an iceberg. The rind itself, while inedible on its own, is an absolutely wonderful addition to a soup or to *pasta e fagiole*, where its flavor is absorbed into the rest of the ingredients. Parmigiano-Reggiano is highly nutritious and very digestible: You would have to eat 185 grams of beef, 225 grams of trout, or 190 grams of pork to get the protein you'd get from eating 100 grams of Parmigiano.

On its own Parmigiano-Reggiano is best served with a big red wine like a Barolo or Barbaresco.

When buying Parmigiano-Reggiano, look for a creamy yellow-ochre color. The cheese can be left in a cool winter storage area, but after a day or two should be placed in plastic wrap and kept in the vegetable storage area of your refrigerator. It will keep well this way for weeks, though it will dry out after a while and lose its texture and nuttiness.

PECORINO ROMANO (peh-koh-REE-noh roh-MAH-noh). While *pecorino* is actually just a generic term for any Italian sheep's milk cheese, the best known is associated with the province of Rome. Still, there's not enough genuine Pecorino Romano to meet demand (the Locatelli brand is probably the most readily available in the United States), so the name may be applied to fine examples made in Sardinia, where it may acquire the stamp *"Pecorino Sardo."* Pecorino can be eaten on its own, but most examples tend to be very strong, somewhat salty, and best reserved for grating.

PROVOLONE (proh-voh-LOH-neh). A cow's milk cheese original-ly from Basilicata, provolone is made in the same way as mozzarella but is shaped into logs—some of them six feet long—and aged to acquire a pungent flavor and a pronounced aroma. Too often bad examples are dry, oily, and, quite frankly, smell bad, but a good, care-fully aged provolone has a sharpness not unlike an aged cheddar. It makes for a fine addition to a hero sandwich, and, as still served in many old-fashioned Italian-American restaurants, it goes well with some olives and a few stalks of celery.

RICOTTA (ree-KOH-tah). This well-known fresh cheese is widely available around the U.S. and, at least in the whole-milk variety, always pretty dependable. It is actually made from the whey (in Italy from cow's or sheep's milk, in America usually just cow's milk) and is already a lightweight cheese, so buying a "skimmed milk" ricotta is the height of dietetic folly.

In a good Italian cheese shop, ricotta will be made fresh and sold by weight, intended to be eaten fresh at home, with perhaps a sprinkling of salt or even sugar. The ricotta you find in plastic con-tainers is creamier in consistency and almost always destined to find its way into lasagna or a pasta with tomato sauce. The best-known domestic ricotta brand is Polly-O, and they do a very good, very consistent job.

RICOTTA SALATA (ree-KOH-tah sah-LA-tah) is a sheep's milk cheese, principally made in Sicily, with a distinct saltiness that in good examples is balanced by the creamy richness of the cheese;

in poor examples, all you'll taste is salt. When purchasing *ricotta salata*, reject any signs of mold on the rind. It is an excellent cheese to serve in shards over pasta and vegetables as an alternative to grated cheese.

ROBIOLA (roh-bee-OH-lah). Rarely found here, this small round of cheese comes both fresh and aged, and may be made from cow's, goat's, or sheep's milk. It is a cheese to be savored with bread and olives, either before a meal or after the main course, with a glass of white wine like Greco di Tufo.

TALEGGIO (tah-LEH-j'yoh). Made from raw cow's milk, this buttery cheese from northern Italy too often comes to the U.S. from giant cheese companies and shows nothing of Taleggio's true character— a richness tempered by nuttiness, ideal with a good sturdy red wine like Dolcetto.

CHICKEN

The Yankee Clipper himself, Joe DiMaggio, was often cited as an Italian-American hero of achievement who, like all American heroes, loved his mother's cooking. Here we see Rosalie DiMaggio, with a plate of homemade ravioli, and Joe's brother Dominic in a 1947 photo.

It is more than likely that the chickens you taste in Italy will be vastly superior in flavor to the commercially produced chickens in the United States, whose mega-companies have created not only a low-flavor bird but also one with a certain degree of salmonella risk. (We do not wish to overstress this problem for two reasons: First, salmonella is killed off when the meat reaches 160°F, so thorough cooking eliminates any possible problem. Second, it has been estimated that your chances of getting salmonella from an egg are about one in 2,000. Depending on your squeamishness about such food-related illnesses, make your choice in chicken and eggs accordingly.)

Kosher chickens may be more flavorful birds, and free-range chickens tend to be. But in the United States none of these compare to the full-flavored chickens in Europe, however scrawny they may look.

COFFEE

Quite honestly, we have never tasted any American coffee that compares with Italian coffee. Starbucks may have upgraded commercial American coffee by a few percentage points, but to us it is still far inferior to even the modest forms of Italian coffee. We therefore recommend buying only imported Italian coffee from companies like Lavazza, Illycaffè, and Danesi. A good domestic brand is Mocca d'Oro.

Of course, neither Italy nor the United States actually grows its own coffee beans, but it is in the selection of the beans and the roasting that the difference lies. Most commercial coffee is made with a mix of inexpensive, fairly harsh *robusta* beans and the more expensive, more delicate *arabica* beans. American coffees tend to be predominantly made from the former, Italian coffees overwhelmingly from the latter. *Arabica* beans have a vivid, lush, almost sweet underpinning and, for those concerned, less caffeine—so even though espresso looks like a "strong" cup of coffee, it actually contains far less acid and caffeine than a regular mug of weak American coffee.

The principal way coffee is consumed in Italy is as espresso. Cappuccino may be taken at breakfast, but espresso is drunk throughout the day. (Incidentally, cappuccino should have a creamy foam of steamed milk on the top, not that shaving cream–type foam you find on American versions.)

Other negligible forms of coffee hyped in the United States include *caffè corretto* (with a shot of grappa or brandy), *caffè latte* (with a dose of milk), *latte macchiato* (more like coffee-flavored milk), *caffè decaffeinato* (decaffeinated), and *caffè freddo* (iced coffee).

In Italy it would a great rarity to find coffee served with lemon peel as is sometimes done in the United States—a practice that probably began when Italian immigrants tried to tame the roughness of American coffee made as espresso.

FLOUR

In Italy flour is called *farina* (fah-REE-nah) and is made from either soft wheat (*Triticum aestivum*), used to make flour for cakes and

breads, or hard durum wheat (*T. durum*), used for pasta. *Farina integrale* is whole-wheat flour, and *farina gialla* is cornmeal flour.

No doubt Italian flour has a different gluten and fiber content than American—even though the wheat for Italian flour probably came from Minnesota—but for a cookbook intended for American usage, American all-purpose unbleached flour is perfectly fine.

GARLIC

Much maligned for its powerful smell, garlic (*aglio*: AHL-yoh) has long been associated with the worst aspects of Italian-American food, and it is true that too many Italian-American cooks seem to add an abundance of garlic to their sauces and other preparations just to comply with Americans' unwitting characterization of Italians as "garlic eaters." The abomination called "garlic salt" was once the standard seasoning for garlic bread, and it is still found in frozen and canned Italian-American food items in the supermarket.

The fact is that garlic is used sparingly throughout Italy, and in many northern regions it is barely used at all. Southern Italians' love of garlic is akin to their love of perfume: A little goes a long way, and too much is a sign of bad taste. In many cases a clove of garlic may be added to hot oil to flavor it and then removed. In other instances the garlic remains, but it is always cooked somewhat to drive off the unappetizing raw taste of this pungent member of the onion family. By the same token, cooking garlic past the point of its taking on a golden color will also increase its bitterness.

Recent scientific studies of the benefits of the so-called Mediterranean diet and the beneficial effects of garlic on the blood have boosted this once lowly seasoning to the top ranks of gastronomy, and, when used in moderation, it is indeed one of the glories of the Mediterranean kitchen.

LAMB

American lamb is now a superb product, with tremendous flavor that far exceeds that of the frozen New Zealand lamb that has made such inroads in American markets. Italian lamb (*agnello:* ahn-n'YEH-loh) is of very good quality too, though it is sometimes not quite so tender or fatted as its American counterpart. The very best lamb, now readily available at good butchers in the United States, is baby lamb, which is milk-fed and usually slaughtered under six weeks of age. In Italy, especially around Rome, where it is called *abbachio* (ah-BAH-k'yoh), baby lamb is succulent and absolutely delicious. The Italians particularly love the lamb riblets they called *scottaditi* (skoh-tah-DEE-tee), which means "finger burners" because they are picked up by the bone and eaten with the fingers. In Italy lamb is most often flavored with garlic and rosemary.

LARD

Lardo (LAHR-doh) was once a major cooking ingredient in Italian kitchens, especially among the poor who could not afford olive oil or butter. Today even the Italians are concerned with the effects of fat on the diet, and they have eschewed using lard in favor of olive oil. Still, lard imparts a flavor and texture to many dishes that would not otherwise take well to olive oil, and a little goes a long way. Combining lard with olive oil will give you a sense of what those old flavors would have been like.

MARJORAM AND OREGANO

Sweet marjoram (*maggiorana:* mah-j'yoh-RAH-nah) is, to our minds, preferable as a flavoring to oregano (*origano:* oh-REE-gah-noh), which is actually a wild variety of marjoram. The former is far milder and more subtle, while oregano can be extremely pungent. In southern Italy, however, some varieties of oregano can be quite sweet, and this may well be the reason why Italian immigrants in

America started using oregano in their food, despite the fact that domestic oregano was less likely to have the aromatic sweetness of the Italian. Oregano may add a more authentic flavor to some Italian-American dishes, but try them with marjoram and we think you'll be pleasantly surprised at the difference. As with all herbs, fresh is better, but dried marjoram or oregano is acceptable.

MINT

Mint is not often thought of as a particularly Italian herb, but it is used widely in Italy in salads, with vegetables, and in the south, on grilled seafood. In Italy spearmint is called *menta* (MEHN-tah), while peppermint is called *mentuccia* (mehn-TOO-ch'yah).

OLIVES

One of the most important food crops of the Mediterranean, the olive (*oliva*: oh-LEE-vah) has been grown in Italy since the sixth century B.C. and is a staple of the diet. Olives are eaten as a snack, as part of antipasti, baked into bread, and, most important, crushed into olive oil (see below). In Sicily black olives are cured in brine. Purple olives, cured in salt, come from Gaeta in Campania.

Never buy canned olives, which have a dreary, musty taste. The increasing number of Mediterranean olives now available in good food stores is very encouraging, and there is no longer any excuse not to buy the good ones. Greek Calamata olives are also excellent and are easy to find here.

OLIVE OIL

Treatises and love poems have been written on the glories of olive oil, so it is ironic that for most of this century, olive oil was regarded by sophisticated cooks as an inferior medium for refined cuisine. One might look in vain in French cookbooks published before the 1980s for any mention of olive oil, despite its use in

Provence. So-called gourmet cooks seem to have "discovered" how wonderful olive oil can be now that the studies of the "Mediterranean diet"—many of them funded by the International Olive Oil Council—show that it may have health benefits in contrast to butter. The tables have turned quickly.

It is, however, easy enough to understand why olive oil was held in such low esteem for so long. For one thing, there was the abiding prejudice against Italian food as being inferior to French cuisine. Second, a great deal of the olive oil used in Italian-American restaurants and homes was of very inferior quality. Often those huge gallon tins contained very little olive at all, the rest being cheaper vegetable oils. Or the oil was made from *pomace*, the residue left after the first and second pressing of the olive to extract the fresh oil. Even in the Old Country, poor people who raised olives would sell the best oil to their affluent landlords and others who could afford it, while they used the dregs that were left—or, more likely, lard.

The appearance—often at ridiculous cost—of "virgin," then "extra-virgin," olive oil in this country altered the oil's image, and even the practitioners of France's nouvelle cuisine began to see the benefits of using good olive oil in their food. These days it seems rarer to find cookbooks recommending butter over olive oil than vice versa, and the olive oil industry has, of course, responded with myriad varieties of oils, some packed in expensive signature bottles. The principal varieties of Italian olive oil (and there are excellent olive oils now coming out of Greece, Spain, France, and California) are regulated by Italy's food laws under the *Denominazione d'Origine Controllata* (D.O.C.) codes, which designate the following:

EXTRA VERGINE: Must be made from the first pressing of the olives by mechanical means only and with an acidity of less than 1 percent. About half of Italy's production of olive oil now falls into this category.

SOPPRAFINO VERGINE: The same as *extra vergine*, with no more than 1.5 percent acidity.

FINO VERGINE: The same, with not more than 3 percent acidity.

VERGINE: The same, with not more than 4 percent acidity.

OLIO D'OLIVA: May contain more than 4 percent acidity and may be a blend of chemically rectified or de-acidified oils.

OLIO DI SANSA DI OLIVA: Olive oil made from the dregs of the pressed olives.

The marketing of extra-virgin and virgin olive oils has been so successful that today it's not easy to find simple 100 percent olive oil this side of the Atlantic, even though it is perfectly fine for cooking. As a matter of fact, few Italians would use expensive extra-virgin or virgin olive oil as a cooking medium, saving it instead as a dressing for various dishes. But given the fact that the cost has come down so mightily, you can use these two high categories with a certain abandon these days.

Be careful to read the fine print on the olive oil can or bottle, however. The more focused the region listed on the product, the better. "Produced in Lucca" (a town in Tuscany famous for its olive oil) is better than "Produced in Tuscany," and "Produced in Italy" is better than "Packaged in Italy," which means that the oil could have come from anywhere in the Mediterranean and was merely bottled in an Italian facility.

Olive oils from different regions of Italy do have different flavors and textures, owing to the different varieties of olives, the differing climates, and the traditional methods used. Tuscan olive oil is quite green, herbaceous, and distinctly peppery. The oils of Puglia and Campania are fruitier and a little zestier, while Ligurian oil is fairly light. Those from Sicily can be heavy but luxurious, and the oils of The Marches, not often seen here, are highly esteemed for their complexity.

PANCETTA

This is the Italian version of our bacon, cut from the belly of the hog, salted, and cured. *Pancetta* (pahn-CHEH-tah), however, has the added flavor of garlic and black pepper, and it is rolled into a sausage-like shape and then cut into disks when ordered at a market. It keeps well in the refrigerator and may be frozen.

Diced, pancetta is sautéed and added to all sorts of dishes to provide a wonderfully saline, lusty flavor. The crispy bits are like cracklings, and may be tossed into salads or even eaten on their own on a piece of Italian bread.

You can buy a chunk of domestic prosciutto or imported *prosciutto cotto* (cooked prosciutto) and use it as you would pancetta.

Guanciale (gwahn-ch'YAHL-leh) is similar to pancetta, but made from the jowl and cheek of the hog.

PARSLEY

There is no problem finding Italian flat-leaf parsley (*prezzemolo*: preh-t'ZEH-meh-loh) at the market, and it is well worth using instead of the curly-leafed parsley that was once ubiquitous. The Italian variety has much more flavor.

PASTA

When Americans say they feel like going out for Italian food, they almost always mean they are in the mood for a plate of pasta. In Italy a restaurant meal without pasta would be unthinkable, and there is no question that Italians eat pasta pretty much on a daily basis: They consume about sixty pounds per person annually, while Americans eat about half that amount. Obviously it would be extremely unusual for an Italian family to make its own pasta each day, and therein lies the myth of fresh pasta's superiority over dried commercial pasta.

Pasta in one form or another has been part of the Italian diet for a thousand years or more. The first printed mention of *maccheroni* is in a Genovese document of the thirteenth century. (There is no truth to the legend that Marco Polo, who arrived back from his trip to the Orient in 1295, brought the idea of pasta from China; for the full story, see page 162.) Stuffed pastas date at least to the fourteenth century, and by 1785 Naples alone had 280 shops selling pasta; that city became the capital of pasta production after the drying process had been perfected just south of Naples at Torre Annunziata. By the end of the nineteenth century, the entire process had been mechanized, and die-cut pasta, created in 1917 by Fereol Sandragne, made commercial pasta available throughout Italy. Thus dried pasta, called *pasta secca* or *pastasciutta*,

made by law from hard durum wheat, has always been the norm in Italian kitchens.

Fresh pasta, called *pasta fresca*, is made from soft wheat, often with an abundance of eggs. While Italians certainly love fresh pasta, it is a special item, easily store-bought but often made at home for special dishes. It is by no means an everyday item in Italian cookery.

Nevertheless the trendy idea that fresh pasta is better took hold in so-called northern Italian restaurants in the United States, and customers were charged accordingly. While fresh pasta has an undeniable appeal in both flavor and texture, most pasta dishes call for a firmer noodle made from hard wheat. Egg-based noodles are very rich and absolutely delightful, but they are saved for only a handful of dishes in the complete pantheon of Italian pasta recipes.

While domestic American pastas are of decent quality, imported Italian pastas are now available at reasonable prices and are the better choice in all cases. Makers we like include the ubiquitous DeCecco, along with Barilla, Colavita, Delverde, and San Giuliano Alghero. Recently Italy has been exporting so-called artisanal pastas, made by small firms like Rustichella d'Abruzzo and Bella Mia, which use old-fashioned metal dies instead of the modern Teflon dies, the result being a nuttier flavor and a rougher texture that picks up sauces better. They can be quite expensive, but once you try them, you may never again be happy with any others.

PEPPER

The black peppercorn is native to India, but it spread early to ancient Greece and Rome, and the appetite for this tantalizing seasoning was one of the main reasons Christopher Columbus set sail. Instead of India he landed in the New World, and instead of black pepper he found chile peppers (see Sweet and Hot Peppers, page 43).

Italians use more black pepper than white (the word for both varieties is *pepe*: PEH-peh), though they do not use pepper all that liberally. It is more likely to be added toward the end of a cooking process. There is no difference between the peppercorns sold here and those found abroad.

Freshly ground black pepper is, of course, the ideal way to season a dish, and there are many peppermills that work perfectly well. Make sure you buy one that lets you adjust the coarseness of the grind.

One of the more ridiculous innovations of Italian-American food service is the oversize pepper mill, brandished even before a guest tastes his or her food. Some restaurateurs seem to think that the bigger the peppermill, the more impressive it will be at the table. In fact, the very biggest have been winkingly named "Rubirosas," after the international playboy of the same name who was known for more than the size of his ego.

PIGNOLI NUTS

P*ignoli* (peeh-n'YOH-lee), also known as pine nuts, are used throughout Italy, as well they might be in a country full of pine trees. Nevertheless, pine nuts are very, very expensive, though less so in this country, where a shorter Chinese variety is more commonly sold. Both can be used interchangeably (the very best pine nuts are grown in Mexico and are a pink color) in recipes in this book. Pine nuts, like most nuts, gain in flavor when lightly toasted in the oven or sautéed without oil in a nonstick pan for a few minutes.

When buying pine nuts, make sure they are very fresh and not rancid. Once home, store them in a closed container in the freezer.

PROSCIUTTO

P**rosciutto** (proh-SHOO-toh) is the great ham of Parma (although it is also made in Friuli under the San Daniele name), where the climate and wind are essential to the careful drying of the hams, which have been praised since the first century B.C. The pigs used in the production must be born and bred in Italy, slaughtered at ten months, and weigh at least 140 kilos (308 pounds). The meat is salted and kept refrigerated in spotless facilities with

controlled humidity, resulting in a luscious sweet-nutty flavor, far more appealing than the overly salty American country ham.

The hams' age and the flow of that wondrous air give them their beautiful color and flavor. They are then aged in cool cellars for at least ten months and usually more, tested frequently for freshness, branded with the Consortium of Parma's ducal crown symbol, and finally shipped to discerning customers around the world.

Extremely nutritious and far less fatty than some assume, a few slices of *prosciutto di Parma* makes an ideal appetizer, but it can be used in cooking too. For decades this extraordinary ham was deliberately kept out of the American market by American pork producers, who have long made a cured ham using the prosciutto name. These domestic varieties can be quite decent—Citterio and Volpi are two dependable brands—but for about ten years now we have been getting the true article, and the delicacy of flavor is noticeable the first moment you taste it. *Prosciutto di Parma* is, of course, more expensive, but one eats very little at a time, and it is worth every penny. With a glass of wine—either a lovely fragrant white or a medium-bodied red—this and a little Parmigiano-Reggiano can make a perfect low-calorie meal.

Ask your Italian butcher to cut paper-thin slices—the thinner the better—but make sure he places each slice on a separate sheet of waxed paper; otherwise they will stick together. And don't buy more prosciutto than you think you'll eat within a day or two, because it will lose its texture, stick to the paper, and become slightly gummy.

SALT

Europeans use sea salt almost exclusively for cooking, and despite its cost, Italians use it quite liberally. It is best as a final seasoning, especially if the salt grain is coarse, adding an additional texture to the dish.

American salt, mostly reclaimed from the earth's salt deposits, is often chemically treated, but kosher salt is not, which is why we highly recommend its use in the recipes in this book.

SEMOLINA

Semolina is the ground endosperm of hard durum wheat, which gives the food made with it, like cakes and pizza dough, its chewy texture. It may also be used to make couscous. Although the word *semolina* means "fine flour," it is actually fairly coarse and is not appropriate for all recipes containing flour; use it only where indicated.

SWEET AND HOT PEPPERS

Chile peppers (*Capsicum annuum*) came to Italy from the Americas, discovered there by Christopher Columbus, who found that the Indians of the New World used them extensively as one of their most revered foods. First brought to Spain in 1514, the chile, which is not taxonomically a pepper like black pepper and white pepper, was named *pimiento*, and was soon exported throughout the Old World. In Italy the chile took various names, including *peperoncino* (peh-peh-rohn-CHEE-noh) and, in Abruzzo, *diavolicchio* (dee-ah-voh-LEE-k'yoh), or "devil" pepper. Italian chile peppers are probably variants of the Anaheim chile, that ranges in hotness from fairly mild to moderately hot.

So-called sweet peppers (*Capsicum frutescens*) took a little longer to reach the Old World, and at first both hot and sweet chiles were considered unfit for refined tables and relegated to the gardens of the poor. Neither gained much favor with the cooks of the noble families until well into the nineteenth century, and even today both sweet and hot peppers are more commonly used in southern Italian home cooking than in the north.

Vinegared peppers are roasted and brined in vinegar and sold in a jar.

We like to use pepperoncini, which come in glass jars and once opened, keep for weeks in the refrigerator.

43

TOMATOES

As closely associated with tomatoes (*pomodori*: poh-moh-DOH-ree) as the Italians are, they were able to live without them for two thousand years before the arrival of the vegetable (actually a fruit) from the New World in the sixteenth century. Even then only the poor Italians of the south, where tomatoes grew best, would eat this member of the deadly nightshade family. The reason there is so much "red sauce" in Italian-American restaurants is because most Italian immigrants came from the south, and they simply adapted one of their principal ingredients to the American larder.

At their peak of ripeness and sweetness, freshly grown summer tomatoes have no equal. By the same token, the anemic tomatoes generally available after September should never be used in a recipe calling for tomatoes. Fortunately we have access to good canned tomatoes, both imported and domestic. The best of these are the so-called plum tomatoes (in Italy, *perini*—peh-REE-nee—meaning "little pears"), also referred to as "Italian-style" tomatoes. The best of the best are said to be those grown at the foot of Mount Vesuvius in an area called San Marzano, though this appellation gets tossed around pretty liberally on labels these days—much as with "Maine lobster," which may come from anywhere along the coast from Nova Scotia to South Carolina.

While canning may be thought to preserve tomatoes for an indefinite length of time, the fact is that tomatoes get mushier in the can, so it's best to check the packing date and use the tomatoes within six months of that date. Tomatoes packed "with puree" are not recommended, because they often have a diluted flavor. If the tomatoes taste a bit too acidic or sour, do as Arthur Schwartz suggests in his wonderful book *Naples at Table* (1998): Don't add sugar, add concentrated tomato paste, which in Italy is called *concentrato* (kohn-chen-TRAH-toh).

Pomodori seccati, sun-dried tomatoes, are not nearly as trendy in Italy as they seem to be here. We find most varieties of these commercially produced dried tomatoes too sour and impossibly chewy. Oven-roasted tomatoes, however (page 332), are delicious, intensely flavorful, and an excellent addition to sauces.

VEAL

American veal has always been of good quality, but now it is of very good quality, certainly comparable in tenderness and flavor to what you'll find in Europe. This was not always the case, and too many cheap Italian-American restaurants depended on veal "cutlets"—ground up and reconstituted lesser cuts of veal. Some unscrupulous restaurateurs—not all of them Italian by a long shot—have even substituted pork cutlets and charged veal prices.

The American veal chop is a gargantuan wonder of the meat world and surpasses any we've had in Italy, where veal chops, when encountered at all, are puny by comparison in size and taste.

VINEGAR

For most of this century, Italian-American and American cooks have gotten along just fine with red wine vinegar. Then the fashion for balsamic vinegar began in the late 1970s, and red wine vinegar is now considered passé. That's a shame, but wholly understandable because even lesser examples of *aceto balsamico* (ah-CHEH-toh bahl-SAHM-ee-koh) can add a sweet-sour measure to any number of dishes.

Balsamico refers to the balsam-like aroma of the vinegars made around Modena for a thousand years—and unknown outside of that region until recently. For centuries *balsamico* was used primarily for medicinal purposes and as a sweetener. It was much prized and very expensive and was given as gifts among families, particularly among the nobility, who believed it could ward off plague. Mere drops would be used to dress a salad or fruit or add flavor to a sauce.

Balsamic vinegar is made by boiling the must (*saba*) of grapes down to one half or one third its original volume, then pouring it into wooden vessels called *sogli* to ferment. Marble powder or ash is added to bring down the acidity and to clarify the liquid, after which it is poured every twelve months into a series of at least three barrels (usually five) called a *batteria*, made from different woods like juniper, oak, chestnut, ash, cherry, or mulberry. These barrels are

set in protected attics called *acetaria* for several years after the "mother" forms on the top. Vinegars are replenished and topped off with new must each year. Some *balsamico* vinegars are aged a hundred years or longer.

Bottles of *balsamico* are submitted to the *Consorteria dell'aceto balsamico* for a D.O.C. designation. Quality ranges from *tradizionale*, to *qualità superiore*, to *riserva* (which must be at least twelve years old), to the highest, *extra vecchia* (at least twenty-five years old). The very best vinegar is described as *da bere* ("for drinking"), although its cost makes it prohibitive to drink more than a few drops. Lesser varieties are referred to as *da condire* ("for dressings"); the *Consoteria* stipulates that only about 8,000 bottles of 3.36 ounces each be offered for sale annually.

Four types of balsamic vinegar are currently made in Italy: the traditional vinegar made according to historic methods in Modena; commercially produced vinegar in the style of Modena vinegars; younger versions of Modena-style vinegar; and imitation balsamic vinegar, primarily made in southern Italy.

Balsamico became a popular item in the American kitchen after Chuck Williams brought some from Modena to sell at his Williams-Sonoma specialty store in San Francisco in 1976, and offered it for sale in his national catalog a year later. The interest in the new product among Italian restaurateurs in the United States sparked an interest among cooks in Italy, and balsamic vinegar has become as much a staple of kitchens and restaurants in Italy, France, Great Britain, and other countries as it is of those in the United States. *Balsamico* is now used liberally in salads, on grilled meats, on fish, and in any of the ways regular vinegar might be used. It is added in droplets to slices of oranges or strawberries.

A SAMPLING OF
ITALIAN WINES

T he enormous improvement and the increased availability
of Italian wines imported into the United States has thoroughly eradicated the idea that they are modest efforts, inferior to French or California bottlings and lacking in any finesse.
The once ubiquitous straw-covered bottle of Chianti—often called
"pizza wine" or "dago red"—was probably valued more for its con-
version to a candle holder than for its contents.

Good Italian wines have been available in the market for
decades, but only in the past twenty years has the quality and variety
of Italian wines been widely recognized worldwide. This is due largely to radical improvements in the technology of Italian winemaking,
including cold fermentation tanks, innovative farming techniques,
and more careful aging; but the real achievements of Italian viniculture are the result of a generation of young Italian winemakers
who, while respectful of regional traditions, have endeavored to
bring complexity, freshness, and varietal character to their wines.

Add to this the strictures imposed by the Italian wine laws
under what is called *Denominazione di Origine Controllata* (D.O.C.)
and *Denominazione di Origine Controllata Garantita* (D.O.C.G.),
which delimit areas of production, authorize only certain grape
varieties to be used within a region, and oversee the technical production of the wines. The "*Garantita*" in the D.O.C.G. is a higher
standard, by which a small number of the thousand or so different
types of wine produced in Italy are guaranteed to be of the highest
quality and represent the best that Italian viniculture has to offer.
When these standards are not met—say, in a bad vintage—the
wines are not entitled to a D.O.C.G. labeling and must simply be
called *vino da tavola*, "table wine."

Currently there are eighteen designated D.O.C.G. wines.
There are many new-style wines that are considered by connois-
seurs to be among the very best yet lack a D.O.C.G. label because
they do not meet the legal requirements for the technical makeup
of a regional wine like Chianti, Barolo, or Barbaresco.

The list below comprises the principal wines available in the American market, from which we have drawn many of our wine suggestions for particular recipes in this book. By no means are our recommendations to be taken as absolute, for there are dozens of wines that go perfectly well with dozens of recipes. Largely we have tried to recommend regional wines that go with dishes from those same regions, for we firmly believe that there is a natural affinity between the wines of, say, Trentino and the foods prepared there.

Nevertheless, the basic rubrics to be followed in drinking certain wines with certain dishes are as follows:

❖ Light, delicate wines go best with light, delicate foods. Therefore, a pleasant fruity or acidic white wine will go best with simple seafood or vegetable dishes.
❖ Fuller-bodied white wines, like Chardonnay, go best with shellfish, cream and butter sauces, and some cheeses.
❖ Deeply flavorful red meats—beef, lamb, venison—require a big red wine with at least a bit of tannin, such as Barbaresco, Barolo, Taurasi, and Brunello di Montalcino.

DRINK WHAT'S GOOD FOR YOU

The evidence supporting the health benefits of wine now seems overwhelming.

❖ Moderate drinking may protect against stroke—Epidemiology (1999).

❖ Moderate drinking may facilitate spontaneous elimination of some bacterial infections—Epidemiology (1999).

❖ Moderate drinking reduces heart attack risk by raising the "good" cholesterol in the blood—New England Journal of Medicine (1993).

❖ Moderate drinking may aid cognitive functioning in the elderly—American Journal of Epidemiology (1996).

❖ Moderate wine drinkers may be protected against upper digestive tract cancer—British Medical Journal (1998).

❖ Moderate drinking reduces the risk of overall mortality in women—New England Journal of Medicine (1995).

❖ Moderate drinking affords protection against atherosclerosis—Stroke (1998).

*Two representatives of Martignetti's in Boston's North End, one holding the small
hot chile peppers known as* diavolicchi, *the other bottles of wine (circa 1933).*

❖ Robust or highly seasoned dishes do not need wines with a great
deal of finesse but do take well to wines that have some power and
lusty flavors, like Gattinara, Montepulciano di Abruzzo, and
Lacrima Christi.

❖ Pork is greatly enhanced by wines with a slight undertone of
sweetness, such as Amarone; lighter meats like veal and chicken, as
well as full-bodied seafood stews and some strong fish like macker-
el and sardines, are best paired with light- to medium-bodied reds
such as Bardolino and Valpolicella.

❖ Sparkling wines are delicious with appetizers and canapés, and with desserts that are not too sweet. Sweet wines are best with cheeses—especially blue-veined varieties like Gorgonzola—and sweeter desserts.

AGLIANICO DEL VULTURE—Basilicata D.O.C. red wine of Greek origins. It is quite big in structure and can be tannic.

ALBANA DI ROMAGNA—Emilia-Romagnan D.O.C. white wine, usually dry but sometimes slightly sweet.

AMARONE RECIOTO DELLA VALPOLICELLA—Veneto D.O.C. red wine made from grapes dried on straw mats to concentrate their sugars, which in turn ferment into alcohol. Big, lush, with a faint sweetness underneath. Recommended labels: Bertani, Tommasi, Allegrini.

ARNEIS DI ROERO—Piedmont D.O.C. white wine regaining popularity after years of neglect. Has a pleasant floral component. Recommended labels: Ceretto, Bruno Giacosa.

ASTI SPUMANTE—Veneto D.O.C.G. sparkling wine made from Muscat grapes grown around the town of Canelli in Asti. The sweetness of a good Asti Spumante should be buoyed by the lush aromatics of the *moscato* grape. Recommended labels: Cinzano, Martini & Rossi.

BARBARESCO—Piedmontese D.O.C.G. red of great power and finesse, often referred to as the feminine counterpart to Barolo (see below). Recommended labels: Gaja, Bruno Giacosa, Michele Chiarlo.

BARBERA—Piedmontese D.O.C. red wine with several variants, including Barbera d'Alba and Barbera d'Asti. Medium- to rich-bodied, it is generally underestimated. It is a wine of wonderful flavors. Recommend labels: Michele Chiarlo, Angelo Gaja, Prunotto.

BARDOLINO—Veneto D.O.C. light red wine grown around Lake Garda. Rarely rises to excellence but is always very drinkable. Recommended labels: Bolla, Bertani.

BAROLO—Piedmontese D.O.C.G. red wine of enormous power and complexity, one of the great wines of Italy for red meat. Recommended labels: Aldo Conterno, Pio Cesare, Michele Chiarlo, Giacomo Conterno.

BIANCO DI CUSTOZA—Veneto D.O.C. white wine, quite light in body and flavor, sometimes made into a sparkling wine.

BRUNELLO DI MONTALCINO—Tuscan D.O.C.G. red wine of tremendous body, plenty of tannin, and long aging prospects. Once made by only a handful of wineries around Montalcino, its fame has caused many newcomers to begin making it, resulting in a somewhat lighter, easier-to-drink style. Recommended labels: Biondi-Santi, Barbi-Colombini, Banfi, Costanti, Il Poggione.

CARMIGNANO—Tuscan D.O.C.G. red wine. Big, bold, intense, somewhat lacking the refinement of Brunello. Recommended labels: Villa di Capezzana, Il Poggiolo.

CERASUOLO—Light red, almost rose-colored wine from various regions, including the Veneto and Sicily, where the Cerasuolo di Vittorio has garnered a D.O.C.

CHIANTI—Once known as the all-purpose Italian wine, the humble Tuscan Chianti Classico has been transformed and is now in the top ranks of the world's wine, with a D.O.C.G. While the Classicos are the best known, Chiantis from other locales within Tuscany—such as Chianti Rufina, Chianti Putto, and Chianti Senesi—can be very enjoyable, though they are rarely exported. Recommended labels: Ruffino, Antinori, Nozzole, Montesodi, Monsanto.

CIRÒ—Calabrian D.O.C. red and rosé wines produced on the island of Ciro off the Ionian coast. Pleasant, light- to medium-bodied reds.

COLLI ALBANI—Latium D.O.C. white that is pleasing and refreshing, but little more.

COLLI ORIENTALI DEL FRIULI—Friulian D.O.C. wines of twenty varieties, ranging from mid-weight cabernets to vivid whites like Riesling Renano. Can be austere.

CORVO—A proprietary name for white and red Sicilian wines made by the Duca di Salaparuta cooperative. They are very well marketed in the U.S., and while early examples were acrid and unsophisticated, current bottlings are good, clean, well-made wines, especially the very fine Duca Enrico red.

DOLCETTO—Piedmontese D.O.C. red wines with several variants, such as Dolcetta d'Alba, Dolcetto d'Acqui, and Dolcetto d'Asti. Despite a name that seems to translate as "little sweet," it is actually a sturdy, medium-bodied red that is extremely versatile. Recommended labels: Fontanafredda, Vietti, Bruno Giacosa.

EST! EST!! EST!!!—Latium D.O.C. white wine whose unusual name derives from the story of a German bishop's servant who was sent along the route to Rome to locate the taverns that had particularly fine wines and mark their doors with the word "Est," meaning "It is." When he tasted the wines of this region, the enthusiastic servant wrote the word on the tavern door three times. Today Est! Est!! Est!!! is a good straw-colored wine that is rarely distinguished. Recommended label: Falesco.

FIANO DI AVELLINO—Campanian D.O.C. white wine with good flavor from its volcanic soil. Excellent with shellfish. Recommended label: Mastroberardino.

THE RIGHT GLASS

Except in the finest deluxe restaurants, Italians and Italian-Americans do not make the kind of fuss over wine glasses that the French seem to. But maybe they should. There is something nostalgic and evocative about drinking a modest Italian wine in a modest glass tumbler, and there is nothing wrong with serving 99 percent of all wines in a standard six-ounce stemmed wine glass. It is the thinness or thickness of a glass that determines its tactile sensitivity, and the thinner the glass the more pleasurable it is to drink from.

FRASCATI—Latium D.O.C. white wine, very light-bodied, fairly refreshing, rarely anything to get excited about. The best-known label in the U.S. is Fontana Candida.

GATTINARA—Piedmontese D.O.C.G. red wine full of tannin and deep color. Though it has a D.O.C.G., it is rarely in the same league with Barbaresco or Barolo. Still, for a brawny, masculine red, Gattinara is usually a good buy. Recommended labels: Travaglini, Nervi.

GAVI—Piedmontese D.O.C. white wine sometimes called Cortese di Gavi. Somewhat overrated, especially Gavi dei Gavi, but at its best a white wine of considerable body.

GHEMME—Piedmontese D.O.C. red of medium body. Not much seen in America.

GRAVE DEL FRIULI—Large D.O.C. zone of Friuli producing fifteen varieties of wine, including Cabernet and Refosco.

GRIGNOLINO—Piedmontese D.O.C. red wine of somewhat light body and pale violet color.

LACRIMA CHRISTI—This widespread name applies to various wines, but the best known are those from around Mount Vesuvius, where a red, white, and rosé are made. None is particularly interesting but they are always very drinkable with simple dishes from the region. Recommended label: Mastroberardino.

LAMBRUSCO—Emilia-Romagnan D.O.C. wine usually made slightly fizzy (*frizzante*), it is best known in the U.S. under the Riunite label, which has a decidedly sweet, almost wine cooler–like flavor.

MARSALA—Sicilian D.O.C. fortified wines made in both sweet and dry versions. They are used in cooking as much as for drinking, but the better examples can be wonderful as a dessert wine. Recommended labels: Florio, Rallo.

MONTEPULCIANO D'ABRUZZO—Abruzzese D.O.C. red wine, usually quite massive and tannic though usually drunk rather young. It is a high-volume wine but one producer, Valentini, makes a superb example.

MÜLLER-THURGAU—Northern Italian wine using a hybrid of Riesling and Sylvaner grapes. It has a distinctly German-Austrian taste that goes well with the foods of the region.

OLTREPÒ PAVESE—Lombardian D.O.C. wines made in red and as a *spumante*. Recommended label: Zonin.

ORVIETO—Umbrian D.O.C. white wine that has shown great strides in modern viniculture. Usually dry, but there are some slightly sweet and sweet versions. Recommended labels: Barberani, Castello della Sala.

PICOLIT—Friulian sweet dessert wine, found in very small quantities in both Italy and the United States. One of the great, rare dessert wines of the world and appropriately expensive.

PINOT BIANCO—Widely planted grape variety—in France called *pinot blanc*—that makes a good everyday white wine for easy drinking.

PINOT GRIGIO—Oceans of mediocre Pinot Grigio came to the United States under the label Santa Margherita and cost far more than it should. Some, however, is quite pleasant. Recommended label: Marco Felluga.

PINOT NERO—Red wine grape, called *pinot noir* in France's Burgundy region. In Italy it rarely attains the status of a good Burgundy.

ROSSO DI MONTALCINO—Tuscan D.O.C. wine made in the same region as Brunello di Montalcino but considered a secondary wine to that illustrious leader. Still, Rosso di Montalcino is a very delicious ruby-red wine with some complexity and has only recently started inching up in price. Recommended label: Barbi-Colombini.

SALICE SALENTINO—Apulian D.O.C. red wine that has a surprisingly good fruited flavor with some decent backbone. It goes very well with spicy seafood. A lovely rosé is also produced. Recommended label: Leone di Castris.

SASSICAIA—Proprietary name for a noble Tuscan red wine made since 1968 and now considered one of Italy's finest.

SFURSAT—Lombardy name for a deeply colored red wine with an almost leathery taste.

SOAVE—Veneto D.O.C. white wine that ranges from the wholly insipid to the bright and refreshing. Mass produced, it is an everyday quaffing wine with just about any kind of fish. Recommended labels: Anselmi, Bolla.

TAURASI—Campanian D.O.C. red wine of superb structure, big body, and lovely bouquet. The pioneer producer of the varietal is Mastroberadino.

TIGNANELLO—Proprietary name of the Antinori wine company in Tuscany for a blend of Sangiovese and Cabernet grapes that produces an extraordinary, much-sought-after red wine considered one of Italy's finest.

TORGIANO—Umbrian D.O.C. zone that produces white and red wines of dependable, simple quality. Lungarotti is the principal and best producer.

TREBBIANO—A workhorse white grape, widely planted throughout Italy. It is a component in many wines as well as a white wine on its own. Trebbiano d'Abruzzo is widely marketed, the finest being made by the firm of Valentini.

VALPOLICELLA—Veneto D.O.C. lightweight to medium-bodied red with no particular distinction except when made into Amarone (see above). Recommended labels: Allegrini, Bolla, Fratelli Tedeschi.

VERDICCHIO—Marches D.O.C. white wine, once known by its green amphora- or fish-shaped bottle, now relegated among the cheaper Italian wines on the market. Pleasing and refreshing with seafood. Recommended label: Umani Ronchi.

VERNACCIA DI SAN GIMIGNANO—Tuscan D.O.C. white wine, now fresh and well balanced, though rarely distinguished. Recommended label: Teruzzi & Puthod.

This photo from the U.S. Office of War Information during World War II shows garment worker Raymond Fazio and his family enjoying an abundant, healthful dinner at their home in Corona, New York. Note that there is wine on the table (but tap water in a pitcher for the children), along with spaghetti and sliced white American bread. The family also shows how Italian-Americans somehow came to adopt the practice of eating spaghetti with both a fork and a spoon.

VINO NOBILE DI MONTEPULCIANO—Tuscan D.O.C.G. red wine of power and finesse that can age for several years to bring out its best qualities. Recommended labels: Valdipiatta, Fattoria del Cerro, Avignonesi.

J. M.

ANTIPASTI

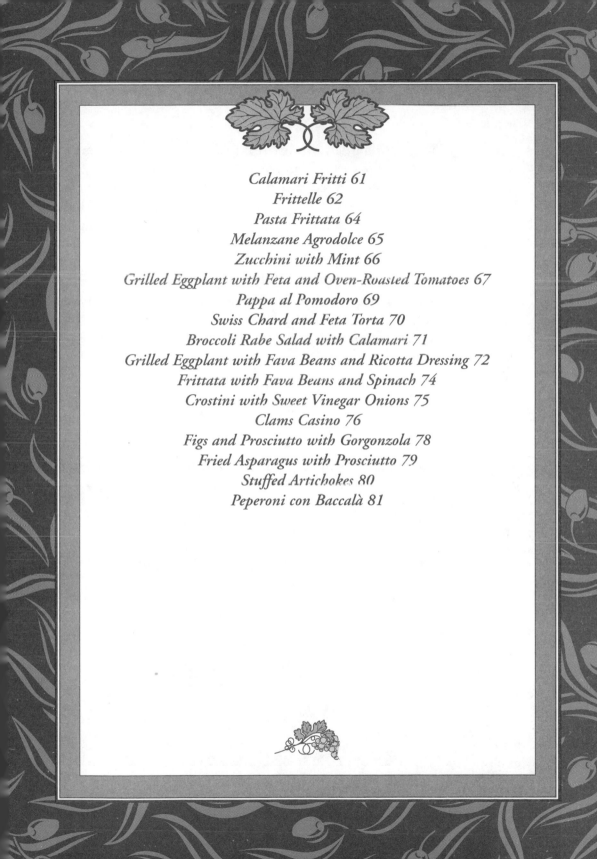

Calamari Fritti 61
Frittelle 62
Pasta Frittata 64
Melanzane Agrodolce 65
Zucchini with Mint 66
Grilled Eggplant with Feta and Oven-Roasted Tomatoes 67
Pappa al Pomodoro 69
Swiss Chard and Feta Torta 70
Broccoli Rabe Salad with Calamari 71
Grilled Eggplant with Fava Beans and Ricotta Dressing 72
Frittata with Fava Beans and Spinach 74
Crostini with Sweet Vinegar Onions 75
Clams Casino 76
Figs and Prosciutto with Gorgonzola 78
Fried Asparagus with Prosciutto 79
Stuffed Artichokes 80
Peperoni con Baccalà 81

ANTIPASTI

The word *antipasto* (ahn-tee-PAH-stoh) does not mean "before the pastas," but rather "before the meal," and refers to any foods served prior to soups, pastas, and main courses. The variety of antipasti is extraordinary, ranging from a few slices of prosciutto with melon or figs to eggplant or zucchini marinated in vinegar, salads, and elaborate dishes like *vitello tonnato* (veal lavished with a creamy tuna sauce).

In Italy, antipasti may well be the most complex items of the meal, with pasta being a form of comfort food and main dishes being quite simple. At home, Italians may have an array of antipasti for the Sunday family meal, while restaurants offer a whole table of antipasti from which to choose. In the United States, antipasti are usually divided into hot and cold appetizers, which may include anything from a cold seafood salad to fried calamari. Many of the recipes in this book fall under categories other than antipasti but may be used as a first course.

Antipasti should never be served cold or chilled, which robs them of their individual flavors. Leave them out in a cool place—a temperature above 75°F is getting too warm—and their flavors will flourish.

The congregational aspect of preparing food for a feast is shown in this photo of women cleaning calamari for a church festival in Illinois (June 1977).

CALAMARI FRITTI

There is no secret to making this extremely easy dish, which is an excellent antipasto or seafood course. The key is not to overcook the calamari or else it will become tough and tasteless. It should be tender and have its own flavor and not be covered with too much of a crust, which will pick up oil and make it taste greasy. The best way to ensure properly fried calamari is to maintain the temperature of the oil—370° to 380°F is best. Mixing a little cornmeal into the dredging flour adds crispness too.

SERVES 4

1 pound cleaned squid (see Note)
5 tablespoons all-purpose flour
5 tablespoons semolina flour or
   stone-ground yellow cornmeal
2 teaspoons salt, preferably kosher

½ teaspoon freshly ground black
   pepper
3 to 4 cups peanut oil
Lemon wedges or 1 cup Marinara
   Sauce (page 126), for serving

1. Cut the squid horizontally into ½-inch-thick rings. Cut the tentacles in half lengthwise. Pat the squid dry with paper towels.

2. In a shallow bowl or a plastic bag, mix the flour, semolina, salt, and pepper. Add the squid pieces, and stir or shake to cover with the flour mixture. Remove the squid, shaking the excess flour off the pieces, and place them on a wire rack. Let them sit for 10 minutes (this allows the coating to adhere well).

3. Pour the oil into a large saucepan (it should be 2 inches deep) and heat until it registers 375°F on a deep-frying thermometer. Carefully add one-quarter to one-third of the squid pieces to the oil, without crowding them, and fry for 1½ minutes. Remove immediately with a slotted spoon and drain on paper towels. Let the oil temperature rise back up to 375°F, and repeat with the rest of the squid.

4. Serve immediately, with lemon wedges or a side dish of Marinara Sauce.

WINE SUGGESTION: SOAVE

NOTE: If your fish market doesn't sell cleaned squid, here's how to clean it yourself. In a large bowl, soak the squid in cold water with a few ice

cubes for 20 minutes. Then, holding the body of the squid with one hand, pull the head off with the other hand. Cut across the head, just above the eyes, and discard the part with the eyes and the innards. In the body part, a hard piece, the cuttlebone, will be protruding. Grab it and pull it out. The outside reddish skin of the squid is edible but can be removed if desired by pulling it off the main body.

FRITTELLE

Frittelle (free-TEH-leh) means "little fried things," and these spaghetti cakes are a good way to use leftover unsauced pasta. In Italy *frittelle* are made fresh in a wide variety of ways and are often offered as part of a lavish antipasto table. They are also terrific as a snack or as a side dish to meat.

Besciamella (beh-sha-MEH-lah), or *balsamella*, is an Italian version of the cream and cheese sauce known as *béchamel* in French cuisine, and is used principally in Rome and northern Italy.

SERVES 4 TO 6

FOR THE BESCIAMELLA
3 tablespoons unsalted butter
3 tablespoons all-purpose flour
1 1/2 cups whole milk
1/2 teaspoon salt, preferably kosher

TO CONTINUE
2 tablespoons plus 1/4 to 1/3 cup olive oil
1 medium yellow onion, chopped
1/2 large or 1 small red bell pepper, cored and diced
2 garlic cloves, minced

Salt, preferably kosher
Freshly ground black pepper
2/3 cup freshly grated Pecorino Romano cheese
1/3 cup chopped salami
8 ounces angel hair pasta, broken into thirds and cooked al dente
1/4 cup chopped flat-leaf parsley
2 large eggs, beaten with 1 1/2 tablespoons water
1 to 1 1/2 cups plain dry bread-crumbs

1. Prepare the *besciamella*: In a medium saucepan, melt the butter over medium heat. Add the flour and cook, stirring, for about 2 minutes. Add the milk and salt and cook, stirring constantly, until the sauce starts to thicken. Keep cooking over low heat, stirring, for 2 minutes. Remove from the heat and set aside.

2. In a medium-size sauté pan, heat the 2 tablespoons olive oil over medium heat. Add the onion and bell pepper and cook, stirring, until soft and lightly browned, 6 to 8 minutes. Add the garlic and cook, stirring, for another 2 minutes. Season with salt and pepper to taste. Remove from the heat.

3. In a large bowl, combine the cooked onion mixture with the Pecorino cheese, salami, cooked pasta, parsley, *besciamella* sauce, and salt and pepper to taste. Stir together well. Grease a 9-inch square baking pan and pour the *frittelle* mixture into the pan; smooth the top. Cover with plastic wrap and refrigerate for 2 hours to set (this facilitates cutting it into squares).

4. Take the pan out of the refrigerator, remove the plastic wrap, and place a cutting board over the pan. Invert the pan with the cutting board, and tap the pan bottom to loosen the *frittelle*. Remove the pan, and with a sharp knife, cut the *frittelle* into 9 or 12 pieces. Dip the pieces into the beaten eggs and then roll them in the breadcrumbs to coat well.

5. In a large sauté pan, heat the remaining ¼ cup olive oil over medium heat for 1 to 2 minutes (when you dip the corner of a *frittelle* into the oil, it should sizzle). Add the *frittelle* pieces to the hot oil and fry them on both sides until nicely browned, 8 to 10 minutes. Between batches, add more olive oil if needed, and heat it thoroughly. Serve immediately.

WINE SUGGESTION:
BARBERA

Parmigiano-Reggiano is an expensive cheese—sometimes $15 a pound—while a good Pecorino costs considerably less. Though sharper and saltier than Parmigiano, Pecorino adds measurably to any hearty, robust dish where you might otherwise be tempted to use Parmigiano. Because of its pungency, you should use a bit less Pecorino. Just make sure you buy a very fine imported Pecorino.

PASTA FRITTATA

I talians are not big egg eaters, and it would be unusual for an
Italian to sit down to a plate of eggs and bacon in the morning.
But this easy-to-make dish might well be served in Italy or here
as a great brunch or lunch dish, or even as an antipasto before the
main course at dinner.

SERVES 4 TO 6

6 tablespoons extra-virgin olive oil
1 medium portobello mushroom,
 stemmed and cut into 1/2-inch
 pieces
1 large yellow onion, thinly sliced
7 large eggs, beaten
2 plum tomatoes, seeded and
 chopped (about 1/2 cup)
2 tablespoons chopped flat-leaf
 parsley

1/2 cup freshly grated Parmigiano-
 Reggiano cheese
1/2 cup soft ricotta salata cheese
 (page 31), cut into 1/4-inch
 pieces
1 cup cooked elbow macaroni or
 other leftover pasta
Salt, preferably kosher
Freshly ground black pepper

1. In a sauté pan, heat 2 tablespoons of the olive oil over high heat.
Add the mushroom pieces and cook, tossing frequently, until browned,
about 4 minutes. Set aside in a bowl.

2. In the same sauté pan, add 1 tablespoon of the olive oil and cook the
onion over medium heat, stirring, until soft and lightly browned, 6 to
8 minutes. Add to the bowl with the mushrooms.

3. In a large mixing bowl, combine the eggs, the plum tomatoes,
parsley, Parmigiano-Reggiano, ricotta salata, onions and mushrooms,
and pasta. Season with salt and pepper, and mix well.

4. In a large nonstick frying pan, heat 2 tablespoons of the olive oil
over medium heat. Add the egg mixture to the pan, distributing the
solids if they are clumped together. Cook the egg mixture, occasionally
poking it with a fork and lifting it when it has set, allowing some of
the liquid to seep to the bottom of the pan to help it cook a bit faster.
When the frittata is lightly browned on the bottom but not completely
set (after 8 to 10 minutes), take a large dish and invert it over the pan.
Turn the heat off, carefully grab the pan and the dish together, and
quickly flip them over. Place the pan back on the stove, and heat the

remaining 1 tablespoon olive oil in it. Gently slide the frittata from the dish into the pan to cook the other side. Cook until lightly browned, about 4 minutes more.

5. Turn the frittata out onto a clean dish, and serve warm or at room temperature.

WINE SUGGESTION: ARNEIS

MELANZANE AGRODOLCE

Agrodolce (ah-groh-DOHL-cheh) dishes are those that have a balance of sweet and sour flavors, the latter usually provided by vinegar. They are among the most beloved dishes of the Mediterranean, found in most of the area's food cultures, so that the farther south in Italy you go, the more *agrodolce* dishes you will find.

SERVES 6 TO 8

2 pounds eggplant, unpeeled, cut into ³/4-inch cubes

2 tablespoons salt, preferably kosher

5 tablespoons plus ¹/4 cup extra-virgin olive oil

2 green bell peppers, cored and cut into ³/4-inch pieces

1 Spanish onion, thinly sliced

2 carrots, halved lengthwise and cut into ¹/4-inch-thick slices

Freshly ground black pepper

¹/3 cup dark raisins

1 bottled pepperoncini pepper, chopped

1¹/2 cups canned Italian-style tomatoes, chopped, with juices

1 bay leaf

¹/4 cup white or cider vinegar

3 teaspoons sugar

1. In a large colander, toss the eggplant cubes while sprinkling 2 tablespoons salt over them. Set aside over a bowl or in an empty sink and let drain for 30 minutes.

2. In a large saucepan, heat 3 tablespoons of the olive oil over medium-high heat. Add the bell peppers and cook, stirring frequently, until softened, about 4 minutes. Add the onion and cook, stirring, until browned, about 4 minutes. Add the carrots and cook, stirring, for 2 to

4 minutes more. Season with salt and pepper to taste. Add the raisins, pepperoncini, tomatoes, and bay leaf, and bring to a boil. Reduce the heat and simmer for 5 minutes.

3. While the onion/tomato mixture is cooking, pat the eggplant dry with paper towels. Heat the ¼ cup olive oil in a large nonstick sauté pan over high heat. When the oil is hot, add half of the eggplant and toss immediately to coat with oil on all sides. Cook, tossing often to brown on most sides, for 6 to 8 minutes. Using a slotted spoon, immediately transfer the eggplant cubes to paper towels to drain. Add the remaining 2 tablespoons olive oil to the sauté pan, add the rest of the eggplant, and brown the same way.

4. Add the eggplant to the onion-tomato mixture and bring to a boil. Reduce the heat and simmer for 15 minutes. Stir in the vinegar and sugar, and cook for 3 minutes. Adjust the seasonings to taste.

5. Let the eggplant cool to room temperature before serving. This can be made a day ahead.

WINE SUGGESTION: TAURASI

ZUCCHINI WITH MINT

Few herbs can enliven a dish or destroy it as dramatically as can mint. When it's fresh, the leaves bright and at their peak, it adds measurably as a flavoring; but when the leaves are tired, brittle, and added in too large an amount, they give an all-too-powerful acrid taste to anything they touch. Here mint is a mere hint in a dish that is typical of the simple cooking of southern Italy and Sicily.

SERVES 4 TO 6

2 pounds zucchini
¼ cup olive oil
Salt, preferably kosher
Freshly ground black pepper
2 garlic cloves, crushed
2 tablespoons coarsely chopped
   fresh mint

1 teaspoon chopped fresh oregano,
   or ½ teaspoon dried
3 tablespoons extra-virgin olive oil
1 tablespoon red wine vinegar

1. On a mandoline or by hand, slice the zucchini lengthwise into ¼-inch-thick strips.

2. In a large sauté pan, heat the ¼ cup olive oil over medium-high heat. When it is hot, add a few of the zucchini slices and sauté until slightly browned, 2 to 4 minutes. Turn the slices over and sauté until browned on the other side, 2 to 4 minutes more. Remove them to a dish and repeat with the rest of the slices. Sprinkle the slices with salt and pepper as you place them in the dish.

3. Using the same sauté pan over low heat, add the garlic and cook, stirring, for 2 minutes. Pour the oil and garlic over the zucchini strips. Add the mint, oregano, extra-virgin olive oil, and vinegar. Tilt the dish to gently blend the ingredients, and spoon the mixture over and between the slices of zucchini. Cover and let marinate for about 6 hours at room temperature. This dish may be prepared up to 1 day in advance (refrigerate it and then let it return to room temperature), but will get soggy if kept any longer than that.

WINE SUGGESTION: EST! EST!! EST!!!

> "Room temperature" is a very imprecise and misleading phrase, especially if one's rooms register at 80°F, which is highly likely in many homes and restaurants. White wines can be served chilled, but red wines should be cool, ideally around 55°F. Cheese loses much of its flavor if it is served straight from the refrigerator, but it will also become too pungent and leaden if served too warm. A good temperature for cheese is about 65° to 70°F.

GRILLED EGGPLANT WITH FETA AND OVEN-ROASTED TOMATOES

Italians don't use goat's cheese (*caprino*) as much as the French or Greeks do, but the piquancy of feta adds measurably to the flavors of this excellent appetizer. You may use regular eggplant instead of the Japanese variety called for below—just cut it into half-inch-thick lengthwise slices and then cut each slice in half lengthwise.

SERVES 4

4 long Japanese eggplants, cut into
   ¹/2-inch-thick lengthwise slices
Salt, preferably kosher
4¹/2 tablespoons olive oil
Freshly ground black pepper
2 tablespoons freshly squeezed
   lemon juice
¹/3 cup Oven-Roasted Tomatoes
   (page 332), cut into ¹/4-inch
   pieces

¹/4 cup Calamata olives, pitted and
   sliced
1 garlic clove, minced
1 tablespoon chopped flat-leaf
   parsley
¹/2 cup crumbled feta cheese

1. Place the eggplant slices in a colander and sprinkle with 1 table-spoon salt. Set the colander over a bowl or in the sink, and let the slices sweat for 30 minutes to 1 hour. Pat them dry with paper towels.

2. Prepare a grill or stovetop grill pan. Brush the eggplant slices with 1¹/2 tablespoons of the oil, and season with salt and pepper to taste. Grill the eggplant slices until they are browned (not charred) and the flesh is soft when pierced. Set aside the grilled slices.

3. In a medium-size bowl, combine the remaining 3 tablespoons olive oil with the lemon juice, tomatoes, olives, garlic, and salt and pepper to taste; mix well. Add the parsley and feta cheese, and toss gently.

4. Place the eggplant slices on a platter, and spoon the tomato-feta mixture on top. Serve at room temperature.

WINE SUGGESTION: BIANCO DI CUSTOZA

NOTE: The eggplant may be grilled in advance, and the topping can be made a little earlier in the day and set aside. Just before serving, toss the topping lightly and spoon it over the eggplant.

A poignant photo from 1905 by Lewis W. Hine showing the stead-fastness, eagerness, and trepidation with which Italian-American immigrants faced their new world as they were about to disembark at Ellis Island.

PAPPA AL POMODORO

Plain and simply put, this is "tomato pap"—one of those easy-to-digest meals for children, and the very soul of Italian peasant cookery. We make this dish only once or twice a year—in August or September, when the tomatoes and basil come straight from our garden and have fabulous sweetness and pungency. This is one of the most rewarding of discoveries—a very basic dish of extraordinary flavor that teaches us a great deal about the importance of seasonal ingredients.

SERVES 4

2¹/2 pounds very ripe tomatoes
2 tablespoons unsalted butter
6 tablespoons extra-virgin olive oil
2 medium yellow onions, chopped
4 garlic cloves, minced
Salt, preferably kosher
Freshly ground black pepper

¹/3 cup sliced fresh basil
2¹/2 cups cubed crusty Italian
    bread (³/4-inch cubes)
Shaved Parmigiano-Reggiano
    cheese
Truffle oil (optional)

1. Fill a medium-size saucepan with water and bring it to a boil. Reduce the heat to medium, add 2 to 3 tomatoes at a time, and leave them in the hot water for 1 minute (test to see if the skins come off easily). Transfer the tomatoes to a bowl filled with cold water and leave them in the water for 1 to 2 minutes. Remove them from the water and place on a cutting board. Repeat with the remaining tomatoes. Slip the skins off, cut the tomatoes in half, remove the seeds, and chop them.

2. In a large saucepan, heat the butter and 1 tablespoon of the olive oil over medium heat. Add the onions and cook, stirring occasionally, until lightly colored, 6 to 8 minutes. Add the remaining 5 tablespoons oil and the garlic, and continue cooking, stirring, for another 2 minutes.

3. Add the chopped tomatoes to the onions, season with salt and pepper to taste, and bring to a simmer. Cook for 5 minutes. Stir in the basil and the bread. Transfer the mixture immediately to a serving dish, sprinkle it with shavings of Parmigiano-Reggiano, and drizzle with truffle oil if desired.

WINE SUGGESTION: TORGIANO ROSSO

SWISS CHARD
AND FETA TORTA

In Italy, Swiss chard may be called either *bietola* (bee-EH-toh-lah) or *erbette* (ehr-BEH-teh), and this hearty, healthy green veg-etable is actually believed to be native to Italy, not Switzerland. It makes a wonderful torta when combined with the fresh saline taste of feta.

SERVES 4 TO 6

FOR THE PASTRY
1¹/3 cups all-purpose flour
¹/8 teaspoon salt, preferably kosher
1¹/2 tablespoons extra-virgin olive oil
4 tablespoons unsalted butter

FOR THE FILLING
8 large Swiss chard leaves, stems removed, thinly sliced
Salt, preferably kosher
2 tablespoons olive oil
1 leek, white part only, washed and thinly sliced

1 medium yellow onion, chopped
1 medium all-purpose potato (or 1 large red), boiled until tender, peeled, and cubed
2 tablespoons chopped flat-leaf parsley
1 cup crumbled feta cheese
¹/3 cup cubed Fontina cheese
Salt, preferably kosher
Freshly ground black pepper
2 large eggs, lightly beaten
4 tablespoons extra-virgin olive oil
2 tablespoons freshly grated Parmigiano-Reggiano cheese

1. Prepare the pastry: In a food processor, combine the flour, salt, oil, and butter, and process briefly. Drizzle in ¹/3 cup cold water and process briefly. Test to see if the dough sticks together. If not, gradually add more water, a tablespoon at a time. Remove the dough from the processor, knead it a few times on a lightly floured surface, and form it into a ball. Flatten it a bit, wrap it in wax paper, and refrigerate for 1 hour or as long as 6 to 8 hours.

2. Meanwhile, prepare the filling: Place the Swiss chard in a colander, sprinkle

---

Never underestimate the subtle power of good, freshly grated Parmigiano-Reggiano to bring out the flavors of a dish. By the same token, Parmigiano does not go with every Italian dish. The basic rule of thumb is that dishes with sauces whose main components are garlic and oil do not need Parmigiano, nor do the vast majority of seafood dishes, including seafood pastas. Sometimes, as with a delicate dish of vegetables like Pappa al Pomodoro (page 69), shavings of Parmigiano are preferable to grated.

with 1½ teaspoons salt, and set the colander aside over a bowl or in the sink for 30 minutes.

3. Preheat the oven to 375°F.

4. In a small saucepan, heat the 2 tablespoons olive oil over medium heat. Add the leek and onion and cook, stirring until softened, about 5 minutes. Transfer to a large bowl.

5. Add the Swiss chard to the bowl, along with the potato, parsley, feta, Fontina, salt and pepper to taste, the eggs, and 2 tablespoons of the extra-virgin olive oil. Mix well.

6. Lightly flour a sheet of plastic wrap, and place the dough on it. Flour the dough lightly, and cover it with another piece of wax paper. Roll the dough out to form a 15-inch circle. Remove the plastic wrap and place the dough on an oiled baking sheet.

7. Spread the filling on the dough, leaving a 1½-inch border all around. Fold the border over the filling, overlapping itself slightly every 2 inches or so. Brush the dough with 1 tablespoon of the extra-virgin olive oil. Sprinkle the filling with the Parmigiano-Reggiano, and drizzle with the remaining 1 tablespoon extra-virgin olive oil. Bake for 30 minutes, or until the crust and filling are lightly browned. Slice, and serve hot or at room temperature.

WINE SUGGESTION: PINOT BIANCO

BROCCOLI RABE SALAD WITH CALAMARI

The bitterness of the broccoli rabe (also known as *broccoli di rape*), dressed with garlic and the bite of red pepper flakes, gives a delightful and unexpected edge to the briny taste of the calamari.

SERVES 4

1 pound broccoli rabe, rinsed,
  trimmed, and cut into 3-inch
  pieces
Salt, preferably kosher
8 ounces cleaned squid bodies
  (see Note, page 61), cut into
  ¹/4-inch-thick rings

2 garlic cloves, minced
7 tablespoons freshly squeezed
  lemon juice
7 tablespoons extra-virgin olive oil
Freshly ground black pepper
¹/2 teaspoon red pepper flakes
1 medium red onion, thinly sliced

1. In a large saucepan, bring 1¹/2 quarts water to a boil. Add the broccoli rabe and boil until the thickest part is done but still firm, 2 to 4 minutes. Drain, rinse under cold water to stop the cooking, and drain again. Pat dry to extract as much water as possible.

2. In the same saucepan, bring 1 quart water to a boil. Add a pinch of salt, add the squid, and boil for no more than 1 minute. Drain, rinse under cold water, drain again, and pat dry.

3. In a medium-size bowl, combine the garlic, lemon juice, olive oil, salt and pepper to taste, and the red pepper flakes. Stir to blend.

4. Add the squid, broccoli rabe, and onion, and toss. Check the seasoning. Serve within 15 minutes.

WINE SUGGESTION: GRECO DI TUFO

NOTE: Everything may be prepared ahead of time. You can cook the broccoli rabe and the squid as directed and set them aside. The dressing may be prepared a day ahead. Before serving, combine the broccoli rabe, calamari, onion, and dressing.

GRILLED EGGPLANT WITH FAVA BEANS AND RICOTTA DRESSING

Whenever we spot fava beans in the market—in the spring, generally in specialty markets—we buy all they have and make several dishes with them, including this one with eggplant and the creamy richness of ricotta.

SERVES 4 TO 6

1 eggplant, cut into ³/8- to
   ¹/2-inch-thick slices
Salt, preferably kosher
3 tablespoons olive oil
1 sweet onion, such as Vidalia, or
   1 small Spanish onion, cut into
   ¹/4-inch-thick slices
4 garlic cloves, unpeeled
1¹/2 pounds fresh fava beans,
   shelled and cooked (see Note)

FOR THE OLIVE OIL DRESSING
¹/4 cup extra-virgin olive oil
4 fresh basil leaves, minced
1 tablespoon balsamic vinegar
Salt, preferably kosher
Freshly ground black pepper

FOR THE RICOTTA DRESSING
¹/2 cup ricotta cheese
4 fresh basil leaves, minced
1¹/2 tablespoons freshly squeezed
   lemon juice
Salt, preferably kosher
Freshly ground black pepper

1. Place the eggplant slices in a colander, salt them generously, and set the colander over a bowl or in the sink. Let the eggplant sweat for 30 minutes to 1 hour. Then pat the slices dry with paper towels.

2. With a pastry brush, brush the olive oil over both sides of the eggplant slices, the onion slices, and the garlic cloves. Prepare a grill or stovetop grill pan and grill the vegetables until they are soft and browned, 6 to 8 minutes. Place the eggplant, onions, and fava beans on a large platter. Set the garlic aside.

3. Make the olive oil dressing: In a small bowl, combine the olive oil, basil, balsamic vinegar, and salt and pepper to taste. Squeeze the softened garlic from 2 of the grilled cloves into the bowl. Stir to blend. Pour the dressing over the eggplant, onions, and fava beans and toss gently.

4. Make the ricotta dressing: In a small bowl, combine the ricotta, basil, lemon juice, and salt and pepper to taste. Squeeze the softened garlic from the other 2 cloves into the bowl and stir to blend. Pour this dressing over the center of the vegetables but do not stir it in. Serve at room temperature.

WINE SUGGESTION:
CABERNET FRANC

Homemade ricotta is remarkably easy to make and worth trying. In a large saucepan, combine 2 quarts whole milk with 1 cup live-culture buttermilk or sour cream. Bring to a boil, reduce the heat, and simmer until the milk curdles, 2 to 5 minutes. Line a large sieve with 2 layers of cheesecloth with a generous overhang down the sides, and pour in the milk. Gather the overhanging cheesecloth to form a bag, squeeze out the excess liquid, tie with a string, and let hang over a bowl for about 1 hour. What you will have is creamy fresh ricotta, to be eaten immediately. Add salt and/or pepper if you like.

NOTE: To prepare the fava beans, cook the shelled beans in a pot of simmering water for 2 to 4 minutes. After 2 minutes, check a bean to see if it is al dente and comes out of the skin easily; if not, continue cooking. Drain, rinse under cold water, and drain again. Slit the skin at the top of each fava bean and squeeze out the bean, discarding the skin.

FRITTATA WITH
FAVA BEANS AND SPINACH

A frittata (free-TAH-tah) is an Italian egg dish that can include any number of ingredients. This is easy to make, very pretty to look at, and a great leftover too. It also serves very well as a brunch or lunch dish.

SERVES 4 TO 6

6 tablespoons olive oil
1 medium yellow onion, thinly
   sliced
6 large eggs, beaten
²/₃ cup freshly grated Parmigiano-
   Reggiano cheese
1¹/₂ pounds fresh fava beans,
   shelled and cooked (see Note,
   above)

1 pound spinach, cooked and
   chopped (see Note, page 75)
7 fresh basil leaves, chopped
Salt, preferably kosher
Freshly ground black pepper

1. In a small sauté pan, heat 2 tablespoons of the olive oil over medium heat and cook the onion, stirring occasionally, until soft and lightly browned, about 5 minutes. Set aside.

2. In a medium-size bowl, combine the eggs, Parmigiano-Reggiano, beans, spinach, basil, salt and pepper to taste, and the sautéed onions. Stir together well.

3. Heat a large nonstick frying pan over medium heat and add 2 tablespoons of the remaining olive oil. Pour in the egg mixture, distributing the solids if they are clumped together. Cook the egg mixture, occasionally poking it with a fork and lifting it when it has set, allowing some of the liquid to seep to the bottom of the pan to help it cook a bit faster. When the frittata is lightly browned on the bottom but not com-

pletely set (after 5 to 8 minutes), take a large dish and invert it over the pan. Turn the heat off, carefully grab the pan and the dish together, and quickly flip them over. Place the pan back on the stove, and heat the remaining 2 tablespoons olive oil in it. Gently slide the frittata from the dish into the pan to cook the other side. Cook for about 4 minutes, until lightly browned.

4. Turn the frittata out onto a clean dish, and serve warm or at room temperature.

WINE SUGGESTION: BARBERA D'ASTI

NOTE: To prepare the spinach, cut off and discard the stems, and rinse and drain the leaves. Add the spinach to a pot of 2 quarts boiling water with 1 teaspoon salt, and boil for 30 seconds. Drain, rinse under cold water, and drain again. Squeeze the water out with your hands, and chop.

CROSTINI WITH SWEET VINEGAR ONIONS

A great way to make toast a feast. Be sure to make plenty of these crostini (kroh-STEE-nee), because people won't be able to stop eating them. Then again, if you make too many, your guests may not eat the main course! Day-old bread works just fine.

SERVES 4

⅓ cup pignoli (pine nuts)	⅓ cup red wine vinegar
¼ cup extra-virgin olive oil	18 fresh sage leaves
1 large Spanish onion, thinly sliced	2 tablespoons chopped flat-leaf
Salt, preferably kosher	parsley
Freshly ground black pepper	6 to 8 pieces crusty bread, grilled
3 tablespoons sugar	

1. Heat a nonstick frying pan over medium heat, add the pignoli, and toast them, for 3 to 5 minutes, shaking the pan to brown them evenly. Keep a close eye on them, because they burn quickly. Set the nuts aside.

2. Heat a sauté pan over medium heat, and add the olive oil. Add the onion and cook, stirring, until golden, about 10 minutes. Season with

salt and pepper to taste, add the sugar, and cook, stirring, for another 3 minutes. Add the vinegar, sage, and parsley, and cook, stirring, for about 4 minutes. Stir in the pignoli.

3. Serve on the grilled bread, either hot or at room temperature.

WINE SUGGESTION:
VERNACCIA DI SAN GIMIGNANO

CLAMS CASINO

L ike Caesar Salad (see page 119), Clams Casino is usually believed to be a classic Italian dish simply because of its Italianate name. In fact, the recipe originated at the Casino at Narragansett Pier in New York around 1917. In his autobiography, *Inns and Outs* (1939), restaurateur Julius Keller described how the society figure Mrs. Paran Stevens asked Keller, then maître d' at the Casino, to create a new dish for a luncheon she was holding for friends. Keller came up with one for clams baked with bacon. When Stevens inquired as to the dish's name, Keller replied, "It has no name, Mrs. Stevens; but we shall call it Clams Casino in honor of this restaurant."

While many recipes for Clams Casino insist on opening up the live clams, we've found that steaming them briefly opens them up and tenderizes the flesh a bit before they're baked.

SERVES 4

4 tablespoons (¹/2 stick) unsalted butter

2 tablespoons minced shallots

2 tablespoons finely chopped fresh or bottled roasted red pepper

¹/2 teaspoon Worcestershire sauce

2 tablespoons finely chopped green bell pepper

4 teaspoons finely chopped flat-leaf parsley

4 teaspoons freshly squeezed lemon juice

Freshly ground black pepper

¹/2 cup white wine, such as Chardonnay

24 littleneck or cherrystone clams, well rinsed

3 strips bacon, each cut into 8 pieces

1. Preheat the oven to 450°F.

2. In a small saucepan, combine the butter, shallots, red pepper, Worcestershire sauce, green pepper, parsley, lemon juice, and black pepper to taste. Place over low heat until the butter melts, then remove from the heat. Stir to blend, and set aside.

3. In a large sauté pan, heat the wine over medium-high heat. Add the clams, bring to a boil, and reduce the heat to medium. Cover the pan with a tight-fitting lid and let steam until the clams open, 3 to 5 minutes. Remove the pan from the heat. Carefully remove the top shell from each clam, being careful not to spill the liquid surrounding the clam. Discard any clams that have not opened.

4. Spoon the butter sauce over each clam, and top with a piece of bacon. Arrange the clams in a baking pan, and bake for 5 minutes. Increase the oven temperature to broil. Heat the clams under the broiler for 2 to 3 minutes, until the bacon crisps a bit, and serve.

WINE SUGGESTION: CHARDONNAY

Writers and journalists of the 1930s and '40s favored the no-nonsense atmosphere of Italian-American restaurants like John's in New York, located on 12th Street and Second Avenue.

FIGS AND PROSCIUTTO WITH GORGONZOLA

Fresh figs—in season now several times a year—should be very tender but not mushy. The prosciutto can be domestic, though imported Prosciutto di Parma or Prosciutto di San Daniele is best. And we are not against using good domestic Gorgonzola that is not too salty; imported Gorgonzola that is too ripe can be acrid, ammoniated, and unpleasant, but when it is in perfect condition, it is superb. The only problem with beginning a meal with these luscious little morsels of sweetness and saltiness: It's a challenge to produce a following course that's as delectable.

SERVES 4

8 fresh figs, cut in half
6 slices prosciutto (not paper-
    thin), each cut into 3 pieces
1 1/2 tablespoons olive oil

4 to 6 ounces Gorgonzola cheese,
    crumbled
Coarsely ground black pepper

1. Wrap a fig half with a piece of prosciutto, and spear it on a skewer so that the prosciutto is secured. Repeat with all the pieces, skewering 4 figs on each skewer. Brush the oil over all the pieces.

2. Heat a stovetop grill pan (or the broiler) over medium heat, and grill the figs for 3 to 4 minutes, turning the skewers to brown on both sides.

3. Divide the Gorgonzola among 4 plates, placing it in the middle of the plate. Place 4 grilled figs on each plate, evenly spaced around the Gorgonzola. Grind some pepper over the dish, and serve.

WINE SUGGESTION:
PROSECCO

FRIED ASPARAGUS WITH PROSCIUTTO

A wonderful first course. The saline taste of the prosciutto and the texture of the breadcrumbs make it a fine accompaniment to slices of fresh unsalted mozzarella and crusty country bread.

SERVES 4

2¹/8 teaspoons salt, preferably kosher

12 large asparagus spears, hard ends cut off and bottoms peeled

6 thin slices prosciutto (about ¹/4 pound), cut in half diagonally

1 large egg

¹/2 cup plain dry breadcrumbs

2 tablespoons freshly grated Parmigiano-Reggiano cheese

¹/2 teaspoon freshly ground black pepper

¹/4 cup olive oil

1¹/2 tablespoons unsalted butter

1. Bring 1¹/2 quarts water to a boil in a large saucepan. Add 2 teaspoons of the salt and the asparagus, reduce the heat, and simmer until the asparagus is cooked but still firm, 2 to 3 minutes. Drain, and immediately submerge in cold water to stop the cooking. Drain again and pat dry.

2. Place an asparagus spear diagonally on a piece of prosciutto, and roll the prosciutto around the asparagus so it covers the spear. Set aside and repeat with the remaining asparagus and prosciutto.

3. In a shallow bowl or on a platter that is as long as the asparagus spears, beat the egg with 1¹/2 tablespoons water. Place the breadcrumbs, Parmigiano-Reggiano, pepper, and the remaining ¹/8 teaspoon salt on a piece of wax paper; mix together.

4. Dip an asparagus spear into the egg wash and then roll it in the breadcrumbs to coat. Set it aside and repeat with the rest of the asparagus.

5. In a large frying pan, heat the oil and the butter over medium-high heat. When the mixture is hot, add the asparagus and sauté, turning to brown on all sides, 4 to 6 minutes. Place on a serving platter and serve immediately.

WINE SUGGESTION:
RIESLING RENANO (COLLI ORIENTALI DEL FRIULI)

NOTE: You can prepare the asparagus through Step 4 up to a day ahead. Place the coated spears on a platter, cover with plastic wrap, and refrigerate until ready to sauté.

STUFFED ARTICHOKES

Ⓞne of the weekly items around the Mariani house, this is always served as a first course, and there is never a leaf left.

SERVES 4

1 1/4 cups homemade plain bread-
    crumbs (see Note)
3 tablespoons freshly grated
    Pecorino Romano cheese
1/2 cup freshly grated Parmigiano-
    Reggiano cheese
2 garlic cloves, minced

2 tablespoons chopped fresh mint
3 tablespoons chopped flat-leaf
    parsley
Salt, preferably kosher
Freshly ground black pepper
1/2 cup extra-virgin olive oil
4 large artichokes

1. In a medium-size bowl, combine the breadcrumbs, Pecorino, Parmigiano-Reggiano, garlic, mint, parsley, and salt and pepper to taste. Mix thoroughly. Add the olive oil in a slow stream, stirring continuously.

2. Cut about 3/4 inch off the tops of the artichokes, and snip off the remaining pointy tips. Cut the stems off so that the artichokes will sit without toppling over. Pry open the artichoke leaves and fill the spaces with the breadcrumb mixture.

3. Place the artichokes in a pot that will hold them snugly. Add water to the depth of 1 inch. Bring it to a boil, cover, and reduce the heat to medium-low. Simmer for 30 to 45 minutes, depending on the size of the artichokes. Test for doneness by pulling out a leaf and tasting for tenderness. Serve hot or at room temperature.

WINE SUGGESTION: PINOT GRIGIO

NOTE: To prepare homemade plain breadcrumbs, take two or three 1/2-inch-thick slices of Italian bread. Slice off the crusts and process in a food processor until finely chopped.

Peperoni con Baccalà

S alting and drying is an ancient method of preserving fish, and *baccalà*—heavily salted, dry-as-leather cod—is a difficult taste for most palates to acquire. But among those who love it— and that includes most old-timers in Italy—it has the ineffable flavor of the sea.

While *baccalà* is usually used in hearty, lusty dishes with plenty of tomato, onions, and garlic, we found a highly refined recipe at Il Cigno, a restaurant in Scarsdale, New York. There, chef-owner Steve DePietro has stuffed roasted peppers with *baccalà* to make a light antipasto that may well convince you that this is a taste you'd enjoy acquiring. Keep in mind that the salt cod must soak for 3 days before you cook it.

SERVES 6 TO 8

FOR THE COD
1 pound skinless, boneless salt cod
2 garlic cloves, minced
1/4 cup extra-virgin olive oil
1/2 cup heavy cream
Freshly ground black pepper
Plain dry breadcrumbs, if needed
6 roasted red peppers (page 332),
    cut in half lengthwise

FOR THE BASIL VINAIGRETTE
1/2 cup extra-virgin olive oil
1/4 cup red wine vinegar
5 fresh basil leaves, chopped
Salt, preferably kosher
Freshly ground black pepper

1. Place the cod in a medium-size bowl, and cover it with water by 2 inches. Cover the bowl with plastic wrap, place it in the refrigerator, and let the cod soak for 3 days, changing the water each day.

2. Remove the salt cod from the soaking water and place it in a medium-size saucepan. Cover it with water and bring to a boil. Reduce the heat to a simmer and cook until the fish flakes to the touch, 5 to 7 minutes. Drain, and let cool.

3. Combine the garlic with the olive oil in a small bowl, and set aside.

4. Put the fish into a food processor, and puree. With the machine running, drizzle in the cream and process until smooth. In the same manner, add the olive oil-garlic mixture. Add pepper to taste. If the

mixture is too thin, add a little bit of breadcrumbs to thicken. Cover and refrigerate for 2 to 3 hours.

5. Divide the baccalà into 12 portions, and form them into cylindrical shapes. Stuff each roasted pepper half with the filling, rolling the peppers over themselves to enclose the filling.

6. Prepare the vinaigrette. In a small bowl, combine the olive oil, vinegar, basil leaves, and salt and pepper to taste, and whisk to mix well. Spoon some vinaigrette over the baccalà-stuffed peppers, and serve.

WINE SUGGESTION: VALPOLICELLA

Italians from seaside towns in the Old Country easily obtained jobs in the fishing industry in the United States, where they eventually bought their own boats, then owned whole fishing fleets.

SOUPS

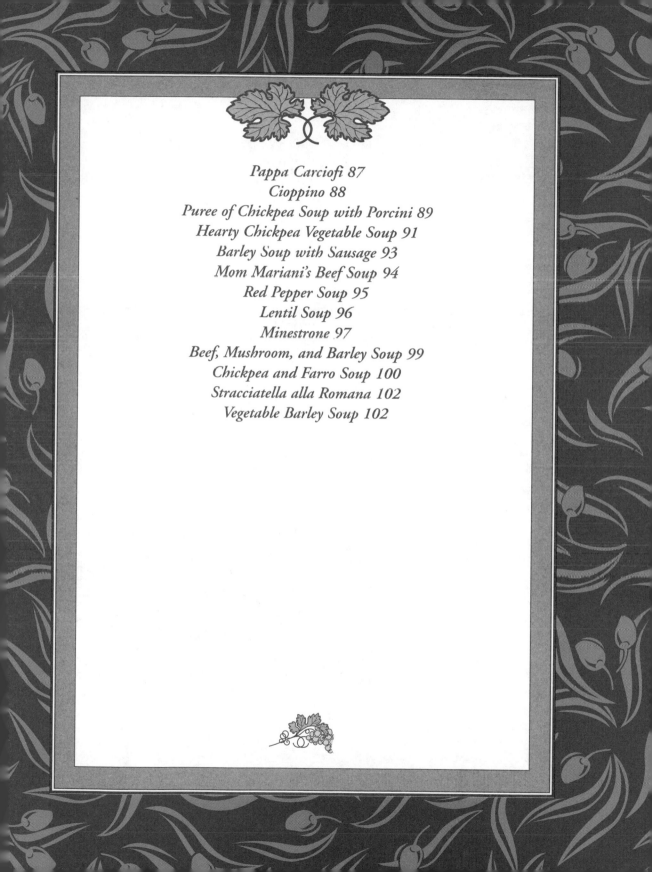

SOUPS

I n Italy, soups fall into four categories: *zuppa*, which is a thick soup that might contain meat, poultry, or seafood, usually served over a slice of bread or toast; *brodo*, broth; *minestra*, which is a broth containing vegetables and/or grains; and *crema*, a cream soup or one with pureed vegetables.

Italians love soup, often substituting it for a pasta course. In the evening, a hearty *zuppa* or *minestra* might form the principal dish of the meal.

S icilian immigrant Vincent Taormina settled in New Orleans and by 1905 was importing food products, principally olive oil, to sell to the Sicilian community in that city. By 1925 the business was rapidly growing, so Taormina merged his company with his cousin's food business to form the Uddo & Taormina Corporation of New Orleans. Later, Vincent Taormina moved to New York to establish his own import business there, merging with the Uddo & Taormina company in 1927 to form the Progresso Italian Food Corporation. When World War II prevented the importation of Italian food products, the family opened their own manufacturing plant in Vineland, New Jersey, and by 1949 they had produced their first canned soup—the first canned ready-to-serve soup in

America—a minestrone based on an old family recipe. In 1969 Imasco Foods bought the company for $30 million, and in turn sold it to the Ogden Corporation in 1979 for $40 million, which built it into a major brand. In fact, Ogden bought two twenty-five-ton clam dredgers in Cape May, New Jersey, just to supply enough clams for their products. Eight years later Ogden sold the company to Pet Inc., which was itself acquired by Grand Metropolitan PLC in 1995.

In an effort to counter stereotypes like "greaseballs," Italian-Americans quickly saw the value in having spotless, sanitary conditions in their food establishments, as shown in this 1933 photo of Frank J. and Frances Russo's spic-and-span, well-ordered Italian-American grocery in St. Paul, Minnesota.

PAPPA CARCIOFI

Here's an interesting twist on Pappa al Pomodoro (page 69) performed by Todd English, chef-owner of Olives restaurant and author of *The Olives Table*, from which this recipe is adapted. Artichokes have an odd effect on wines, making them all taste sweet, so we have not given a wine suggestion with this dish. This is one of those useful soups that's delicious either hot or cold.

SERVES 4 TO 6

1 tablespoon extra-virgin olive oil
1 tablespoon chopped garlic
1/2 Spanish onion, thinly sliced
1 1/2 tablespoons chopped prosciutto
6 large fresh or canned artichoke
  bottoms, chopped
2 1/2 cups chicken broth

1 1/2 cups cubed day-old bread
3 tablespoons chopped fresh basil
1/4 cup freshly grated Parmigiano-
  Reggiano cheese
Freshly grated Parmigiano-
  Reggiano cheese, for serving
Extra-virgin olive oil, for serving

1. Place a cast-iron skillet over medium heat. When it is hot, add the oil, garlic, onion, and prosciutto, stirring well after each addition. Cook until the onion has softened but not discolored, 2 to 3 minutes.

2. Add the artichokes and cook for 2 minutes. Then add the chicken broth. Increase the heat to medium-high, bring to a low boil, and cook until the artichokes are soft, 5 to 7 minutes. Add the bread cubes and cook for 2 minutes. Remove from the heat and stir in the basil and the Parmigiano-Reggiano.

3. Transfer the mixture to a blender or food processor, and process until smooth. Serve hot or chilled, in small bowls. Sprinkle each serving with Parmigiano-Reggiano and drizzle with olive oil.

TO GRATE OR NOT TO GRATE?

Although grating cheese onto one's food is a good way to make sure the cheese is at its freshest, Italians do indeed pre-grate cheese and serve it in a bowl on the table for people to spoon onto their food. But it is always grated just prior to being placed on the table, never far in advance or at the store.

CIOPPINO

Cioppino (choh-PEE-noh) is a corruption of the Ligurian word *ciuppin*, referring to a fish stew similar to this, one of the classics of San Francisco cooking brought by Ligurian immigrants to that great American city. Sadly, cioppino is not easy to find anymore in San Francisco or anywhere else; it fell out of favor because so many weak examples made it seem outdated. While the seafood used in cioppino may vary, crabs are essential; Dungeness crabs from the Pacific are best of all, but eastern blue crabs work almost as well.

SERVES 6

¹/₃ cup plus 2 tablespoons extra-virgin olive oil
3 medium yellow onions, diced
1 leek, white and light green parts only, chopped
1 carrot, diced
1 celery stalk, diced
Salt, preferably kosher
Freshly ground black pepper
7 garlic cloves, minced
Sprig of fresh oregano, or ¹/₄ teaspoon dried
Sprig of fresh thyme, or ¹/₄ teaspoon dried
2 bay leaves
¹/₄ to ¹/₂ teaspoon saffron threads, crushed in a mortar and diluted with 2 tablespoons hot water
1 large or 2 small tomatoes, peeled and diced (see Note)

2 cups dry white wine, such as Soave
3 cups fish stock
¹/₂ teaspoon red pepper flakes, or to taste
6 whole crabs (see headnote)
12 ounces monkfish, cut into 6 pieces
12 ounces halibut, cut into 6 pieces
12 ounces cleaned squid bodies (see Note, page 61), sliced into rings
1 pound mussels, scrubbed and debearded
1 pound small clams, scrubbed
¹/₃ cup chopped flat-leaf parsley
3 medium all-purpose or large red potatoes, cubed and boiled until tender

1. In a large stockpot, heat the ¹/₃ cup olive oil over medium heat. Add the onions, leek, carrot, and celery. Season with salt and pepper to taste, and cook, stirring occasionally, until the vegetables are softened and lightly colored, about 10 minutes. Add the garlic and cook, stirring, for another 2 minutes.

2. Add the oregano, thyme, bay leaves, saffron, tomatoes, and wine, and bring to a boil. Reduce the heat to medium and cook to evaporate the alcohol and slightly reduce the liquid, about 10 minutes.

3. Add 1 cup of the fish stock and the red pepper flakes, and simmer for 5 minutes.

4. Add the remaining 2 cups fish stock. Ladle 3 cups of the soup into a food processor, and process until pureed. Pour it back into the stockpot. Check the seasoning.

5. Add the crabs, cover, and simmer for 3 minutes. Add the monkfish, halibut, squid, mussels, and clams. Cover and simmer for another 3 minutes or until the shells open. Add the parsley, the remaining 2 tablespoons olive oil, and the potatoes. Stir well. Transfer the cioppino to a large serving bowl and serve it at the table.

WINE SUGGESTION: BARDOLINO

NOTE: To peel tomatoes, submerge them in a pot of boiling water to cover for about 1 minute. Remove, and place in cold water to cool them down. The skins should peel off easily.

PUREE OF CHICKPEA SOUP WITH PORCINI

The humble chickpea and the noble porcini are combined for a wonderful marriage of complementary flavors.

SERVES 6

FOR THE SOUP

1¹/2 cups dried chickpeas, soaked
  in cold water overnight
1 ounce dried porcini mushrooms
¹/3 cup extra-virgin olive oil
2 medium yellow onions, coarsely
  chopped
2 carrots, coarsely chopped
3 garlic cloves, chopped
2 fresh sage leaves, chopped,
  or 1 teaspoon dried
1 medium all-purpose or red
  potato, peeled and cubed

1¹/2 cups coarsely chopped canned
  Italian style-tomatoes, with their
  juices
7 cups chicken broth
1 teaspoon salt, preferably kosher
¹/2 teaspoon freshly ground black
  pepper
3 tablespoons unsalted butter

FOR THE CROUTONS
¹/4 cup extra-virgin olive oil
3 cups cubed Italian bread

1. Rinse and drain the chickpeas.

2. Put the porcini into a small bowl, cover with 1¹/2 cups hot water, and let stand for 20 minutes or until tender.

3. In a soup pot, heat the olive oil over medium heat. Add the onions and carrots, and cook, stirring, until lightly browned, about 10 minutes. Add the garlic and sage, and cook, stirring, for another 2 minutes.

4. Meanwhile, using your hands, squeeze the water from the porcini, reserving the liquid. Strain the liquid through a sieve lined with cheesecloth, and set it aside. Coarsely chop the porcini.

5. Add the porcini to the soup pot, and toss with the onions and carrots. Add the potato, tomatoes, chickpeas, chicken broth, and the porcini liquid. Season with the salt and pepper, and bring the soup to a boil. Cover, reduce the heat to a gentle simmer, and cook until the chickpeas are tender, about 2 hours.

6. While the soup is cooking, prepare the croutons: Heat the olive oil in a large skillet over medium-high heat. Add the bread cubes, quickly tossing them in the oil to coat most sides. Cook, tossing often to brown evenly on all sides, for 6 to 8 minutes. Set aside.

The idea that imported canned tomatoes, especially those labeled as coming from the region of San Marzano, are always better than American varieties has little or no truth to it. The tomato, after all, came from the Americas, and we grow great ones. "San Marzano" has become an umbrella term, like "Maine lobster," for an item that may in fact come from anywhere within a wide territory. We've found canned tomatoes grown and packed in the U.S. to be just as good, on the whole, as the imported Italian brands. We particularly like Red Pack and Contadina. Just make sure you select plum (or "Italian-style") tomatoes.

7. Transfer the soup to a blender or food processor in batches, and puree. Adjust the seasonings as needed. Just before serving, stir in the butter. Scatter a few croutons over each serving.

SUGGESTED WINE: GRIGNOLINO

NOTE: If it's made a day in advance, the flavors in this soup will improve.

HEARTY CHICKPEA VEGETABLE SOUP

Michael Romano, chef at Union Square Café in New York, has always moved his menus closer to the kind of food that is eaten by Italians at home. Nothing could be more wholesome than this rich chickpea soup of his.

SERVES 6

1 pound dried chickpeas, soaked in cold water overnight

1 sprig fresh rosemary (4 to 5 inches long), or 1/2 teaspoon dried

1 bay leaf

6 black peppercorns

1/4 cup coarsely chopped flat-leaf parsley, stems and leaves combined

3 tablespoons plus 1/4 cup extra-virgin olive oil

1 medium yellow onion, chopped

1 large carrot, chopped

1 celery stalk, chopped

1 teaspoon red pepper flakes

Salt, preferably kosher

Freshly ground black pepper

5 large garlic cloves, chopped

1/2 cup sundried tomatoes (either dry or oil-packed), chopped

3 ounces rind of Pecorino Romano or Parmigiano-Reggiano cheese (optional)

4 ounces ditalini or other small pasta, cooked al dente

1/4 cup chopped flat-leaf parsley, for serving

3 tablespoons freshly grated Pecorino Romano or Parmigiano-Reggiano cheese, for serving

1. Rinse and drain the chickpeas.

2. Place the rosemary, bay leaf, peppercorns, and the parsley on a piece of cheesecloth, and wrap in a bundle. Tie with a piece of string, and set aside.

3. In a large stockpot over medium-low heat, heat the 3 tablespoons olive oil. Add the onion, carrot, celery, red pepper flakes, salt and pepper to taste, and the garlic. Cook, stirring, until the vegetables are softened and lightly colored, about 10 minutes. Add the sundried tomatoes, cheese rind if using, chickpeas, and the herb bundle. Add 2 quarts water and bring to a boil. Reduce the heat to a simmer and cook until the chickpeas are tender, about 2 hours. If the soup is too thick, add another 1 to 2 cups water.

4. Remove 1½ cups of the cooked chickpeas and vegetables from the soup, and set aside. Discard the cheese rind and the herb bundle. Transfer the rest of the soup to a food processor or blender in batches and puree. Return the soup to the pot, and add the reserved chickpeas and vegetables, the cooked pasta, and the remaining ¼ cup olive oil. Check the seasonings. Serve with a sprinkling of chopped parsley and grated Pecorino cheese.

WINE SUGGESTION: AGLIANICO DEL VULTURE

Said to be America's oldest Italian restaurant, Fior d'Italia was established in 1886 by Angelo del Monte and "Papa" Maronette at 492 Broadway in San Francisco's North Beach neighborhood, primarily to serve food to the clients of the bordello in the same building. Increasingly popular with the general public, it burned down in 1893 but was soon rebuilt. During the earthquake of 1906 it was destroyed once again—and was set up in a tent the next day, feeding stunned and homeless San Franciscans from soup kettles. Today Fior d'Italia is located at 601 Union Street and still retains a wealth of memorabilia from its Barbary Coast beginnings.

BARLEY SOUP WITH SAUSAGE

A good hearty soup for cold weather. You may use hot Italian sausage for more of a kick, or mix sweet and hot for a good balance of flavors. While many Americans may not think of barley as being a particularly Italian ingredient, it is one of the oldest grains of the Mediterranean, known in Europe by 3000 B.C. It was one of the principal grains used by the ancient Romans, who called it *hordeum*. Over time, with the increased knowledge about leavening, Europeans came to favor wheat, which interacts with yeast far better than barley. Still, the poor of Italy continued to use this cheaper, more available grain for their porridges, breads, and soups, and barley soup has had something of a comeback owing to the increased interest in older regional cuisines.

SERVES 6

7 tablespoons olive oil
1 large yellow or Spanish onion, chopped
2 small carrots, cubed
1/2 celery stalk, chopped
3 garlic cloves, chopped
1 cup barley (about 8 ounces)
3 tablespoons chopped flat-leaf parsley
1 1/2 to 2 quarts chicken broth

1/4 teaspoon dried oregano
3/4 teaspoon chopped fresh rosemary
Salt, preferably kosher
Freshly ground black pepper
8 ounces sweet Italian sausage without seeds, casings removed, cut into 1/2-inch pieces
1 medium all-purpose or red potato, cubed

1. In a large stockpot, heat 3 tablespoons of the olive oil over medium heat. Add the onion and cook, stirring frequently, until lightly browned, about 10 minutes. Add the carrots, celery, and garlic, and cook, stirring, for another 3 to 4 minutes.

2. Add the barley, parsley, 1 1/2 quarts chicken broth, oregano, rosemary, and salt and pepper to taste. Bring the soup to a boil. Reduce the heat to a simmer and cook for 30 minutes.

3. In the meantime, heat 2 tablespoons of the remaining olive oil in a sauté pan over high heat. Add the sausage

Always have a little server of sea salt on the table for those who want a touch more. It's delightful to pick up a few grains with one's fingers.

and cook, stirring, until it is nicely browned, 6 to 8 minutes. Set aside on paper towels.

4. Add the sausage and potato to the soup, and simmer for an additional 20 minutes. Check the seasoning—the soup should be peppery. If the soup is too thick, add some extra chicken broth. Just before serving, stir in the remaining 2 tablespoons olive oil.

WINE SUGGESTION: MONTEPULCIANO D'ABRUZZO

MOM MARIANI'S
BEEF SOUP

My mother made this soup about once a month, and she could never make enough of it. It is the kind of soup that's so satisfying, it can be a main course for lunch or a light dinner, especially when accompanied by good Italian bread.

—J.M.

SERVES 6

5 tablespoons olive oil
2 pounds beef short ribs
Salt, preferably kosher
Freshly ground black pepper
2 tablespoons unsalted butter
2 or 3 leeks, white and light green parts only, washed and cut into ¼-inch-thick slices (2½ to 3 cups)

¼ cup chopped celery
2 garlic cloves, minced
½ teaspoon dried oregano
2 cups canned crushed tomatoes
3 ounces ditalini, cooked al dente
⅓ cup freshly grated Parmigiano-Reggiano cheese

1. In a large sauté pan, heat 2 tablespoons of the olive oil over high heat. Season the short ribs with salt and pepper, and brown the ribs on all sides in the sauté pan, about 10 minutes total.

2. While the ribs are browning, heat the remaining 3 tablespoons olive oil and the butter in a stockpot over medium heat. Add the leeks and celery, season with salt and pepper to taste, stir well, and cook, covered, for 10 minutes, stirring occasionally. Add the garlic and cook, stirring, for another 2 minutes.

3. When the ribs have browned, add them to the stockpot along with the oregano, 5 cups water, and salt and pepper to taste. Bring the soup to a boil and skim off any foam. Add the tomatoes, reduce the heat to low, and let simmer, covered, until the meat is very tender, 1³/4 to 2 hours.

4. Remove the ribs, cut the meat from the bones, discarding any fat or gristle, and cut the meat into ¹/2-inch pieces. Return the meat to the stockpot. Add the cooked pasta, bring to a boil, sprinkle with the Parmigiano-Reggiano, and serve.

WINE SUGGESTION: MONTEPULCIANO D'ABRUZZO

NOTE: This soup can be made the day before without the ditalini. The flavor will improve overnight. Add the ditalini and Parmigiano-Reggiano just before serving.

RED PEPPER SOUP

D on't expect a fiery chile-hot red pepper soup—this is a savory-sweet soup, and very beautiful too. The last-second addition of cool ricotta cheese is the icing on the soup!

SERVES 6

¹/4 cup olive oil	3 roasted red peppers (page 332), coarsely chopped
2 medium yellow onions, chopped	1 medium all-purpose potato, peeled and cubed
¹/2 fennel bulb, sliced	2¹/2 tablespoons tomato paste
2 large garlic cloves, chopped	5¹/2 cups chicken broth
Salt, preferably kosher	²/3 cup ricotta cheese
Freshly ground black pepper	

1. In a large stockpot, heat the olive oil over medium heat. Add the onions and fennel, toss to coat the vegetables with oil, and cook, stirring, until the vegetables are softened and lightly browned, about 8 minutes. Add the garlic and cook, stirring, for another 2 minutes.

2. Season the vegetables with salt and pepper to taste, and add the red peppers, potato, tomato paste, and chicken broth. Stir, and bring to a boil. Then reduce the heat and simmer for 25 minutes.

3. Transfer the soup in batches to a food processor or blender and puree. Return the soup to the pot and reheat it as needed. Adjust the seasonings to taste. Add a large dollop of ricotta to each serving.

WINE SUGGESTION: BIANCO DI CUSTOZA

LENTIL SOUP

Lentils represent good luck in Italy and are traditionally eaten in one form or another on New Year's Day. Once considered a food of the poor, lentils now appear on the menus of every trattoria in Italy and of many of the finest Italian *ristoranti* in the U.S. For a cold-weather soup, there is nothing better, and by adding a small pasta like ditalini, it becomes a rich and satisfying main course.

SERVES 6

1/3 cup olive oil
2 large yellow onions, chopped
1 celery stalk, chopped
1 carrot, diced
3 garlic cloves, chopped
2 ounces pancetta, cut into
   1/4-inch dice
2 bay leaves
1/3 cup chopped flat-leaf parsley

1 ham bone, or 1 smoked ham
   hock
1/4 cup tomato paste
1 pound dried lentils
Salt, preferably kosher
Freshly ground black pepper
Extra-virgin olive oil, for serving
Freshly grated Parmigiano-
   Reggiano cheese, for serving

1. In a large stockpot, heat the olive oil over medium-low heat. Add the onions, celery, carrot, and garlic, and cook, stirring occasionally, until the vegetables are softened, about 10 minutes.

2. Push all the vegetables to one side of the pot and add the pancetta. Increase the heat to medium-high and cook the pancetta, stirring, until browned, 3 to 4 minutes. At the same time stir the vegetables to keep them from burning.

3. Add the bay leaves, parsley, ham bone, tomato paste, and lentils to the pot. Season to taste with salt and pepper.

Many cooks soak lentils for hours to plump and soften them. Just as easy is a quick blanching in salted water for a few minutes.

Add 2¹/₂ quarts water, stir well, and bring to a boil. Then reduce the heat to a simmer and cook for 1 hour.

4. Adjust the seasonings if needed. The soup should be thick, but if it's too thick, just stir in a little more water. Serve with a drizzle of olive oil and some Parmigiano-Reggiano.

WINE SUGGESTION: SPANNA

MINESTRONE

Minestrone (mee-neh-STROH-neh) means "big soup," and you may in fact find everything in the kitchen in a pot of this rich elixir. In Italy, the ingredients will vary not only from region to region, but from household to household. The consistency should be fairly thick; a watery minestrone is a poorly made or diluted minestrone.

SERVES 8

8 ounces dried cannellini beans
1 large piece of Parmigiano-
 Reggiano cheese rind (3-inch
 square or bigger, optional)
¹/₃ cup plus 2¹/₂ tablespoons olive
 oil
1 large yellow onion, diced
3 ounces pancetta, cut into
 ¹/₄-inch pieces
4 garlic cloves, minced
2 carrots, diced
1 medium celery stalk, diced
2 teaspoons fresh rosemary, or
 1 teaspoon dried
3 tablespoons chopped flat-leaf
 parsley

10 fresh basil leaves, chopped
4 cups canned Italian-style
 tomatoes with juices, passed
 through a strainer or food mill
4 ounces white mushrooms, halved
 and sliced
Salt, preferably kosher
Freshly ground black pepper
8 ounces Savoy cabbage, cored
 and thinly sliced
6 ounces ditalini or other small
 pasta, cooked until al dente
Freshly grated Parmigiano-
 Reggiano cheese
Extra-virgin olive oil

1. In a medium-size saucepan, combine the beans with 1 quart water. Bring to a boil, reduce the heat, and simmer for 2 minutes. Cover and remove from the heat. Let stand for 1¹/₂ hours. Then drain, rinse, and drain again.

2. In a large pot, combine the beans, Parmigiano-Reggiano rind if using, and 3 quarts cold water. Bring to a boil, then boil over medium heat until the beans are al dente, 30 to 40 minutes.

3. About 10 minutes before the beans are done, heat the $1/3$ cup olive oil in a medium saucepan over medium heat. Add the onion, and cook, stirring, until softened, about 5 minutes. Add the pancetta and continue cooking for another 3 minutes. Add the garlic and cook, stirring, for 2 minutes. Add the carrots and celery, and toss with the other vegetables for 1 minute. Transfer the mixture to the large pot with the beans. Add the rosemary, parsley, basil, and tomatoes, and bring to a boil.

4. Using the same medium saucepan, heat the remaining $2 1/2$ tablespoons olive oil over high heat. Add the mushrooms and cook, stirring often, until browned, 4 to 6 minutes. Add the mushrooms to the soup. Season the soup with salt and pepper to taste, and simmer for 10 minutes. Then add the cabbage and continue cooking for another 15 minutes. Taste the beans and the cabbage to check for doneness.

5. Shortly before serving, add the cooked pasta to the soup. Serve with the grated Parmigiano-Reggiano cheese and a drizzle of extra-virgin olive oil.

Bread peddlers on Mulberry Street in New York's Little Italy.

SUGGESTED WINE: SASSELLA OR BONARDA

NOTE: If it is made a day in advance (through Step 4), the flavors in this soup will improve.

BEEF, MUSHROOM, AND BARLEY SOUP

Another winning combination of textures and rich flavors.

SERVES 6 TO 8

2 to 3 pounds beef bones
1 pound beef chuck or beef chicken steak
3 tablespoons olive oil
Salt, preferably kosher
Freshly ground black pepper
1 celery stalk, cut into 4 pieces
1 carrot, halved lengthwise
1 small yellow onion, cut into 4 pieces
3 sprigs flat-leaf parsley
7 black peppercorns
2 tablespoons tomato paste
5 tablespoons extra-virgin olive oil

1 large yellow onion, chopped
2 garlic cloves, chopped
8 ounces white mushrooms, sliced
1 small portobello mushroom, chopped
$^1/_3$ cup dried porcini mushrooms, soaked in 1 cup hot water for 30 minutes
$^1/_2$ cup barley
1 large carrot, cut into $^1/_4$-inch cubes
1 all-purpose or Yukon Gold potato, peeled and cubed
1 cup canned or frozen corn

1. Preheat the oven to 400°F.

2. Prepare the soup base: Place the beef bones and meat in a roasting pan. Add the olive oil and toss to coat. Season with salt and pepper to taste. Roast for 20 to 25 minutes, or until browned, tossing every 10 minutes.

3. In a large stockpot, combine the bones, meat, celery, carrot, onion, parsley, peppercorns, and tomato paste. Add 2$^1/_2$ quarts water and bring to a boil. Partially cover, reduce the heat to low, and simmer for about 1$^1/_2$ hours or until the meat is tender. Discard the bones. Remove

Mushrooms must be treated gently to remove the surface dirt that may cling to them. Do not wash them under water, although a quick rinsing won't hurt them if dried immediately. It's best to use a soft brush to get rid of the dirt.

the beef and cut it into small pieces. Set the meat and the soup base aside.

4. Heat a large flameproof casserole or stockpot over medium heat. Add 2 tablespoons of the olive oil and the onion, and cook, stirring, until softened, about 6 minutes. Add the garlic and cook, stirring, for another 2 minutes. Transfer to a bowl.

5. Add the remaining 3 tablespoons olive oil to the same casserole or stockpot and set it over high heat. Add the white and portobello mushrooms and cook, tossing often, until lightly browned, 4 to 6 minutes. Return the onions and garlic to the casserole. Strain the soup base into the casserole, crushing the vegetables to extract as much flavor as possible.

6. Reserving the soaking liquid, chop the porcini. Strain the liquid through a cheesecloth-lined sieve. Add the porcini and the strained liquid to the soup, along with the reserved beef and the barley. Season with salt and pepper to taste. Bring to a boil, then reduce the heat to low and simmer for 15 minutes.

7. Add the carrot, potato, and corn, and simmer until the potato is tender, 10 to 15 minutes. If the soup is too thick, add a little more water. Serve the soup hot.

WINE SUGGESTION: GATTINARA

NOTE: This soup is even tastier when it is made a day before serving.

CHICKPEA AND FARRO SOUP

Farro is an ancient grain, known in English as "spelt" (*Triticum spelta*). It was one of the principal foods of the Roman legions. As wheat became more available, *farro* was relegated to the category of poor people's food. In the last decade there has been a renewed interest in this excellent source of fiber and texture.

There are so many flavors in this soup, which is adapted from Paula Wolfert's book, *Mediterranean Grains & Greens*, we are tempted to list them all in its name, but the chickpea and *farro* underpin all the rest, so we'll let it go at that.

SERVES 4 TO 6

1/2 cup dried chickpeas, soaked in cold water overnight

Salt, preferably kosher

2 bay leaves

1/4 cup extra-virgin olive oil

1 large yellow onion, chopped

1 small leek, white and light green parts only, washed and chopped

3 tablespoons minced pancetta

1/2 celery stalk, finely chopped

3/4 cup spelt, soaked in cold water overnight

1 all-purpose potato, peeled and cubed

1 quart chicken broth

1/2 teaspoon dried oregano

1/8 teaspoon freshly grated nutmeg

Freshly ground black pepper

Extra-virgin olive oil, for serving

1. Rinse and drain the chickpeas. Place them in a large soup pot, cover with plenty of fresh water, and add salt and the bay leaves. Bring to a boil. Reduce the heat to medium and boil until the chickpeas are soft, about 1 1/2 hours.

2. Meanwhile, in another large soup pot, heat the olive oil over medium heat. When it is hot, add the onion, leek, prosciutto, and celery. Cook, stirring occasionally, until softened, about 8 minutes.

3. Drain the spelt and add it to the onion mixture. Add the potatoes and the chicken broth, oregano, nutmeg, and pepper, and bring to a boil. Reduce the heat to low, cover partially, and cook for about 1 hour.

4. Drain the chickpeas, reserving the liquid. Place half the chickpeas in a food processor or blender, add 3/4 cup of the reserved cooking liquid, and process until the mixture is smooth. Repeat with the remaining chickpeas. Add the pureed chickpeas to the pot with the spelt, adding more of the chickpea cooking liquid if the soup is too thick. The soup should have a creamy consistency. Adjust the seasonings as needed, and top each serving with a drizzle of extra-virgin olive oil.

WINE SUGGESTION:
AGLIANICO DEL VULTURE

STRACCIATELLA ALLA ROMANA

*S*tracciatella (strah-chah-TEH-lah) means "little shreds," referring to the appearance of the egg in this soup of broth, eggs,
and Parmigiano-Reggiano. Nothing could be simpler, but be
careful about adding the egg mixture: It should be drizzled with a
fork into the hot broth to achieve the correct texture, so they do
indeed look like little shreds.

SERVES 4

2 large eggs
1/2 cup freshly grated Parmigiano-
  Reggiano cheese
1 quart chicken or beef broth
Salt, preferably kosher
Freshly ground black pepper

Freshly grated Parmigiano-
  Reggiano cheese (optional),
  for serving
Chopped flat-leaf parsley
  (optional), for serving

1. In a bowl, whisk the eggs together with the 1/2 cup Parmigiano-
Reggiano until well blended.

2. Bring the broth to a boil in a large stockpot. Lower the heat to
a simmer. Using a fork, drizzle the egg-cheese mixture into the
broth (the broth will cook the mixture into shreds). Add salt and
pepper to taste.

3. Pour the soup into individual soup bowls. If desired, add more
Parmigiano-Reggiano, and garnish with parsley.

WINE SUGGESTION: SOAVE

VEGETABLE BARLEY SOUP

*A*nice throw-together dish for which you need not keep too
close to the instructions. You are invited to put in whatever
you like—the results are bound to be delicious. It is the
barley that makes this unusual and hearty.

SERVES 8

1/4 cup olive oil

3 medium yellow onions, thinly sliced

2 leeks, white and light green parts only, washed and sliced into 1/2-inch pieces

3 garlic cloves, chopped

1 carrot, cubed

1 cup canned Italian-style tomatoes, crushed, with juices

2 bone-in chicken breast halves

7 cups chicken broth

Large piece of Parmigiano-Reggiano cheese rind (about 3 x 5 inches, optional)

Salt, preferably kosher

Freshly ground black pepper

1/2 cup barley

1/4 cup chopped flat-leaf parsley

Extra-virgin olive oil, for serving

Freshly grated Parmigiano-Reggiano cheese, for serving

1. In a large soup pot, heat the olive oil over medium-high heat. Add the onions and cook, stirring often, until browned, about 10 minutes. Add the leeks, garlic, and carrot. Reduce the heat to medium and cook, stirring, for 8 minutes.

2. Add the tomatoes, chicken breasts, chicken broth, Parmigiano-Reggiano rind if using, and salt and pepper to taste. Bring to a boil. Then reduce the heat to low, partially cover, and simmer for 10 minutes.

3. Add the barley and parsley, and continue to simmer until the barley is cooked, about 30 minutes. Remove the chicken breasts, discard the

The epitome of the Italian immigrant raised to affluence and prominence. "Big Nick" Tartaglione of Providence, Rhode Island, was known as a "Champion Eater," although his repast looks fairly meager in this photo from 1925, with the exception of an entire gallon of wine.

skin and bones, and cut the meat into $^1/_2$- to $^3/_4$-inch pieces. Return the chicken pieces to the soup.

4. Serve with a drizzle of extra-virgin olive oil over each plate, and some grated Parmigiano-Reggiano if the rind was not used in the soup.

WINE SUGGESTION: CHIANTI CLASSICO

NOTE: This soup tastes even better when it is made a day ahead.

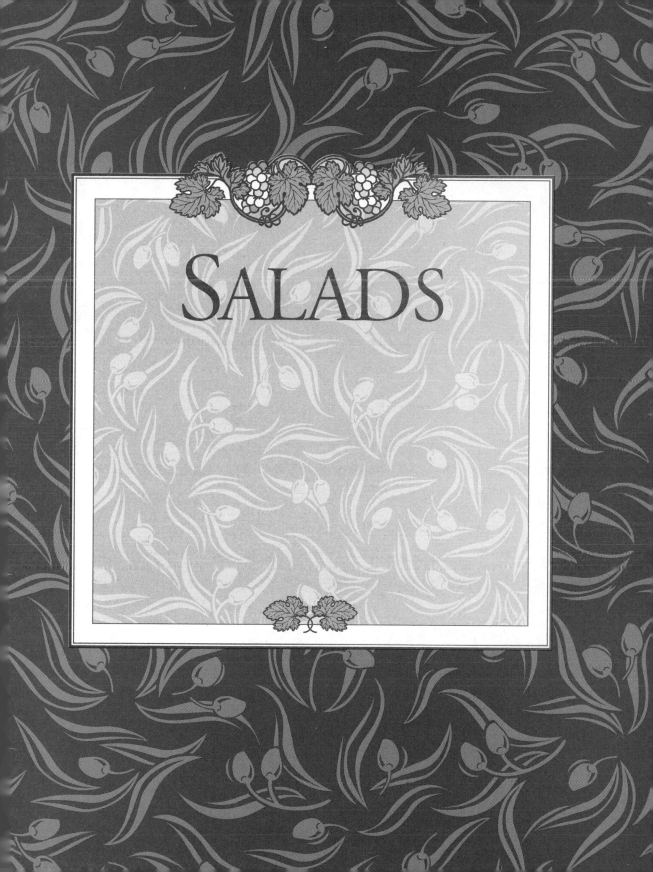

SALADS

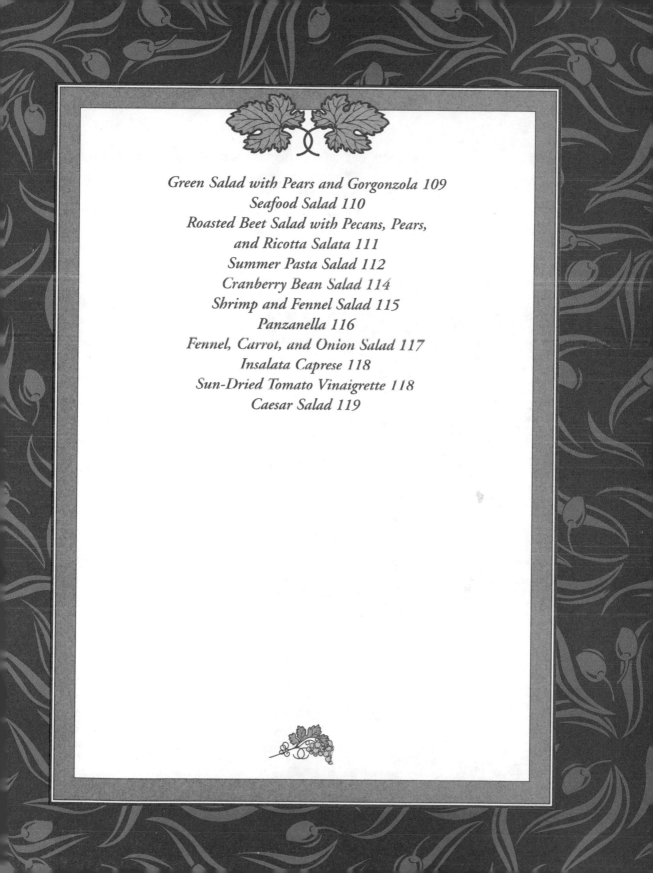

SALADS

Italians rarely eat salads the way some Americans do, as part
of a weight-loss diet or as a main course—and never as a first
course, with the possible exception of a seafood salad, which
would probably not contain any lettuce. When they do eat a salad
of greens it is usually after the main course and before cheese or
dessert. Usually it is dressed very simply, with salt (the word "salad"
derives from the Latin word *sal*, for salt), pepper, lemon juice or
vinegar, and a touch of olive oil.

Italian-Americans have
adopted the American way
of eating salad, which might
well be as a luncheon dish or a
main course, especially when
meat or poultry is added. Pasta
salads are almost unknown in
Italy, though in America they
are part of every deli counter
and buffet banquet's list of
requisite dishes.

*The grocery business was one that
Italian immigrants entered into with
relative ease, usually within their
own neighborhoods, like this food
store on First Avenue and Tenth
Street in New York, pictured in 1943.
Such grocers carried a wide variety
of Italian products, although during
the war importation from Italy was
almost impossible. Many of the
products pictured were produced
in America. Note the sign: "We are
helping the farmers of America move
surplus food."*

GREEN SALAD WITH PEARS AND GORGONZOLA

Sweetness, saltiness, creaminess, nuttiness, green flavors—here's a salad that has it all.

SERVES 4

FOR THE SALAD
1/2 cup walnut halves
6 red-leaf lettuce leaves, torn into
   bite-size pieces
1 small head radicchio, cut into
   4 wedges, each wedge cut into
   1/2-inch-thick slices
1 large Belgian endive, cut into
   1/2-inch-thick slices and
   separated
2 tablespoons chopped flat-leaf
   parsley

8 ounces Gorgonzola cheese,
   crumbled
1 ripe pear, preferably Bartlett or
   Comice

FOR THE VINAIGRETTE
1 1/2 teaspoons Dijon mustard
2 tablespoons red wine vinegar
Salt, preferably kosher
Freshly ground black pepper
1/3 cup plus 2 tablespoons extra
   virgin olive oil

1. Preheated an oven to 350°F.

2. Place the walnuts in a shallow pan and toast in the oven for about 8 minutes. Let cool. Grind a few walnuts in a food processor—you need about 2 tablespoons. Break the remaining walnuts into large pieces.

3. In a salad bowl, toss together the lettuce, radicchio, endive, parsley, and walnut pieces.

4. Prepare the vinaigrette: In a small bowl, combine the mustard, vinegar, and salt and pepper to taste; stir to blend. Slowly add the oil, whisking constantly until the oil is incorporated. Stir in the ground walnuts.

5. Peel, core, and quarter the pear. Cut each quarter in half crosswise, and then slice the pieces 1/8 inch thick.

6. Pour the dressing over the salad and toss. Add the Gorgonzola and the pears, toss gently, and serve immediately.

WINE SUGGESTION: DOLCETTO

SEAFOOD SALAD

Italians who live near the sea are likely to serve this *insalata di marina* (een-sah-LAH-tah dee mah-REE-nah) on a regular basis as an antipasto. If you make it at home, be sure you have a good fishmonger. The absolute freshness of the seafood is crucial, or you'll end up with a fishy-smelling salad. Italian-American chefs seem to favor adding celery to such seafood salads. That's up to you. Either way, make sure you serve some fresh bread alongside.

SERVES 4 TO 6

FOR THE SALAD
8 ounces baby octopus, cleaned
3 teaspoons salt, preferably kosher
8 ounces shrimp, peeled and
    deveined
8 ounces cleaned squid (see Note,
    page 61), body sliced into
    1/4-inch-thick rings, tentacles
    cut in half
8 ounces sea scallops, cut in half
    horizontally

FOR THE DRESSING
1/2 cup extra-virgin olive oil
1/4 cup freshly squeezed lemon
    juice
3 tablespoons freshly squeezed
    orange juice
3/4 teaspoon red pepper flakes
2 garlic cloves, minced
3 tablespoons chopped flat-leaf
    parsley
1 celery stalk, finely chopped
    (optional)
Salt, preferably kosher
Freshly ground black pepper

1. In a small saucepan, combine the octopus, 1 teaspoon of the salt, and enough water to cover. Bring to a boil, reduce the heat, and simmer until tender, 20 to 25 minutes. Drain and rinse under cold water to stop the cooking. Drain again. Cut the octopus into bite-size pieces.

2. In a medium-size saucepan, combine 1 quart water and the remaining 2 teaspoons salt, and bring to a boil. Add the shrimp and boil until pink, about 1 1/2 minutes. Remove the shrimp with a slotted spoon, rinse under cold water, and drain. Add the squid to the same saucepan, and cook for 45 seconds. Remove it with the slotted spoon, rinse under cold water, and drain. Cook the scallops in the same manner for about 1 1/2 minutes; drain, and rinse under cold water. Pat all the seafood dry and set aside. Cut the shrimp in half lengthwise, and cut the scallops in half if they are not too small.

3. Prepare the dressing: In a medium-size bowl, combine the olive oil, lemon juice, orange juice, red pepper flakes, garlic, parsley, celery if you are using it, and salt and pepper to taste. Whisk to mix. Add the seafood and mix. Cover and refrigerate for 2 to 4 hours. Let the salad come to room temperature before serving.

WINE SUGGESTION: VERMENTINO

ROASTED BEET SALAD WITH PECANS, PEARS, AND RICOTTA SALATA

Brian Whittmer has proven himself one of this country's most innovative chefs working within certain Mediterranean and French traditions, first as chef at New York's noted Montrachet, then in California at the Pacific's Edge in Carmel, the trend-setting Montrio in Monterey, and the best tavern-restaurant in the U.S.—Moose's in San Francisco. His combination of ingredients is always enlightening and delicious. Verjus is unsweetened, unfermented grape juice. It is available in specialty stores.

SERVES 4

1¹/2 pounds medium beets

FOR THE VERJUS VINAIGRETTE
¹/4 cup white verjus
¹/4 cup extra-virgin olive oil
¹/2 shallot, minced
Salt, preferably kosher
Freshly ground black pepper

1 ripe Bosc pear
4 ounces baby greens (6 to 8 cups)
2¹/2 ounces ricotta salata cheese, grated (³/4 cup)
¹/2 cup pecans, toasted (see Note)
¹/3 cup chopped fresh chives

1. Preheat the oven to 375°F.

2. Into a small roasting pan, put the beets and ¹/4 cup water, cover, and roast in the oven until tender, about 45 minutes. Remove from the oven and allow to cool.

3. Meanwhile, prepare the vinaigrette: In a mixing bowl, whisk the verjus slowly into the oil. Whisk in the shallot, and salt and pepper to taste. Set aside.

4. When the beets have cooled, peel them and cut them into eighths. Toss them with a little of the vinaigrette.

5. Peel and core the pear, and slice it thinly. Toss the slices with a little vinaigrette.

6. Combine the pears, beets, greens, and the remaining vinaigrette, and toss. Divide the salad among 4 plates and top each serving with some of the ricotta salata, pecans, and chives.

WINE SUGGESTION: VERNACCIA DI SAN GIMIGNANO

NOTE: To toast the nuts, place them in a shallow pan and set it in a 325°F oven for about 8 minutes, or until the nuts are lightly browned.

SUMMER PASTA SALAD

I talian cooking teacher Marcella Hazan once said that she prayed nightly for God's forgiveness after including a cold pasta salad in her first cookbook, *The Classic Italian Cookbook* (still one of the best in the field), because Italians never made such a dish. But pasta salads have become very much a part of American menus. Far too many are ill conceived and seem to ignore that the pasta itself should shine through the other ingredients. In the following recipe the pasta does just that, and we think even Marcella would love it.

SERVES 3 TO 4

FOR THE SALAD
2 heaping teaspoons salt,
  preferably kosher
6 ounces penne pasta
3 tablespoons extra-virgin olive oil
1 small red bell pepper, cored and
  cut into 1/2-inch pieces
1 small sweet onion, such as
  Vidalia, thinly sliced
1 garlic clove, chopped

Freshly ground black pepper
1 cup cherry tomatoes, cut in half
  or quarters
1/2 cup canned or cooked frozen
  corn, drained
1/2 cup crumbled Gorgonzola
  cheese
1/2 cup cubed fresh mozzarella
  cheese
1/2 cup coarsely chopped fresh basil

FOR THE VINAIGRETTE
1¹/2 tablespoons red wine vinegar
¹/2 tablespoon balsamic vinegar
1 teaspoon Dijon mustard

Salt, preferably kosher
Freshly ground black pepper
1 garlic clove, minced
5 tablespoons extra-virgin olive oil

1. In a large stockpot, bring 2 quarts water to a boil. Add the salt and the pasta. Cook until the pasta is al dente, rinse once under cold water, drain, and transfer to a large bowl.

2. In a sauté pan, heat the olive oil over high heat. Add the bell pepper and the onion, and cook, stirring, until softened, about 3 minutes. Reduce the heat to low, add the garlic and salt and pepper to taste, and cook, stirring, for 30 seconds. Transfer the mixture to the bowl with the pasta, and toss.

3. Add the tomatoes, corn, Gorgonzola, mozzarella, basil, some salt, and a good amount of pepper to the pasta mixture and toss.

4. Prepare the vinaigrette: In a small bowl, combine the red wine vinegar, balsamic vinegar, mustard, salt and pepper to taste, and garlic, and stir with a whisk. Stirring constantly, slowly add the olive oil in a stream. Whisk to blend.

5. Pour the vinaigrette over the pasta salad, mix well, and serve.

WINE SUGGESTION: ORVIETO

DID SHE OR DIDN'T SHE?

It has long been asserted that Caterina de' Medici (1519–1589) of Florence had a great influence on the cooking of France after marrying King Henry and becoming Queen of France in 1547 (afterward taking the name Catherine de Medicis). Recently, however, some food authorities have questioned this, noting that she was but fourteen years old when she married Henry and therefore could hardly have had such an impact on the established court cuisine. But her age does not seem particularly pertinent to the discussion, for it would have been her own chefs from Florence who brought their talents to bear on the French court, and many techniques that became standard in French kitchens were used first in Italian ones.

CRANBERRY BEAN SALAD

I n Italy, cranberry beans are called *borlotti* (bohr-LOH-tee) and are used widely. They take a little work to shell, but the results are much better than if you used canned beans.

SERVES 6

FOR THE SALAD
12 ounces fresh cranberry beans,
shelled (1¹/2 to 2 pounds
unshelled)
2 bay leaves
5 fresh sage leaves
1 tablespoon olive oil
1 large sweet onion, such as
Vidalia, sliced
¹/3 cup chopped roasted red
peppers (page 332)
¹/4 cup thinly sliced pitted
Calamata olives

FOR THE VINAIGRETTE
1 garlic clove, minced
5 tablespoons extra-virgin olive oil
3 tablespoons red wine vinegar
Salt, preferably kosher
Freshly ground black pepper
3 ripe tomatoes, cubed
¹/2 cup loosely packed sliced fresh
basil

1. In a large saucepan, combine the beans, bay leaves, and sage. Add enough water to cover the beans. Bring to a gentle boil, and boil until the beans are tender, 15 to 25 minutes. Drain and let cool in a large bowl. Discard the bay and sage leaves.

2. In a sauté pan heat the 1 tablespoon olive oil over high heat. When it is hot, add the onion and cook, stirring, just to sear and brown lightly, 2 to 3 minutes. Add the onion to the beans. Add the roasted peppers and olives, and stir.

3. Prepare the vinaigrette: In a small bowl, combine the garlic, extra-virgin olive oil, vinegar, and salt and pepper to taste, and mix. Add this dressing to the bean mixture, and stir to coat all the ingredients. Set aside for at least 30 minutes or for as long as 3 hours. Just before serving, add the tomatoes and basil, and stir to mix.

WINE SUGGESTION: BIANCO DI CUSTOZA

SHRIMP AND FENNEL SALAD

Here's the kind of dish you'll encounter all over Italy, though sitting on a terrace overlooking the Bay of Sorrento is possibly the best place to find it. That pinch of cayenne or red pepper flakes at the end makes a subtle but big difference.

SERVES 4

1 pound shrimp
2 navel oranges
1/2 sweet onion, such as Vidalia, thinly sliced, and separated into rings
1/2 fennel bulb, cored and thinly sliced
1 1/2 tablespoons chopped fresh mint

1/4 cup extra-virgin olive oil
2 tablespoons freshly squeezed lemon juice
Salt, preferably kosher
Freshly ground black pepper
Pinch of cayenne pepper or red pepper flakes

1. Bring 1 quart water to a boil in a large saucepan. Add the shrimp and boil until pink, about 4 minutes. Drain and plunge the shrimp into cold water to cool them. Peel the shrimp and set them aside.

2. Using a sharp knife, cut off the outer peel and the inner pith of the oranges, exposing the orange sections. Holding an orange in the palm of your hand, cut down along the side of one of the sections, and then along the other side, to remove the flesh without the membrane. Repeat until all sections are cut out. With your hand, squeeze the remaining membrane to extract any remaining juice. Reserve the juice. Repeat with the other orange.

3. In a large bowl, combine the orange segments and juice with the onion, fennel, mint, olive oil, lemon juice, salt and lots of pepper, cayenne, and the shrimp. Mix well and serve.

WINE SUGGESTION: VERNACCIA DI SAN GIMIGNANO

PANZANELLA

Simple goodness *in excelsis*! With a glass of wine on a summer's evening, there is nothing lovelier than this Italian-style salad.

SERVES 4 TO 6

7 tablespoons extra-virgin olive oil
3 garlic cloves, sliced
3 cups cubed Italian country bread
    (1/2-inch pieces)
1 1/2 pounds ripe tomatoes, cut into
    medium-size cubes
1 medium red or sweet onion,
    such as Vidalia, thinly sliced

1 1/2 tablespoons balsamic vinegar
2 teaspoons red wine vinegar
Salt, preferably kosher
Freshly ground black pepper
1/4 to 1/2 teaspoon red pepper flakes
1/2 cup sliced fresh basil leaves

1. In a large sauté pan, heat 4 tablespoons of the olive oil over low heat. Add the garlic and cook, stirring, to extract the flavor without browning the slices, 2 to 3 minutes. Remove the garlic and set aside.

2. Turn the heat to medium-high. Add the bread to the sauté pan and toss quickly to coat the cubes on all sides with the oil. Cook, tossing the cubes frequently, until they are evenly browned and crisp, 6 to 8 minutes. Set aside.

3. In a large bowl, combine the tomatoes, onion, balsamic vinegar, red wine vinegar, salt and a generous amount of pepper, red pepper flakes, the sautéed garlic, and the remaining 3 tablespoons olive oil. Toss to coat well. Just before serving, add the bread cubes and basil. Toss quickly, and serve immediately in soup bowls.

WINE SUGGESTION:
BARDOLINO

> "It is impossible to think of the Mediterranean without the olive tree, rising gnarled from a parched, rocky, calcareous soil, its silvery green leaves shimmering against a gaudy azure sky. Giver of light and solace, nourishment and blessedness, the fruit of the olive has brought a unique flavor to the cuisines of the birthplace of Western civilization." —Maggie Blyth Klein, co-owner of Oliveto restaurant in Oakland, California; from Olive Oil: From Tree to Table (1997).

FENNEL, CARROT, AND ONION SALAD

The increasing availability of good fennel in American markets makes fine antipasto salads like this one possible. In Italy, fennel is called *finocchio* (fee-NOH-k'yoh)—and sometimes it is called "Florence fennel" because of its association with Florentine cookery. Italians eat it mainly as a cooked vegetable, while *finocchietto*, a wild variety, is used as an herb. For a salad, Italians prefer a variety called *carosella*. Fennel seeds, *semi di finocchio*, are widely used in breads and sausages.

SERVES 4

1/4 teaspoon Dijon mustard
3 tablespoons freshly squeezed
   lemon juice
1 teaspoon balsamic vinegar
Salt, preferably kosher
Freshly ground black pepper
3 1/2 tablespoons extra-virgin olive
   oil
1 fennel bulb, cut in half vertically,
   cored, and thinly sliced

1 large carrot, grated
1 small sweet onion, such as
   Vidalia, thinly sliced and
   separated into rings
1 small bunch arugula, rinsed and
   dried
Bruschetta, for serving (page 361
   or 362)

1. In a large bowl, whisk together the mustard, lemon juice, balsamic vinegar, and salt and pepper to taste. Gradually add the oil, whisking all the time. Add the fennel, carrot, and onion, and toss to mix.

2. Arrange the arugula on 4 plates, and place the fennel salad on top of the arugula. Serve with bruschetta on the side.

WINE SUGGESTION:
FIANO DI AVELLINO

INSALATA CAPRESE

Nothing more than a layering of mozzarella, tomato, and basil, if this wonderful example of the classic dishes of Capri is not made at its freshest, it fails to show its true colors—which just happen to be those of the Italian flag. Use only the best-quality fresh mozzarella for this dish, never the packaged kind, and only in-season ripe tomatoes. Serve it with some crusty bread.

SERVES 4

1 pound fresh mozzarella cheese
2 large ripe tomatoes
1/2 cup loosely packed fresh basil
  leaves

Extra-virgin olive oil
Salt, preferably kosher
Freshly ground black pepper

Slice the mozzarella and tomatoes into 1/2-inch-thick slices. Layer them on a platter, and dress with basil sprigs and a sprinkling of extra-virgin olive oil. Add salt and pepper to taste, and serve.

WINE SUGGESTION: FIANO DI AVELLINO

SUN-DRIED TOMATO VINAIGRETTE

This lovely amalgam of sweet and sour flavors makes an ideal dipping sauce for bread, a fine salad dressing, or a delicious condiment alongside poultry and seafood dishes.

SERVES 4

1/4 cup chopped oil-packed
  sun-dried tomatoes
3 tablespoons balsamic vinegar

1/3 cup extra-virgin olive oil
Salt, preferably kosher
Freshly ground black pepper

In a blender or mini food processor, process the tomatoes and balsamic vinegar. With the blender running, slowly pour in the olive oil to emulsify. Season with salt and pepper to taste.

NOTE: This will keep for up to 2 weeks in the refrigerator.

CAESAR SALAD

This famous mix of romaine lettuce, garlic, olive oil, croutons, Parmesan cheese, Worcestershire sauce, and, often, anchovies sounds like the most Italian of all salads. It was in fact created by an Italian, but he was an immigrant—Caesar Cardini, who owned a series of restaurants in Tijuana, Mexico, just across the border from San Diego. At Caesar's Place, on the July Fourth weekend in 1924, Cardini, having run out of ingredients for main courses, concocted the salad as a main course, arranging the lettuce leaves on a plate with the intention that they would be eaten with the fingers. Later Cardini shredded the leaves into bite-size pieces. It was the first main-course salad in the United States, where salads had previously been served only as a side dish.

Caesar salad became particularly popular with the Hollywood movie crowd that frequented Tijuana during Prohibition, and it was a featured dish at Chasen's and Romanoff's in Los Angeles. Caesar Salad went on to be voted the "greatest recipe to originate from the Americas in fifty years" by the International Society of Epicures in Paris.

Cardini, who died in 1956, was always adamant that the salad should be subtly flavored, and argued against the inclusion of anchovies, whose faint flavor in his creation he believed may have come from the Worcestershire sauce. He also decreed that only Italian olive oil and imported Parmigiano be used. In 1948 he established a patent on the dressing, which is still packaged and sold as "Cardini's Original Caesar Dressing Mix," distributed by Caesar Cardini Foods in Culver City, California.

The following recipe is the original and does not include anchovies.

SERVES 6

4 garlic cloves
12 tablespoons olive oil
2 cups diced Italian bread
2 medium heads romaine lettuce
1/2 teaspoon salt, preferably kosher
2 large eggs

Freshly ground black pepper
Juice of 1 lemon
1 teaspoon Worcestershire sauce
1/4 cup freshly grated Parmigiano-
   Reggiano cheese

1. Preheat the oven to 250°F.

2. In a small bowl, mash 2 of the garlic cloves in 3 tablespoons of the olive oil. Baste the diced bread with the oil and garlic mixture, and place the cubes in a shallow baking pan. Bake, basting two more times, until the croutons are crisp, 8 to 12 minutes.

3. Meanwhile, separate the lettuce leaves, rinse them gently, shake them dry, and refrigerate in a plastic bag until ready to serve.

4. Mash the remaining 2 garlic cloves, and combine them with 1/4 teaspoon of the salt and 3 tablespoons of the olive oil in a mini processor or a mortar. Process to a puree, and then strain.

5. Place the strained garlic oil in a sauté pan over medium heat. Add the croutons, heat briefly, and toss. Then turn them into a serving bowl and set aside.

6. Bring a small pot of water to a boil, add the eggs, and boil for exactly 1 minute. Remove the eggs from the water.

7. Place the lettuce leaves in a very large bowl, and pour 4 tablespoons of the olive oil over them. Stir with large motions to coat. Sprinkle the lettuce with the remaining 1/4 teaspoon salt, 8 grindings of black pepper, and the remaining 2 tablespoons olive oil. Toss again, and add the lemon juice and Worcestershire sauce. Break the eggs into the salad, toss, and add the Parmigiano-Reggiano. Toss again and top with the croutons. Serve on chilled plates.

WINE SUGGESTION: FRASCATI

GIVE US A BETTER GRATER

Much to our dismay, we have almost given up ever finding a good Italian cheese grater. Mouli is the best-known company that makes cheese graters, and for more than forty years we used one handed down in the family from the 1940s. But when it finally broke down, the Mouli replacement never came close to doing the job well. The metal is too light, the construction flimsy, the results uneven. We have tried all manner of graters and have found none better than adequate. You may use one of those rectangular four-sided graters, but they tend to be unwieldy, are tough on the knuckles, and do a less than satisfactory job with hard cheeses. You may also grate cheese in a food processor, but do so only minutes before serving it. Never have your cheese grated in advance at the store. It will begin to dry out and lose flavor immediately.

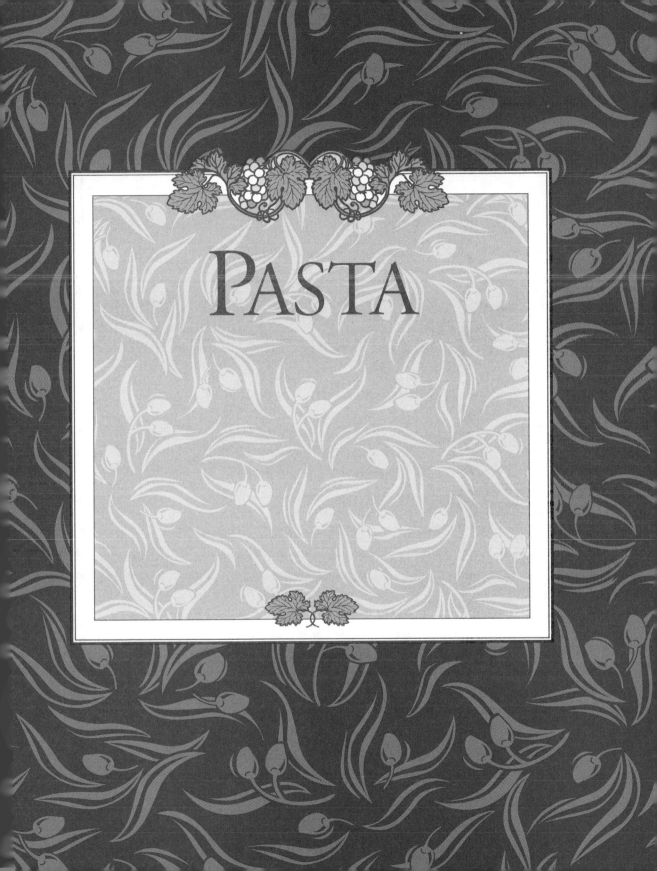

PASTA

PASTA

No food is more closely associated with Italy than pasta—not because Italians are the only people in the world who eat noodles made from a basic mixture of flour, water, and sometimes egg, but because Italians from every region have made it the backbone of their cookery. Rarely does a day go by without a plate of pasta being served at lunch or dinner. Italians consume about sixty pounds per person annually—twice what Americans, who are big pasta eaters, consume.

While Italians loosely lump farinaceous dishes including risotto and polenta under the general term *pasta*, for our purposes it seems more reasonable to treat macaroni, spaghetti, and other noodle dishes separately.

In one form or another, pasta has been known in Italy since Roman times. An Arab text of A.D. 1154 mentions pasta-making in Sicily, and by the fourteenth century many shapes of pasta had acquired their Italian names, the most popular being *vermicelli*. By the late eighteenth century, Naples alone had 280 pasta-making shops; the first commercially produced pastas were made in that city. However, it was not until mechanized pasta-making was perfected in the early twentieth century that pasta became something just about every Italian could afford on a daily basis.

Pasta takes two basic forms in Italy: *pasta fresca*, fresh pasta, made from soft wheat (*Triticum vulgare aestivum*); and *pasta secca* or *pasta asciutta*, dried pasta, which under law must be made from hard wheat (*Triticum durum*). Pasta dough made with eggs—*pasta all'uovo*—is increasingly popular because of the availability and relative cheapness of eggs, though in the past egg-based pasta would have been a luxury.

In the United States, much has been made of the "superiority" of fresh pasta, especially in restaurants that wish to charge more for dishes made with it, but in Italy and among the best Italian cooks there is great respect for commercially produced dried pasta. Indeed certain shapes of dried pasta are essential to particular dishes, and fresh egg pasta would be all wrong in certain preparations. The quality of the pasta now imported from Italy is excellent, and the texture of cooked dried pasta is preferable to fresh pasta in many cases.

The term *al dente* ("to the teeth") means that the cooked pasta should be tender but still retain a slight chewiness. In Italy that chewiness can seem almost too raw to Americans, but Italians believe, rightly, that there is much more flavor to the pasta in that state of tenderness than when it is overcooked into a limp mess. For that same reason Italians do not oversauce their pasta, insisting that the pasta itself, not the sauce mixed in with it, is the main ingredient.

Portion sizes of pasta are a highly individual thing. In Italy pasta is usually eaten as a course prior to the main course, although the former may be more sumptuous in portion and richness than the entree. In America pasta is very often served as a main course, in which case second helpings may even be in order for a big eater. In our notes on serving portions we indicate what we think is a substantial, satisfying first course, about 3 ounces per person. Four to 5 ounces would serve as a good main-course portion.

MARINARA SAUCE

Ope of the basic, all-purpose tomato sauces, marinara has been the defining element of Italian-American cookery for decades. It falls between a long-simmered sauce like the ragù on page 196 and a quickly cooked tomato sauce such as the one on page 139. The amount of garlic and oregano used is really up to the individual cook. Many will remove the garlic cloves after they have been sautéed in the oil, which gives the marinara a brighter flavor, while others prefer to retain them so the bold taste of the garlic remains vibrant.

SERVES 8

¹/₂ cup extra-virgin olive oil
5 garlic cloves, crushed
Two 28-ounce cans Italian-
style tomatoes, with
juices, crushed or chopped

³/4 teaspoon dried oregano
Salt, preferably kosher
Freshly ground black
pepper
¹/₂ teaspoon sugar

1. In a large saucepan, heat the olive oil over medium-low heat. Add the garlic and cook, stirring, until lightly browned, squashing the cloves every minute to release more flavor into the oil, about 4 minutes. The garlic cloves may be left in the sauce or removed.

2. Add the tomatoes, oregano, salt and pepper to taste, and sugar, and bring to a boil. Reduce the heat to a simmer and cook for 20 minutes. Adjust the seasonings as needed. The sauce may be stored in the refrigerator for up to 5 days.

WHEN BURNING CAN BE A VIRTUE

One afternoon while making a very quick tomato sauce, we forgot that it was on the stove. When we returned ten minutes later, it had simmered down into what appeared to be a thick paste. Upon tasting it, however, we found the intense smoky flavor was very appealing. We used it both as a condiment and, thinned with just a little water, as a pasta sauce with a wonderful smoky taste.

GALINA'S MEAT SAUCE

When we first met and started cooking together, we used to make a big pot of meat sauce—which Italian-Americans often refer to as "gravy"—that was as much chopped beef as it was tomato. This is in contrast to a *ragù alla bolognese*, which has little tomato, a mix of veal, beef, and pork, and plenty of vegetables. Now, decades later, we still think of this as "Galina's meat sauce," and it is always well received as our personal comfort food. It is very rich, goes a long way, and freezes easily.

SERVES 8 TO 10

1 cup olive oil	2 pounds chopped beef chuck
3 large yellow onions, chopped	3 bay leaves
2 large carrots, chopped	2 teaspoons dried oregano
1 celery stalk, chopped	2 teaspoons sugar
6 garlic cloves, chopped	Three 28-ounce cans Italian-style
4 teaspoons salt, preferably kosher	tomatoes, with juices, crushed
1¹/2 teaspoons freshly ground black	or coarsely chopped
pepper	One 6-ounce can tomato paste

1. In a large stockpot, heat 1/2 cup plus 2 tablespoons of the olive oil over medium heat. When it is hot, add the onions, carrots, and celery. Cook, stirring occasionally, until lightly browned, about 10 minutes. Push the vegetables to the side a bit, add the garlic, season the vegetables with 2 teaspoons of the salt and 3/4 teaspoon of the pepper, and cook for another 2 minutes.

2. While the vegetables are cooking, heat the remaining 2 tablespoons of the olive oil in a large sauté pan over high heat. When it is very hot, add half of the meat and cook, breaking up the clumps, until browned, about 8 minutes. Transfer the meat to the pot with the cooked vegetables. Repeat with the other half of the meat.

3. Add the bay leaves, oregano, 1 cup water, the sugar, tomatoes and their liquid, and tomato paste to the meat and vegetables. Mix well and bring to a boil. Season with the remaining 2 teaspoons salt and 3/4 teaspoon pepper. Reduce the heat to low or medium-low, and cook for 45 minutes. Adjust the seasonings. Serve with the pasta of your choice, or use in making lasagna.

WINE SUGGESTION: VINO NOBILE DI MONTEPULCIANO

NOTE: The sauce improves if made the day before.

> "*Learn to eat anything, if you wish to avoid being resented by the rest of your family. . . . Don't let yourself become a slave to your stomach; it's a capricious organ that takes offense for naught and seems to take special pleasure in tormenting those who overeat, a vice that's common among those not held by circumstance to a frugal diet. . . . If you haven't given your stomach reason to complain by overindulging, fight back hand to hand in an attempt to persuade it that you run the show. However, if it absolutely rebels against a given food, concede victory and desist.*"
> —Pellegrino Artusi, The Art of Eating Well (1891; trans. by Kyle M. Phillips II, 1991).

RED PEPPER AND ONION SAUCE

T his is a savory, creamy sauce that goes as well with vegetables
or meats as it does with pasta.

SERVES 4

^{1}/4 cup olive oil
4 tablespoons (^{1}/2 stick) unsalted
   butter
2 large yellow onions, thinly sliced
2 garlic cloves, minced
Salt, preferably kosher
Freshly ground black pepper

3 roasted red peppers (page 332),
   with juices, coarsely chopped
^{1}/2 cup chicken broth
^{1}/2 cup heavy cream
2 tablespoons minced flat-leaf
   parsley

1. In a large saucepan, heat the olive oil and the butter over medium
heat. Add the onions and cook, stirring, until lightly browned and soft,
about 10 minutes. Add the garlic and cook, stirring, for an additional
2 minutes. Add salt and pepper to taste.

2. Meanwhile, in a blender, combine the red peppers, chicken broth,
and cream, and puree until smooth. Pour this mixture in the saucepan
with the onions. Stir, bring to a boil, and reduce to a simmer. Cook
for about 8 minutes to blend the flavors. Adjust the seasonings. Add
the parsley just before serving. Serve over any pasta.

SUGGESTED WINE: CHIANTI CLASSICO

TRENETTE WITH PESTO

T he word *pesto* (PEH-stoh) derives from the pestle used to
grind the ingredients in a mortar, an ancient technique for
making this classic Ligurian sauce. Although American
chefs have stretched the definition of pesto to include just about
any green sauce containing any number of ingredients, the true
pesto is made primarily with fresh basil, garlic, olive oil, and
cheese—although the addition of green beans and potatoes, as well
as pine nuts, is very common.

Genoa claims that it is the rightful home of pesto, or at least the best of all possible pestos, and, as Colman Andrews points out in *Flavors of the Riviera*, one can get into a pretty loud argument as to which neighborhood—even which street!—in Genoa produces the most authentic pesto.

Pesto goes with a wide variety of pastas, but it is by tradition combined with trenette, which in other parts of Italy approximates tagliarine or linguine. If you use fresh pasta, it will bulk up when it's cooked—so you may need less pasta or more sauce.

SERVES 4

1 teaspoon plus 1 heaping table-spoon salt, preferably kosher
1 large (8 ounce) all-purpose or Yukon Gold potato, cut into 2-inch pieces
8 ounces thin green beans
12 ounces trenette, tagliarine, or linguine
1 large garlic clove, coarsely chopped

3 tablespoons pignoli (pine nuts)
2 cups loosely packed fresh basil leaves
$\frac{1}{2}$ cup freshly grated Pecorino Romano cheese
$\frac{1}{2}$ cup freshly grated Parmigiano-Reggiano cheese
Freshly ground black pepper
$\frac{1}{2}$ cup extra-virgin olive oil

1. In a medium-size saucepan, bring 1 quart water to a boil. Add 1 teaspoon of the salt and the potatoes, and simmer until tender, 8 to 10 minutes. Remove the potatoes with a slotted spoon, and set them aside to cool.

2. Cook the green beans in the same simmering water until tender, 4 to 6 minutes. Plunge the beans into cold water to cool, and drain. Cut the beans into 2-inch pieces, and set aside.

3. When they have cooled, cut the potatoes into $\frac{3}{8}$-inch cubes.

4. In a large stockpot, bring 4 quarts water to a boil. Add the remaining tablespoon salt and the pasta, and cook until al dente. Reserving $\frac{1}{2}$ cup of the cooking water, drain the pasta.

5. In a food processor, combine the garlic, pignoli, and basil and process until coarsely ground. Add the Pecorino, Parmigiano-Reggiano, and salt and pepper to taste. With the processor running, pour in the oil in a steady stream. Add $\frac{1}{3}$ cup of the reserved pasta water, and process for 3 seconds more.

6. In a large serving bowl, combine the pasta, potatoes, green beans, and pesto. Toss well to blend. If the mixture looks a bit too dry, add a touch more of the remaining pasta water and toss again. Serve immediately.

WINE SUGGESTION: BARBERA D'ASTI

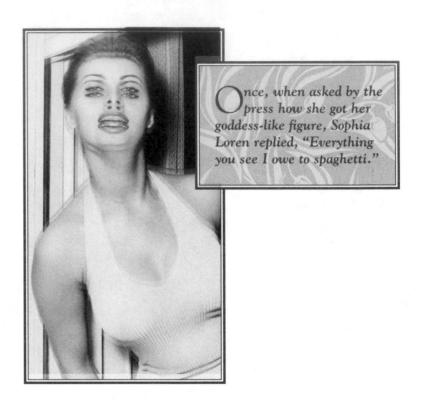

Once, when asked by the press how she got her goddess-like figure, Sophia Loren replied, "Everything you see I owe to spaghetti."

SPAGHETTI ALL'AMATRICIANA

This famous pasta dish, named after a town on the border of Latium and Abruzzo, displays those regions' preference for robust flavors quickly melded. By tradition the dish is served on the first Sunday after August 15, an Italian public holiday. Spaghetti is a good pasta to serve with this sauce, though bucatini is even better.

SERVES 4

1/4 cup extra-virgin olive oil
2 medium yellow onions, thinly
  sliced
3 ounces pancetta, cut into
  1/4 x 1/2-inch pieces
1 pepperoncini, minced
One 28-ounce can Italian-style
  tomatoes, crushed, with their
  juices

Salt, preferably kosher
Freshly ground black pepper
12 ounces spaghetti or bucatini
2 tablespoons unsalted butter
Freshly grated Parmigiano-
  Reggiano cheese, for serving

1. In a medium-size saucepan, heat the olive oil over medium-high heat. Add the onions and cook, stirring, until lightly browned, about 8 minutes. Push the onions aside, add the pancetta to the pan, and cook, stirring, until browned and crisp, about 4 minutes.

2. Add the pepperoncini, tomatoes, and salt and pepper to taste. Bring to a boil, then reduce the heat and simmer for about 10 minutes.

3. Meanwhile, bring 4 quarts water to a boil in a large stockpot. Add the 1 heaping tablepoon salt and the pasta, and boil until the pasta is al dente. Drain the pasta and toss with the butter. Serve the pasta with the sauce and some Parmigiano-Reggiano cheese.

WINE SUGGESTION:
MONTEPULCIANO D'ABRUZZO

About that Macaroni in "Yankee Doodle Dandy": Everyone knows the lyric in "Yankee Doodle Dandy" about the fellow who stuck a feather in his cap "and called it macaroni"—which is not an early citation of Italian pasta in American history. "Macaroni" was a slang term for a dandy, derived from a gentlemen's club called the London Macaroni Club.

SPAGHETTI ALLA PUTTANESCA

The story of how this pasta dish got its name—that *puttante* (prostitutes) would make this quick sauce between appointments with clients—is surely concocted, but it does give this lusty dish a certain notoriety. It is found throughout Italy but is most closely associated with Naples and Calabria.

SERVES 6

1/4 cup olive oil
2 large garlic cloves, minced
1 pepperoncini pepper, minced
4 anchovies, rinsed if packed in salt, and chopped
1 tablespoon capers, rinsed if packed in salt, and chopped
2/3 cup Calamata olives, pitted and chopped

One 28-ounce can Italian-style tomatoes, chopped, with juices
Salt, preferably kosher
1 pound spaghetti
2 tablespoons unsalted butter
1/2 cup freshly grated Parmigiano-Reggiano cheese

1. In a large saucepan, heat the olive oil over medium heat. Add the garlic, pepperoncini, and anchovies. Cook, stirring occasionally, for 3 minutes.

2. Add the capers, olives, and tomatoes. Stir, bring to a boil, and reduce the heat. Simmer for 10 minutes. Taste, and add salt if needed (the olives, capers, and anchovies are all quite salty).

3. Meanwhile, bring 6 quarts water to a boil in a stockpot. Add 1 1/2 heaping tablespoons of salt and the spaghetti, and boil until al dente. Drain, return the pasta to the stockpot, and stir in the butter. Add half the sauce to the pasta, and stir briefly over medium heat. Transfer it to a serving platter, and pour the rest of the sauce on top of the pasta. Serve immediately, with the Parmigiano-Reggiano on the side.

WINE SUGGESTION: TAURASI

NOTE: An open jar of pepperoncini or anchovies, because they are packed in oil, will keep indefinitely in the refrigerator.

LINGUINE WITH ASPARAGUS

Atouch of cream, coupled with that slight bite of lemon zest, makes this a surprisingly tasty dish.

SERVES 4

1 pound fresh asparagus spears,
 bottoms peeled
3 tablespoons unsalted butter
1 small yellow onion, chopped
1 cup heavy cream
3/4 teaspoon freshly grated lemon
 zest

Salt, preferably kosher
Freshly ground black pepper
12 ounces linguine
2/3 cup freshly grated Parmigiano-
 Reggiano cheese

1. Cut the asparagus spears in half. Cut the halves into 1-inch pieces, keeping the bottoms and tops separate.

2. In a medium saucepan, melt 2 tablespoons of the butter over medium heat. Add the onion and the asparagus bottoms. Cook, stirring, until the onion has softened, 5 to 7 minutes. Add the cream, lemon zest, and salt and pepper to taste, and heat through, 2 to 4 minutes. Transfer the mixture to a food processor or blender, and process until smooth. Return the mixture to the pan and keep it warm.

3. In a large stockpot, bring 4 quarts water to a boil. Add 1 heaping tablespoon salt and the linguine, and boil until al dente. Drain.

4. While the pasta is cooking, in a sauté pan melt the remaining 1 tablespoon butter over medium-high heat. Add the asparagus tops and cook, stirring, until tender but still firm, 3 to 4 minutes. Add them to the hot pureed sauce, stir in the Parmigiano-Reggiano, pour over the cooked linguine, and serve immediately.

WINE SUGGESTION: PINOT GRIGIO

When a dish is called all'Abruzzese (Abruzzo style), it usually means the dish is made with hot chile peppers, which in Abruzzo are called diavolichii. We've found that placing a single small dried red chile pepper in a tomato sauce will add measurably to the flavor without tasting in any way hot.

VENISON BOLOGNESE

Despite the exceptionally rich flavor the venison sauce gives to this pasta dish, it is actually quite low in fat because venison is such a lean meat. We adapted this idea after having a fabulous Venison Bolognese prepared by Greg Topper, a brilliant young American chef at the Ajax Tavern in Aspen, Colorado, where the Rocky Mountain atmosphere is ideal for this kind of hearty pasta.

SERVES 4 TO 6

1 1/2 to 2 ounces fatback, cut into 1/4-inch-thick strips (see Note)
4 tablespoons olive oil
1 pound ground venison (your butcher can do this for you)
7 tablespoons unsalted butter
4 cups chopped yellow onions
1 1/2 cups chopped carrots
2 cups chopped celery
One 28-ounce can Italian-style tomatoes, with their juices, passed through a food mill

1/2 cup full-bodied red wine, such as Chianti
1 cup beef broth
1 bay leaf
1 1/2 heaping tablespoons salt, preferably kosher
Freshly ground black pepper
1/4 teaspoon freshly grated nutmeg
1/4 teaspoon ground cinnamon
1 pound fettuccine or other wide, flat pasta

1. In a small saucepan, cover the fatback with water. Bring to a boil, then reduce the heat and simmer for 5 minutes. Drain and refresh in cold water. Drain again, and grind or mince the fatback, using a small food processor or a sharp knife. Set it aside.

2. In a large sauté pan, heat 2 tablespoons of the olive oil over high heat. When it is very hot, add the venison and the fatback and sauté, breaking up the meat, until browned, 12 to 15 minutes. Remove from the heat.

3. Heat a large saucepan over medium heat, and add the remaining 2 tablespoons olive oil and 4 tablespoons of the butter. When it is hot, add the onions and carrots, and cook, stirring, until lightly browned, about 10 minutes. Add the celery and cook, stirring, until browned, about 10 minutes more.

4. Transfer the meat to the onion mixture. Add the tomatoes, wine, beef broth, and bay leaf, and bring to a boil. Partially cover, reduce the heat to low, and simmer for 1½ hours, stirring every 20 minutes.

5. Stir in the nutmeg and cinnamon, and simmer for another 30 minutes.

6. Meanwhile, bring 6 quarts water to a boil in a large pot. Add the salt and the fettuccine, and cook until al dente. Drain, toss with the remaining 3 tablespoons butter, and serve with the sauce.

WINE SUGGESTION: VINO NOBILE DI MONTEPULCIANO

NOTE: The flavor of the ragù improves if it is prepared a day in advance. Instead of fatback, you can buy salt pork in the supermarket, cut it into ¼-inch-thick slices, cover them with water in a saucepan, and simmer for 8 minutes. Drain and rinse.

FARFALLE WITH SAUSAGE, TOMATO, AND PORCINI SAUCE

Filling and irresistible—a pasta course for a hearty appetite or a main course.

SERVES 4

1 ounce dried porcini mushrooms
3 tablespoons extra-virgin olive oil
1 tablespoon unsalted butter
1 small yellow onion, chopped
8 ounces sweet Italian sausage, casing removed, cut into pieces
Salt, preferably kosher
Freshly ground black pepper
One 28-ounce can Italian-style tomatoes with juices, passed through a food mill or pressed through a strainer

¼ teaspoon red pepper flakes
12 ounces farfalle
½ cup heavy cream
2 tablespoons chopped flat-leaf parsley
⅔ cup freshly grated Parmigiano-Reggiano cheese

1. In a small bowl, cover the porcini with ³/4 cup hot water, and set aside for 20 minutes.

2. Meanwhile, in a medium-size sauté pan heat 1 tablespoon of the olive oil and the butter over medium-low heat. Add the onion and cook, stirring, until softened, 5 to 7 minutes. Using a slotted spoon, remove the onion and set aside.

3. In the same sauté pan, heat the remaining 2 tablespoons olive oil over medium-high heat. Add the sausage and cook, tossing and breaking up the meat into ¹/2-inch pieces, until browned, 5 to 7 minutes.

4. While the sausage is cooking, drain the porcini, reserving the soaking liquid. Using your hands, squeeze the porcini to extract the excess liquid. Chop the porcini.

5. Add the porcini to the sausage and cook, stirring, for 2 minutes.

6. Strain the reserved porcini liquid into the sauté pan through a sieve lined with cheesecloth. Add the reserved onions and simmer over low heat for 10 minutes.

7. Season the sausage mixture with salt and pepper to taste. Add the tomatoes and red pepper flakes, bring to a boil, and reduce the heat. Simmer for 10 minutes.

8. Meanwhile, bring 4 quarts water to a boil in a large stockpot. Add 1 heaping tablespoon salt and the farfalle, and boil until al dente. Drain.

9. While the pasta is boiling, add the cream to the sauce and heat through. Just before serving, stir the parsley and ¹/3 cup of the Parmigiano-Reggiano into the sauce. Add the drained pasta, mix well, and serve immediately. Pass the extra Parmigiano-Reggiano.

WINE SUGGESTION: DOLCETTO

PASTA USED AS A REFRIGERATOR DOOR MAGNET

There is a ridiculous but persistent piece of advice that says, to test if a piece of spaghetti is cooked al dente, throw a strand against the refrigerator and see if it sticks. If it does, it's ready; if it slips off, it's not. Sounds like a waste of pasta to us, especially since the term al dente means "to the tooth," referring the tender but chewy texture it should have when tested by tasting a strand in one's own mouth.

FARFALLE WITH PORCINI AND SPINACH

This is a good example of how a specific pasta shape makes for optimum flavor with certain ingredients. You could combine this sauce with any number of pastas, but farfalle, (bow-ties) seem to pick up the flavors best and give their own pleasing texture in the mouth.

SERVES 6

1 ounce dried porcini mushrooms
8 tablespoons (1 stick) unsalted butter
1 small yellow onion, chopped
1 garlic clove, minced
1 heaping tablespoon salt, preferably kosher
1 pound farfalle

One 10-ounce package frozen chopped spinach, thawed and drained
Freshly ground black pepper
2/3 cup heavy cream
2/3 cup freshly grated Parmigiano-Reggiano cheese

1. In a small bowl, cover the porcini with 3/4 cup hot water, and stir. Set aside for 20 minutes.

2. In a medium-size saucepan, heat 3 tablespoons of the butter over medium-low heat. Add the onion and cook, stirring, until softened, about 8 minutes. Add the garlic and cook, stirring, for another 2 minutes.

3. Meanwhile, drain the porcini, reserving the soaking liquid. Using your hands, squeeze the porcini to extract the excess liquid. Coarsely chop the porcini.

4. Add the porcini to the onion and cook, stirring, for 2 minutes.

5. In a large stockpot, bring 4 quarts water to a boil. Add the salt and the farfalle, and boil until al dente.

6. While the pasta is boiling, press the spinach to remove as much liquid as possible, and add it to the onion/porcini mixture. Season with salt and pepper to taste, and stir to mix. Strain the porcini liquid into the saucepan through a sieve lined with cheesecloth. Simmer for 3 minutes. Add the cream, bring to a boil, then reduce the heat and simmer for 2 minutes. Add 2 tablespoons of the butter and stir to blend.

7. Drain the pasta and transfer it to a serving bowl. Add the remaining 3 tablespoons butter, and stir. Add the onion/porcini mixture, and mix. Add ¹/₂ cup of the Parmigiano-Reggiano, and serve. Pass the remaining cheese.

WINE SUGGESTION: CANNONAU

FARFALLE WITH WALNUT SAUCE

This is one of the richest pastas you'll ever enjoy—a little goes a long way. After hazelnuts and chestnuts, walnuts are among Italians' favorite nuts; they use them in sauces, desserts, and liqueurs. While we like this sauce with farfalle, you might also consider using pappardelle or penne.

SERVES 6

1¹/₄ cups walnut halves (4 ounces)
2 garlic cloves, minced
¹/₃ cup chopped flat-leaf parsley
1 cup heavy cream
1¹/₂ heaping tablespoons salt,
  preferably kosher

1 pound farfalle
Freshly ground black pepper
2 tablespoons unsalted butter
²/₃ cup freshly grated Parmigiano-
  Reggiano cheese

1. Preheat the oven to 325°F.

2. Spread the walnuts in a shallow baking pan and toast in the oven for 8 minutes. Let cool.

3. In a food processor, combine the walnuts, garlic, and parsley; process until chopped. Add ¹/₂ cup of the cream and process until the walnuts are finely chopped. Set aside.

4. Bring 6 quarts water to a boil in a large stockpot. Add the salt and the farfalle, and boil until al dente.

5. While the pasta is cooking, heat the remaining ¹/₂ cup cream in a small saucepan over medium heat. Add the walnut mixture, season with salt and pepper to taste, and bring just to a boil. Immediately remove from the heat.

6. Drain the pasta, reserving ¹/₂ cup of the cooking water. Return the pasta to the stockpot, add the butter, and toss. Add the walnut mixture, about ¹/₄ cup of the reserved pasta water, and the Parmigiano-Reggiano. Toss to blend. If the dish is not moist enough, add some more of the pasta water. Serve immediately.

WINE SUGGESTION: PINOT NERO

SPAGHETTI WITH FRESH TOMATO SAUCE

It is difficult to imagine a dish that better expresses the wholesomeness of Italian cooking than good spaghetti cooked al dente and lavished with the freshest of uncooked sauces. Curiously enough, this is a dish you'd rarely find on an old-fashioned Italian-American menu, which would instead use oceans of overcooked marinara sauce on every pasta dish. The ripeness of the tomatoes is essential to this dish. If necessary, wait until summer rolls around, when tomatoes are at their very best.

SERVES 4

2 to 3 ripe tomatoes, cut into 1-inch pieces (2¹/₂ cups)
1 cup cubed fresh mozzarella cheese (¹/₄-inch pieces)
2 garlic cloves, minced and mashed
2 teaspoons plus 1 heaping table-spoon salt, preferably kosher

1 teaspoon freshly ground black pepper
¹/₂ teaspoon red pepper flakes
¹/₂ cup extra-virgin olive oil
12 ounces spaghetti
²/₃ cup coarsely chopped fresh basil

1. In a medium-size bowl, combine the tomatoes, mozzarella, garlic, the 2 teaspoons salt, black pepper, red pepper flakes, and olive oil. Stir gently to mix, and let marinate for 30 minutes.

2. Bring 4 quarts water to a boil in a stockpot. Add the remaining salt and the spaghetti, stir, and cook until al dente. Drain.

3. Return the spaghetti to the stockpot, add the marinated tomato mixture and the basil, and stir to mix. Serve immediately.

WINE SUGGESTION: VERNACCIA DI SAN GIMIGNANO

SPAGHETTI ALLA CARBONARA

One of the most delectable of Roman dishes, *spaghetti alla carbonara* (kahr-boh-NAH-rah) has a name that has defied all attempts to trace its origins. Some say it derives from a nineteenth-century secret political society called the Carbonari; others believe it memorializes the coal miners of Abruzzo and Lazio; one Italian food authority insists it was originally made with squid ink, giving it a black carbon color.

Whatever its origins, it is a thoroughly Roman dish, served in every trattoria with variations that include adding a little garlic, onion, hot pepper, and parsley. Others make the dish with rigatoni. In Italian-American restaurants *carbonara* is too often sullied by the cloying addition of heavy cream.

We think this dish is best at its purest, with only the flavors of the pancetta and the cheeses to enhance the velvety texture of the egg-coated spaghetti. Some cookbooks say you can substitute American smoked bacon, but the flavor of *carbonara* should be fairly subtle and lush, not smoky.

The salmonella problem is a real one, though it has probably been overemphasized as a widespread threat. Salmonella bacteria are killed off when eggs are thoroughly cooked, and the whole point of *carbonara* is to have the hot spaghetti cook the eggs. But because you can't be absolutely sure that the safe temperature of 140°F will be reached in the preparation of this dish, *please do not make this dish if you are worried about salmonella*. By all means, do *not* attempt to make it with packaged pasteurized liquid eggs or with precooked eggs. You'll get nothing like the flavor and texture that define *carbonara*.

SERVES 4 TO 6

> "*I* have been campaigning to have the national Thanksgiving dish changed from turkey to spaghetti carbonara." —*Calvin Trillin*, Third Helpings (1983).

1 heaping tablespoon salt,
   preferably kosher
1 pound spaghetti
$1/2$ cup olive oil
6 ounces pancetta, diced
$2/3$ cup freshly grated Parmigiano-
   Reggiano cheese

$2/3$ cup freshly grated Pecorino
   Romano cheese
4 large eggs
Freshly ground black pepper
Freshly grated Parmigiano-
   Reggiano and Pecorino Romano
   cheeses, mixed, for serving

1. Fill a large serving bowl with hot water to warm it.

2. Bring 4 quarts water to a boil in a stockpot, and add the salt and the spaghetti. Boil until the pasta is almost al dente.

3. While the spaghetti is cooking, pour the olive oil into a large saucepan and heat it for about 30 seconds over medium-high heat. Add the pancetta and sauté until browned but still tender and not yet crisp, 3 to 5 minutes. Remove from the heat.

4. In a small bowl, whisk together the Parmigiano-Reggiano, Pecorino, and eggs until blended.

5. Just before the spaghetti is al dente, pour the water from the heated serving bowl, place a colander in the bowl, and drain the spaghetti in it. Pour the water from the serving bowl, and add the drained spaghetti, the egg/cheese mixture, the pancetta, and the oil from the pan. Add salt and pepper to taste, and mix well until the egg is completely incorporated and coats the spaghetti. The heat of the spaghetti will cook the egg. There should be a silky sauce at the bottom.

6. Serve immediately, offering more salt, pepper, and grated cheese at the table.

SUGGESTED WINE: SALICE SALENTINO

CAPELLINI WITH
CALAMARI AND SHRIMP

Tony's restaurant in Houston, Texas, is one of the finest of any kind in this country, and although he has many French and American items on his menu, owner Tony Vallone puts his heart and soul into the Italian dishes. This is a rare example of the successful wedding of seafood with pasta. The addition of walnuts gives it even more flavor and crunch.

SERVES 4

1/4 cup chopped walnuts
1/4 cup extra-virgin olive oil
2 large garlic cloves, minced
1 1/2 cups chicken broth
One 28-ounce can Italian-style
   tomatoes, drained and chopped
1/4 cup dry white wine, such as
   Soave
1/4 cup chopped flat-leaf parsley
1 1/2 teaspoons dried oregano

Salt, preferably kosher
1/4 teaspoon freshly ground black
   pepper
12 ounces capellini
8 ounces large shrimp, peeled,
   deveined, and cut into thirds
10 ounces cleaned squid bodies
   (see Note, page 61), sliced into
   thin rings
1/4 teaspoon red pepper flakes

1. Preheat the oven to 350°F.

2. Place the walnuts in a shallow baking pan and toast in the oven for 10 minutes. Let cool.

3. In a medium-size sauté pan, heat the olive oil over low heat. Add the garlic and cook, stirring, for 2 minutes. Add the chicken broth, tomatoes, wine, parsley, oregano, 1/2 teaspoon salt, and the pepper. Bring to a boil, reduce the heat, and simmer to reduce for about 8 minutes.

4. In a large stockpot, bring 4 quarts water to a boil. Add 1 heaping tablespoon salt, and boil the capellini until al dente.

5. While the pasta is boiling, add the shrimp to the tomato sauce and simmer until barely cooked, about 1 minute. Then add the squid and simmer for 30 seconds to 1 minute.

6. Drain the pasta, toss it with the seafood sauce, and sprinkle with the red pepper flakes and walnuts. Serve immediately.

WINE SUGGESTION: GRECO DI TUFO

PASTA AL BURRO

Comfort food Italian-style: nothing more than pasta and butter. Sounds simple, but the difference between good and poor versions of *pasta al burro* (BOO-roh) lies, as always with Italian food, in the quality of the ingredients. Arrigo Cipriani, owner of Harry's Bar in Venice and several *ristoranti* in New York, says he judges the overall quality of an Italian restaurant by ordering this simple dish. If the pasta and butter are both of good quality, and the kitchen cooks it correctly, he knows that they care about the lesser dishes just as much as they do the rest of the menu, Cipriani explains.

To that end, use a first-rate dried pasta. Or, if you prefer fresh, use a pasta with not too many egg yolks because of the sheer richness of the dish. Just about any pasta shape—from tiny ditalini and pastina to fat ziti and bigoli—goes well with butter, as long as the butter is of excellent quality and very fresh.

SERVES 6

1 heaping tablespoon salt, preferably kosher
1 pound pasta (see headnote)

6 to 8 tablespoons (3/4 to 1 stick) unsalted butter, cut into pieces
Freshly ground black pepper

1. Bring a large pot of water to a boil, add the salt and the pasta, and cook until al dente. Drain, reserving a little of the pasta water.

2. Place the butter in the still-hot pasta pot, return the pasta to the pot, and toss. Add a little of the pasta water for a creamy consistency. Cook and toss over medium heat just until the pasta is well coated with the butter. Add salt and pepper to taste, and serve immediately in a large bowl.

WINE SUGGESTION: CHIANTI CLASSICO

SPAGHETTI AGLIO E OLIO

After Pasta al Burro (page 143), Spaghetti Aglio e Olio (AHL-yoh eh OHL-yoh, "garlic and oil") must be the simplest of all southern Italian pasta dishes—and made correctly, one of the most delicious. Poorly made, it is a pungent, oily dish of either uncooked or burnt garlic.

The key here is to cook the garlic and chile peppers in the oil very slowly, and to remove the pan from the heat when the garlic is just starting to turn golden (golden garlic imparts a nuttiness to the dish; browned garlic will be bitter). Since the pasta is going to be cooked slightly in the oil and garlic, make sure it is on the firmer side of al dente when you remove it from the boiling water.

Adjust the quantities of garlic and chile pepper to your taste. Some people like to spark the dish further with red pepper flakes.

SERVES 4 TO 6

1 cup olive oil
8 to 10 garlic cloves, chopped
1 to 2 dried red chile peppers
1 heaping tablespoon salt,
 preferably kosher

1 pound spaghetti or linguine
Freshly ground black pepper
1 to 3 tablespoons extra-virgin
 olive oil
Red pepper flakes, for serving

1. In a large saucepan, heat the 1 cup olive oil for a minute or so over low heat. Add the garlic and chile peppers. Shake the pan and stir the garlic and peppers continuously until the garlic just begins to take on a golden color, 3 to 5 minutes. Remove the pan from the heat.

2. Bring a large pot of water to a boil. Add the salt and the pasta, and boil until al dente. Drain well, and pour the pasta into the saucepan with the oil, garlic, and peppers. Place the saucepan over medium heat, and toss the pasta slowly (being careful not to get any of the hot oil on your hands or face) until the sauce is well incorporated. Add salt and pepper to taste.

3. Swirl the extra-virgin olive oil into the pasta, remove the chile peppers, and transfer the pasta to a warmed bowl. Have people help themselves, offering red pepper flakes on the side.

WINE SUGGESTION: ORVIETO

SPAGHETTI WITH POTATOES AND GARLIC

This dish was the result of finding a leftover baked potato in the refrigerator. It's a variation on Spaghetti Aglio e Oglio (page 144), and it's a good hearty dish. You need not bake the potatoes (we boil them when there are no leftovers), but baking or roasting them can add a nice nutty flavor, as long as they've not been cooked until they are dry and mealy.

SERVES 4

Salt, preferably kosher
1 large all-purpose potato, cut into 6 pieces
12 ounces spaghetti
1 cup extra-virgin olive oil
12 garlic cloves, coarsely chopped

1 dried red chile pepper, or ¹/₄ to ¹/₂ teaspoon red pepper flakes
¹/₄ cup chopped flat-leaf parsley
¹/₄ teaspoon freshly ground black pepper

1. Bring a medium-size saucepan of water to a boil. Add 2 teaspoons salt and the potato, and boil until tender. Drain and cut into ¹/₄-inch pieces.

2. In a large stockpot, bring 4 quarts water to a boil. Add 1 heaping tablespoon salt and the spaghetti, and cook until al dente, about 8 minutes.

3. While the pasta is cooking, in a large saucepan, heat the olive oil over medium heat. Add the garlic, chile pepper, and the potatoes, and cook, stirring frequently, until the ingredients are lightly golden, about 5 minutes. Remove the chile pepper if used.

4. Drain the spaghetti, and add it to the saucepan with the potato mixture. Add the parsley, season with salt to taste and the black pepper, and toss to mix well. Serve immediately.

WINE SUGGESTION: ROSSO DI MONTALCINO

FIRST THINGS FIRST

Beware any Italian-American restaurant that describes pasta dishes with the other ingredients first, as in "grilled chicken with red and yellow peppers over fettuccine." Italians consider the pasta to be the main ingredient and so they would write, "fettuccine with grilled chicken and red and yellow peppers." (Not that any real Italian would ever think of mixing grilled chicken with pasta in the first place.)

SPAGHETTI ALLA NORMA

A triumph of simple flavors from the south of Italy, this is named after the opera *Norma* by Vincenzo Bellini, who was born in Catania in eastern Sicily. Some authorities say the dish commemorated the first performance of the opera in Sicily.

SERVES 4

1 eggplant (about 1½ pounds),
  cut into ½-inch-thick slices
Salt, preferably kosher
6 tablespoons olive oil
3 garlic cloves, minced
One 28-ounce can Italian-style
  tomatoes, drained and passed
  through a food mill or pressed
  through a strainer

Freshly ground black pepper
12 ounces spaghetti
10 fresh basil leaves, thinly sliced
⅔ cup cubed ricotta salata cheese
  (¼-inch cubes)

1. Put the eggplant slices in a large colander, and sprinkle 1½ tablespoons salt evenly over both sides. Set the colander in a large bowl or in the sink, and let the eggplant sweat for 1 hour. Then rinse the slices, pat them dry, and cut them into ½-inch cubes.

2. In a sauté pan, heat 2 tablespoons olive oil over medium-high heat. Add half of the eggplant and cook, tossing often, to brown evenly on all sides, 8 to 10 minutes. Drain on paper towels. Repeat with the second batch of eggplant and 2 tablespoons more of the olive oil.

3. In a medium-size saucepan, heat the remaining 2 tablespoons olive oil over low heat. Add the garlic and cook, stirring, until golden, 1 to 2 minutes. Add the tomatoes and salt and pepper to taste. Simmer, stirring occasionally, over medium-low heat for 15 minutes.

4. In a large pot, bring 4 quarts water to a boil. Add 1 heaping tablespoon salt and the spaghetti, and cook until al dente. Drain.

5. While the pasta is cooking, add the eggplant and the basil to the tomato sauce and cook over low heat for 3 minutes.

6. Toss the spaghetti with the eggplant sauce and the ricotta salata. Serve immediately.

WINE SUGGESTION: CORVO ROSSO

NOTE: There are two kinds of ricotta salata: a harder one, good for grating, and a softer one that is better for this dish.

PENNE WITH SPINACH AND GORGONZOLA

If you enjoy Gorgonzola, this is the dish for a real feast. Imported Gorgonzola tends to be more pungent than domestic. *Gorgonzola dolce* (sweet Gorgonzola) is even less pungent and deliciously creamy—the choice is yours. This sauce works better with a short pasta like penne than with strands like spaghetti.

SERVES 4

3 tablespoons unsalted butter
2 shallots, minced
2 small garlic cloves, minced
15 ounces (1¹/₂ packages) frozen
  chopped spinach, thawed and
  drained

1 heaping tablespoon salt,
  preferably kosher
12 ounces penne
¹/₂ cup heavy cream
6 ounces Gorgonzola cheese,
  coarsely chopped
Freshly ground black pepper

1. Heat a medium-size saucepan over low heat. Add the butter, shallots, and garlic, and cook, stirring, until softened, about 3 minutes. Press the spinach to remove as much liquid as possible, and add it to the pan. Add 3 tablespoons water, cover, and cook for 5 minutes. Set aside.

2. In a stockpot, bring 4 quarts water to a boil. Add the salt and the penne, and cook until al dente.

3. While the pasta is boiling, return the spinach mixture to medium-low heat and add the cream, Gorgonzola, and salt and pepper to taste; stirring until it is heated through.

4. Drain the pasta, reserving some of the cooking water. Toss the pasta with the sauce. If it seems dry, add some of the reserved pasta liquid. Serve at once.

WINE SUGGESTION: FRANCIACORTA ROSSO

PENNE WITH BROCCOLI RABE AND CROUTONS

Penne is an excellent pasta for any country-style sauce because it holds the sauce so well. The vegetal flavor of the broccoli rabe and the crunchiness of the croutons make this a dish that will please and surprise everyone.

SERVES 4

FOR THE CROUTONS
1/4 cup extra-virgin olive oil
2 cups cubed Italian bread (crusts removed, 1/3-inch-pieces)

6 tablespoons extra-virgin olive oil
3 garlic cloves, finely chopped

1 bunch (about 1 pound) broccoli rabe, chopped
Salt, preferably kosher
Freshly ground black pepper
2/3 cup chicken broth
12 ounces penne
3 tablespoons unsalted butter
1/2 teaspoon red pepper flakes

1. In a stockpot, bring 4 quarts water to a boil.

2. While the water is heating, prepare the croutons: In a sauté pan, heat the olive oil over medium heat. Add the bread cubes, and toss quickly to coat with the oil. Cook, tossing often, until the croutons are nicely browned, 4 to 6 minutes. Set aside.

3. Next, set a large saucepan over low heat and add 4 tablespoons of the olive oil. Add the garlic and cook, stirring, until golden, 2 to 3 minutes. Add the broccoli rabe and toss it in the oil. Season with salt and pepper to taste. Add 1/4 cup water and the chicken broth, cover, and cook over medium heat until the broccoli is done, 5 to 7 minutes.

4. While the broccoli rabe is cooking, add the penne and 1 heaping tablespoon salt to the boiling water. Cook until al dente, and drain. Toss the penne with the butter.

5. Stir the red pepper flakes into the broccoli rabe. Add the penne and toss to mix. Serve immediately, drizzling some of the remaining 2 tablespoons olive oil and scattering some croutons over each dish.

WINE SUGGESTION: CHIANTI CLASSICO

STRANGOLAPRETI

Strangolapreti (strahn-goh-lah-PREH-tee) means "priest stranglers," a fanciful name that pokes fun at local priests who would come to dinner at a family's house and eat greedily, gobbling down so much of this dish that they would be strangled by their own gluttony.

In some parts of Italy the term (often seen as *strozzolopreti*) refers either to long curled pastas like farfalle or to small gnocchi-like pasta tossed with a very rich sauce. Our variety of *strangolapreti* is from Trentino, and after one bite you'll readily understand the reason for the name.

SERVES 4

8 ounces frozen chopped spinach, thawed and drained

8 ounces ricotta cheese

3/4 cup plus 3 tablespoons freshly grated Parmigiano-Reggiano cheese

2 tablespoons unsalted butter, melted

1/2 cup all-purpose flour

1 tablespoon plain dry breadcrumbs

1 large egg, beaten with 1 large egg yolk

1/8 teaspoon freshly grated nutmeg

1 teaspoon plus 1 heaping tablespoon salt, preferably kosher

1/2 teaspoon freshly ground black pepper

4 tablespoons (1/2 stick) unsalted butter

6 fresh sage leaves, quartered

1. In a medium-size bowl, combine the spinach, ricotta, the 3/4 cup Parmigiano-Reggiano, melted butter, flour, breadcrumbs, beaten eggs, nutmeg, 1 teaspoon salt, and the pepper. Mix well. Cover, and refrigerate for 1 hour.

2. In a stockpot, bring 4 quarts water to a boil.

3. While the water is heating, uncover the ricotta mixture. Scoop out 1 tablespoon of the mixture and quickly roll it into a ball. Flatten it slightly and place it on a piece of floured wax paper. Repeat with the rest of the mixture. Flour your hands while you work to avoid too much stickiness.

4. When the water comes to a fast boil, add the tablespoon of salt and drop in the *strangolapreti*. Boil for 5 minutes.

5. While the *stangolapreti* are boiling, in a small saucepan, melt the butter and add the sage.

6. Preheat the broiler.

7. Drain the *strangolapreti*, and transfer them to a flameproof 8 x 12-inch baking dish. Pour the butter and sage over them, and sprinkle the remaining 3 tablespoons Parmigiano-Reggiano over the top. Put the dish under the broiler just to brown the tops, 2 to 3 minutes. Serve immediately.

WINE SUGGESTION: MERLOT

FETTUCCINE ALL'ALFREDO

Fettuccine all'Alfredo is one of the most misunderstood and most corrupted of all Italian dishes. It originated in Rome in 1914 at a restaurant named Alfredo, owned by Alfredo Di Lelio, whose wife had lost her appetite after the birth of their son. Alfredo restored it with a simple dish of egg-rich fettuccine, triple-rich butter, and the heart of a wheel of Parmigiano-Reggiano cheese.

Di Lelio featured the dish at his restaurant on the Via della Scrofa, but he was hardly prepared for the fame that came when Hollywood movie stars Mary Pickford and Douglas Fairbanks arrived in Rome on their honeymoon in 1927, and upon sampling Fettuccine all'Alfredo, ate it at every meal at Di Lelio's restaurant, presenting him at the end of their stay with a gold-plated fork and spoon inscribed "To Alfredo the King of the Noodles, July 1927." (The original utensils were supposedly later melted down for Mussolini's war efforts.) Upon their return to Los Angeles, the stars popularized the dish among the Hollywood community, and within a year there was a recipe printed in *The Rector Cook Book*.

Because American butter and "Parmesan" cheese did not provide the richness of the original recipe, American cooks began adding heavy cream to

> The time-honored technique of reserving a small amount of water from the pot in which pasta has been cooked is based on a simple principle: The salt and starch in the water has the effect of amalgamating the flavors and the silkiness of the pasta and sauce when stirred in at the very end.

the dish, which tended to make it unfortunately heavy and excessive—though pretty delicious at the same time. After a while "Alfredo sauce" came to mean a cream-and-cheese sauce that American cooks might lavish on chicken, vegetables, or anything else—which is about as far from the original concept of Fettuccine all'Alfredo as one could imagine.

To this day, descendants of the Di Lelio family operate an Alfredo's restaurant in Rome (now on the Piazza Imperatore), and Italian-American entrepreneur Guido Bellanca opened a franchise at EPCOT in Walt Disney World in Florida, where the dish is still made correctly, with only butter and cheese. In Italy the addition of cream to the dish is a rarity, and in that case the dish would be called *fettuccine alla panna* or *alla crema*.

Here are two recipes for Fettuccine all'Alfredo—Di Lelio's original, and an Italian-American version.

ALFREDO DI LELIO'S ORIGINAL VERSION

SERVES 6

1 pound egg fettuccine (preferably fresh)
6 to 8 tablespoons (3/4 to 1 stick) unsalted butter, cut into pieces

2/3 cup freshly grated Parmigiano-Reggiano cheese
1 heaping tablespoon salt, preferably kosher
Freshly ground black pepper

1. In a large pot bring 4 quarts water to a boil. Add the salt and the fettuccine, and cook until al dente. Drain, reserving a little of the pasta water.

2. In a large saucepan, melt the butter over medium heat until it is just barely foamy. Add the fettuccine and toss with the butter. Add the Parmigiano-Reggiano and a little of the pasta water, and mix until well incorporated and creamy. Add salt and pepper to taste. Serve immediately, in individual dishes.

WINE SUGGESTION: A CHIANTI CLASSICO RISERVA OR A MERLOT FROM TRENTINO

AMERICAN-STYLE
FETTUCCINE ALFREDO

SERVES 4

4 tablespoons (¹/2 stick) unsalted
   butter
1 cup heavy cream
Pinch of freshly grated nutmeg
Salt, preferably kosher

Freshly ground black pepper
12 ounces fresh fettuccine
²/3 cup freshly grated Parmigiano-
   Reggiano cheese

1. In a large stockpot, bring 4 quarts water to a boil.

2. While the water is heating, combine the butter, cream, nutmeg, and salt and pepper to taste in a 12-inch sauté pan, and bring to a simmer over medium-low heat.

3. Add 1 heaping tablespoon salt and the fettuccine to the boiling water, bring back to a boil, and cook for 1 minute. Drain the pasta, reserving ¹/2 cup of the cooking water. Add the pasta to the sauce and toss. Sprinkle the Parmigiano-Reggiano over the pasta and toss gently for 30 seconds. If the sauce is a bit dry, add some of the reserved pasta water to moisten it. Serve immediately.

SUGGESTED WINE: DOLCETTO

Farfalle with Leek Sauce

When leeks are at their best, they have a fine sweet onion flavor. When they are not, they are bland and not worth the trouble of cleaning them. This sauce is excellent for pasta, but it could be used even as a luxurious sauce for seafood or poultry.

Serves 4

3 tablespoons unsalted butter
2 tablespoons olive oil
2 large or 4 small leeks, white and light green parts only, washed and cut into 1/4-inch-thick slices
1 medium sweet onion, such as Vidalia, thinly sliced

Salt, preferably kosher
Freshly ground black pepper
3/4 cup chicken broth
12 ounces farfalle
1/2 cup heavy cream
1 1/2 tablespoons freshly squeezed lemon juice

1. In a large stockpot, bring 4 quarts water to a boil.

2. While the water is heating, heat the butter and olive oil in a large saucepan over low heat. Add the leeks and onion, tossing well to coat with the oil. Season with salt and pepper to taste, cover, and sweat for 10 minutes, stirring occasionally so as not to brown.

3. Add the chicken broth, cover, and cook until the leeks are tender, 5 to 8 minutes.

4. Meanwhile, add 1 heaping tablespoon salt and the pasta to the boiling water. Cook until al dente. Drain the pasta.

5. Add the cream to the leeks and cook for another 5 minutes. Just before serving, add the lemon juice and adjust the seasoning. Toss with the farfalle, and serve immediately.

Wine Suggestion: Tocai Friulano

Spaghetti with White Clam Sauce

Is there an Italian-American restaurant that doesn't make linguine with white or red clam sauce? It seems to be one of the requisite dishes on every menu, and as long as the clams are fresh, most places do quite a good job with this simple, delicious dish. Our preference for the pasta, however, is spaghetti, which somehow seems to pick up the ingredients better. At home be careful not to overcook the clams, and have the pasta truly al dente.

SERVES 4

*1/3 cup plus 2 tablespoons extra-
virgin olive oil*
1 large garlic clove, chopped
*1/3 cup dry white wine, such as
Soave*
Pinch of red pepper flakes
*36 littleneck clams, scrubbed if
necessary and rinsed*

*1 heaping tablespoon salt,
preferably kosher*
12 ounces spaghetti or linguine
*2 tablespoons chopped flat-leaf
parsley*
2 tablespoons unsalted butter

1. In a large sauté pan, heat the olive oil over medium heat. Add the garlic and cook, stirring, for about 1 minute without browning. Add the wine, red pepper flakes, and clams, and let the alcohol evaporate by boiling it off for 1 minute. Cover, and simmer over medium heat until all the clams have opened, 4 to 6 minutes. Those that have not opened should be thrown away.

2. Meanwhile, in a large pot, bring 4 quarts water to a boil. Add the salt and the spaghetti. Cook until al dente. Reserve 1/2 cup of the cooking water, drain the rest, and set the pasta aside.

3. Carefully remove the meat from the clams, reserving any liquid. Coarsely chop the clams, and return them to the sauté pan along with the juices. Add the spaghetti and parsley, and simmer for 2 minutes, adding some of the pasta water if the mixture is not moist enough. It should be somewhat soupy. Stir in the butter and serve immediately.

VARIATION: Linguine with Red Clam Sauce

This alternative uses the same ingredients plus 1 cup crushed canned Italian-style tomatoes. Follow the instructions for the white clam sauce, adding the tomatoes when you add the white wine and clams in Step 1.

WINE SUGGESTION: BARDOLINO

Cooked to tender goodness, ready to be quickly served, with all the savoriness of the home-cooked dish— Beech-Nut Prepared Spaghetti graces the family board and spares the busy house keeper.

The sauce, in which it is cooked, boasts an inimitable *Beech-Nut flavor*— the tang of sun-kissed tomatoes, blended with mellow cheese, spiced and seasoned to your taste.

Beech-Nut Spaghetti is a convenient emergency dish. An economical family meal. A time-saver for the busy woman. Just heat it and it's ready for serving. Beech-Nut Packing Company, Canajoharie, N.Y.

Beech-Nut
Prepared Spaghetti

WITH CHEESE AND TOMATO SAUCE

A RICH MAN'S DISH

As much as Italians are identified with pasta eating, only upper- and middle-class Italians could afford to do so more than occasionally before the twentieth century. Wheat flour was very expensive in Italy until the beginning of the nineteenth century, and commercial pasta-making cut the cost still further by mid-century. Today, however, it is not at all unusual for an Italian to eat pasta twice a day.

The appeal of Italian food as "quick and easy" was a major selling point to the postwar "busy woman" who had little time to prepare elaborate meals for her family. Note how the Beech-Nut ad tries to elevate a once lowly dish to a higher status by using an elegant casserole and silver candleware.

PASTA E FAGIOLE

Here is the greatest of all peasant dishes, and one that has traveled well to America. Every Italian cook has his or her version of the dish, and every Italian-American restaurant has it on the menu. It is most closely associated with the Veneto region, but it is found throughout the south as well.

The key to a good *pasta e fagiole* (PAH-stah eh fah-JOH-leh, "pasta and beans") is its final texture, for while some may prefer it to be more souplike others more stewlike, there are certain ways the dish should *not* be made. First, it should not be so thickened by reduction as to be like a sludgy porridge, nor should it be so diluted it resembles a soup. Second, the best *pasta e fagiole* is made, as below, with dried (not canned) beans, which provide a perfect consistency of flavor and texture. Third, too many cooks put too much tomato into *pasta e fagiole*, making it yet another Italian-American dish dependent on the tomato. Last, the beans and pasta should be more or less equal in volume, with neither overpowering the other.

SERVES 6 TO 8

1 pound dried cannellini beans
1/3 cup extra-virgin olive oil
3 medium yellow onions, chopped
4 large garlic cloves, chopped
1/4 to 1/2 teaspoon red pepper flakes
1 1/2 cups chopped canned Italian-
    style tomatoes
One 48-ounce can chicken broth
Salt, preferably kosher
Freshly ground black pepper

2 bay leaves
One 3-inch sprig fresh rosemary,
    or 1 teaspoon dried and crushed
One 4- to 5-inch piece of
    Parmigiano-Reggiano cheese
    rind (optional)
4 ounces ditalini or other small
    pasta, cooked al dente
Extra-virgin olive oil, for serving

1. In a large bowl, soak the cannellini beans in 2 quarts water for 12 to 18 hours, changing the water once or twice. Drain.

2. In a large casserole or stockpot, heat the olive oil over medium heat. Add the onions and cook, stirring, until softened, about 8 minutes. Add the garlic and red pepper flakes and cook, stirring, for another 4 minutes. Add the cannellini, tomatoes, chicken broth, salt and pepper to taste, bay leaves, rosemary, and Parmigiano-Reggiano rind (if using—the rind gives the soup a wonderful flavor), and bring to a boil.

Reduce the heat and simmer gently until the beans are tender, 30 to 45 minutes. The cooking time will depend on the length of time the beans have soaked. Discard the cheese rind, rosemary, and bay leaves.

3. Transfer 2¹/₂ cups of the soup to a food processor or blender, and puree. Return the pureed soup to the pot. Adjust the seasonings, and add the cooked ditalini. Heat thoroughly. Serve with a drizzle of extra-virgin olive oil.

WINE SUGGESTION: VALPOLICELLA

VARIATION: You may wish to add some diced ham or pancetta that has been sautéed until golden brown. This gives more flavor, though we think it is a finer dish without meat.

NOTE: This soup tastes even better when prepared a day ahead.

PASTA ALLA PRIMAVERA

Now here's a dish one would think to be the epitome of Italian vegetable cookery, yet its creation was an accident. We even know the exact moment of creation: On October 2, 1975, Sirio Maccioni, a Tuscan who owns the chic Le Cirque 2000 restaurant in New York, was in Canada with several visiting chefs who, at the end of a long evening at a restaurant there, were ravenous for something to eat. Maccioni picked up a few fresh vegetables from the kitchen and made the dish up as he went along. Everyone liked it so much that he put it on the menu at Le Cirque, serving it to some local food writers who began to sing its praises in print, calling it a wonderfully light evocation of springtime (*primavera* means "springtime"). The dish became the most popular item on Le Cirque's menu (so much so that it is no longer listed and will be made only on request) and was copied everywhere.

SERVES 6

1 cup sliced zucchini
1 cup sliced broccoli
1 1/2 cups snow peas
1 cup baby peas
6 asparagus spears, sliced
10 white mushrooms, sliced
1 heaping tablespoon salt,
   preferably kosher
1 pound fettuccine
2 tablespoons olive oil

1/3 cup pignoli (pine nuts)
2 teaspoons minced garlic
1/2 cup chopped flat-leaf parsley
Freshly ground black pepper
1/2 cup freshly grated Parmigiano-
   Reggiano cheese
5 1/2 tablespoons unsalted butter
1 cup heavy cream
1/3 cup chopped fresh basil
2 tomatoes, coarsely chopped

1. Fit a steamer basket into a large pot. Add a small amount of water to the pot and bring to a boil. Place the zucchini, broccoli, snow peas, baby peas, asparagus, and mushrooms in the steamer basket, cover, and steam until tender, about 3 minutes. Rinse the vegetables under cold water and allow to drain.

2. Bring a large pot of water to a boil. Add the salt and the fettuccine. Cook until al dente.

3. Meanwhile, in a sauté pan, heat 1 tablespoon of the olive oil over medium heat. Add the pignoli and garlic and cook, stirring, until they begin to turn golden, 2 to 3 minutes. Add the remaining 1 tablespoon olive oil, and then the steamed vegetables. Next add the parsley and salt and pepper to taste. Cook until all the ingredients are heated through, 2 to 3 minutes.

4. Drain the spaghetti and add it to the sauté pan. Add the Parmigiano-Reggiano, butter, cream, and basil, and heat thoroughly. Toss, then scatter the tomatoes on top. Serve immediately.

WINE SUGGESTION: BARBERA D'ALBA

PENNE ALLA VODKA

It's puzzling why this dish became such an enormous hit in "northern Italian" restaurants in the United States. It's certainly not a dish Italians would think of making, for vodka is not one of their favorite spirits. We suspect it was an American infatuation with vodka and its upscale image that made this dish so popular here. We've had bland versions and we've had very good versions—the latter always dependent upon spiking things with a nice dose of red pepper. (If you like, you can make your own pepper vodka by steeping half a dozen dried red chile peppers, or a teaspoon of red pepper flakes, and a tablespoon of black peppercorns in a bottle of vodka—no need for an expensive name brand—for several days or even weeks.)

SERVES 6

3 tablespoons unsalted butter
1 medium yellow onion, chopped
3 garlic cloves, minced
1/4 cup vodka
1/2 teaspoon red pepper flakes
One 28-ounce can Italian-style
    tomatoes, chopped or pureed
    with some of the tomato juices

Salt, preferably kosher
Freshly ground black pepper
1 pound penne
1/2 cup heavy cream

1. In a medium-size saucepan, heat the butter over medium heat. Add the onion and cook, stirring, until softened, about 7 minutes. Add the garlic and cook, stirring, for 2 minutes more.

2. Add the vodka, red pepper flakes, tomatoes, and salt and pepper to taste. Stir and bring to a boil. Reduce the heat to low, and simmer for 10 to 12 minutes.

3. Meanwhile, in a large stockpot, bring 4 quarts water to a boil. Add 1 heaping tablespoon salt and the penne. Cook until al dente, and drain.

4. Add the cream to the tomato sauce, and simmer for 2 minutes. Transfer the penne to a serving dish, add the vodka sauce, toss well, and serve.

WINE SUGGESTION: PREDICATO

MOST UNUSUAL NAMES OF PASTA SHAPES

vermicelli—*little worms*

lingue di battone—*whores' tongues*

elicoidali—*helixes*

denti d'elefante—*elephants' teeth*

radiatori—*radiators*

gemelli—*twins*

strangolapreti—*priest stranglers*

malfatti—*badly made*

pansoti—*little bellies*

PENNE WITH
CABBAGE AND POTATOES

Cabbage—*cavolo* (KAH-voh-loh)—is not much used in southern Italian cookery, but it is very much a part of the repertoire in the northern regions of Trentino–Alto Adige and Friuli, whose proximity to and domination by Austria affected the cooking there. Indeed, many dishes in those regions retain Germanic names, like *spaetzle* (egg dumplings) and *Speck* (bacon). The widespread use of cabbage there adds yet another layer of food culture to Italy's rich gastronomic heritage.

SERVES 4

2 small all-purpose, Yukon Gold, or red potatoes, cubed
Salt, preferably kosher
12 ounces penne
3 tablespoons olive oil
4 tablespoons (1/2 stick) unsalted butter
12 ounces green cabbage, cut into 1/2-inch-wide strips

2 medium yellow onions, sliced
3 garlic cloves, chopped
Freshly ground black pepper
1/3 cup chicken broth
4 ounces mozzarella cheese, cut into 1/4-inch cubes
Freshly grated Parmigiano-Reggiano cheese

1. Place the potatoes in a small saucepan, cover with water, and add 1 teaspoon of the salt. Bring to a boil and cook until the potatoes are tender, 6 to 8 minutes. Drain, let cool a bit, and then cut into 1/2-inch pieces. Set aside.

2. Bring 4 quarts water to a boil. Add 1 heaping tablespoon salt and the penne, and cook until al dente. Drain, reserving 1/2 cup of the cooking water.

3. Meanwhile, heat a large sauté pan over medium-high heat. Add the olive oil and 2 tablespoons of the butter. When the mixture is hot, add the cabbage and the onions, and toss well to coat with the oil. Cook, stirring often, until browned, about 10 minutes. Push some of the vegetables to one side, add the garlic, and cook, stirring, for 2 minutes. Mix all together. Season with salt and pepper to taste, and add the chicken broth. Stir, reduce the heat to medium-low, and cook for another 5 minutes. Add the potatoes and stir.

4. Return the drained penne to the pot it was cooked in, and toss with the remaining 2 tablespoons butter. Add the cabbage mixture, the mozzarella, and if it seems a little dry, some of the reserved pasta water. Heat for 30 seconds and serve, sprinkled with the Parmigiano-Reggiano.

WINE SUGGESTION: RIESLING RENANO

RIGATONI WITH TOMATO, SAUSAGE, AND MUSHROOM SAUCE

Big, fat rigatoni are best with hearty sauces like this because the hole in the pasta collects the ingredients and turns each bite of pasta into a little nugget bursting with flavor.

SERVES 4

6 tablespoons olive oil
2 medium yellow onions, sliced
1 yellow bell pepper, cored and
   diced
1 pound thin (³/4-inch-diameter)
   sweet Italian sausage, cut into
   1-inch pieces (if unavailable,
   use regular Italian sausage and
   cut into ¹/2-inch pieces)
2 garlic cloves, chopped
10 ounces white mushrooms,
   sliced

¹/2 teaspoon dried oregano
Salt, preferably kosher
Freshly ground black pepper
One 28-ounce can Italian-style
   tomatoes, crushed, with juices
12 ounces rigatoni
2 tablespoons unsalted butter
¹/2 cup gently packed fresh basil
   leaves, chopped
¹/2 cup freshly grated Parmigiano-
   Reggiano cheese

1. In a large sauté pan, heat 3 tablespoons of the olive oil over medium heat. Add the onions, bell pepper, and sausage and cook, stirring frequently, until browned, about 15 minutes. Add the garlic and cook, stirring, for another 2 minutes.

2. In a medium-size sauté pan, heat the remaining 3 tablespoons olive oil over medium-high heat. Add the mushrooms, toss immediately to coat with the oil, and cook, stirring, until browned, about 8 minutes.

Add to the sausage-onion mixture, and season with the oregano and salt and pepper to taste. Add the tomatoes, stir, and bring to a boil. Reduce the heat to a simmer and cook for 15 minutes.

3. Meanwhile, in a stockpot, bring 4 quarts water to a boil. Add 1 heaping tablespoon salt and the rigatoni, and cook until al dente. Drain, and toss with the butter.

4. Stir the basil into the sauce. Serve the sauce with the rigatoni, and sprinkle Parmigiano-Reggiano on top.

WINE SUGGESTION: CANNONAU

NO, HE DID NOT.

The notion that Marco Polo brought pasta back from his trip to China is sheer nonsense. Various forms of pasta, from lasagne to maccheroni, were known in Italy long before Marco Polo's return in 1292. Much of what was recorded by Marco Polo of his travels has been under scholarly dispute for centuries. The book known as The Travels of Marco Polo was a collaboration between Marco, while captive in a prison in Genoa, and a cellmate named Rustichello of Pisa, a romance writer who may well have added a good deal of fantasy to the notes Marco provided him, and the work is full of stock romance conventions of the time; indeed, the original manuscript was in all probability written in French.

In any case, the only reference to pasta in the entire book is a single sentence about the diet of the people of the city of Khan-balik, the central city of Kublai Khan's empire. Having spoken of their abundance of rice, panic grass, and millet, Marco continues (in Ronald Latham's translation for Penguin Books, 1958): "Wheat in their country does not yield such an increase; but such of it as they harvest they eat in the form of noodles or other pasty foods," a passage that clearly indicates Marco's assumption that his readers were familiar with such foods.

SPAGHETTI WITH GREEN TOMATOES

We came across this dish at Scopa, a fine Italian restaurant in New York. The idea of combining spaghetti with green tomatoes, that icon of the American South, turns out to be a capital one. Be aware that you may have to adjust all your seasonings in this dish, depending on the seasonal flavor and sweetness of the green tomatoes. The garlic and the touch of ginger are very important to bringing the flavors together.

SERVES 4

3 tablespoons olive oil
5 tablespoons unsalted butter
1 Spanish onion, sliced
3 garlic cloves, minced
2 tablespoons minced fresh ginger
1 heaping tablespoon salt,
  preferably kosher
12 ounces spaghetti

1 pound green tomatoes, cubed
¼ teaspoon red pepper flakes
Freshly ground black pepper
¾ cup chicken broth
3 tablespoons chopped flat-leaf
  parsley
½ cup freshly grated Parmigiano-
  Reggiano cheese

1. In a large sauté pan, heat 1 tablespoon of the olive oil and 1 tablespoon of the butter over medium heat. Add the onion and cook, stirring, until browned, about 10 minutes. Add the garlic and ginger and cook, stirring, for another 2 minutes. Transfer to a platter and set aside.

2. Bring 4 quarts water to a boil in a stockpot. Add the salt and the spaghetti, and boil until al dente. Drain, return to the pot, and toss with 2 tablespoons of the butter.

3. Meanwhile, in the same sauté pan you used for the onions, heat the remaining 2 tablespoons olive oil and 2 tablespoons butter over medium-high heat. Add the tomatoes and cook, stirring, until browned, 8 to 10 minutes.

4. Return the onions to the sauté pan, add the red pepper flakes, season with salt and pepper to taste, and add

Flavored pastas have become rather trendy in recent years, and, while you do see them all over Italy in pasta shops, they are really more show than flavor. Ninety-nine percent of the time the stuff is dreadful. One percent of the time it's only colorful. The essence of good pasta is in its nutty, wheaty taste, which squid's ink, tomato, spinach, and basil compromise. We feel it's better to add such ingredients as a sauce rather than submerge them within the pasta itself.

the chicken broth. Bring to a boil, reduce to a simmer, and cook for 5 minutes.

5. Just before serving, toss the parsley into the sauce. Serve the sauce with the spaghetti, sprinkled with the Parmigiano-Reggiano.

WINE SUGGESTION: VERMENTINO

BUCATINI WITH FILETTO DI POMODORO

The quickly cooked sauce in this dish retains the full flavor of the tomato. We have adapted this recipe from Amerigo's restaurant in the Bronx, which was one of the great Italian-American success stories from 1934 until its closing in 1998. Bucatini are fat macaroni; this is also good with perciatelli, fusilli, or spaghetti.

SERVES 4

Salt, preferably kosher
12 ounces bucatini
2/3 cup extra-virgin olive oil
2 large yellow onions, chopped
5 ounces prosciutto, chopped
1/2 cup dry Marsala
Freshly ground black pepper
1/2 teaspoon red pepper flakes

One 28-ounce can Italian-style
  tomatoes, sliced vertically into
  1/4-inch-thick slices, with juices
3 tablespoons chopped fresh basil
1 1/2 tablespoons chopped flat-leaf
  parsley
2 tablespoons unsalted butter
Freshly grated Parmigiano-
  Reggiano cheese

1. In a large sauté pan, heat the olive oil over medium-high heat. Add the onions and cook, stirring, until golden, 6 to 8 minutes. Add the prosciutto and cook, stirring, for another 5 minutes. Add the Marsala, a little salt and pepper, and the red pepper flakes. Simmer for 2 minutes.

2. Add the tomatoes and bring to a boil. Reduce the heat to medium-low and simmer, stirring occasionally, for 15 to 20 minutes. Stir in the basil and parsley, and simmer for another 2 minutes.

3. While the sauce cooks, bring 4 quarts water to a boil in a large stockpot. Add 1 heaping tablespoon salt and the bucatini. Cook until al dente.

4. Drain the pasta, toss it with the butter, and stir with the sauce. Pass the Parmigiano-Reggiano.

WINE SUGGESTION: ROSSO DI MONTALCINO

ORECCHIETTE WITH SAUSAGE AND PESTO

This is one of our favorite pasta shapes. The *orecchiette*, or "little ears," hold sauce beautifully—and you'll want to get as much of this fine sauce as you can.

SERVES 6

4 tablespoons olive oil
1 pound sweet Italian sausage, casing removed, coarsely chopped
2 medium yellow onions, thinly sliced
4 garlic cloves, minced
1/4 teaspoon dried thyme
1 cup dry white wine, such as Soave
One 14 1/2-ounce can chicken broth
2 anchovies, rinsed if packed in salt, and chopped
One 28-ounce can Italian-style tomatoes, crushed, with their juices
Salt, preferably kosher
1 pound orecchiette

FOR THE PESTO
2 cups loosely packed fresh basil leaves
1 garlic clove, chopped
1/4 teaspoon salt, preferably kosher
1/2 cup plus 2 tablespoons extra-virgin olive oil

One 15- to 19-ounce can cannellini beans, rinsed and drained
1/2 teaspoon freshly ground black pepper
3 tablespoons unsalted butter
1/2 cup freshly grated Parmigiano-Reggiano cheese

1. In a large sauté pan, heat 2 tablespoons of the olive oil over medium-high heat. Add the sausage and cook, stirring and breaking up the pieces, until lightly browned, about 5 minutes. Add the remaining 2

tablespoons olive oil and the onions, reduce the heat to medium, and cook, stirring occasionally, until the onions have softened, 5 minutes. Add the garlic and thyme and cook, stirring, for another 2 minutes.

2. Pour in the wine, stirring and scraping up the brown bits on the bottom of the pan. Add the chicken broth and bring to a boil. Reduce the heat to medium-low and simmer until the liquid has reduced by half, about 10 minutes.

3. Add the anchovies, tomatoes, and $1/2$ teaspoon salt. Simmer for 20 minutes.

4. While the sauce is cooking, bring 6 quarts water to a boil in a large stockpot. Add $1^1/2$ heaping tablespoons salt and the orecchiette, and cook until al dente.

5. Meanwhile, prepare the pesto: In a food processor, combine the basil and garlic and pulse to chop the leaves. Add the salt. With the machine running, gradually add the olive oil. Process until smooth.

6. Add the cannellini and pepper to the tomato sauce, and simmer for 5 minutes. Just before serving, stir in the butter.

7. Drain the pasta and mix it with the sauce. Serve with a drizzle of pesto and the Parmigiano-Reggiano.

WINE SUGGESTION: MERLOT

PAGLIA E FIENO

One of the quintessential "northern Italian" dishes that began appearing in New York restaurants in the late 1960s. The popularity of *paglia e fieno* (PAHL-yah eh fee-EH-noh)—"straw and hay," because of the colors of the white and green pastas—is probably due as much to the introduction of spinach pasta as to its similarity to Fettuccine all'Alfredo (see page 150) with the addition of ham and peas.

SERVES 4

Just how much do Americans love pasta? Apparently a lot. Italians consume about sixty pounds of pasta per person each year. Americans currently eat about half that amount but are gaining on the Italians.

According to the National Pasta Association,

❖ *40 percent of respondents in a survey said they eat more pasta now than five years ago.*

❖ *77 percent said they eat it at least once a week, and 36 percent of those aged 30 to 50 eat it three or more times a week.*

❖ *15 percent of the orders in fine dining restaurants of every stripe is pasta.*

❖ *The most popular choices are spaghetti, lasagna, macaroni and cheese, fettuccine, linguine, and angel's hair.*

4 tablespoons (¹/2 stick) unsalted
  butter
2¹/2 tablespoons chopped shallots
1 cup heavy cream
Pinch of freshly grated nutmeg
Salt, preferably kosher
Freshly ground black pepper

¹/2 cup frozen peas, thawed
6 ounces fettuccine
6 ounces spinach fettuccine
3 ounces ham, cut into ¹/4 x ¹/2-
  inch pieces
²/3 cup freshly grated Parmigiano-
  Reggiano cheese

1. Bring 3 quarts water to a boil in a large stockpot.

2. While the water is heating, melt 2 tablespoons of the butter in a large saucepan over medium heat. Add the shallots and cook, stirring, for 2 minutes. Add the cream, the remaining 2 tablespoons butter, the nutmeg, salt and pepper to taste, and the peas. Simmer gently over low heat for 2 minutes.

3. Add 2 heaping teaspoons salt and the fettuccine to the boiling water. Cook until al dente, and drain.

4. Add the ham and Parmigiano-Reggiano to the sauce, and stir. Add the fettuccine, mix, and serve.

WINE SUGGESTION: DOLCETTO

One curious exception to the Volstead Act regulations of Prohibition (Section 29) was to allow householders to produce up to 200 gallons each year of "non-intoxicating cider and fruit juices exclusively for use in his home." Though originally designed to help apple farmers, soon "juice grape" prices rose from $10 a ton to $100, indicating that a lot of grapes were being pressed at home. Here two Chicagoans, Nicola Salvucci and Andrea DeLuca, happily partake of the results of their pressing in their backyard at 225 East 22nd Street.

PENNE ALL'ARRABIATA

This is *not* pasta made "Arab-style," as some claim. *Arrabiata* means "hot" or "mad," referring to the number of spicy ingredients in the sauce. It is typical of the regions from Rome southward, and as lusty a pasta dish as you'll find. The sauce is also good with the fat macaroni called *bucatini*.

SERVES 6

1/4 cup extra-virgin olive oil
2 ounces sliced pancetta, cut into
  1/4-inch pieces
3 garlic cloves, chopped
3/4 teaspoon red pepper flakes, or
  to taste
One 28-ounce can Italian-style
  tomatoes, chopped or put
  through a coarse food mill, with
  their juices

Salt, preferably kosher
1 pound penne
2 tablespoons unsalted butter
3 tablespoons chopped flat-leaf
  parsley
1/3 cup freshly grated Pecorino
  Romano cheese

1. In a large saucepan, heat the olive oil over medium-high heat. Add the pancetta and sauté until lightly browned, about 3 minutes. Reduce the heat to low, add the garlic, and cook, stirring, until it is softened and lightly colored, about 2 minutes. Add the red pepper flakes, tomatoes, and salt to taste. Stir and bring to a boil. Then reduce the heat to medium-low and cook for 12 minutes.

2. Meanwhile, bring 6 quarts water to a boil in a large stockpot. Add 1 1/2 heaping tablespoons salt and the penne, and cook until al dente. Drain, and toss with the butter.

3. Add the parsley and the pasta to the sauce, mix, and heat for 1 minute. Serve with the Pecorino.

WINE SUGGESTION: CORVO ROSSO

PERCIATELLI WITH PUREED VEGETABLE SAUCE

A great dish for spring—light, tantalizing, and ideal for lunch. Perciatelli are tubular spaghetti with a small hole down the center.

SERVES 6

¼ cup extra-virgin olive oil
2 large yellow onions, coarsely chopped
4 large garlic cloves, coarsely chopped
2 carrots, coarsely chopped
1 small celery stalk, chopped
Salt, preferably kosher
Freshly ground black pepper

One 28-ounce can Italian-style tomatoes, crushed, with their juices
½ teaspoon red pepper flakes, or to taste
½ teaspoon sugar
1 pound perciatelli
2 tablespoons chopped fresh basil (optional)
3 tablespoons unsalted butter

1. In a large saucepan, heat the olive oil over medium-high heat. Add the onions, garlic, carrots, and celery, mix to coat the vegetables in the oil, and then reduce the heat to medium. Season with salt and pepper to taste, cover, and cook for 10 minutes, stirring a couple of times.

2. Add the tomatoes, red pepper flakes, and sugar, and cook over medium-low heat for 15 minutes.

3. Meanwhile, bring 6 quarts water to a boil in a large stockpot. Add 1½ heaping tablespoons salt and the perciatelli, and boil until al dente. Drain.

4. Combine the sauce and the basil (if you are using it) in a food processor, and puree. Blend in the butter.
Toss with the pasta, and serve.

WINE SUGGESTION:
MÜLLER-THURGAU

CREOLE SPAGHETTI BORDELAISE

Here's a perfect example of how American immigrant food cultures meld. In the nineteenth century, New Orleans, and southern Louisiana in general, was home to large settlements of French and Italian immigrants, each of whom lent their culinary traditions to the mix called Creole cuisine (along with Spanish, African, and Indian influences). This dish, the most famous version of which is served at Mosca's in Waggaman, is basically southern Italian Spaghetti Aglio e Olio (page 144) to which the French Creoles add butter and, in a nod toward refinement, remove the browned bits of garlic. The white, rather than black, pepper also gives it more of a French twist.

The term *bordelaise* in classic French cuisine refers to a dish, usually a sauce, made with Bordeaux red wine, but there is none in spaghetti bordelaise—suggesting that the dish may have originated with a cook from Bordeaux who named it after his hometown.

We've made the dish with the garlic removed and with the garlic left in. The latter gives a little bite of garlic; the former tastes more of flavored butter. In either case, the parsley gives it a slight green flavor at the end. We do not recommend adding grated cheese to this dish.

SERVES 4

Salt, preferably kosher
12 ounces spaghettini or capellini
3/4 cup (1 1/2 sticks) unsalted butter
6 tablespoons olive oil
10 garlic cloves, coarsely chopped
3 tablespoons minced flat-leaf parsley
Ground white pepper

1. Bring a large pot of water to a boil. Add 1 heaping tablespoon salt and the spaghettini, and cook until al dente.

2. Meanwhile, heat a saucepan over medium heat, and add the butter and olive oil. When the butter has melted, add the garlic, blending well. Just as the garlic begins to take on a golden color, remove the pan from the heat and using a slotted spoon, remove the garlic from the oil and butter mixture. (You may reserve the garlic and use it later on the spaghettini if you like.)

3. Stir the parsley into the oil and butter. Add salt and white pepper to taste.

4. Drain the spaghettini, retaining a little bit of the cooking water, and place it in a large bowl. Pour in the oil-butter mixture and toss until well coated. If the mixture seems dry, stir in a little of the reserved cooking water. Serve immediately.

WINE SUGGESTION: CHARDONNAY

SPAGHETTI ALLA CARUSO

Like Chicken Tetrazzini (page 314), this is an Italian-American dish named after a famous opera singer—in this case, the great tenor Enrico Caruso. Or is it? The origins of the dish have long been disputed, as has the all-important ingredient—chicken livers—that in Italian-American cookbooks and restaurants defines the dish. In the 1955 book *Spaghetti Dinner*, author Giuseppe Prezzolini says the dish was originally made by Caruso himself while living at the York Hotel in New York City, and that he made it for a visiting reporter. Prezzolini's recipe contains tomato, basil, red pepper, garlic, and zucchini, but no livers.

In *The New York Times Food Encyclopedia*, Craig Claiborne cites two undated sources giving recipes *with* chicken livers. Claiborne says that a couple named the Truaxes claimed that Caruso once made the dish for them in their kitchen. Despite such assertions, we have found a New York restaurant guide, *Where to Dine in '39*, that attributes the dish to a chef named Antonio With, of the Caruso restaurant chain in New York.

Whoever created Spaghetti alla Caruso, it was once very popular on Italian-American menus, though absent from most over the past twenty years. It's time to bring it back, for it is a rich, lusty dish—one we like to think Caruso would have enjoyed mightily.

SERVES 4

1 heaping tablespoon salt,
   preferably kosher
12 ounces spaghetti
1/4 cup olive oil
1 medium yellow onion, finely
   chopped
6 garlic cloves, chopped

9 to 10 ounces chicken livers,
   coarsely chopped
10 ounces tomatoes, peeled (see
   Note, page 89), seeded, and
   coarsely chopped
Freshly ground black pepper
2 tablespoons balsamic vinegar

1. Bring 4 quarts water to a boil in a large pot. Add the salt and the spaghetti, and cook until al dente.

2. Meanwhile, heat a large saucepan over low heat and add the olive oil. Add the onion and cook, stirring, until it begins to turn golden, 8 to 10 minutes. Add the garlic and cook, stirring, for 2 to 3 minutes more. Using a slotted spoon, remove the garlic and onion from the saucepan and set aside.

3. Add the chicken livers to the saucepan, and sauté until they lose their color and start to become slightly seared on the outside, 4 to 6 minutes.

4. Return the garlic and onion to the pan, add the tomatoes and salt and pepper to taste, and then add the balsamic vinegar. Cook until the liver is cooked through and the tomatoes have disintegrated into the sauce, about 5 minutes.

5. Drain the pasta and serve it immediately with the sauce.

WINE SUGGESTION:
AGLIANICO DEL VULTURE

Sicilian-born restaurateur Tony May, owner of the renowned San Domenico in New York, tells his chefs, "I buy you the best ingredients in the world; now don't screw them up."

SPAGHETTI WITH EGGPLANT, TOMATOES, AND OLIVES

The addition of eggplant to a dish almost always earns it the association *alla Sorrentino*, "in the style of Sorrento." And it is certainly true that the sunny vegetable is beloved by the people of that region. And those Gaeta olives are the soul of the south. So who are we to quibble? Call the dish *Spaghetti alla Sorrentino* and enjoy it to the hilt.

SERVES 6

1 pound eggplant, peeled and cut into ¹/2-inch cubes
Salt, preferably kosher
5 tablespoons extra-virgin olive oil
1 medium yellow onion, chopped
3 garlic cloves, chopped
One 28-ounce can Italian-style tomatoes, with juices, chopped or passed through a food mill

2 tablespoons minced pitted Calamata or Gaeta olives
¹/8 to ¹/4 teaspoon red pepper flakes
1 pound spaghetti
2 tablespoons chopped flat-leaf parsley
8 ounces plain or smoked mozzarella cheese, or a combination

1. Place the eggplant in a colander, and generously sprinkle with salt, tossing the cubes to coat them. Set the colander in a large bowl or in the sink to drain for 30 minutes.

2. Bring 6 quarts water to a boil in a large stockpot.

3. While the water is heating, heat 2 tablespoons of the olive oil in a large skillet over medium heat. Add the onion and cook, stirring, until softened and lightly colored, about 5 minutes. Add the garlic and continue to cook, stirring, for another 2 minutes. Transfer the onion and garlic to a bowl.

4. Dry the eggplant cubes with paper towels. In the same large skillet, heat the remaining 3 tablespoons olive oil over medium-high heat. When it is very hot, add the eggplant, tossing immediately to coat the pieces with the oil. Cook, stirring, until browned, 3 to 5 minutes. Return the onion and garlic to the skillet, and add the tomatoes, olives, red pepper flakes, and a little salt. Cook over medium-low heat for about 8 minutes to blend the flavors.

5. While the sauce is cooking, add 1¹/₂ heaping tablespoons salt and the spaghetti to the boiling water, and cook until al dente.

6. Add the parsley to the sauce and adjust the seasonings.

7. Drain the pasta, return it to the stockpot, and add the sauce and the mozzarella. Toss to mix, and serve.

WINE SUGGESTION: TAURASI

SPAGHETTI WITH CAULIFLOWER

Although you don't often see cauliflower used in Italian-American restaurants, it is a significant vegetable in the Italian diet, where it may find its way into an antipasto, a pasta, or a side dish. The anchovy fillets are essential to the authentic southern Italian flavor of this formidable pasta dish, and the saffron evokes the luxuries of Mediterranean cookery.

SERVES 4

¹/₂ cup dried currants
Salt, preferably kosher
2 pounds cauliflower, cut into
   pieces
¹/₈ teaspoon saffron threads
5 tablespoons extra-virgin olive oil
1 large yellow onion, thinly sliced
3 garlic cloves, minced
6 anchovy fillets (rinsed if packed
   in salt), chopped

1¹/₂ cups chopped canned Italian-
   style tomatoes, with juices
Freshly ground black pepper
12 ounces spaghetti
¹/₃ cup pignoli (pine nuts)
2 tablespoons freshly grated
   Pecorino Romano cheese
2 tablespoons freshly grated
   Parmigiano-Reggiano cheese

1. In a small saucepan, cover the currants with water, and bring to a boil. Simmer for 30 seconds. Then remove from the heat, and set aside.

2. Bring 2 quarts water to a boil in a large pot. Add a pinch of salt and the cauliflower. Boil until al dente but quite firm, 2 minutes. Drain, rinse in cold water, and drain again. When it is cool enough to handle, cut the cauliflower into small florets.

3. Using a mortar and pestle, crush the saffron. Add 2 tablespoons hot water, and set aside.

4. In a medium-size saucepan, heat 2 tablespoons of the olive oil over medium heat. Add the onion and cook, stirring, until softened, about 6 minutes. Add the garlic and anchovies, and cook for another 2 minutes. Add the tomatoes and bring to a boil. Reduce the heat to low and simmer for 15 minutes.

5. Drain the currants and add them to the pan along with the cauliflower. Add the saffron (stir another 2 tablespoons water in the mortar to extract all the saffron), pepper to taste, and a little salt (be careful not to oversalt, because anchovies have a fair amount of salt). Stir, and simmer for another 20 to 30 minutes to blend the flavors.

6. Meanwhile, bring 4 quarts water to a boil in a large stockpot. Add 1 heaping tablespoon salt and the spaghetti, and boil until al dente. Drain, reserving ½ cup of the pasta water.

7. Toss the pasta with the cauliflower sauce, the pignoli, the remaining 3 tablespoons olive oil, and a few tablespoons of the reserved pasta water to make it moist. Stir the cheeses together, and sprinkle over the pasta.

WINE SUGGESTION: TOCAI FRIULANO

Spaghetti was a good, low-cost food when meat, eggs, and other products were rationed during World War II. Here a woman rakes dried pasta to keep it from clogging the flow at the Atlantic Macaroni Company, maker of Caruso Brand Products in Long Island City, N.Y., in 1943.

BAKED MACARONI AND CHEESE

O ne of the great childhood comfort foods, the essential wholesomeness of this dish was compromised forever when the Kraft food company introduced the "Kraft Dinner" in 1937 (the company still sells 300 million boxes a year). This goop became the standard for inexpensive, toss-it-together macaroni and cheese, but ours, made from scratch, restores this wonderful dish to the goodness it deserves.

SERVES 2 TO 4

2 heaping teaspoons salt,
  preferably kosher
8 ounces elbow macaroni
4 1/2 tablespoons unsalted butter
1 small yellow onion, minced
2 tablespoons all-purpose flour
2 cups whole milk

Freshly ground black pepper
Pinch of freshly grated nutmeg
1/8 teaspoon cayenne or other
  ground hot chile
2 1/4 cups grated sharp cheddar
  cheese
2 tablespoons plain dry
  breadcrumbs

1. Preheat the oven to 350°F.

2. In a large pot, bring 3 quarts water to a boil. Add the salt and the elbow macaroni, and cook until the pasta is al dente. Drain and set aside.

3. In a large saucepan, heat 3 tablespoons of the butter over low heat. Add the onion and cook, stirring, until softened, about 8 minutes. Add the flour and cook, stirring, for 3 minutes. Add the milk all at once, and season with salt and pepper to taste. Cook over medium-low heat, stirring almost constantly, until the mixture begins to bubble. Then simmer for 2 minutes. Remove from the heat, and add the nutmeg, cayenne, and 2 cups of the cheese. Stir. Add the macaroni and mix.

4. Pour the macaroni mixture into a baking dish about 8 by 8 inches in size, and sprinkle with the remaining 1/4 cup cheese. Sprinkle with the breadcrumbs, and dot with the remaining 1 1/2 tablespoons butter. Bake in the oven for 20 to 25 minutes, or until the top is browned.

WINE SUGGESTION: ROSSO DI MONTALCINO

AMERICA'S FAVORITE PASTA

L ittle did traveling sales-man Harry Weishaar of St. Louis, Missouri, know when he started to tie two-ounce packages of Kraft grat-ed cheese to boxes of maca-roni as a promotional gim-mick that he was the father of the most famous American pasta dish of them all. His employer, Kraft, took the idea one step further, putting the two foods in one blue box. Soon they were selling 12 million boxes a year, for 19 cents. Kraft Macaroni & Cheese Dinner now costs a bit more, but it still sells 300 million boxes each year.

LASAGNA

S pelled with an "e"—*lasagne*—in Italy, this is a dish that has traveled very well across the Atlantic. Lasagna has become almost a staple at get-togethers in this country, from soccer team parties to anniversary celebrations. There are scores of variations on this layered pasta dish, the most famous being from Bologna, where a *besciamella* sauce is used instead of tomato. Our version is typically Italian-American and has served our family and others well for decades.

SERVES 6

1 heaping tablespoon salt, preferably kosher

1 pound fresh pasta sheets, each cut into 3 lengthwise strips

4 cups Galina's Meat Sauce (page 126)

2 tablespoons olive oil

One 15-ounce container ricotta cheese

1 pound mozzarella cheese, diced or shredded

2 cups freshly grated Parmigiano-Reggiano cheese

1. Bring 4 quarts water to a boil in a large pot. Add the salt and 4 of the pasta strips, and boil for 2 minutes. Remove the pasta strips with tongs or a fork, and submerge them in a bowl of cold water to stop the cooking. Rinse, drain, and spread them out on a clean kitchen towel. Repeat with the remaining pasta.

2. Preheat the oven to 350°F.

3. Spread 3 to 4 tablespoons of the sauce over the bottom of an 8x11-inch baking pan. Drizzle the olive oil over the sauce. Arrange 3 pasta strips, overlapping, in the pan. Spread one-third of the ricotta over the pasta, followed by one-fourth of the mozzarella and one-fourth of the Parmigiano. Dot with ⅔ cup of the sauce.

4. Repeat the layers of pasta and cheeses two times. For the final layer, scatter mozzarella, Parmigiano, and the remaining sauce over the pasta (you will have used all the ricotta).

5. Bake in the oven until bubbly and hot, 25 to 30 minutes. Let stand for 10 minutes before cutting.

WINE SUGGESTION:
LACRIMA CHRISTI DEL VESUVIO ROSSO

ONION LASAGNA

This lasagna, adapted from *Cucina Simpatica* (HarperCollins), is probably the most luxurious we've ever tasted. It's a signature dish of Johanne Killeen and George Germon, owners of one of this country's most innovative restaurants—Al Forno, in Providence, Rhode Island. Non-Italians who fell in love with the food of Italy, this former photographer and graphic designer opened a tiny trattoria fifteen years ago in this historic city (which has its own "Little Italy" on Federal Hill) to augment their income. Soon they were well known locally. Within five years they were famous nationally for the way they adapted Italian cuisine to their own style. They are probably most famous for their grilled pizzas.

Besciamella is a northern Italian version of the cream and cheese sauce known as *béchamel* in France.

SERVES 4

FOR THE BESCIAMELLA
3 tablespoons unsalted butter
3 tablespoons all-purpose flour
1 bay leaf
1²/3 cups whole milk
¹/2 teaspoon salt, preferably kosher

8 tablespoons unsalted butter
4 large sweet, such as Vidalia, or Spanish onions (2 pounds in all), halved vertically and thinly sliced

1 leek, white and light green parts only, washed and thinly sliced
Salt, preferably kosher
3 sheets fresh lasagna (about 1 pound), each sheet cut into 3 lengthwise strips
¹/4 cup heavy cream
1 cup freshly grated Parmigiano-Reggiano cheese

1. Prepare the *besciamella*: In a medium-size saucepan, melt the 3 tablespoons butter over medium heat. Add the flour and cook, stirring, for 3 minutes. Add the bay leaf and then milk all at once. Add the salt and stir continuously until the *besciamella* starts to thicken and comes to a boil. Reduce to a simmer and cook for 2 minutes. Set aside.

2. In a large sauté pan, heat 7 tablespoons of the butter over medium heat. Add the onions, leeks, and 1 teaspoon salt, toss to coat, and cook, stirring occasionally, until soft and lightly browned, about 25 minutes. Set aside.

3. Preheat the oven to 400°F.

4. Bring 4 quarts water to a boil in a large stockpot. Add 1 heaping tablespoon salt. Drop in 6 lasagna strips and boil for 1 minute. Remove the strips and let them drain, reserving the water for the next batch. Refresh the strips in cold water, and drain again. Spread the strips on kitchen towels. Repeat with the remaining strips.

5. To assemble: Remove the bay leaf. Spread 3 tablespoons of the *besciamella* in an 8 x 12-inch baking dish. Drizzle the cream over the *besciamella*. Cover with 3 pasta strips, overlapping. Spread a few more tablespoons of the *besciamella*, half of the onion mixture, and half of the Parmigiano-Reggiano over the pasta. Cover with 3 more pasta strips and repeat as before, reserving 2 tablespoons of the Parmigiano. Cover with the remaining 3 pasta strips, and spread the remaining *besciamella* over them. Sprinkle with the reserved 2 tablespoons Parmigiano, and dot with the remaining 1 tablespoon butter.

6. Bake for 20 minutes, or until the top is golden brown and the lasagna is bubbling hot. Remove it from the oven and let stand for 5 minutes before cutting.

WINE SUGGESTION: TIGNANELLO

NOTE: The *besciamella* (Step 1) can be prepared up to 2 days in advance. Cover and refrigerate.

> *Midnight Lasagna is not a recipe or the title of an Italian movie. It is a term that describes the phenomenon of eating lasagna cold out of the refrigerator late at night. This occurs principally, but not exclusively, after the lasagna was served at an early afternoon family gathering, then stored in the refrigerator for the next day.*

BRIAN WHITTMER'S ROCK SHRIMP CANNELLONI

Creamy, lush, and irresistible after the first bite, this California-style twist on cannelloni comes via chef Brian Whittmer, who first made his mark in the Burgundian style of New York's Montrachet restaurant, then moved to northern California, where he distinguished himself at the Pacific's Edge in Carmel and the Montrio in Monterey. This is as modern an Italian-American dish as one might hope for.

SERVES 4

FOR THE TOMATO SAUCE

1/4 cup extra-virgin olive oil
1 small yellow onion, chopped
2 garlic cloves, chopped
One 28-ounce can Italian-style
　tomatoes, crushed, juices
　reserved
1 cup chicken broth
Salt, preferably kosher
Freshly ground black pepper
1/4 teaspoon red pepper flakes
2 tablespoons chopped fresh basil

FOR THE CANNELLONI

Salt, preferably kosher
2 sheets (about 8 ounces) fresh
　pasta, cut in half lengthwise
2 1/2 tablespoons unsalted butter
1 large leek, white and light green
　parts only, washed and chopped
Freshly ground black pepper
1 1/4 pounds rock shrimp (see
　Note), rinsed, coarsely chopped,
　and patted dry
1/2 cup heavy cream
1 tablespoon tomato paste
1 teaspoon chopped fresh tarragon,
　or 1/2 teaspoon dried
1 tablespoon chopped fresh chives
2/3 cup freshly grated Parmigiano-
　Reggiano cheese

1. Prepare the sauce: In a medium-size saucepan, heat the olive oil over low heat. Add the onion and garlic and cook, stirring, until softened, about 5 minutes. Add the tomatoes and 1/3 cup of the reserved juices, the chicken stock, salt and pepper to taste, and the red pepper flakes. Bring to a boil. Reduce the heat to low and simmer for 30 minutes. Add the basil, transfer the sauce to a food processor, and puree. Set aside.

2. For the cannelloni, bring 2 quarts water to a boil in a large saucepan. Add 2 teaspoons salt and the pasta sheets, and cook until al dente, about 1 1/2 minutes. Remove, rinse in cold water, drain, and set aside. Cut each sheet into 3 strips.

3. Prepare the filling: In a small saucepan, melt 1 tablespoon of the butter over low heat. Add the leek and salt and pepper to taste, and cook, stirring, until softened, 4 to 5 minutes. Set aside.

4. In a large saucepan, heat the remaining 1 1/2 tablespoons butter over high heat. Add the shrimp and sauté until opaque, about 2 minutes. Using a slotted spoon, transfer the shrimp to the saucepan with the leeks, reserving the liquid. Season with salt and pepper to taste, and set aside.

5. Add the cream, tomato paste, and tarragon to the saucepan that was used to cook the shrimp. Bring to a simmer, and add the shrimp liquid. Cook until reduced by a little less than half, 3 to 5 minutes. Let cool for 10 minutes.

6. Add the cream mixture to the rock shrimp mixture, and stir in the chives.

7. Preheat the oven to 375°F.

8. Prepare the cannelloni: Sprinkle ½ cup of the Parmigiano-Reggiano over the 12 pasta rectangles. Divide the shrimp filling among the pasta pieces. Spread 2 to 3 tablespoons of the tomato sauce over the bottom of a 9 x 13 x 2-inch baking dish. Roll each cannelloni up, overlapping the ends, and place them, seam side down, in the baking dish. Cover with the remaining sauce, and sprinkle the rest of the Parmigiano-Reggiano over the top. Bake for 15 minutes, and serve hot.

WINE SUGGESTION: BARDOLINO

NOTE: Rock shrimp are a firm, very meaty variety of shrimp from Florida that has much more flavor and sweetness than the regular pink shrimp. If you can't find them, however, regular shrimp will do.

MANICOTTI

The lovely Italian word *manicotti*, pronounced "mah-nih-KOH-tee," sounds awful the way it's usually pronounced by Americans, as "man-ih-KAHDEE"—but it's still an Italian-American comfort food that just about everyone adores. Once a staple of Italian-American restaurants, it went out of fashion in favor of the very similar cannelloni, which are usually somewhat more slender and are filled with ground meat. Manicotti are wider, and while they may be filled with ground veal, pork, and/or beef, the most common form is stuffed with a ricotta mixture and sauced with a tomato sauce.

181

The following recipe is from one of the grand old Italian-American restaurants of Chicago, the Italian Village, run for four generations by the Capitinini family. This version is somewhat lighter than others, because it's made with a crepe batter rather than a pasta dough.

SERVES 4

FOR THE CREPES
3 large eggs
³/4 cup whole milk
1 teaspoon salt, preferably kosher
1 cup all-purpose flour
Olive oil

FOR THE SAUCE
3 cups Marinara Sauce or
   Galina's Meat Sauce (page
   126)

FOR THE FILLING
2 extra-large eggs
Salt, preferably kosher
Freshly ground white pepper
Pinch of freshly grated nutmeg
3 cups ricotta cheese, drained
¹/4 cup freshly grated Parmigiano-
   Reggiano cheese

1. Prepare the crepes: In a bowl, whisk the eggs together adding the milk in a steady stream. Add the salt and the flour, and whisk to make a light, thin batter. Refrigerate for 30 minutes.

2. Brush an 8-inch nonstick sauté pan with some olive oil and place over medium heat. Add ¹/4 cup of the batter, tilt to coat the bottom of the pan, and cook until lightly browned on one side, 1 to 2 minutes. Flip the crepe over and cook the other side until lightly browned, 1 to 2 minutes more. Set the crepe aside. Repeat this process until all the batter is used (about 18 crepes).

3. Prepare the filling: In a large bowl, lightly beat the eggs. Add salt and white pepper to taste, the nutmeg, and the two cheeses. Mix well.

4. Preheat the oven to 450°F.

5. Prepare the manicotti: Lay one of the crepes on a work surface. Spoon 4 to 5 tablespoons of the filling on the

"*Amici e pasta, se non sono caldi, non sono buoni.*" One of the most serious of Italian sayings regarding their favorite food is as true on this side of the Atlantic as on the other: "Friends and pasta—if they are not warm, they are not good."

bottom third of the crepe. Roll it up gently to form a flattened tube. Repeat until all of the crepes are filled.

6. Place the manicotti in a casserole or ovenproof baking dish. Cover with the tomato sauce and bake for about 15 minutes, until a toothpick inserted in the center comes out clean. Serve immediately.

WINE SUGGESTION: BARBERA D'ASTI

STUFFED SHELLS WITH MEAT SAUCE

Ｏne of the ubiquitous foods of backyard patio parties, graduations, even funerals, stuffed shells—always served in an aluminum pan!—are very American and express the Italian-American love of big portions and good, gooey pasta.

SERVES 6 TO 8

4 ounces mozzarella cheese, cut into ¼-inch cubes
1 cup freshly grated Parmigiano-Reggiano cheese
15 ounces ricotta cheese

½ teaspoon plus 1 heaping table-spoon salt, preferably kosher
Freshly ground black pepper
32 jumbo shells
2½ cups Galina's Meat Sauce (page 126)

1. In a large bowl, combine the mozzarella, ¼ cup of the Parmigiano-Reggiano, the ricotta, ½ teaspoon of the salt, and pepper to taste. Mix thoroughly.

2. Bring 4 quarts water to a boil in a large stockpot. Add the remaining tablespoon of salt and the shells, and boil until just al dente (do not overcook). Drain, rinse under cold water, and drain again thoroughly.

3. Meanwhile, preheat the oven to 350°F.

4. Spread ¼ cup of the meat sauce over the bottom of a 9 x 13-inch baking pan.

5. Fill the shells with the ricotta filling, and place them in the baking dish. Spoon the remaining sauce over the shells, and sprinkle the remaining ¾ cup Parmigiano-Reggiano over the sauce. Bake in the

oven until a nice brown crust has formed on the top, about 20 minutes. Serve immediately.

WINE SUGGESTION: LACRIMA CHRISTI ROSSO

ST. LOUIS "TOASTED" RAVIOLI

Although you can find fried ravioli in Italian cookbooks, so-called toasted ravioli is a specialty of the Italian-American restaurants on what is called The Hill in St. Louis, Missouri. They are not in fact toasted at all, but the crisp outer coating of breadcrumbs does give them a toastiness. The day after we made them, we popped some leftover ravioli in a toaster oven. After a few minutes they came out very much toasted and delicious—so maybe that's how the name came about. These are very rich, but you'll find that they're a big hit, so be generous.

SERVES 4 TO 6

¹/2 cup evaporated milk
1 cup plain dry breadcrumbs
24 small cheese ravioli
Vegetable oil for deep-frying

¹/2 cup freshly grated Parmigiano-
*   Reggiano cheese*
1 cup Marinara Sauce (page 126)
*   or simple tomato sauce (optional)*

1. Pour the evaporated milk into a shallow bowl. Put the breadcrumbs into another shallow bowl.

2. Dip each ravioli into the evaporated milk, and then coat it with breadcrumbs. Set the ravioli aside on a large piece of wax paper to rest for 10 minutes.

3. In a large saucepan, pour the oil to a depth of 2 inches. Heat the oil to 375°F, and fry the ravioli (do not crowd the pan—cook in batches if necessary) until golden brown, 3 to 4 minutes. Remove the ravioli with a slotted spoon and drain on paper towels. Place them on a heated platter, sprinkle with the Parmigiano-Reggiano, and serve with the sauce on the side, if desired.

WINE SUGGESTION: BARBERA D'ALBA

RAVIOLI WITH
FRESH PEA SAUCE

This is one of the prettiest, lightest sauces for springtime and summer, and it can be used for a wide variety of pastas or as a sauce for vegetables, meats, or fish. We were inspired to make this sauce after enjoying a fresh pea soup created by Jean-Georges Vongerichten, the Alsatian-born chef at Restaurant Jean-Georges in New York. He serves it with fried bread. We changed the thyme to a bay leaf, and serve it with cheese ravioli with a sprinkling of Parmigiano.

SERVES 4

1¼ pounds fresh peas (in pods)
6 tablespoons (¾ stick) unsalted
   butter
1 large yellow onion, coarsely
   chopped
1 leek, white and light green parts
   only, washed and chopped
1 bay leaf

2 tablespoons chopped flat-leaf
   parsley
Salt, preferably kosher
Freshly ground black pepper
2 cups chicken broth
32 small cheese ravioli
⅓ cup freshly grated Parmigiano-
   Reggiano cheese

1. Shell the peas, reserving the pods.

2. In a large saucepan, heat 3 tablespoons of the butter over low heat. Add the onion, leek, bay leaf, and parsley, and mix to coat all the vegetables with the butter. Season with salt and pepper to taste, and cook, stirring, until the vegetables are softened, about 5 minutes.

3. Add the empty pea pods to the onion mixture, cover with the chicken broth, and raise the heat. Bring to a boil. Cover the saucepan, reduce the heat to a simmer, and cook for 20 minutes.

4. Meanwhile, bring 2 quarts water to a boil in a large pot.

5. In a small saucepan, heat 3 cups water to a gentle boil. Add a pinch of salt and the shelled peas, and cook until the peas are tender, about 5 minutes. Drain and immediately refresh in cold water two times to stop the cooking. Set aside.

Charles de Gaulle once moaned about his beloved France, "One can simply not bring together a country that produces 265 kinds of cheese." What would he have made of a country that produces more than 500 shapes of pasta?

6. Strain the pea pod mixture into a saucepan, pressing the vegetables to extract as much liquid as possible. Discard the solids.

7. Add 2 heaping teaspoons salt and the ravioli to the boiling water, and cook until done, 5 to 6 minutes. Drain, and toss with 1 tablespoon of the butter.

8. Set aside ¹/2 cup of the peas. In a blender, combine the remaining peas and 1 cup of the strained sauce; puree. Add this puree to the rest of the sauce along with the reserved ¹/2 cup peas, and heat to a simmer. Cut the remaining 2 tablespoons butter into pieces and stir into the sauce. Adjust the seasoning to taste, and serve over the cooked ravioli. Sprinkle with the Parmigiano-Reggiano before serving.

WINE SUGGESTION: FRASCATI

KRAFI

Lidia Bastianich is one of the most ardent advocates of regional Italian food, particularly the food from her home region of Istria, near Trieste, which shows as much Austrian as Italian influence. *Krafi* is an Istrian pasta she introduced at Felidia, her award-winning *ristorante* in New York.

SERVES 6 TO 8

FOR THE DOUGH
2³/4 cups all-purpose flour
3 large eggs plus 1 large egg yolk
¹/4 teaspoon plus 1 heaping tablespoon salt, preferably kosher

FOR THE FILLING
¹/2 cup golden raisins (if dry, soak
in ³/4 cup hot water for 20 minutes and drain)
2 tablespoons dark rum
2 large eggs
Pinch of salt, preferably kosher
2 teaspoons sugar

¹/2 teaspoon freshly grated lemon
zest
¹/2 teaspoon freshly grated orange
zest
12 ounces Fontina cheese,
shredded
¹/2 cup freshly grated Parmigiano-
Reggiano cheese
¹/4 cup plain dry breadcrumbs

FOR THE FINISHING SAUCE
6 tablespoons (³/4 stick) unsalted
butter, softened
6 tablespoons freshly grated
Parmigiano-Reggiano cheese

1. Prepare the dough: In a food processor, combine the flour, eggs, egg yolk, and the ¼ teaspoon salt and process until the dough comes together. If needed, add a few tablespoons of water, little by little. Remove the dough from the processor, place it on a lightly floured surface, and knead it by hand for a few minutes. Wrap it in plastic wrap and let it rest for 30 to 45 minutes.

2. Meanwhile, prepare the filling: In a small bowl, combine the raisins and the rum and set aside to soak.

3. In a medium-size bowl, stir the eggs, salt, and sugar together. Add the lemon and orange zest, and mix well. Add the Fontina, Parmigiano-Reggiano, and breadcrumbs, and stir well to blend the ingredients. Mix in the raisin-rum mixture. Set aside.

4. Divide the dough into 3 or 4 pieces. Roll one piece out on a floured board to form a rectangle about ¹⁄₁₆-inch thick. (Rewrap the remaining dough.) Spoon the filling by teaspoons, 3 inches apart, onto the bottom half of the dough. Fold the other half over the filling, pressing the edges together. Using a 3-inch cookie cutter, cut each ravioli in the top row in a half-circle shape. Set them aside. Using a knife, cut straight across the top of the dough. Repeat until the sheet of dough is used up, and then repeat with the remaining dough and filling. The scraps of dough can be put together and rerolled. Seal the ravioli well, using a bit of water along the edges if needed.

5. Bring 4 quarts water to a boil in a large stockpot. Add the remaining tablespoon salt and the *krafi*, and boil for 6 minutes. Drain, reserving ½ cup of the cooking water. Return the ravioli to the stockpot. Add the butter, some of the reserved pasta water, and the Parmigiano-Reggiano, and gently mix. The butter sauce should be thick and creamy. Serve immediately.

WINE SUGGESTION: RIBOLLA GIALA

FIRST RULE OF ITALIAN COOKERY

If the pasta is overcooked, throw it out! There is no way to save or restore overcooked pasta.

EGG-FILLED RAVIOLI
WITH WHITE TRUFFLES

I f ever there was a voluptuous, even decadent, and defining dish
of modern Italian cuisine, this is it—a single, large *raviolo* stuffed
with spinach, cheese, and an egg yolk that spills forth into a
sauce of brown butter under a mantle of white truffles.

The dish was created by chef Valentino Mercatilii at
the trend-setting San Domenico restaurant in Imola, outside of
Bologna—a city known for its gastronomic excess. When Gianluigi
Morini, the owner of San Domenico, went into partnership with
Naples-born New York restaurateur Tony May to open a branch in
Manhattan, this signature dish became the centerpiece for a kind of
exquisite Italian cooking never before seen in the United States.

Although Morini is no longer associated with the New York
San Domenico, Tony May and his chef Odette Fada have kept
this glorious pasta dish on the menu. It is not particularly difficult
to make at home. The shavings of white truffles, which are out-
rageously expensive, are optional of course, but this is one special
dish that deserves full-tilt, spare-no-expense hedonism.

SERVES 4

Pasta dough, rolled into very thin
  sheets (pages 190–91)
1/2 cup cooked spinach
1/2 cup ricotta cheese
2/3 cup freshly grated Parmigiano-
  Reggiano cheese
5 large eggs

Pinch of freshly grated nutmeg
Salt, preferably kosher
Ground white pepper
7 tablespoons unsalted butter
2 ounces white truffles, shaved
  (optional)

1. Cut 8 5- to 6-inch circles from the pasta dough, using a cookie cutter,
or a knife with a saucer as a template.

2. Chop the spinach finely. In a bowl, thoroughly combine the spinach
with the ricotta, half the Parmigiano-Reggiano, and 1 of the eggs.
Season with the nutmeg and salt and white pepper to taste.

3. Place 4 rounds of the pasta dough on 4 sheets of wax paper. Divide
the ricotta-spinach mixture among the rounds.

4. One at a time, separate the yolks from the whites of the remaining 4 eggs. Make a slight indentation in each mound of the spinach mixture, and carefully place 1 egg yolk and $^1/_2$ of its white in the indentation. Season with salt and pepper.

5. Brush the edges of the pasta rounds with a little cold water, cover with the remaining 4 pasta rounds, and press together to seal, eliminating as much air as possible from the inside.

6. Bring a large pot of water to a boil. Add 2 heaping teaspoons salt, and carefully ease the ravioli into the water. Cook for 2 minutes.

7. While the ravioli are cooking, melt the butter in a saucepan over high heat and cook just until the butter takes on a light brown color.

8. Drain the ravioli and place them on 4 individual heated plates. Sprinkle with the shaved white truffles, if using, and the remaining Parmigiano-Reggiano. Then pour the browned butter over the ravioli, and serve.

WINE SUGGESTION: GAVI DEI GAVI

PASTA WAITS FOR NO MAN

We were once privileged to be at a banquet dinner feting the great tenor Luciano Pavarotti at New York's San Domenico restaurant. We were seated at a long oval table for about twenty people, and since he was guest of honor, the first dish of pasta was set before him; then everyone else was served. Trying as hard as he could to do as the Americans did, the huge tenor sat quietly looking down at his plate, rolling his eyes and fidgeting as the pasta dishes were set down before the other guests—a process that took about three minutes. When everyone was served, Pavarotti put his fork into his pasta, tasted it, and could hold himself back no longer. He let the fork drop on the table, looked up, and said in that extraordinary voice of his: "The pasta eet eez cold! You must eat the pasta when eet eez served to you. Presto! Immediately! Pasta waits for no man!" He then demanded a new, hot plate of pasta as everyone else dove into the lukewarm dishes in front of them.

DUCK RAVIOLI

For some reason we cannot wholly figure out—aside from the fact that it tastes delicious—ravioli stuffed with duck meat has become quite trendy at upscale Italian-American restaurants. In our version the addition of porcini mushrooms and the duck liver gives this sumptuous dish complexity and depth of flavor.

SERVES 4

FOR THE PASTA
2 cups all-purpose flour
3 extra-large eggs, at room temperature
1 tablespoon salt, preferably kosher

FOR THE FILLING
1/2 ounce dried porcini mushrooms
3 tablespoons unsalted butter
1 large yellow onion, chopped
1 medium carrot, chopped
1/2 duck liver (optional), chopped
2 tablespoons chopped flat-leaf parsley

1 1/2 cups chopped cooked duck
  (cut into small pieces)
1/4 cup dry Marsala
1/4 cup beef broth
Salt, preferably kosher
Freshly ground black pepper
1/4 cup freshly grated Parmigiano-
  Reggiano cheese

TO SERVE
6 tablespoons (3/4 stick) unsalted
  butter
1/2 cup freshly grated Parmigiano-
  Reggiano cheese

1. Prepare the pasta: Place the flour in a mound on a work surface. With your fingers, create a well in the middle of the mound. Break the 3 eggs into the well. Using a fork, beat the eggs, incorporating the flour little by little from the sides of the well. When most of the flour is incorporated, put the fork aside and knead the dough until smooth, about 8 minutes. Wrap it in plastic wrap and set it aside to rest for 20 minutes.

2. Next, prepare the filling: In a cup, combine the porcini with 1/2 cup hot water, and let soak for 20 minutes. Then squeeze the liquid out of the porcini, reserving the liquid. Chop the porcini and set aside. Strain the liquid through a cheesecloth-lined sieve and set it aside.

3. In a medium-size sauté pan, heat the butter over medium heat. Add the onion and carrot and cook, stirring, until softened, about 8 minutes. Add the mushrooms and the duck liver, if using, and cook, stirring, for 3 minutes. Add the parsley and stir.

4. Add the duck meat, strained mushroom liquid, Marsala, broth, and salt and pepper to taste. Stir, and simmer for 5 minutes over medium heat. Transfer the mixture to a food processor and coarsely chop. Adjust the seasonings. Return the mixture to the sauté pan and heat until the mixture is somewhat thick but not dry. Stir in the Parmigiano and set it aside.

5. Flatten the pasta dough by hand and cut it into 6 pieces. Take 1 piece and wrap the rest in the plastic wrap. Set a pasta machine to the widest setting and roll the dough through the machine. Take the dough and fold it into thirds. Run it through the machine again. Repeat this process three times. Go to the next setting on the machine and roll the dough through the machine. Then move the setting to next setting, and repeat until you reach the thinnest setting. When you are finished, your pasta strip should be 4 to 5 inches wide. (Leave the remaining dough until you have made ravioli with this piece. If you roll it all out at once, the pasta will dry too quickly.)

6. To make the ravioli, cut a straight edge at one end of the pasta strip. Place 2 scoops of filling, about 1 teaspoon each, about 1$^{1}/_{2}$ inches from one long edge and a couple of inches apart. Fold the edge over the stuffing and cut with a knife to make the 2 ravioli. Moisten the inside edges with a little water and seal them with your fingers. Place the ravioli on a semolina- or cornmeal-sprinkled pan. Repeat the process until the pasta sheet is used up. Then repeat the rolling and filling with each of the remaining pieces of dough. You should have 28 to 32 ravioli in all.

7. Bring 4 quarts water to a boil in a large stockpot. Add 1 heaping tablespoon salt, and drop in the ravioli. Bring the water back to a boil and cook for 1 minute. Reserve $^{1}/_{2}$ cup of the pasta cooking water and drain the rest.

8. In the same stockpot, melt the 6 tablespoons butter over medium heat. Transfer the ravioli to the butter, add $^{1}/_{3}$ cup of the reserved pasta water, and gently toss with a wooden spoon, so as not to puncture the ravioli. Add the Parmigiano-Reggiano and stir again, adding a little more water if necessary. The ravioli should be moist with the sauce. Serve immediately.

W I N E   S U G G E S T I O N :   B A R O L O

RAVIOLI WITH
ACORN SQUASH SAUCE

I talians love to make variations of this sumptuous ravioli at Christmastime, and the Jewish community of Ferrara makes it at Yom Kippur with a little added citron. The spices indicate that it probably originated in the eastern regions, possibly the Veneto, through which such spices were imported. These same spices—once very expensive—explain why this was a traditional feast-day dish, when people would spend extra money on their food. You may also use pumpkin for this dish.

SERVES 4

6 tablespoons (³/4 stick) unsalted butter
1 large yellow onion, chopped
8 fresh sage leaves
1 acorn squash, peeled, cut into large pieces, and steamed until tender
Salt, preferably kosher

40 small cheese ravioli
¹/4 teaspoon ground cinnamon
Large pinch of freshly grated nutmeg
2 teaspoons sugar
Freshly ground black pepper
¹/2 cup freshly grated Parmigiano-Reggiano cheese

1. In a medium-size saucepan, heat 3 tablespoons of the butter over medium-low heat. Add the onion and cook, stirring, until soft and translucent, about 7 minutes. Add the sage leaves and cook, stirring, for another minute.

2. Meanwhile, cut the acorn squash into ¹/4-inch cubes.

3. Add the cinnamon, nutmeg, sugar, salt and pepper to taste, and the squash to the onion, and stir well. Add ³/4 cup water, and simmer over medium-low heat until the liquid has reduced a bit and the sauce is thick, 6 to 8 minutes.

4. While the sauce thickens, bring 3 quarts water to a boil in a large pot. Add 2 heaping teaspoons salt and the ravioli, and cook until done, 4 to 6 minutes. Drain, and toss with 1 tablespoon of the butter.

5. Stir the remaining 2 tablespoons butter into the sauce. Divide the ravioli among 4 plates, spoon the squash sauce on top, and sprinkle with the Parmigiano-Reggiano.

WINE SUGGESTION: TIGNANELLO

LOBSTER RAVIOLI

Lobster ravioli became one of the trendy dishes of the '90s at upscale Italian restaurants in the U.S. (It's almost unknown in Italy, where they don't have American lobsters to begin with.) Gradually lobster ravioli filtered down to less expensive Italian-American restaurants, which charged a much lower price for a dish that has to cost a lot because of the main ingredient. One has to wonder—who in their right minds would cut up a whole lobster just to make ravioli? Which leads to the next question: Can the run-of-the-mill Italian-American restaurant actually afford to make ravioli with lobster? Or are they using a substitute, like surimi, which is a minced fish paste, usually made from cheap pollock, flavored to taste like lobster?

Frankly we thought that lobster ravioli were just a waste of good lobster, but after experimenting, we found that the following dish has become one of our favorites, with the true flavor of the lobster coming through with the lovely taste of the potato. This is a dish for a special occasion.

SERVES 4

FOR THE RAVIOLI
4 tablespoons (¹/2 stick) unsalted
   butter
1 shallot, finely chopped
1 garlic clove, minced
1 cup chopped cooked lobster meat
¹/4 cup cubed cooked all-purpose
   potato
1 tablespoon minced flat-leaf
   parsley
Salt, preferably kosher
Freshly ground black pepper
25 to 30 Chinese wonton skins or
   dumpling wrappers
1 large egg, beaten with 1
   teaspoon water

FOR THE SAUCE
4 tablespoons (¹/2 stick) unsalted
   butter
1 tablespoon finely chopped
   shallots
1 small garlic clove, minced
¹/4 cup chicken broth
2 tablespoons dry white wine
2 tablespoons chopped Italian-style
   canned tomatoes, drained
¹/3 cup heavy cream
Salt, preferably kosher
Freshly ground black pepper

1. Prepare the ravioli: Heat a small saucepan over low heat. Add 2 tablespoons of the butter, the shallot, and the garlic, and cook, stirring, until the vegetables are soft but not browned, about 3 minutes. Set aside.

2. In a small bowl, combine the lobster, potato, parsley, salt and pepper to taste, and the shallot-garlic mixture, and stir to combine.

3. One at a time, place 1 heaping teaspoon of the lobster filling in the center of a wonton skin. Wet half of the outer rim of the wonton skin with the egg wash, fold, and seal well. Set it aside and repeat with the remaining skins and filling.

4. In a large pot, bring 3 quarts of water to a boil.

5. Meanwhile, prepare the sauce: In a small saucepan, melt the butter over low heat. Add the shallots and garlic, and cook, stirring, until softened, about 2 minutes. Add the chicken broth, wine, and tomatoes, and bring to a boil. Then reduce the heat to a simmer and cook for 3 minutes. Add the cream and salt and pepper to taste, and cook over low heat for another 3 minutes. Set aside.

6. Add 2 heaping teaspoons salt and the ravioli to the boiling water, bring back to a boil, and boil for 3 to 4 minutes. Drain, and return the ravioli to the pot. Add the remaining 2 tablespoons butter, toss gently, and add the sauce. Bring to a boil, and serve immediately.

WINE SUGGESTION: CHARDONNAY

While Italian waters offer up nothing as delectable as a Maine lobster, American cooks should treat the live lobster both carefully and tenderly. They must be alive when they are cooked, and the more lively they seem when handled—their tails and claws flapping—the better. If you must keep a lobster for more than a day, wash it off, drain the water from it, cover with a damp towel, and store in a pan in the refrigerator.

GNOCCHI

When I was a kid and my family went out to an Italian-American restaurant, I never ordered anything but gnocchi because my mother rarely made them at home. She led me to believe that these wondrous, light potato dumplings were difficult to prepare, but nothing can be further from the truth. It's O.K.—there were plenty of other things she gladly made, and there were plenty of Italian-American restaurants where I could get gnocchi.

—J.M.

SERVES 4 TO 6

2 pounds (about 4) Idaho potatoes
1 large egg, lightly beaten
1 tablespoon heavy cream
Salt, preferably kosher
1¹/₂ to 2 cups all-purpose flour

3 tablespoons unsalted butter
About 2 cups Fresh Tomato Sauce
(page 139), Alfredo Sauce
(page 151), or Galina's Meat
Sauce (page 126)

1. In a large pot, cover the potatoes with 1 inch water, cover the pot, and bring to a boil. Reduce the heat to a simmer and cook until the potatoes are tender, 20 to 30 minutes. (The time will depend on the size of the potatoes.) Drain, and let the potatoes cool. Then peel them and pass them through a ricer or food mill.

2. In a large bowl, combine the potatoes, egg, cream, and 2 teaspoons salt. Blend thoroughly, until smooth. Add 1¹/₂ cups of the flour, and mix to form a soft dough. Turn the dough out onto a floured board and knead it gently, adding more flour if the dough is too sticky.

3. Divide the dough into 6 pieces. Roll each piece into a ³/₄-inch-thick rope, and cut the rope into ³/₄-inch pieces. Holding a wire whisk in one hand, with the other hand take a gnocchi and roll it up the wires near the handle of the whisk to form little grooves in the dough. (You can also use the tines of a fork to press grooves into the gnocchi, rolling them slightly as you press.) Place the grooved gnocchi on a floured board. Repeat the process with the rest of the dough.

4. Bring 6 quarts water to a boil in a large stockpot. Add 1¹/₂ heaping tablespoons salt, and drop the gnocchi into the boiling water. Once the gnocchi have risen to the top, boil for 3 minutes. Taste for doneness, and drain. Toss gently with the butter and serve with the sauce of your choice.

WINE SUGGESTION: CHIANTI CLASSICO

POTATO GNOCCHI
WITH
WILD MUSHROOM RAGÙ

When he opened the restaurant named Simposio in 1998, Alberto Baffoni brought authentic Italian food to Houston. This is one of his masterful dishes.

Veal *jus* is available in specialty gourmet shops. If you can't find it, use good-quality beef stock.

SERVES 4

FOR THE MUSHROOM RAGÙ
2 tablespoons extra-virgin olive oil
3 shallots, finely chopped
2 garlic cloves, mashed
6 ounces portobello mushrooms, stemmed and sliced
6 ounces cremini mushrooms, stemmed and sliced
3 ounces dried porcini mushrooms, soaked in hot water for about 20 minutes, drained, and chopped
2 cups dry white wine, such as Soave
1 cup veal jus or beef stock

³/4 cup finely chopped flat-leaf parsley
3 tablespoons unsalted butter
Salt, preferably kosher
Freshly ground black pepper

FOR THE GNOCCHI
Salt, preferably kosher
1¹/2 pounds Idaho potatoes, peeled and quartered
1 large egg, beaten
Pinch of freshly grated nutmeg
1³/4 cups all-purpose flour

1. Prepare the ragù: In a sauté pan, heat the olive oil over low heat. Add the shallots and garlic and cook, stirring, until softened, about 2 minutes. Increase the heat to medium, add all the mushrooms, and cook, tossing, until softened, about 5 minutes. Add the wine and simmer for 10 minutes. Add the veal *jus* and the parsley, and simmer to reduce a bit, 10 minutes. Add the butter, season with salt and pepper to taste, and set aside.

2. Prepare the gnocchi: Bring a large pot of water to a boil, add 2 teaspoons salt and the potatoes, and cook until tender, 8 to 12 minutes. Drain, and mash the potatoes while they are still hot.

3. In a mixing bowl, combine the mashed potatoes, the egg, the 1 tablespoon salt, and the nutmeg. Stir to incorporate the ingredients. Stirring with a fork, slowly add the flour, and then knead until a smooth dough is formed.

4. Dust a wooden cutting board with flour, and roll portions of the dough into ropes about $^3/4$ to 1 inch in diameter. Cut each rope into bite-size pieces.

5. Bring a large pot of water to a rolling boil. Drop in 2 heaping teaspoons salt and the gnocchi, and when the gnocchi have risen to the top, cook for 2 to 3 minutes (taste to check for doneness). While they are cooking, quickly reheat the ragù. Drain the gnocchi and serve immediately with the mushroom ragù.

WINE SUGGESTION: SALICE SALENTINO

MORELS AND PEA-SHOOT GNOCCHI IN A LIGHT BROTH

Daniel Boulud is widely recognized as one of the finest chefs in the world, and as owner of Restaurant Daniel in New York he is constantly coming up with dishes at the height of haute cuisine. But at his more casual Café Boulud, where Andrew Carmellini is the on-premises chef, Boulud harks back to the dreamy dishes of his childhood in a small town outside of Lyons, France. At the same time, he loves Italian food, which he gives his own Gallic twist, as in these lovely ricotta-light gnocchi just moistened with a light broth. In *Daniel Boulud's Café Boulud Cookbook* he writes of his gnocchi dish: "You can tinker with the selection of vegetables—I always do—but I like to keep the earthy flavors and crunch of carrots and radishes, and the sweetness of fresh peas." This recipe is adapted from his book.

SERVES 4

FOR THE GNOCCHI

3/4 cup ricotta cheese
Salt, preferably kosher
5 1/2 ounces pea shoots (see Note),
  leaves and tender stems only
3 tablespoons extra-virgin olive oil,
  plus a little more
2 tablespoons plus 1 teaspoon all-
  purpose flour
Ground white pepper

FOR THE BROTH

1 tablespoon unsalted butter
4 scallions, white and green parts
1 large shallot, cut diagonally into
  very thin slices
1 sprig fresh rosemary
2 long, thin carrots, cut diagonally
  into very thin slices
2 garlic cloves, thinly sliced
1 1/2 cups unsalted vegetable stock,
  canned vegetable broth, or water
2 pounds morels, rinsed and patted dry
Salt, preferably kosher
Ground white pepper
1 1/2 pounds English sweet peas,
  shelled
1 ounce pea shoots, leaves and
  tender stems only
1 tablespoon extra-virgin olive oil
4 small pink radishes, scrubbed
  and cut into very thin rounds
1 tablespoon finely chopped fresh
  chives

1. Prepare the gnocchi: Place the ricotta in a tea towel and squeeze to force out the excess moisture. Set it aside.

2. Bring a pot of salted water to a boil, and plunge in the pea shoots. Cook until the leaves are tender but still green, 2 to 3 minutes. Drain the leaves in a strainer and run them under cold water to set their color and cool them. Press the leaves between your hands to remove the excess water, and pat dry between paper towels.

3. In a small food processor or blender, combine the leaves with the ricotta and olive oil. Process until smooth. Add the flour, season with salt and white pepper to taste, and pulse just to blend. Then taste, and adjust the salt and pepper if necessary. Press the gnocchi mixture through a sieve into a bowl.

4. Bring 1 quart of water to a boil in a saucepan, and add 1 1/2 heaping teaspoons salt. Then lower the heat to a gentle simmer. Set a bowl filled with ice cubes and water close to the stove. Using two teaspoons, make gnocchi dumplings, about 1 inch in diameter, by picking up some of the gnocchi mixture on one spoon and scraping it off into the simmering water with the other. Poach the gnocchi in three batches, cooking each batch for 4 to 5 minutes. With a slotted spoon, transfer the gnocchi to the ice-water bath.

5. When the gnocchi are cold, use the slotted spoon to transfer them to a plate. Drizzle a little olive oil over them, cover with plastic, and refrigerate until needed. (They can be prepared up to 6 hours in advance.)

6. Prepare the broth: In a medium sauté pan, heat the butter over medium heat. Toss in the scallions, shallot, and rosemary and cook, stirring, until the shallots are translucent but not colored, 3 to 4 minutes. Add the carrots, garlic, and stock, and cook for 3 minutes. Add the morels and salt and white pepper to taste, cover, and cook for another 5 minutes. Uncover the pan, add the peas, and cook for 4 to 5 minutes more.

7. Check the liquid in the pan to make sure it is at a very gentle simmer. Then add the gnocchi, pea shoot leaves, and olive oil. Heat the gnocchi gently for 3 minutes, then add the radishes. Taste the broth, and add more salt and pepper, stock, or olive oil, if needed. Remove the pan from the heat.

Broadway showgirls (from left) Geraldine Shay, Pat Gale, Bonnie Blair, Gennie Courtney, and Toni Tucci show their spaghetti-eating skills (with their hands behind their backs) for a publicity photo for a New York restaurant (1948).

8. Lift the gnocchi and vegetables from the pan with a slotted spoon, and divide them among 4 warmed shallow soup plates. Pour an equal amount of broth over each serving, sprinkle with the chives, and serve immediately.

WINE SUGGESTION: MÜLLER-THURGAU

NOTE: Pea shoots can be found in Asian and specialty produce markets during the spring and summer.

TWO RESTAURANT REVIEWS FROM TWO DIFFERENT ERAS:

ENRICO & PAGLIERI RESTAURANT, 66 West 11th Street; Phone: ALgonquin 4-4658.

Type of Cooking: Italian-Continental. This is one of the oldest and best of the Italian restaurants in New York serving full-course dinners. The eight-course menu ($1.25) is a treat and is warmly recommended to all who like fine Italian cooking. There is no form of spaghetti, ravioli, gnocchi or similar dishes which cannot be found here at its best and Enrico will always be glad to advise if you are uncertain as to what to order." —G. Selmer Fougner, Dining Out in New York: What to Order (1939)

SAN MARINO * * * 236 East 53rd Street. PL 9-4130.

An East Side, 53rd Street version of '21' Club—you might call it a spaghetti eaters' 21. . . . From long and extensive observations, Forbes Magazine's Restaurant Guide can state as a fact that in San Marino there are more highly custom-made suits on the males than in any other restaurant in New York. If you're dressed off the rack, you'll feel positively dowdy. . . . The minestrone Milanese is beautifully seasoned and filled with vegetables. The Italian sausage served at lunch should be tried. Veal scaloppine, fine.

The restaurant is noted for its fine pasta and fish. The pasta dishes are made fresh; all the various spaghettis, as great as spaghetti can be. Pompano almondine upholds the other end of that reputation. . . . The shrimp in the jumbo shrimp Fra Diavolo are delicious, but the dish, though spicy by nature, is too much so. . . . The approximate cost of lunching here will be $20. Dinner is a la carte; with wine, drinks and tip, it can run an additional $15 or $20. The wine list is good." —Forbes Magazine's Restaurant Guide (1971).

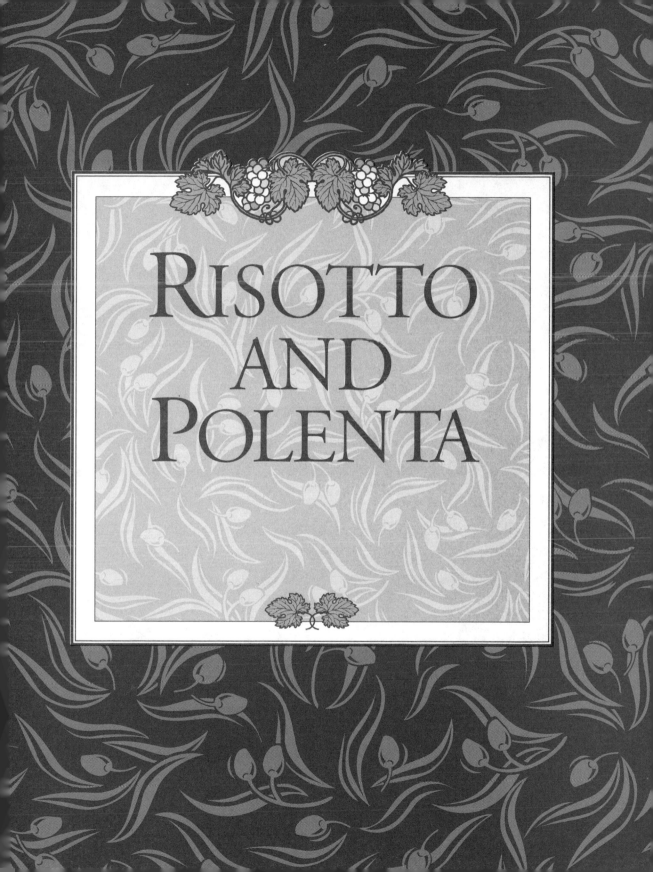

RISOTTO AND POLENTA

RISOTTO

Pesto Risotto 205
Risotto with Spinach, Porcini, and Peas 206
Risotto al Finocchio e Pancetta 208
Risotto with Roasted Red Peppers 209
Risotto with Apples and Saffron 214
Risotto alla Milanese 215
Risotto with Corn 217
Mushroom Risotto 218

POLENTA

Polenta with Fontina 220
Polenta with Mushroom Sauce 221
Semolina Gnocchi with Tomato Sauce 223

Risotto and Polenta

Risotto

Risotto (re-SOH-toh) is not just rice—which Italians call *riso* (REE-soh). Risotto is the cooking of rice with broth and other ingredients to achieve a creamy consistency called *all'onda,* "wavelike." And that is what you should aim for when cooking risotto.

Rice was first brought to Italy, probably from Spain, in the tenth century, but there was no significant production until the sixteenth, and then only in the Po Valley of the north. For this reason rice dishes, and risotti in particular, flowered in northern Italy and were, until the present century, not much in favor in the south, where pasta was preferred as a farinaceous dish.

In the United States, risotto rarely appeared on restaurant menus until the 1980s, when it suddenly became quite fashionable—and quite expensive, based on the restaurants' insistence that each dish of risotto was made from scratch and constantly stirred for twenty minutes. While made-to-order risotto is the ideal, it is rarely the reality in restaurant kitchens, and in Italy it would be highly unusual to wait twenty to thirty minutes for a plate of risotto. In the homes of Italian-American families who emigrated from southern Italy, risotto would be made only on rare occasions, for it's principally a northern dish.

Today Italy produces several kinds of rice suitable for risotto, and you will hear arguments as to which is best for which specific dish. By far the most widely available in the United States is *Arborio* (ahr-BOH-ree-oh), which works extremely well in all the risottos you could possibly want to make.

A good broth, be it chicken or beef, is essential to making a tasty risotto, because the rice absorbs whatever flavor the broth possesses.

PESTO
RISOTTO

As with Trenette with Pesto (page 128), the verdant color and the flavors of basil and garlic make this one of the favorite dishes of northern Italy, where risotti are more widely cooked than in the south.

SERVES 4 TO 6

One 48-ounce can chicken broth
2 tablespoons olive oil
4 tablespoons (¹/2 stick) unsalted
 butter
1 small yellow onion, chopped
2 cups Arborio rice
¹/2 cup dry white wine, such as
 Soave
1 large garlic clove, chopped
2 tablespoons pignoli (pine nuts)

1¹/2 cups packed fresh basil leaves
Salt, preferably kosher
¹/3 cup extra-virgin olive oil
1 medium-size all-purpose potato,
 boiled and cut into ¹/4-inch cubes
²/3 cup freshly grated Parmigiano-
 Reggiano cheese
¹/3 cup freshly grated Pecorino
 Romano cheese

1. In a medium-size saucepan, bring the chicken broth to a boil. Then reduce the heat to very low, and keep it warm.

2. In a large flameproof casserole, heat 2 tablespoons olive oil and 1 tablespoon of the butter over medium heat. Add the onion and cook, stirring, until softened, about 5 minutes. Add the rice, stir to coat the grains with the oil and butter, and cook, stirring, for 2 minutes. Add the wine and cook, stirring, until it's almost absorbed, 1 to 2 minutes.

3. Add about ¹/2 cup of the hot chicken broth to the rice and cook, stirring often, over medium-low heat until the liquid is almost absorbed, 3 to 4 minutes. Add another ¹/2 cup of broth and continue to cook, stirring. Repeat this procedure, stirring often. It will take about 20 minutes for the rice to cook until done, or al dente; start checking it after 15 to 18 minutes.

4. Meanwhile, in a food processor, combine the garlic, pignoli, and basil, and pulse to chop the ingredients. Add salt to taste, and with the machine running, pour in the ¹/3 cup olive oil in a slow stream.

5. Add the basil mixture and the potato to the risotto, and stir. Add the

cheeses and the remaining 3 tablespoons butter, stir to blend, and serve immediately.

WINE SUGGESTION: SPANNA

RISOTTO WITH SPINACH, PORCINI, AND PEAS

A good, hearty risotto for the winter months.

SERVES 4 TO 6

3/4 ounce dried porcini mushrooms
One 48-ounce can chicken broth
1 tablespoon olive oil
4 tablespoons (1/2 stick) unsalted butter
1 medium yellow onion, chopped
2 small garlic cloves, minced
2 cups Arborio rice
1/2 cup dry white wine, such as Soave

Salt, preferably kosher
2 cups chopped fresh spinach
1/2 cup peas, fresh and parboiled, or frozen and thawed
2 tablespoons chopped flat-leaf parsley
1/4 cup heavy cream
2/3 cup freshly grated Parmigiano-Reggiano cheese

1. In a small bowl, pour 1 cup hot water over the porcini. Set aside to soak for 30 minutes.

2. In a large saucepan, bring the chicken broth to a boil. Reduce the heat to very low and keep it warm.

3. In a large casserole, heat the olive oil and 2 tablespoons of the butter over medium heat. Add the onion and cook, stirring, until softened, about 5 minutes. Add the garlic and cook, stirring, for another 2 minutes. Add the rice and stir to coat with the butter and oil. Then add the wine and a little salt, stir, and cook until the wine is almost absorbed, 1 to 2 minutes.

4. Add about 1/2 cup of the chicken broth to the rice and cook, stirring often, over medium-low heat until the liquid is almost absorbed, 2 to

4 minutes. Add another ¹/₂ cup broth and continue to cook, stirring. Repeat this procedure until you have added 2 cups of the broth.

5. Meanwhile, using your hands, squeeze the water out of the porcini, reserving the soaking liquid. Coarsely chop the porcini. Strain the soaking liquid through a cheesecloth-lined sieve.

6. Add the porcini and strained liquid to the risotto, and stir. Continue adding the chicken broth, stirring often.

7. After the risotto has cooked for a total of 15 to 18 minutes, taste it for doneness. It should be tender but firm, not soft. When it is almost done, add the spinach, peas, and parsley, and cook for 1 minute. Stir in the cream and the remaining 2 tablespoons butter. Add the Parmigiano and stir. Check to see if more salt is needed, and serve.

WINE SUGGESTION: BARBARESCO

Michael Lomonaco rose from failed actor to the top of the world—the 107th floor of the World Trade Center in New York City, where he is now chef at the acclaimed Wild Blue dining room.

"I was born in Brooklyn, and my parents were both from Sicily. I was going to be an actor. I did some Off Off Broadway and struggled like every young actor. Both my brothers were doctors, but my parents accepted me as a struggling actor, at a time when guys like Al Pacino and Robert DeNiro were just getting some attention. But when I told my parents I wanted to become a chef, my God! You can't believe the hue and cry that went up! It was like my mother and father had expected a priest in the family, and I had renounced my religion to become a cook! My mother cried her eyes out, moaning, 'That's what I do every day for the family, and I hate it!' But they finally came around and were very supportive.

"I went to a New York City technical school for my culinary training, then worked for eighteen months at Monte's Venetian Room, one of the old Brooklyn Italian restaurants. Nick Monte owned the place, as well as Guerney's Inn in Montauk, and he was a great restaurateur and raconteur, and he knew how to keep his customer base. I learned how to do everything in a restaurant from Nick, and that's where I learned to cook southern Italian food. But I knew I wanted to go toward American food, and I wanted to define myself professionally through American food culture. In my private life I'm still so Italian. I cook Italian at home and it's what I eat on my day off. For me it's still my greatest comfort food."

RISOTTO AL FINOCCHIO E PANCETTA

The tantalizing anise flavor of *finocchio* (fee-NOH-k'yoh)—fennel—can overpower a dish, but the salty pancetta tames it, and the combination makes this a very unusual risotto.

SERVES 4

One 48-ounce can chicken stock
1/4 cup olive oil
4 tablespoons (1/2 stick) unsalted
  butter
1 small yellow onion, finely
  chopped
1 garlic clove, minced
3 ounces pancetta, cut into
  1/4-inch dice

1 fennel bulb, thinly sliced
Salt, preferably kosher
Freshly ground black pepper
1 3/4 cups Arborio rice
1/2 cup dry white wine, such as
  Soave
3/4 cup freshly grated Parmigiano-
  Reggiano cheese

1. In a large saucepan, bring the chicken broth to a boil. Reduce the heat to very low and keep warm.

2. Heat a medium-size flameproof casserole over medium heat. Add the olive oil and 1 tablespoon of the butter, and heat. Add the onion and garlic and cook, stirring, until soft but not browned, about 4 minutes. Add the pancetta and cook, stirring, for about 2 minutes or until lightly browned. Add the fennel, stir well, and cook until slightly softened, about 4 minutes. Add salt and pepper to taste.

3. Add the rice and cook, stirring with the vegetables, for 2 minutes. Add the wine and stir until it is almost absorbed, 1 to 2 minutes. Add 1/2 cup of the hot chicken broth and cook, stirring often, until the liquid is almost completely absorbed, 3 to 4 minutes. Add another 1/2 cup broth and repeat the process, stirring frequently, until the rice is al dente, about 20 minutes in all. Start checking it after 15 to 18 minutes.

4. Stir in the remaining 3 tablespoons butter and the Parmigiano, and adjust the salt and pepper to taste. Serve immediately.

WINE SUGGESTION: DOLCETTO

RISOTTO WITH ROASTED RED PEPPERS

A very fine, somewhat unusual risotto, a kind you'd probably find more easily on this side of the Atlantic than on the other.

SERVES 4 TO 6

2 roasted red peppers (page 332)
1 tomato, peeled (see Note, page 89) and seeded
One 48-ounce can chicken broth
3 tablespoons olive oil
5 tablespoons unsalted butter
1 large yellow onion, finely chopped

1/2 celery stalk, finely chopped
2 cups Arborio rice
1/2 cup dry white wine, such as Soave
1/4 cup heavy cream
2/3 cup freshly grated Parmigiano-Reggiano cheese

1. In a blender or food processor, combine the peppers, tomato, and 1/2 cup of the chicken broth. Process until smooth, and set aside.

2. In a large saucepan, bring the remaining broth to a boil. Reduce the heat to very low and keep warm.

3. In a large flameproof casserole, heat the olive oil and 2 tablespoons of the butter over medium heat. Add the onion and celery and cook, stirring, until soft but not browned, about 8 minutes.

4. Add the rice, stir to coat, and cook, stirring, for 2 minutes. Stir in the wine, and cook until it has been almost completely absorbed, 1 to 2 minutes. Add 1/2 cup of the hot chicken broth, and let it simmer, stirring, over medium-low heat. When the liquid is almost all absorbed, add another 1/2 cup broth and stir. Add the red pepper puree. Continue adding the chicken broth, stirring often, until the rice is al dente, about 20 minutes in all (start checking for doneness after 15 to 18 minutes).

5. Add the remaining 3 tablespoons butter, the cream, and the Parmigiano-Reggiano. Stir to blend. The risotto should be creamy, not soupy and not dry. If it is too thick, add a little more broth. Serve immediately.

WINE SUGGESTION: CARMIGNANO

How to Tell
an Italian Restaurant from
an Italian-American restaurant

Y*ou've just finished the lobster ravioli in vodka sauce and can't wait for the waiter to bring the sixteen-ounce veal chop with the portobello mushrooms. You dip your bread into a dish of extra-virgin olive oil and survey the dining room of mottled walls, dark red carpet, and a reproduction of Michelangelo's David in the foyer. "The Three Tenors" are singing their hearts out on the stereo. You finish with a full cup of decaf espresso with lemon peel and a shot of Sambuca, and you sit back and say, "This is one terrific Italian restaurant!"*

But you would be wrong. Almost nothing about the scene I've just described has any resemblance to a restaurant in Italy, whether it's a posh dining salon in Bologna or a humble trattoria in Naples.

Don't get me wrong: There are plenty of inauthentic Italian restaurants in the United States where I love to eat. But the reason people return from Italy moaning that the food here is never as good as the food there has as much to do with entrenched clichés of Italian-American dining as it does with the difference in the quality of the mozzarella.

To understand Italian-American restaurants, you must know that the vast majority of Italians who emigrated to the United States between 1890 and 1910 were from southern Italy—more than 5 million of them, most settling in New York and other northern cities. Miserably poor in the Old Country, subsisting on a diet skimpy in meat and seafood, even in pasta, these immigrants found that food was abundant and cheap in America. Few had any experience cooking or working in a restaurant; indeed, almost none had ever set foot in one. But they found that opening a grocery or pizzeria offered easy access to American entrepreneurship. Thus was the Italian-American restaurant born, pandering to Americans' stereotype of fat, fun-loving Italians lapping up platters of macaroni in oceans of "red sauce." Everything came in portions that would have fed a family for a week back in Salerno. Meatballs grew to the size of tennis balls. Six-inch pizzas grew to twelve inches, inundated with ingredients Italian pizza-makers would never dream of putting on their pies. And cooks named dishes anything they wanted—veal "parmesan," fettuccine Alfredo, chicken Tetrazzini, shrimp scampi, and sole Marichiare—nothing anyone in Italy had ever heard of.

Red checkered tablecloths, candles in Chianti bottles, Alitalia posters, and mustachioed waiters became fixtures both expected and cherished, until replaced by the upscale faux-trattorias of the 1980s with mottled walls, track lighting, dark wood wainscoting, out-of-work-actor waiters, and menus full of new dishes that would leave a visitor from Palermo or Venice scratching his head—fettuccine primavera, tri-colored ravioli in "pink sauce," veal scaloppine with chopped salad on top, smoked salmon and caviar pizzas, and Chilean sea bass drizzled with balsamic vinegar and white truffle oil.

Americans lap it up, and it can be pretty tasty stuff, served with style. But it ain't really Italian at all. Let me count the ways.

First of all, in Italy, restaurant decor, except in the most elegant establishments, is usually quite modest, even nondescript, with fairly bright lighting, tile floors, a jumble of artwork, and no hint that a designer ever set his mind to the job. Statues of Michelangelo's Greatest Hits would be hard to find. Rarely will you ever hear music.

Usually the restaurant, especially if it's a smaller, inexpensive trattoria, is family owned, and family members are always present. The menu is regional and seasonal and has its own specialties. You may well find spaghetti with tomato and basil on as many menus in Genoa as you will in Sorrento, but it's unlikely that a specialty like marubini (pork-stuffed pasta rounds) from Cremona would be found on a menu in Bari or Pescara. In Italy, menus do not say "northern Italian" or "southern Italian." There is Roman, Venetian, Neapolitan, and Sardinian cooking, but when such regions appear on Italian-American menus, they are often meaningless.

When you sit down, the table will be covered with good linen, often damask. Napkins of the same quality will be large. Sliced bread and skinny, crisp breadsticks (grissini) will already be on the table, so you don't have to ask for it. There is no butter and no olive oil set out, because Italians don't butter or dip their bread. Nor is bread ever served with pasta!

There may be water glasses for bottled water, not ice water poured from a pitcher. There will always be wine glasses, and the house wines in most Italian restaurants will be far superior to the plonk most Italian-American restaurants pour from a jug at the bar. The wine list will be placed on the table as a matter of course.

The day's specials, keyed to the season, will be appended to the menu. If it's May, you'll see artichokes and asparagus. If it's not, you won't. If it's autumn, there will be wild game like boar, venison, even chamois. They will not serve cuttlefish (seppie) out of season, so don't expect black pasta made from cuttlefish ink year-round.

And don't expect the waiter to read off a dozen nightly specials (which are invariably the same as last night's) with that ridiculous singsong of American waiters, as in "My personal favorite is the fresh sea bass lightly sautéed with just a touch of fresh garlic, a touch of white wine, some balsamic vinegar, and some fresh artichokes." In fact, I've never heard a waiter in Italy use the word "fresh" (fresco), simply because everyone assumes everything will be.

If you are in need of a fork or napkin, the waiter will grab one in about two seconds from a well-placed nearby service table, not run to the kitchen to get one. No waiter in Italy would announce his name, then say, "I'll be right back to take your drink order." He will merely give you the menus, return in a few minutes to take your food order (Italians don't take forever to order their meal), then ask if you wish to go to the antipasti table and help yourself, where an extraordinary array of items—prosciutto, peppers, buffalo mozzarella, marinated vegetables, chickpeas (all at room temperature for maximum flavor)—are set out for your delectation.

By the time you finish your antipasto, the pasta course will arrive—an ample, not excessive, portion as a precursor to the main course. The pasta will be lightly dressed, not soaked in sauce, because in Italy the pasta—the individual shape and texture—is the focus of the dish; sauce is meant to enhance, not drown it. One sure way of knowing a kitchen hasn't the foggiest idea how to cook pasta is to read how it is described on the menu: If it says "Grilled chicken over freshly made fettuccine," the place is a fake. Pasta takes precedence over the next ingredient, not the other way around, in Italy. And no Italian cook would ever plop grilled chicken on fettuccine anyway.

Italians do not twirl their spaghetti on a tablespoon, so don't expect one. Learn to use the fork alone.

Moments after you finish your pasta, the main course will be presented, and it will be very, very simple: A piece of perfectly grilled fish (preferably on the bone, never previously filleted); perhaps a regional stew made with lamb, vegetables, and red wine served over hot polenta; roast chicken with pan-roasted potatoes; or veal scaloppine with a slice of lemon on the side. There may be some buttered spinach too, but that's about it. If you're lucky and you're in a northern city like Modena, Mantua, or Parma, you may have bollito misto—steaming pots of meats like beef, chicken, and veal boiled in vegetable stock—a dish you almost never see in American restaurants.

In Italy don't look for veal slathered with tomato sauce and melted cheese, fish flanked with clams and mussels in tomato sauce, or any main course accompanied by "your choice of vegetable or [overcooked] spaghetti." In Italy bistecca alla fiorentina (Florentine steak) is a specific cut (lombata) of barely aged beef, glossed with olive oil and grilled over charcoal. It is never glopped up with mushrooms, Port wine sauce, parsley, or garlic butter. And Italian cooks never, ever use a universal "brown sauce" poured over their meats or bottled clam juice over their seafood. Never.

Incidentally, there are no portobello or cremini mushrooms in Italy—these are American terms for bigger versions of simple white mushrooms, rarely used in Italian cooking. Italians favor wild mushrooms like porcini, which in their fresh form are eaten uncooked in a salad or lightly sautéed in olive oil.

Even Italy has become entranced with tiramisù, the espresso-and-mascarpone biscuit dessert created at El Toulà in Treviso but popularized in restaurants in the United States. So tiramisù is all over the place in Italy; cheesecake, part of every Italian-American dessert cart, is not. Italians prefer fresh ripe—and I emphasize ripe—fruit or cheese after the main course, saving sweets for late afternoon or a weekend family dinner.

Espresso, taken very seriously in Italy, is served in small heated cups filled no more than halfway—usually less—and it will be an almost syrupy elixir, invariably from one of two superb producers—Illycaffè or Lavazza. There will be no lemon peel—an Italian-American idiocy used to make poor-quality coffee taste better—and no cheap licorice-flavored cordial to disturb the pure taste of the coffee.

RISOTTO WITH
APPLES AND SAFFRON

Some years ago the conjurers of "*la nuova cucina*," following the lead of the more eccentric of France's *nouvelle cuisine* chefs, started adding fruits to savory dishes—an idea not wholly incompatible with traditional cooking. But these Italian chefs seemed to go out of their way to be novel—does risotto with raspberries and kiwi made any sense? Most of those dishes failed to last more than their season in the media sun. But the fragrant, mild sweetness of apples in this risotto dish, coupled with the ineffable scent of saffron, makes it a winner, whether it's old or new.

SERVES 4

One 48-ounce can chicken broth
5 tablespoons unsalted butter
4 tablespoons olive oil
1 medium yellow onion, chopped
12 ounces Arborio rice
1/2 cup dry white wine, such as
   Soave
2 cups peeled, cored, and cubed
   Golden Delicious apples
   (1/4-inch pieces)

1/4 teaspoon saffron threads,
   pulverized in a mortar
Salt, preferably kosher
Freshly ground black pepper
1/4 cup heavy cream
1 1/4 cups freshly grated
   Parmigiano-Reggiano cheese

1. Bring the chicken broth to a boil in a large saucepan. Reduce the heat to very low and keep warm.

2. In a large flameproof casserole, heat 1 tablespoon of the butter and 3 tablespoons of the olive oil over medium-low heat. Add the onion and cook, stirring, until soft and translucent, about 8 minutes. Add the rice, stir, and cook for 2 minutes. Stir in the wine and cook until it has been almost completely absorbed, 1 to 2 minutes. Add 1/2 cup of the chicken broth and simmer, stirring often, over medium-low heat until it is almost all absorbed. Continue adding the broth to the rice, 1/2 cup at a time, stirring frequently.

3. Meanwhile, in a medium-size sauté pan, heat the remaining 1 tablespoon olive oil and 1 tablespoon of the butter of the over medium heat. Add the apples and cook, stirring, until they are tender but not browned, about 5 minutes. Set aside.

4. After the risotto has been cooking for about 10 minutes, add the apples and the saffron. (Stir a little chicken broth into the mortar to make sure you get all the saffron out of it.) Taste the risotto for doneness after 15 to 18 minutes—the rice should be tender but firm (al dente).

5. When the rice is done, add the remaining 3 tablespoons butter and the cream, and stir. Stir in ³/4 cup of the Parmigiano-Reggiano, and serve immediately. Pass the remaining Parmigiano-Reggiano on the side.

WINE SUGGESTION: MÜLLER-THURGAU

RISOTTO ALLA MILANESE

This is one of the dishes that defines the simple greatness of Milanese cookery. The combination of ingredients is alchemical, with the saffron lending its golden beauty. The careful tending of a well-made risotto, so that it has a creamy "waviness" the Italians call *all'onda*, is what distinguishes this fabulous dish. This risotto is a traditional accompaniment to that other great Lombardian dish, Osso Buco (page 275), but can also be eaten on its own.

SERVES 4

One 48-ounce can chicken broth
¹/2 teaspoon saffron threads
3 tablespoons olive oil
4 tablespoons (¹/2 stick) unsalted
    butter
1 small yellow onion, finely
    chopped
1³/4 cups Arborio rice

Salt, preferably kosher
Freshly ground black pepper
¹/2 cup dry white wine, such as
    Soave
¹/4 cup heavy cream
1¹/4 cups freshly grated
    Parmigiano-Reggiano cheese

1. Bring the chicken broth to a boil in a large saucepan. Reduce the heat to very low and keep warm.

2. Place a small saucepan over medium heat, add the saffron, and toss until the saffron has darkened slightly (be careful not to burn it), 2 to 4 minutes. Immediately transfer the saffron to a mortar and grind it with a pestle. Stir in a few tablespoons of the hot chicken broth to loosen any saffron from the mortar bottom.

3. Heat a large flameproof casserole over medium heat, and add the olive oil, 1 tablespoon of the butter, and the onions. Cook, stirring, until softened but not browned, about 5 minutes.

4. Add the rice and stir with the onions for 2 minutes. Season with salt and pepper to taste. Add the wine and cook, stirring, until it has been almost completely absorbed, 1 to 2 minutes. Then add about $1/2$ cup of the hot chicken broth and cook, stirring often, for 2 to 4 minutes. Add the saffron. Add another $1/4$ cup chicken broth to the mortar to get the rest of the saffron essence, and add it to the risotto. When the liquid is almost absorbed, add another $1/2$ cup chicken broth. Repeat this process, stirring frequently, until the rice is al dente, about 20 minutes in all. Start checking after 15 to 18 minutes.

5. When the rice is done, stir in the remaining 3 tablespoons butter, the cream, and $3/4$ cup of the Parmigiano-Reggiano. Adjust the salt and pepper, and serve immediately. Pass the remaining Parmigiano-Reggiano on the side.

WINE SUGGESTION: BARBARESCO

My grandmother, who lived to be ninety-seven years old, used to tell me that if it gets too hot in the kitchen, simply run your wrists under cold water. Know something? It really works.

Robert Mondavi was one of many Italian-Americans in California who pioneered modern American wine-making. Formerly involved with his family's Charles Krug Winery, Mondavi opened his own namesake winery in the Napa Valley in 1966, which was the first new winery built there since Prohibition.

RISOTTO
WITH CORN

Y ou won't find many risotti in Italy made with American corn,
but their numbers are increasing here and abroad. The first
time we had such a dish was at Valentino in Santa Monica,
California. Sicilian-born owner Piero Selvaggio has worked for more
than twenty years to elevate the image of Italian food while giving
it a colorful tinge of California ingredients. Thus, the creation of
this wondrously creamy first course.

SERVES 4

One 48-ounce can chicken broth
3 tablespoons olive oil
4 tablespoons ($^{1}/_{2}$ stick) unsalted
    butter
2 medium yellow onions, chopped
2 small garlic cloves, finely
    chopped
$1^{3}/_{4}$ cups Arborio rice

1 cup full-bodied red wine, such as
    Dolcetto
One 15-ounce can creamed corn
Salt, preferably kosher
Freshly ground black pepper
$^{1}/_{3}$ cup heavy cream
$^{3}/_{4}$ cup freshly grated Parmigiano-
    Reggiano cheese

1. In a large saucepan, bring the chicken broth to a boil. Reduce the
heat to very low and keep warm.

2. Heat a large flameproof casserole over medium heat, and add the
olive oil and 1 tablespoon of the butter. Add the onions and garlic and
cook, stirring, until softened but not browned, about 5 minutes.

3. Add the rice, and stir with the onions for about 2 minutes. Stir in the
wine, and simmer for 2 to 3 minutes. Then add about $^{1}/_{2}$ cup of the hot
chicken broth and cook, stirring often, until it is almost absorbed. Add
another $^{1}/_{2}$ cup broth and repeat the process, stirring frequently, until
the rice is al dente, about 20 minutes in all. Start checking after 15 to
18 minutes.

4. Add the corn and heat through. Season with salt and pepper to
taste. Add the cream and the remaining 3 tablespoons butter, stir,
and heat through. Add the Parmigiano-Reggiano, stir, and serve
immediately.

WINE SUGGESTION: DOLCETTO

217

MUSHROOM RISOTTO

To our minds this is one of the best *risotti* ever, even more so than the well-known Risotto alla Milanese (page 215), because the chewy al dente texture of the rice, the creaminess of the sauce, and the woodsy flavors of the mushrooms combine in perfect balance.

SERVES 4

1¹/2 ounces dried porcini mushrooms
¹/4 cup olive oil
8 ounces assorted fresh wild mushrooms (shiitake, cremini, oyster, chanterelle), sliced
2 garlic cloves, minced
1 cup dry white wine, such as Soave
Salt, preferably kosher

Freshly ground black pepper
One 48-ounce can chicken broth
4 tablespoons (¹/2 stick) unsalted butter
1 medium yellow onion, finely chopped
2 cups Arborio rice
¹/3 cup heavy cream
1¹/3 cups freshly grated Parmigiano-Reggiano cheese

1. In a small bowl, cover the porcini mushrooms with ³/4 cup hot water. Stir, and let soak for 20 to 30 minutes. Then, using your hands, squeeze the liquid from the porcini, reserving the liquid. Chop the porcini and set aside. Strain the liquid through a cheesecloth-lined sieve, and set it aside.

2. Heat a large sauté pan over medium-high heat. Add the olive oil, and when it is hot, add the fresh mushrooms. Cook, stirring often, for 2 to 3 minutes. Add the garlic and the chopped porcini and cook, stirring, for another 1 to 2 minutes. Add ¹/2 cup of the wine, season with salt and pepper to taste, and simmer until the wine is almost all reduced, 1 to 2 minutes. Set aside.

3. In a large saucepan, bring the chicken broth to a boil. Reduce the heat to very low and keep warm.

4. Place a large flameproof casserole over medium heat, add the butter, and when it is hot, add the onion. Cook, stirring, until soft but not browned, about 5 minutes.

5. Add the rice to the casserole with the onions and stir for 2 minutes. Stir in the remaining ¹/₂ cup of the wine, and cook until it is almost completely absorbed, 1 to 2 minutes. Then add ¹/₂ cup of the hot chicken broth. Cook, stirring often, until the liquid is almost absorbed, 2 to 4 minutes. Add another ¹/₂ cup broth.

6. Add the mushroom mixture and the porcini liquid to the rice, and stir. When that liquid is almost absorbed, continue adding the chicken broth, stirring frequently. Taste the rice for doneness after 15 to 18 minutes. It should be al dente.

7. When the rice is done, stir in the cream and ²/₃ cup of the Parmigiano-Reggiano. Adjust the seasonings. Serve immediately, with the remaining Parmigiano-Reggiano on the side.

WINE SUGGESTION: SPANNA

Polenta is really nothing more than cornmeal, but in Italy the cornmeal is stone-ground and, often, organically raised. It is almost always yellow, while in the American South, cornmeal is often white, especially when intended for grits. If you have access to stone-ground cornmeal, you will notice a difference in flavor—it does make for first-rate polenta.

POLENTA

Before corn was brought to Italy in the sixteenth century, there was no such thing as *polenta* (poh-LEHN-tah). The ancient Romans ate a porridge called *pulmentum*, made with farro (spelt), which was a major part of the Roman legions' diet and which lent its name to what eventually was called polenta, made with cornmeal. While polenta is now enjoyed throughout Italy, it was once considered a very ordinary food. In recent years it has taken on a kind of retro-chic, and you find myriad recipes for it—boiled, baked, cut into squares, grilled, or made into gnocchi.

POLENTA WITH FONTINA

Plain polenta can be pretty bland, so we always like to gussy it up a bit with other flavors—in this case, the creamy richness of Fontina cheese.

SERVES 6

5 cups chicken broth
1²/₃ cups stone-ground yellow
  cornmeal
Salt, preferably kosher

3 ounces Fontina cheese, cubed
4 tablespoons (¹/₂ stick) unsalted
  butter

1. Pour the chicken broth into a large saucepan with a heavy bottom. Add the cornmeal in a steady stream, stirring continually to incorporate it into the broth. Stir in salt to taste. Turn the heat to medium and bring the polenta to a simmer, stirring constantly. Reduce the heat to the lowest setting and continue cooking, stirring often, for 20 to 25 minutes.

2. Add the Fontina and butter, and stir until the cheese has melted. Serve immediately, or transfer the polenta to a double boiler and keep it warm over low heat for up to 1 hour.

WINE SUGGESTION: CHIANTI CLASSICO

POLENTA WITH MUSHROOM SAUCE

Here's a recipe that shows the versatility of polenta in absorbing some flavors and adding its own.

SERVES 6

³/4 ounce dried porcini mushrooms
6 tablespoons extra-virgin olive oil
1 tablespoon unsalted butter
2 medium yellow onions, finely chopped
3 garlic cloves, minced
4 ounces white mushrooms, cut into ¹/4-inch cubes
1 portobello mushroom, stemmed and cut into ¹/2-inch cubes

Salt, preferably kosher
Freshly ground black pepper
4 fresh sage leaves, sliced
1 cup dry white wine, such as Soave
1 cup beef broth
¹/2 cup heavy cream
1 recipe Polenta with Fontina (page 220), kept hot

1. In a small bowl, cover the porcini mushrooms with 1 cup hot water. Set aside for 30 minutes.

2. Using your hands, squeeze the water from the porcini, reserving the liquid. Chop the porcini and set aside. Strain the liquid through a cheesecloth-lined sieve and set it aside.

LEAVE IT TO POLENTA

It is a very curious thing that Europeans ecstatically embraced New World corn as an ideal food for cattle but, except in Italy, almost completely ignored the grain at the dinner table. Not that Italians, who first acquired corn from the Americas in the sixteenth century, thought much of eating corn kernels on or off the cob, but they did make it into a meal that was then made into the porridge called polenta, as well as into a flour for cakes and breads.

Polenta was a natural enough leap of culinary necessity. For two millennia the Romans ate a similar dish called puls or pulmentum, made from the grain called farro. The Italians merely adapted corn to the job, finding ways of shaping it, sautéing it, saucing it, and grilling it to various advantage.

3. In a large sauté pan, heat 2 tablespoons of the olive oil and the butter over medium heat. Add the onions and cook, stirring, until lightly browned, about 10 minutes. Add the garlic and cook, stirring, for another 2 minutes. Remove to a bowl.

4. In the same sauté pan, heat the remaining 4 tablespoons olive oil over medium-high heat. Add the white mushrooms and the portobello, and quickly toss to coat in the oil. Cook, stirring often, until lightly browned, about 5 minutes. Season with salt and pepper to taste, and add the sage, chopped porcini, onion mixture, and wine. Bring to a boil, reduce the heat to a simmer, and cook for 5 minutes. Add the porcini liquid and the beef broth, and simmer for another 12 minutes. Remove from the heat.

Much of the wine industry before, during, and after Prohibition (when they made "medicinal" and "sacramental" wines for use in Mass) was controlled by Italians— who also made the wine vats, barrels, and presses shown in this 1924 photo.

5. Transfer ¹/2 cup of the mushroom mixture to a food processor or food mill, and puree. Return the puree to the sauté pan. Add the cream, adjust the seasoning, and simmer for 2 minutes. If the mushroom sauce is very thick, add a little water. (This entire recipe can be made the day before.)

6. Serve over the polenta.

WINE SUGGESTION: SPANNA

NOTE: When adding mushrooms to hot oil to sauté, as soon as they are put into the pan, toss them rapidly to coat them evenly with oil. If you don't, the pieces of mushroom will soak up the oil on only one side. Because of their porousness, they act like a sponge and soak up any liquid very quickly.

SEMOLINA GNOCCHI
WITH TOMATO SAUCE

W hile potato gnocchi (page 196) are well known throughout Italy, gnocchi made with semolina flour are particularly popular in Rome and southern Italy. When topped with Parmigiano-Reggiano and tomato sauce and browned in the oven, they make quite an impression.

SERVES 4 TO 6

FOR THE GNOCCHI
1 quart whole milk, chilled
*1¹/3 cups semolina flour or stone-
  ground yellow cornmeal*
Pinch of freshly grated nutmeg
Salt, preferably kosher
Freshly ground black pepper
3 tablespoons unsalted butter

FOR THE TOMATO SAUCE
¹/4 cup extra-virgin olive oil
*1 large yellow onion, coarsely
  chopped*
¹/4 cup chopped celery
¹/4 cup chopped flat-leaf parsley
*2 cups chopped canned Italian-
  style tomatoes, with juices*
Salt, preferably kosher
Freshly ground black pepper
3 tablespoons unsalted butter
*1²/3 cups freshly grated
  Parmigiano-Reggiano cheese*

223

1. Prepare the gnocchi: Pour the milk into a large saucepan and place it over medium heat. While stirring with a whisk, add the semolina flour in a steady stream. Add the nutmeg and salt and pepper to taste, and cook, stirring constantly, as the polenta starts to thicken. When it begins to simmer, reduce the heat to low and cook for 15 minutes. Remove the pan from the heat and stir in the butter.

2. Pour the hot polenta into a 9 x 13-inch baking dish and smooth the surface. Let cool.

3. Meanwhile, prepare the sauce: Heat a medium-size saucepan over low heat and add the olive oil. Add the onion and celery and cook, stirring, until softened, about 8 minutes. Add the parsley and cook, stirring, for an additional 2 minutes.

4. Add the tomatoes and salt and pepper to taste. Bring to a boil, reduce the heat to a simmer, and cook for 15 to 18 minutes.

5. While the sauce is cooking, preheat the oven to 400°F.

6. Transfer the sauce to a food processor and puree (or use a hand blender). Add the butter and adjust the seasonings.

7. Remove the polenta from the pan, and cut it into 2½- to 3-inch squares. Cut each square into 2 triangles. Spoon the sauce into a 9 x 13-inch baking pan, spreading it evenly. Arrange the polenta triangles, with the broad point up, overlapping, in rows on top of the sauce. Sprinkle the polenta with the Parmigiano-Reggiano, and place in the upper third of the oven. Bake for 8 to 10 minutes to heat through. Then turn on the broiler and brown the top for 2 to 3 minutes, watching carefully so the polenta doesn't burn. Serve immediately.

WINE SUGGESTION: SASSELLA

NOTE: Stirring the semolina into cold milk—not hot, as usually suggested—creates a smoother mixture. As the milk heats, the semolina thickens, so it is essential to stir constantly.

IS IT A SIN TO ADD SUGAR TO A TOMATO SAUCE?

Not at all, as long as you don't add too much, as is the case in most bottled commercial sauces (which may also contain sucrose, glucose and all kinds of other -coses). The reason to add a little sugar—perhaps a teaspoon or two—is to give sweetness to tomatoes that haven't quite enough on their own. If they are sweet, then there's no rationale for adding sugar.

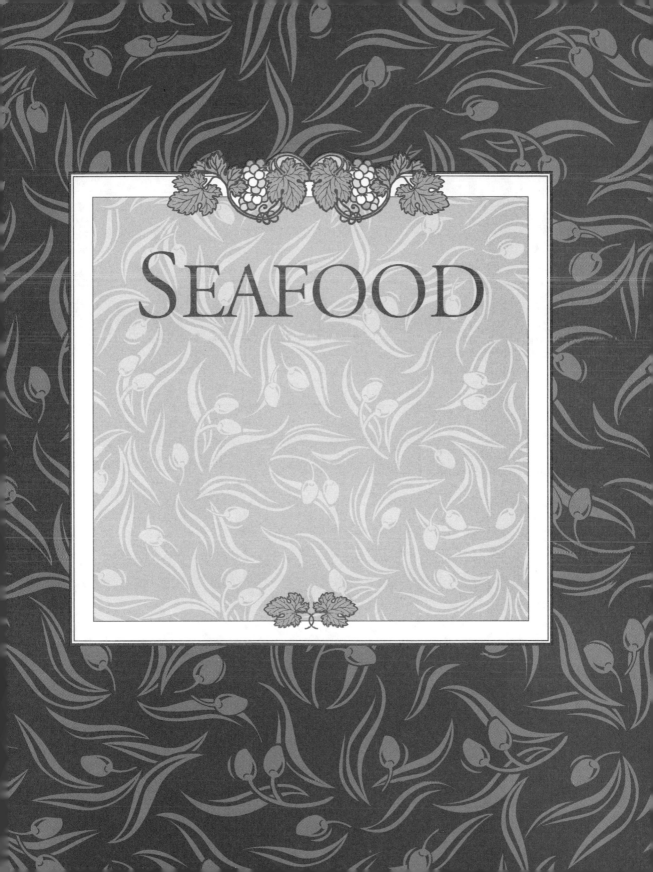

SEAFOOD

Shrimp alla Caprese 229
Shrimp Sardi 230
Grilled Shrimp with Peperoncini Oil 232
Shrimp Fra Diavolo 233
Creole Barbecued Shrimp 234
Shrimp Scampi 235
Shrimp and Langoustines with Israeli Couscous 236
Grilled Langoustines 237
Sea Scallops with Pignoli Breadcrumbs 238
Halibut with Pureed Potatoes and Arugula 243
Tuna Carpaccio with Chives 244
Tuna with Grilled Vegetable Relish 246
Swordfish Agrodolce 248
Sea Bass with White Wine and Tomato 249
Cod with Tomatoes and Olives 250

SEAFOOD

Italian-American seafood has, until recently, shown little of the variety that you'd find in Italy. The American species of fish used have been few—overwhelmingly lemon or gray sole, striped bass, and sea bass—and too heavily sauced with tomato, garlic, and oil. The same has been true of shellfish, which was too often cooked in spicy marinara sauce or fried and served with marinara sauce on the side.

In the last ten years or so, however, Italian seafood has been treated with the respect it has always enjoyed in Italy, where a simply grilled piece of fish, often cooked whole, is given nothing more than a benediction of lemon and olive oil, perhaps with a few herbs placed in its cavity. To be sure, Italians love seafood stews, usually made with lesser species, and fried shellfish is as relished there as it is here. But now the leading Italian restaurants in this country have cut back on their saucing of seafood and have developed excellent sources for Mediterranean species like *branzino* (sea bass), *San Pietro* (John Dory), *orta* (gilthead bream), and others. Tuna is again plentiful, and cod has made a comeback in popularity. You can even find delicacies like *bottarga* (dried tuna or mullet roe) in Italian-American restaurants now, usually sliced very thin and served with lemon and oil or crumbled over pasta.

Curiously enough, Italians have in the past tended to overcook seafood, but this too has begun to change as Italian cooks on both sides of the Atlantic follow the modern French and American technique of cooking seafood until just past translucence, which retains the succulence of the fish and prevents it from becoming tough. And the European tradition of cooking fish whole on the bone is gathering support at fine restaurants whose clients are not terrified to look the cooked fish in the eye. (You can always have the waiter fillet the fish for you at or away from the table.)

ITALIANS ARE NOT PERFECT

Italians tend to overcook fish by the standards of modern cuisine. It would be out of character for an Italian to serve a fish whose flesh is still translucent, as chefs often do in France, but if you like your fish to have real flavor and texture, do not cook it much past that point where the translucence and bloodiness disappear.

SHRIMP ALLA CAPRESE

One of the few chefs presenting real Capri-style food in this country is Andrea Apuzzo. Every Italian food lover from New Orleans eats at his always busy *ristorante*, Andrea's, in Metairie, Louisiana. This shrimp dish is typical of Apuzzo's lively style. Try it on its own, or over angel hair pasta.

SERVES 4

1 1/2 pounds shrimp, peeled and
   deveined
Salt, preferably kosher
Freshly ground black pepper
5 tablespoons extra-virgin olive oil
2 garlic cloves, minced
2 tablespoons brandy
1 1/2 cups dry white wine, such as
   Soave

1 1/2 cups fish stock
2 sprigs fresh rosemary
2 sprigs fresh oregano
4 fresh basil leaves, chopped
1/8 teaspoon red pepper flakes
2 tablespoons freshly squeezed
   lemon juice
4 tablespoons (1/2 stick) unsalted
   butter

1. Season the shrimp with salt and pepper. In a large sauté pan, heat 4 tablespoons of the olive oil over high heat. When it is hot, add the shrimp and quickly sear on all sides, 2 to 3 minutes. Transfer the shrimp to a platter.

2. In the same sauté pan, heat the remaining 1 tablespoon olive oil over low heat. Add the garlic and cook, stirring, for 1 to 2 minutes. Increase the heat to medium-high, add the brandy, and let it evaporate, about 30 seconds. Add the white wine and simmer until it has reduced by half, 3 to 5 minutes. Add the fish stock, rosemary, oregano, basil, and red pepper flakes, and bring to a simmer. Cook over medium-low heat for 5 minutes.

3. Return the shrimp to the sauté pan, add the lemon juice, and heat for 2 to 3 minutes. Correct the seasoning, if necessary, and remove the rosemary and oregano sprigs. Blend in the butter, 1/2 tablespoon at a time. Serve immediately.

WINE SUGGESTION: GRECO DI TUFO

When mincing garlic, add a few grains of salt to the clove, which will help the chopped pieces stay off your knife and on the chopping board.

SHRIMP SARDI

One of the most famous restaurants in New York, and the requisite site for the opening-night theater party when actors, directors, and producers shudder as the newspaper reviews come in, Sardi's is going as strong as ever. Its signature dishes, like this Shrimp Sardi, are as requested as ever. The caricatures on the walls are celebrated, and the decor hasn't changed much in decades, but the food, once mediocre, has taken on a new vibrancy in recent years. At Sardi's this shrimp is served with rice.

SERVES 4

8 tablespoons olive oil
1 yellow onion, chopped
1 carrot, chopped
1 celery stalk, chopped
5 garlic cloves, minced
1 1/2 pounds shrimp, peeled and deveined, shells reserved
1 cup dry white wine, such as Soave
1 1/2 cups chicken broth
1 large tomato, chopped
1 sprig fresh thyme, or 1/2 teaspoon dried

1 small bay leaf
3 sprigs flat-leaf parsley, chopped
3 sprigs fresh tarragon
1 tablespoon tomato paste
Salt, preferably kosher
Freshly ground black pepper
1/2 teaspoon red pepper flakes (optional)
6 tablespoons (3/4 stick) unsalted butter, softened
4 pieces crusty bread, grilled or toasted
2 tablespoons chopped fresh chives

1. In a medium-size saucepan, heat 6 tablespoons of the olive oil over medium-low heat. Add the onion, carrot, celery, and 1 garlic clove, and cook, stirring occasionally, until softened, about 10 minutes.

2. Add the shrimp shells and the wine, bring to a boil, and simmer until reduced by half, 4 to 6 minutes. Add the chicken broth, tomato, thyme, bay leaf, parsley, tarragon, tomato paste, and salt and pepper to taste. Bring to a boil, reduce the heat to a simmer, cover, and cook for 20 minutes.

3. Strain the shrimp sauce through a sieve, pressing as much of the liquid from the solids as possible with the back of a wooden spoon. Add the crushed red pepper to the sauce. Then add the butter, incorporating it into the sauce 1 tablespoon at a time. Set aside.

4. Heat a large sauté pan over high heat, and add the remaining 2 tablespoons olive oil. Season the shrimp with salt and pepper to taste, and sauté them quickly until just done, 2 to 3 minutes. Quickly add the remaining 4 garlic cloves and cook, stirring, over medium heat for 1 minute. Stir the shrimp into the sauce. Sprinkle with the chives, and serve with the toast alongside.

WINE SUGGESTION: SASSELLA

Although unknown as a species in Italy, lobsters were abundant on this side of the Atlantic and became a staple of Italian restaurants like this one, Pieroni's in Boston, where chef Jimmy Ritztano (pictured in 1949) would go through 500 pounds of the creatures over a weekend.

Marinades should not be used as a gravy or sauce base unless the marinade has been boiled to kill any possible contaminants that would otherwise be killed off in the cooking of the food itself.

GRILLED SHRIMP WITH PEPERONCINI OIL

Absolutely one of our favorite summer dishes, as perfect as an appetizer as for a main course. It has a good bite to it, and a chilled brisk white wine is a perfect match.

SERVES 4

FOR THE SHRIMP
3 tablespoons olive oil
3 tablespoons freshly squeezed lemon juice
1 tablespoon chopped fresh oregano, or $1/2$ teaspoon dried
3 tablespoons chopped fresh chives or scallions (white and green parts)
$3/4$ teaspoon salt, preferably kosher
$1/2$ teaspoon coarsely ground black pepper
$1^1/2$ pounds shrimp, peeled and deveined

FOR THE SAUCE
$1/3$ cup extra-virgin olive oil
2 small shallots, chopped
2 garlic cloves, minced
3 bottled pepperoncini peppers, seeded and thinly sliced
$1/4$ teaspoon salt, preferably kosher
$1/8$ teaspoon freshly ground black pepper
2 tablespoons minced flat-leaf parsley
1 tablespoon balsamic vinegar

1. In a nonreactive bowl, combine the olive oil, lemon juice, oregano, chives, salt, pepper, and shrimp. Stir to coat, cover, and refrigerate for 30 minutes.

2. Prepare the sauce: In a small saucepan, heat the extra-virgin olive oil over medium-low heat. Add the shallots and garlic and cook, stirring, until softened, about 2 minutes. Add the pepperoncini, salt, and pepper, and stir for 30 seconds. Set aside.

3. Prepare a stovetop or outdoor grill. Thread the shrimp on skewers, and grill over high heat until done, about 2 minutes on each side.

4. Just before serving, return the sauce to medium-low heat, add the parsley and balsamic vinegar, and stir for 1 minute. Serve over the shrimp.

WINE SUGGESTION: RIESLING RENANO

Never thaw any perishable frozen food by placing it out on a counter at room temperature. Throughout the day there is the danger of bacterial infection and growth. Thawing is best done slowly over a twenty-four-hour period in the refrigerator.

SHRIMP FRA DIAVOLO

I n Italy the phrase *"alla fra diavolo"* (AH-lah dee-AH-voh-loh), which means "in Brother Devil's style," refers to a dish in which chicken is sprinkled heavily with black pepper and then grilled—a recipe you'll find on page 324. In America, lobster fra diavolo became a popular restaurant dish in the 1930s—it was unknown in Italy, where they do not have American lobsters. It was one of the dishes my mother had to learn from my father's mother, and cook properly, before she would believe that my mother was fit to marry her son.

The reference to "brother Devil" refers both to the red color of the lobster and the tomato sauce and to the hot bite provided by chile pepper in some form, which suggests that this might have originated with Abruzzese cooks who came to this country. While you may use cayenne pepper, the dried chile peppers give it a better flavor—adjust it to your degree of tolerance for hot peppers.

We've substituted shrimp for the lobster, but the dish may be made with either shellfish.

SERVES 4

1/4 cup extra-virgin olive oil	Salt, preferably kosher
1 small yellow onion, diced	Freshly ground black pepper
3 garlic cloves, crushed	1/4 teaspoon sugar
One 28-ounce can Italian-style tomatoes, crushed or coarsely chopped, with juices	1/2 teaspoon red pepper flakes or cayenne
3/4 teaspoon dried oregano	1 1/4 pounds shrimp, peeled and deveined

1. In a medium-size saucepan, heat the olive oil over low heat. Add the onion and garlic and cook, stirring, until softened, about 7 minutes.

2. Add the tomatoes, oregano, salt and pepper to taste, sugar, and red pepper flakes. Bring to a boil and cook, stirring occasionally, for 15 minutes.

3. Add the shrimp, increase the heat to medium, and cook until the shrimp are done, 3 to 5 minutes. Adjust the seasonings and serve at once.

WINE SUGGESTION: VALPOLICELLA

CREOLE BARBECUED SHRIMP

Here's a dish with a big misnomer, since the shrimp don't go anywhere near a barbecue. The dish was created at Pascal's Manale restaurant in New Orleans—where they leave the heads on the shrimp and bake, not barbecue, them with plenty of butter. (If you can find fresh shrimp with the heads on, by all means use them—but the flavor will still be fine with "headless" shrimp.) This is a very rich dish, but it will go fast.

SERVES 4

8 tablespoons (1 stick) unsalted butter
1/4 cup extra-virgin olive oil
2 tablespoons finely chopped garlic
1 tablespoon coarsely cracked black pepper
1 tablespoon Worcestershire sauce

1/4 teaspoon dried thyme
2 teaspoons Louisiana-style hot pepper sauce
1 1/2 pounds shrimp, peeled and deveined
Salt, preferably kosher
Crusty Italian bread, for serving

1. Preheat the oven to 375°F.

2. Heat an ovenproof sauté pan, or a flameproof baking dish that's large enough to hold the shrimp in one layer, over medium heat. Add the butter, oil, garlic, pepper, Worcestershire sauce, thyme, and hot pepper sauce. Stir, and cook for 1 minute. Add the shrimp, toss them in the sauce, and spread them out in a single layer. Sprinkle with salt to taste and place in the oven. Bake, tossing them once, until they are just done, 3 to 5 minutes.

3. Serve the shrimp in soup bowls, topped with the sauce, and with crusty Italian bread alongside.

WINE SUGGESTION: BARDOLINO

SHRIMP SCAMPI

A real misnomer if there ever was one. Shrimp are shrimp and *scampi* is a Venetian dialect word for the small lobster called a prawn. Somehow, in Italian-American restaurants "scampi" evolved into a term for the sauce used to make this shrimp dish. Although there is no such thing as a "scampi sauce" in Venice or anywhere else, every Italian-American menu lists the dish as "shrimp scampi," and Americans know what to expect when they order it—a juicy dish of garlic-rich shrimp sautéed in a little oil and white wine. Whatever you call it, it's a classic.

SERVES 4

1/4 cup extra-virgin olive oil
3 tablespoons unsalted butter
1 1/2 pounds shrimp, peeled and deveined
3 garlic cloves, minced
Salt, preferably kosher

Freshly ground black pepper
1/3 cup dry white wine, such as Soave
1/4 cup chopped flat-leaf parsley
3 tablespoons freshly squeezed lemon juice

1. Heat a large sauté pan over high heat, and add the olive oil and the butter. When it is hot, add the shrimp and sauté, tossing often, for 1 minute. Add the garlic and sauté until the shrimp have turned pink, 1 to 2 minutes more.

2. Reduce the heat to medium, season the shrimp with salt and pepper to taste, and add the wine. Bring to a boil. Then reduce the heat and simmer for 2 minutes. Add the parsley and lemon juice, toss with the shrimp, and serve immediately.

WINE SUGGESTION: PINOT GRIGIO

SHRIMP AND
LANGOUSTINES WITH
ISRAELI COUSCOUS

Here's one of those recipes that very clearly shows what
Italian-American food has become in the second century
of its existence. Chef Fabrizio Aielli, owner of two of the
finest Italian restaurants in Washington, D.C., Goldoni and Teatro
di Goldoni, served this to us one day, and we dreamt about reproducing it at home. In its use of Israeli couscous (which is really just
a small-grain pasta resembling a large-grain couscous), shrimp, and
langoustines, this is a lavish example of combining Mediterranean
flavors and ingredients in a stunning modern format. Langoustines
are a species of prawn now available, frozen, from Iceland, New
Zealand, and other parts of the world, albeit at a high price. You
may substitute morsels of lobster or jumbo shrimp for the langoustines, and pastina would be a reasonable substitute for the
Israeli couscous, but the dish is at its best when made according to
Aielli's formula.

SERVES 4

3 teaspoons extra-virgin olive oil
1/2 cup finely chopped yellow onion
6 fresh basil leaves, finely chopped
2 cups Israeli couscous or pastina
Pinch of saffron threads
Salt, preferably kosher
Freshly ground black pepper
8 ounces small shrimp (rock
   shrimp if available)
2 garlic cloves, thinly sliced
1/2 cup dry white wine, such as
   Soave

1 tablespoon chopped flat-leaf
   parsley
1/4 cup all-purpose flour
4 langoustines, thawed, rinsed,
   and patted dry
1/2 cup grapeseed oil or corn oil
1/2 cup olive oil
2 tablespoons unsalted butter
1/2 cup freshly grated Parmigiano-
   Reggiano cheese

1. Heat a medium-size saucepan over medium heat. When it is hot,
add 1 1/2 teaspoons of the extra-virgin olive oil and the onion. Cook,
stirring, until softened, about 5 minutes. Then add the basil and stir.
Add the couscous and stir the mixture thoroughly. Pour in 4 cups

water, and add the saffron. Season with salt and pepper to taste. Stir until blended, cover, and reduce the heat to low. Cook for 8 minutes, stirring occasionally.

2. Meanwhile, in a small sauté pan, heat the remaining 1^1/$_2$ teaspoons extra-virgin olive oil over high heat. Add the shrimp and cook, stirring, for 2 minutes. Add the garlic and cook, stirring, for another minute, until the shrimp turn pink. Add the wine and cook until it has evaporated, 2 to 4 minutes. Stir in the parsley and remove from the heat.

3. Place the flour in a shallow dish, and season it with salt and pepper to taste. Remove the shells from the langoustines, and dredge the langoustines in the seasoned flour.

4. In a small sauté pan, heat the grapeseed oil and olive oil over high heat until very hot. Add the langoustines and deep-fry for 2 minutes. Then remove them from the oil and allow to drain on paper towels.

5. Add the shrimp to the couscous. Then add the butter and Parmigiano, and stir until blended to a creamy consistency. Spoon the couscous-shrimp mixture onto individual plates, and place a langoustine on top of each serving.

WINE SUGGESTION: ARNEIS

GRILLED LANGOUSTINES

We once spent five days on the Amalfi Coast, where we ate langoustines at nearly every meal. After so much feasting on langoustines, however, we felt like eating meat on our last night in Sorrento. But when we walked through the door of the restaurant Caruso, we spotted an enormous platter of huge langoustines and immediately changed our minds: We ordered the langoustines.

Sweet-fleshed and buttery, larger than a shrimp and smaller than an American lobster, these sharp-clawed, pink crustaceans are among the great treasures of the Mediterranean. Langoustines are not readily available in the United States, and then only in frozen

If you wish to get that wonderful flavor of the outdoor grill into your fish cookery, here are a couple of suggestions: First, use hardwoods or charcoal, if possible, which throw off a more intense heat than briquets or a gas grill. Second, use a very clean grill so the fish does not stick. Third, delicately fleshed fillets should be grilled on only one side. The fish is actually better off being finished on the other side in a hot oven, where its texture and structure will be better kept intact.

form. They are usually imported from Iceland or New Zealand, and they are very expensive—but as an occasional treat, they are well worth it. They should not be sullied with a sauce of any kind—just grilled with some olive oil, salt, and pepper, and perhaps dipped in melted butter.

SERVES 2

12 langoustines, thawed, rinsed,
  and patted dry
3 tablespoons extra-virgin olive oil
Salt, preferably kosher

Freshly ground black pepper
4 tablespoons (^{1}/2 stick) unsalted
  butter, melted

1. Preheat the broiler.

2. Split the langoustines in half lengthwise with a cleaver or a large sharp knife. Place them, split side up, on a rack in a shallow roasting pan. Drizzle or brush the olive oil over them. Season with salt and pepper to taste, and place under the broiler, 5 to 6 inches from the heat source. Broil for 3 to 4 minutes.

3. Serve with the melted butter.

WINE SUGGESTION: CHARDONNAY

SEA SCALLOPS WITH PIGNOLI BREADCRUMBS

The lovely nutty flavor of pignoli adds so much to many Italian dishes, but combining it with seafood is unusual, and unusually delicious.

SERVES 4

9 tablespoons unsalted butter
2 large garlic cloves, minced
^{1}/4 cup pignoli (pine nuts)
2 cups homemade plain breadcrumbs (see Note)
Salt, preferably kosher

Freshly ground black pepper
1^1/4 teaspoons freshly grated lemon
  zest
3 tablespoons chopped flat-leaf
  parsley

1¹/4 to 1¹/2 pounds sea scallops, rinsed and patted dry

6 tablespoons freshly squeezed lemon juice

1. In a large sauté pan, melt 2 tablespoons of the butter over medium-low heat. Add the garlic and the pignoli and cook, stirring, for about 2 minutes. Add another 4 tablespoons butter. When it has melted, add the breadcrumbs. Cook, stirring often, over medium heat until the breadcrumbs become golden in color, 3 to 5 minutes. Season lightly with salt and pepper, add the lemon zest and parsley, and mix.

2. Meanwhile, season the scallops with salt and pepper. In a large sauté pan, heat the remaining 3 tablespoons butter over medium-high heat. When it is hot, add the scallops and sauté for about 2 minutes on each side (do this in two batches if necessary, to avoid overcrowding). Check the inside of a scallop for doneness. Do not overcook.

3. Just before serving, stir 4 tablespoons of the lemon juice into the breadcrumbs. Divide the scallops among 4 plates, sprinkle with the remaining 2 tablespoons lemon juice, and top with the breadcrumbs.

WINE SUGGESTION: VINTAGE TUNINA

NOTE: To prepare 2 cups homemade plain breadcrumbs, take ¹/3 to ¹/2 loaf of Italian bread. Slice off the crusts, and process the bread in a food processor until finely chopped.

Because of certain microbe problems in America's aquasystems, tiny, sweet bay scallops are difficult, if not impossible, to find in the market. In fact, the only remaining area where safe bay scallops may be harvested is in a small section around Nantucket. Beware of any restaurant or fishmonger who advertises bay scallops but cannot readily tell you where they are from. Often they are actually selling calico scallops, referred to in the industry as "pencil erasers"—for their size, not their texture. But while they can be tasty, they don't compare with true bay scallops. Fortunately, readily available, larger sea scallops are also wonderful and can be cooked in innumerable ways. Whatever variety you buy, look for scallops that are sitting on ice, not in any kind of liquid, which is either melted ice or a solution used to plump up the scallops and make them look fat and juicy.

CHRISTMAS IN THE BRONX

Maybe it didn't snow for Christmas every year in the Bronx back in the 1950s. But my memory of at least one perfect snowbound Christmas Eve makes me think it did often enough—I still picture my neighborhood as white as Finland in those days when I lived along the choppy waters of Long Island Sound.

But for all the decorations and the visits to stores and Rockefeller Center, it was the sumptuous Christmas feasts that helped maintain our families' links to the Old Country long after most other immigrant traditions had faded away. Food was always central to everyone's thoughts at Christmas, and the best cooks in each family were renowned for specific dishes no one else dared make.

The assumption that everything would be exactly the same as last year was as comforting as knowing that Christmas Day would follow Christmas Eve. The finest ancestral linens were ironed and smoothed into place, dishes of hard candy were set out on every table, and the kitchen ovens hissed and warmed our homes for days. The reappearance of the old dishes, the irresistible aromas, tastes, and textures, even the seating of family members in the same spot at the table year after year anchored us to a time and a place that was already changing more rapidly than we could understand.

It's funny now to think that my memories of the food and the dinners are so much more intense than those of toys and games I received, but that seems true for most people. The exact taste of Christmas cookies, the sound of beef roasting in its pan, and the smell of evergreen mixed with the scent of cinnamon and cloves and lemon in hot cider were like holy incense in church, unforgettable, like the way you remember your parents' faces when they were young.

No one in our neighborhood was poor but few were rich. Yet we mounted feasts as lavish as any I could imagine, and in the days preceding Christmas people took enormous joy in spending their money on foods eaten only during that season.

It was still a time when the vegetable man would sell his produce from an old truck on Campbell Drive, and Dugan's and Krug's bread men came right to your door with special holiday cupcakes and cookies. The butcher on Middletown Road usually carried fresh fish only on Fridays, but was always well stocked with cod, salmon, lobster, and eel during the holidays. The pastry shops worked overtime to bake special Christmas breads and cakes, which would be gently wrapped in a swaddling of very soft pink tissue paper tied up with ribbons and sometimes even sealed with wax to deter anyone from opening them before Christmas.

By Christmas Eve the stores ran out of everything, and pity the poor cook who delayed in buying her chestnuts, ricotta cheese, or fresh yeast until it was too late. Weeks in advance the women would put in their order at the live poultry market for a female rabbit—not a male—or a goose that had to weigh exactly twelve pounds.

You always knew what people were cooking for Christmas because the aromas hung in the hallways of the garden apartments and the foyers of their homes—garlicky tomato sauces, roast turkeys, rich shellfish stews, and the sweet, warm smells of pastries and breads that could make you dizzy with hunger. When you went out into the cold, those aromas would slip out the door and mingle with the biting sea-salted air and the fresh wet snow swept in off the Sound.

At the Italian homes in the Bronx ancient culinary rituals were followed long after they'd lost their original religious symbolism. The traditional meatless meal of Christmas Eve—La Vigilia—which began centuries ago as a form of penitential purification, developed into a robust meal of exotic seafood dishes that left one reeling from the table. According to the traditions of Abruzzi, where my father's family came from, the Christmas Eve dinner should be composed of seven or nine dishes—mystical numbers commemorating the seven sacraments, and the Holy Trinity multiplied by three. This was always my Auntie Rose's shining moment. She would cook with the zeal and energy of a dozen nuns, beginning with little morsels of crisply fried calamari. She made spaghetti on a stringed cutting utensil called a ghitarra (it resembles the strings of a guitar) and served it with a sauce teeming with shellfish. Next came an enormous pot of lobster fra diavolo—a powerful coalescence of tomato, garlic, onion, saffron, and hot red peppers, all spooned into soup plates around shiny, scarlet-red lobsters that some guests attacked with daunting, unbridled gusto, while others took their dainty time extracting every morsel of meat from the deepest recesses of the body, claws, and legs.

Few children would eat baccalà, a strong-smelling salted cod cooked for hours in order to restore its leathery flesh to edibility; and stewed eel, an age-old symbol of renewal was a delicacy favored mostly by the old-timers. But everyone waited for the dessert—the yeasty egg bread called panettone, shaped like a church dome and riddled with golden raisins and candied fruit.

Christmas Day came too early for everyone but the children, but as soon as presents were exchanged, my mother and grandmother would begin work on the lavish dinner to be served that afternoon. It was always a mix of regional Italian dishes and American novelties, like the incredibly rich bourbon-laced eggnog my father insisted on serving before my grandmother's lasagna, in which were hidden dozens of meatballs the size of hazelnuts. Then my mother would set down a massive roast beef, brown and crackling on the outside, red as a poinsettia within, surrounded by sizzling roast potatoes and Yorkshire pudding glistening from the fat absorbed from the beef. Dessert reverted to venerable Italian tradition with my grandmother's prune-and-chocolate-filled pastries and honeyed cookies called struffoli.

After such a meal, we needed to go for a walk in the cold air. In other homes up and down our block, people were feasting on Norwegian lutefisk, Swedish meatballs, German stollen, Irish plum pudding, and American gingerbread. If you stopped and listened for a moment, you could hear the families singing carols in their native tongues.

By early evening guests were getting ready to leave and leftovers were packed up to take home, belying everyone's protest that they wouldn't be able to eat for days.

By then the snow had taken on an icy veneer and the wind had died down to a whisper. I remember how the cold air magnified sounds far, far away, so that as I crept into bed I could hear the waves lapping the seawall and the rattling clack-clack, clack-clack of the El running from Buhre Avenue to Middletown Road. It was a king of lullaby in those days, when it never failed to snow on Christmas in the Bronx.

—J.M.

HALIBUT WITH PUREED POTATOES AND ARUGULA

Тhis is a good choice for those who feel a little tentative about fish cookery. It's quite simple and delicious.

SERVES 4

2 medium all-purpose potatoes, cut into pieces
Salt, preferably kosher
4 tablespoons olive oil
1 large yellow onion, chopped
2 garlic cloves, chopped

3 tablespoons extra-virgin olive oil
2 tablespoons unsalted butter
Freshly ground black pepper
1 1/2 pounds halibut steak, cut into 4 servings
1 cup chopped arugula

1. In a large saucepan, cover the potatoes with 1 1/2 quarts water, add a little salt, and bring to a boil. Lower the heat and simmer until the potatoes are tender, about 8 minutes.

2. While the potatoes are cooking heat 2 tablespoons of the olive oil in a sauté pan over medium-low heat. Add the onion and cook, stirring, until soft and translucent (not browned), about 7 minutes. Add the garlic and cook, stirring, for another 2 minutes. Remove from the heat.

3. Drain the potatoes, reserving 1 cup of the cooking water. Pass the potatoes, onion, and garlic through a food mill into a bowl. Add the extra-virgin olive oil, butter, and enough of the potato water to make a thin potato puree. Blend thoroughly. Season with salt and pepper to taste. Cover and keep warm.

4. Season the halibut steaks with salt and pepper to taste. Heat a sauté pan over medium-high heat, and add the remaining 2 tablespoons olive oil. Sauté the halibut on both sides until just done, 6 to 8 minutes.

5. Mix the arugula into the potato puree. Place a portion of the puree in the middle of each plate, and arrange a piece of the halibut on top of the puree.

WINE SUGGESTION: VERNACCIA DI SAN GIMIGNANO

TUNA CARPACCIO
WITH CHIVES

Fourteen years ago, Gilbert and Maguy Le Coze literally revolutionized seafood cookery around the world when they left Le
Bernardin, their Michelin two-star restaurant in Paris, to open
a branch in New York (they later closed the Paris original). Gilbert's
masterful, simple way of cooking—or not cooking—fish and his
exacting demands for quality had a tremendous influence on
American chefs. He was also a great champion of American seafood.
His sister, Maguy, ran Le Bernardin with a glamour and elegance
she seemed to invent. To this day Le Bernardin is arguably the greatest seafood restaurant in the world.

Tragically, Gilbert died four years ago, leaving the kitchen
duties to his redoubtable chef de cuisine Eric Ripert (now a partner
in the restaurant with Maguy), who has not just kept Gilbert's flame
alive but has given his own modern spark to everything that happens at Le Bernardin.

One of the startling innovations Gilbert set in motion was
his use of raw fish—a technique only Japanese sushi bars had dared
to perform until then. Gilbert even went so far as to call some of
his raw fish dishes by the name *carpaccio*, derived from the famous
beef carpaccio created at Harry's Bar in Venice (page 420). In the
Le Bernardin Cookbook, Maguy describes how Gilbert worked to
create several dishes with cooked tuna, always unsuccessfully, to his
sister's taste. "Getting it right wasn't easy," she writes. "After several tasting experiments, I told Gilbert the tuna was so bad, it would
be better raw. And that's how tuna carpaccio was born." This recipe
is adapted from *Le Bernardin Cookbook*.

SERVES 4

Four ¹/₂-inch-thick slices tuna
  (4 ounces each)
¹/₂ cup extra-virgin olive oil
Sea salt
Ground white pepper
1¹/₂ teaspoons finely diced shallot

2 tablespoons finely chopped fresh
  chives
1 lemon, cut in half
4 slices country-style bread,
  toasted and quartered

1. Trim any blood from the tuna. Then rub about $^1/_2$ teaspoon of the oil in the center of a work surface and cover it with a large sheet of plastic wrap. Place 1 tuna steak in the center of the plastic and cover it with another sheet of plastic.

2. Flatten the tuna with a pounder, using a fluid motion that combines hitting the tuna in the center and sliding the pounder over the tuna, pressing it outward. Continue pressing out the tuna in this manner until you have a very thin, even circle about 10 inches in diameter. (The oil under the plastic wrap keeps it from sliding and bunching up while you do this.)

3. Place a 9-inch plate over the tuna, and using a sharp knife, cut through both layers of plastic, leaving a perfect 9-inch round of tuna. Leave the tuna in the plastic. Repeat with the remaining pieces of tuna.

4. Stack the tuna rounds in the refrigerator and chill for 30 minutes.

5. Pull the top sheet of plastic off 1 tuna round, center a large plate upside-down over the tuna, and invert the plate and tuna. Pull the plastic off the top of the tuna. Repeat with the remaining pieces.

6. To serve, with your fingers several inches above the plate, sprinkle the tuna with sea salt and pepper. Dip a pastry brush into the olive oil and coat the tuna generously with it. Sprinkle with the shallot and chives, then squeeze the lemon juice over the tuna.

7. Tilt the plates over a sink to allow any excess lemon juice to run off. Serve immediately, passing the toast separately.

WINE SUGGESTION: BARDOLINO

TUNA WITH
GRILLED VEGETABLE RELISH

T he quality of tuna in the United States has improved sharply over the past few years, and American waters even provide much of what the Japanese call "sushi-grade" tuna, which can get up to $25 or $30 a pound at the market. While it is unreasonable to expect anyone to pay that kind of money for tuna to be served at home—except on rare occasions—tuna is one of those fishes for which a truly knowledgeable fishmonger is necessary. Good tuna is never cheap. Look for a bright red color, with no dark, gray flesh, and no smell of fishiness whatsoever. Since tuna can be eaten raw, as in the Tuna Carpaccio recipe (page 244), it is at its best when cooked rare. Once the flesh is cooked past the pink color, it will lose a great deal of its succulence, flavor, and texture.

The recipe here might be found in any southern Italian coastline restaurant, where little is done to the tuna and the savoriness comes from the simply grilled vegetable relish tinged with sweet-sour balsamic vinegar.

SERVES 4

FOR THE TUNA
2 tablespoons extra-virgin olive oil
2 tablespoons freshly squeezed
  lemon juice
1 teaspoon freshly ground black
  pepper
1¹/2 pounds tuna steak, cut into 4
  pieces
Salt, preferably kosher

FOR THE GRILLED VEGETABLES
2 zucchini, cut into ³/4-inch-thick
  slices
2 red bell peppers, cored and cut
  into 6 wedges

1 sweet, such as Vidalia, or
  Spanish onion, cut into 6 to 8
  wedges
2 tablespoons olive oil
Salt, preferably kosher
Freshly ground black pepper

FOR THE SAUCE
2 tablespoons extra-virgin olive oil
2 garlic cloves, minced
1 cup chicken broth
¹/2 cup balsamic vinegar
3 tablespoons unsalted butter,
  softened

1. Prepare the tuna: In a shallow bowl, combine the olive oil, lemon juice, and pepper. Stir to blend. Add the tuna steaks and cover well with the marinade. Cover and refrigerate for 30 minutes.

2. Prepare the vegetables: Thread the zucchini, bell peppers, and onion onto skewers. Brush with the 2 tablespoons olive oil, and season with salt and pepper to taste. Prepare a stovetop grill pan or an outdoor barbecue, and grill the vegetables over medium-high heat for 6 to 8 minutes or until al dente. Remove from the heat.

3. Prepare the sauce: In a small saucepan, heat the 2 tablespoons extra-virgin olive oil over low heat. Add the garlic and cook, stirring, for 2 minutes. Add the chicken broth and simmer over medium heat until reduced by half, 4 to 6 minutes. Add the balsamic vinegar, bring to a boil, and simmer for 3 to 4 minutes. Keep warm.

4. Remove the tuna from the marinade and season it with salt. Cook the tuna on the grill until rare or medium-rare, 3 to 4 minutes in all.

5. Meanwhile, dice the grilled vegetables into 1/4-inch pieces, sprinkle with some salt and pepper, and toss to mix.

6. Just before serving, add the butter, a little at a time, to the sauce, stirring to incorporate it after each addition.

7. To assemble: Place a piece of tuna in the middle of each plate, spoon some of the sauce around it, and distribute some of the vegetables around the tuna. Serve immediately.

WINE SUGGESTION: CERASUOLO

SWORDFISH AGRODOLCE

Sweet and sour *agrodolce* (ah-groh-DOHL-cheh) flavors are widespread throughout the entire Mediterranean, and from Rome southward Italians use them for everything from vegetables to seafood. In this recipe, the piquancy and sweetness give a luster to swordfish without compromising the fresh flavor of the fish.

SERVES 4

¹/4 cup pignoli (pine nuts)
Extra-virgin olive oil
2 medium yellow onions, thinly
  sliced
¹/4 cup dry white wine, such as
  Soave
¹/4 cup red wine vinegar
¹/2 cup balsamic vinegar

Salt, preferably kosher
Freshly ground black pepper
3 tablespoons chopped flat-leaf
  parsley
Four 6-ounce swordfish steaks
All-purpose flour, for dredging
3 tablespoons olive oil

1. Heat a small skillet over medium heat. Add the pignoli and cook, shaking the skillet often, until the nuts have browned, 4 to 6 minutes. Remove from the heat and set aside.

2. Heat a medium saucepan over medium heat, and add ¹/4 cup oil. Add the onions and cook, stirring, until golden brown, 10 to 12 minutes. Add the wine, red wine vinegar, balsamic vinegar, and salt and pepper to taste. Bring to a boil, then reduce the heat and simmer until the sauce has reduced by half, 6 to 8 minutes. Add the parsley and the toasted pignoli, stir, and remove from the heat.

3. Season the swordfish with salt and pepper. Dredge the steaks in the flour, and shake off any excess. In a large sauté pan, heat 3 tablespoons olive oil over medium-high heat. Add the swordfish and sauté for about 2 minutes on each side. Do not overcook. Quickly reheat the sauce, and serve it with the swordfish.

WINE SUGGESTION: SALICE SALENTINO

> It is often said that the best way to tell if fish is fresh is to look it in the eye and make sure the eye is clear, not opaque. This is helpful, but the only true test of whether a fish is fresh is to put your nose as close to it as possible and smell it. If it smells fresh, it is fresh. Also, fishmongers who cover their fish in crushed or shaved ice are being more careful about the freshness and quality than those who just lay their fish on top of the ice and don't replenish it.

SEA BASS WITH WHITE WINE AND TOMATO

Very easy to make in very little time, and very typical of Italian seafood cookery for that reason.

SERVES 4

1/4 cup extra-virgin olive oil
2 garlic cloves, minced
2 tablespoons chopped flat-leaf parsley
2 to 3 canned Italian-style tomatoes, drained and chopped
1 scallion, white and light green parts, chopped

1/2 cup dry white wine, such as Soave
1/2 cup chicken broth
1/2 dried red chile pepper
Salt, preferably kosher
Freshly ground black pepper
1 1/2 to 1 3/4 pounds thick sea bass fillet

Cioppino—a San Francisco fish stew adapted from a Ligurian model—includes fresh crabs, and this 1938 photo shows Italian-Americans at the city's Fisherman's Wharf clamoring for crabs just brought in by the Crab Fisherman's Protective Association.

1. Preheat the oven to 375°F.

2. In a flameproof baking dish that is large enough to hold the fish, combine the olive oil, garlic, parsley, tomatoes, scallion, wine, chicken broth, and chile. Season with salt and pepper to taste. Place the baking dish over low heat, and simmer for 5 minutes to blend the flavors.

3. Season the fish with salt and pepper to taste, and add it to the baking dish, spooning some of the liquid over the fish. Bake in the oven for 10 to 15 minutes, or until just done. (The cooking time will depend on the thickness of the fillet.) Remove the chile pepper, and serve.

WINE SUGGESTION: GRECO DI TUFO

COD WITH TOMATOES AND OLIVES

You will certainly find fresh cod on menus in Italy, though there they use far more salt cod (*baccalà*). In the United States, cod used to be considered a common fish of little culinary interest—until contemporary chefs discovered that it is among the most lustrous, loveliest, and lightest species in the sea and highly adaptable to all sorts of recipes, like this southern-style rendition.

SERVES 4

1 large tomato, cored
2/3 cup dry white wine, such as Soave
3/4 teaspoon salt, preferably kosher
1 teaspoon freshly grated lemon zest
3 tablespoons extra-virgin olive oil

1 1/4 pounds cod fillet, cut into 4 pieces
1/2 cup chopped tomatoes
2 1/2 tablespoons sliced pitted Calamata olives
1/3 cup packed sliced fresh basil
Freshly ground black pepper

1. In a food processor or food mill, process the tomato. Press the tomato through a strainer into a large shallow saucepan or a sauté pan. Add the wine, salt, lemon zest, and olive oil. Place over medium heat, bring to a boil, and cook for 5 minutes.

Barbetta is the oldest continually operating family-owned restaurant in New York (it opened in 1906). Located in two historic townhouses in the Theater District, it has long been host to all the greats of the musical and theatrical world. Today Barbetta is still in the Maioglio family, run by Laura Maioglio.

2. Add the cod, seasoned with salt and pepper, reduce the heat, and cover. Simmer for 2 to 3 minutes. Carefully turn the cod over and simmer for 1 to 2 minutes more.

3. Arrange the fish in 4 soup plates.

4. Add the chopped tomatoes, olives, basil, and pepper to the tomato-wine sauce, heat for 30 seconds, and then spoon over the 4 servings. Serve immediately.

WINE SUGGESTION:
TREBBIANO D'ABRUZZO

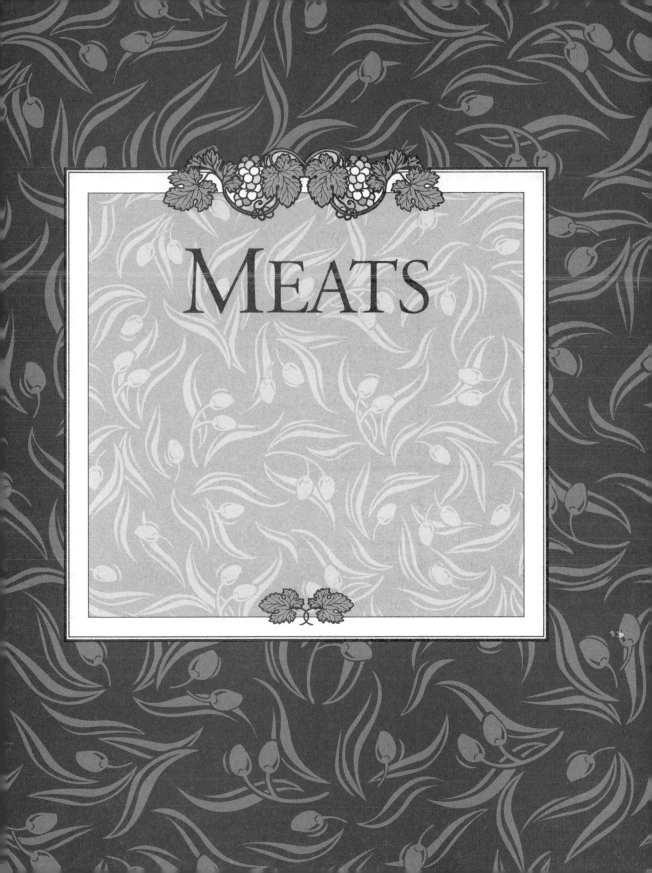

MEATS

MEATS

I n so many ways meat is the defining food for the Italian-American immigrant experience, because most of those who came from impoverished towns and farms in southern Italy ate meat only on the rarest of occasions. Meat was what the rich people ate, while the poor peasants might never have had access to beef, veal, lamb, or game. If they were well-off enough to own pigs, one would be slaughtered, with ritualistic ceremony, and every part of the animal used. The lesser cuts went into stews, the bones were used as flavoring, and the rendered lard would be used throughout the year as a principal source of fat. In fact, olive oil was quite expensive for most Italians, so lard was used at least as often in their cookery.

Beef cattle were in short supply in Italy until the twentieth century, and, just as in Japan after World War II, consumption of beef rose as Italy became more prosperous and Italians were able to afford foods that were once considered luxuries. In America, however, the immigrants found the price of and access to meat one of the boons to settling in their new country. Once unimaginable, meat might be served two or three times a week, and on Sunday a great roast of beef or pork or lamb was expected to follow the antipasto and pasta courses. So, too, the new Italian-American restaurants found plenty of customers for traditional veal dishes as well as for new ideas like Steak Pizzaiolo (page 258) and huge meatballs with spaghetti.

There is, however, no dish more symbolic of Italian-American restaurant cooking than the massive, two-inch-thick veal chop requisite to every menu. Simply grilled, it is a meal fit for Gargantua. But stuffed with prosciutto and mozzarella *alla Valdostana* (page 276), or lavished with portobello mushrooms, it is a triumph of Italian cookery taken to its most delectable extreme.

FILET MIGNON AND GORGONZOLA SALAD

Themes granddaddy of all Italian-style New York steakhouses is the Palm (so called because of a mistake by a civil scribe who recorded the family name "Parma" as Palm), originally a speakeasy during Prohibition, then a restaurant whose clientele includes everyone in journalism, many of whom are caricatured on the walls of the original restaurant on Second Avenue. In fact, many of the great newspaper cartoonists painted their own characters on the Palm's walls.

Today the Palm has about a dozen branches, from New York to Mexico City, and while most customers order the classic meal of tomato and onions, sixteen-ounce sirloin, cottage-fried potatoes, and cheesecake to finish, the Palm does offer several Italian-American dishes, including this hefty piece of filet gilded with Gorgonzola salad.

SERVES 4

Four 5-ounce filets mignons
Salt, preferably kosher
Freshly ground black pepper
2 tablespoons chopped fresh
  rosemary
1 1/2 tablespoons olive oil
1/2 cup extra-virgin olive oil
1/2 cup red wine vinegar

12 Belgian endive leaves
12 ounces arugula leaves
12 ounces radicchio, broken into
  large pieces
2 red tomatoes, quartered
2 yellow tomatoes, quartered
12 ounces imported Italian
  Gorgonzola cheese, sliced

1. Rub the filets mignons with salt and pepper to taste, the rosemary, and the olive oil.

2. Heat an outdoor or stovetop grill, and grill the filets mignons to the desired doneness. Remove the filets from the grill and let them cool to room temperature, 20 to 25 minutes. Slice the filets mignons, and set aside.

3. Prepare the dressing: In a small bowl, combine the olive oil, vinegar, and salt and pepper to taste and blend well.

4. On each dinner plate, arrange 4 endive leaves in an X pattern. Place wedges of tomato between the endive leaves, alternating red and yellow.

5. Toss the arugula and the radicchio with the salad dressing, and pile the salad high in the middle of the plates. Fan the filet mignon slices on top of the salad, and top with the Gorgonzola. Serve immediately.

WINE SUGGESTION: TIGNANELLO

STEAK PIZZAIOLO

Pizzaiolo (peet-zye-OH-loh) means "in the style of the pizza-maker," apparently because the sauce used on the steak resembles the pizza sauce used by some pizza-makers. In any case, the dish is better known in Italian-American restaurants, where it often comes out steamy and overcooked. The key to making this full-flavored dish is to brown the beef but not to cook it through before removing it from the pan.

Serve this with mashed potatoes or pasta.

SERVES 4

6 tablespoons olive oil
2 medium yellow onions, thinly
   sliced vertically
1 green bell pepper, cut in half,
   cored, each piece cut in half
   horizontally, then slivered
4 garlic cloves, minced
Salt, preferably kosher
Freshly ground black pepper

One 28-ounce can Italian-style
   tomatoes, crushed, with juices
3/4 teaspoon dried oregano
1/3 cup chopped flat-leaf parsley
1 1/2 to 1 3/4 pounds London broil,
   cut diagonally into 1/2-inch-thick
   slices
1/3 cup dry white wine, such as
   Soave

1. Preheat the oven to 350°F.

2. In a sauté pan over medium-high heat, heat 4 tablespoons of the olive oil. Add the onions and bell pepper and cook, stirring, until browned, 8 to 10 minutes. Add the garlic and cook, stirring, for another 2 minutes. Season with salt and pepper to taste. Add the tomatoes, oregano, and parsley, and bring to a boil. Remove from the heat.

3. In another sauté pan, heat 1 tablespoon of the olive oil over high heat. Add half of the beef and sauté until browned, 2 to 3 minutes on each side. Set those slices aside. Add the remaining 1 tablespoon oil to the pan and repeat with the remaining beef. Remove the beef from the pan. Deglaze the pan by adding the wine and scraping up all the brown bits. Pour this into the tomato mixture.

4. Coat the bottom of an 8 x 11-inch roasting pan with $^1/_2$ cup of the tomato sauce. Arrange the beef slices evenly over the sauce, and cover with the remaining sauce. Cover the pan with aluminum foil, and bake in the oven for $1^1/_4$ hours.

WINE SUGGESTION: CANNONAU

NOTE: This can be prepared the day before and reheated.

BISTECCA ALLA FIORENTINA

You probably won't be able to find the exact cut of meat Florentines use for this dish—it's a massive T-bone called *lombata*. The beef in Italy is un-aged and much leaner than ours. You might approximate the taste of Italian beef by buying USDA Choice, which is leaner and not as well aged as USDA Prime. But Prime is the best meat you can buy, and its fat marbling gives tremendous flavor to the meat. In Tuscany steak is served blood-rare, and we do recommend that you not cook it past medium-rare if you want the best possible flavor.

SERVES 4

One $1^1/_2$- to 2-pound porterhouse
  steak
1 teaspoon salt, preferably kosher
$^1/_2$ teaspoon freshly ground black
  pepper

2 teaspoons fresh rosemary leaves
$^1/_3$ cup olive oil
$^1/_2$ lemon (optional)

1. Place the steak in a glass 8 x 8-inch baking dish, and season it on both sides with the salt and pepper. Add the rosemary and the olive oil, coating all sides. Set aside to marinate for 30 minutes.

There are those Italians who insist that cooking with extra-virgin olive oil, however expensive, is justified by the flavor. We respectfully disagree: Just as it is unreasonable to cook with high-priced Burgundies of Bordeaux (or super Tuscan wines, for that matter), so, too, it is ridiculous to use high-priced extra-virgin olive oil. The application of heat to both wine and olive oil drives out their delicacy and subtlety. This is not to say, however, that you should use inferior, cheap olive oil in cooking. Make sure it is of good quality, produced and packed in the region mentioned on the can or bottle.

2. Meanwhile, heat an outdoor or stovetop grill or an oven broiler.

3. Scrape off the rosemary, and grill or broil the steak over high heat until medium-rare. Let it rest for 5 minutes, and then slice it. Squeeze lemon juice over the steak if desired. Serve immediately.

WINE SUGGESTION: BRUNELLO DI MONTALCINO

CHOPPED BEEF WITH ONION SAUCE

This is a very savory example of an Italian-American hamburger, which you might serve on a wedge of Italian bread.

SERVES 4

1 slice sandwich
   bread, soaked in
   1/2 cup water
1 1/4 pounds ground
   beef
1 shallot, chopped
Salt, preferably
   kosher
1/4 teaspoon freshly
   ground black
   pepper
1 1/2 tablespoons
   chopped flat-leaf
   parsley

1 cup freshly grated
   Parmigiano-
   Reggiano cheese
1 large egg yolk
2 tablespoons olive oil
3 tablespoons
   unsalted butter
2 yellow onions,
   thinly sliced
2 tablespoons
   balsamic vinegar
1/2 cup heavy cream

1. Squeeze most of the water out of the bread, and place it in a medium-size bowl. Add the beef, shallot, 3/4 teaspoon salt, pepper, parsley, Parmigiano, and egg yolk. Mix thoroughly. Divide the mixture into 8 portions and form them into rectangular patties about 1/2 inch thick.

2. In a medium-size saucepan, heat 1 tablespoon of the olive oil and 2 tablespoons of the butter over medium heat. Add the onions and cook, stirring, until browned, about 8 minutes. Season with salt and pepper to taste. Add the vinegar and the cream, bring to a boil, and reduce to low heat. Simmer for about 5 minutes, or until slightly reduced and thickened. Set aside.

3. In a large sauté pan, heat the remaining 1 tablespoon olive oil and 1 tablespoon butter over medium heat. When it is hot, add the beef patties and sauté until nicely browned and cooked inside, about 3 minutes per side. Arrange them on a platter, and pour the sauce over them.

WINE SUGGESTION: SPANNA

JOHNNY MARZETTI

You'll find Johnny Marzetti recipes throughout the Midwest. The original was created at the Marzetti Restaurant in Columbus, Ohio, back in the 1920s, and was named after the owner's brother, Johnny. It's a Sloppy Joe–type adaptation, with an Italian twist.

SERVES 6

10 tablespoons olive oil
2 medium yellow onions, chopped
3 garlic cloves, chopped
8 ounces white mushrooms, sliced
Salt, preferably kosher
Freshly ground black pepper
1 1/2 pounds ground beef
One 28-ounce can Italian-style
    tomatoes, crushed or chopped,
    with juices
1 teaspoon dried oregano

2 tablespoons chopped flat-leaf
    parsley
10 ounces wide noodles
2 tablespoons unsalted butter
8 ounces sharp cheddar cheese,
    shredded
3 ounces mozzarella cheese,
    shredded
3 tablespoons plain dry
    breadcrumbs

1. In a large sauté pan, heat 3 tablespoons of the olive oil over medium heat. Add the onions and cook, stirring, until lightly browned, about 7 minutes. Add the garlic and continue to cook, stirring, for another 2 minutes. Transfer to a bowl.

2. In the same sauté pan, heat another 3 tablespoons of the olive oil over medium-high heat. When it is hot, add the mushrooms and toss to coat in the oil. Cook, stirring, until nicely browned, about 5 minutes. Season with salt and pepper to taste, and transfer to the bowl with the onions.

3. In the same pan, heat 2 tablespoons of the olive oil over medium-high heat. Add the beef and cook, mixing and breaking up the clumps of meat, until browned, 5 to 7 minutes. Season with salt and pepper to taste. Remove the excess fat and oil from the pan. Add the onions and mushrooms to the meat. Stir in the tomatoes and oregano, and bring to a boil. Reduce the heat and simmer for 15 minutes. Adjust the seasoning. Mix in the parsley.

4. In a large stockpot, bring 4 quarts water to a boil. Add 1 teaspoon salt and the noodles, and boil until just barely al dente. Drain, return to the pot, and toss with the butter.

5. Meanwhile, preheat the oven to 325°F.

6. In a 9 x 13-inch baking pan, spread about ²/₃ cup of the meat sauce on the bottom. Spread the noodles over the sauce, and sprinkle about two thirds of the cheddar over the noodles. Top with the rest of the meat sauce. Sprinkle with the rest of the cheddar, then the mozzarella and the breadcrumbs. Drizzle with the remaining 2 tablespoons olive oil. Bake for 15 to 18 minutes or until hot. Put under the broiler for about 2 minutes to brown the cheese.

WINE SUGGESTION: MONTEPULCIANO D'ABRUZZO

MEATBALLS

No dish shares affection and scorn more equally than spaghetti and meatballs, which once seemed to symbolize what Italian-American food was all about: abundance, love of meat, and lavish use of tomato sauce. Indeed, for a long time, uninformed food critics insisted that meatballs were not even Italian at all. They were wrong. *Polpette* (pohl-PEH-teh) is the Italian word for meatballs, and they are well loved in the south. True, they are usually much smaller than the generously proportioned meatballs you find on most Italian-American tables, but they are popular nonetheless, especially with layered pasta dishes like Lasagna (page 177).

The following recipe uses the traditional mix of two or more meats, in this case pork, beef, and veal. The size of the meatballs depends completely on your own preference. If you're baking them into lasagna, they should be about the size of a nickel in diameter. If you're making them Italian-American style, with spaghetti, they might range from the size of a nickel up to a half-dollar in diameter.

SERVES 4 TO 6

4 slices Italian bread, about ½ inch thick, crusts removed
10 ounces ground pork
10 ounces ground beef
10 ounces ground veal
2 garlic cloves, minced
3 tablespoons chopped flat-leaf parsley
8 fresh sage leaves, chopped
1 medium yellow onion, chopped

½ cup freshly grated Pecorino Romano cheese
Salt, preferably kosher
Freshly ground black pepper
4 large eggs
1 cup plain dry breadcrumbs
½ cup olive oil
2 cups Marinara Sauce (page 126)

1. In a bowl, soak the bread in 1½ cups water for 10 minutes.

2. In another bowl, combine the meat, garlic, parsley, sage, onion, Pecorino, salt and pepper to taste, ⅓ cup water, and 2 of the eggs. Using your hands, squeeze the excess water from the bread. Add the bread, crumbled, to the meat mixture. Mix well to blend all the ingredients. Scoop out heaping tablespoons of the mixture, and roll each one to form a ball about 1½ inches in diameter; you should have approximately 24 meatballs.

3. In a shallow bowl, beat the remaining 2 eggs with 2 tablespoons water. Place the breadcrumbs in another shallow bowl. Roll the meatballs in the egg mixture and then in the breadcrumbs to coat them.

4. In a large nonstick sauté pan, heat ¼ cup of the olive oil over medium-high heat. Fry half of the meatballs, turning them to brown on all sides, 8 to 10 minutes. When they are browned, transfer them to a large saucepan. Add the remaining ¼ cup oil to the sauté pan, and repeat with the rest of the meatballs.

Some unscrupulous restaurateurs have substituted cheaper pork for more expensive veal and sold it as veal scaloppine on their menus. When one deluxe Italian restaurant in Nashville was exposed by the local newspaper for pulling such a switch, other Italian restaurants in town took out ads proclaiming, "Our veal don't squeal."

5. Add the Marinara Sauce to the meatballs and bring to a boil. Reduce the heat to a simmer and cook for 10 minutes.

WINE SUGGESTION: AGLIANICO DEL VULTURE

BEEF BRACIOLA

In Italy, the term *braciola* (brah-j'YOH-lah) refers to a slice or chop of any kind of meat, whereas in America the word has taken on the meaning of a slice of meat that has been wrapped around other ingredients. It is typical of the Italian-American tradition of enriching what was already considered something of a luxury. It's a very hearty dish that will feed a crowd, and it tastes even better if it sits overnight, so the flavors are absorbed into the meat. Serve the braciola with polenta or pasta.

SERVES 6

2 pounds beef top or bottom round

FOR THE FILLING
1/3 cup fresh breadcrumbs (see Note, page 239)
3 garlic cloves, chopped
1/3 cup chopped flat-leaf parsley
3 tablespoons pignoli (pine nuts), coarsely chopped
2 ounces salami, chopped

1/3 cup freshly grated Pecorino Romano cheese
Salt, preferably kosher
Freshly ground black pepper
6 tablespoons olive oil
1 yellow onion, chopped
1 garlic clove, chopped
One 28-ounce can Italian-style tomatoes, crushed, with juices
1/2 teaspoon red pepper flakes

1. Cut the beef into 1/4-inch-thick slices. Place the slices between plastic wrap and pound them with a meat mallet (using the flat side) to flatten the slices. (Or your butcher may do this for you.)

2. To make the filling, combine the breadcrumbs, garlic, parsley, pignoli, salami, Pecorino, and salt and pepper to taste in a medium-size bowl. Stir to mix.

3. Distribute the filling among the beef slices, and spread it out on each slice. Roll each slice up tightly, and secure with either string or, preferably, two toothpicks.

4. In a heavy flameproof casserole, heat 4 tablespoons of the olive oil over medium-high heat. Add half the beef rolls and brown on all sides, 4 to 6 minutes. Remove them to a platter and repeat with the remaining beef rolls.

5. While the beef rolls are browning, in a small sauté pan, heat the remaining 2 tablespoons olive oil over medium heat. Add the onion and cook, stirring, until softened, about 5 minutes. Add the garlic and cook, stirring, for another 2 minutes.

6. When all the beef rolls have browned, add $\frac{1}{4}$ cup water to the empty casserole and scrape up all the brown bits on the bottom of the pan. Return the beef rolls to the casserole. Add the onions, tomatoes, salt and pepper to taste, and the red pepper flakes. Stir, bring to a boil, and reduce the heat to low. Cover and simmer for $1\frac{1}{2}$ to $1\frac{3}{4}$ hours, stirring occasionally.

WINE SUGGESTION: BAROLO

BRAISED BEEF

Braising is a fine enough way to use the lesser cuts of meat, but it is also a terrific way to impart enormous flavor to meat, making it far more savory than, say, a slab of prime rib. Serve this with polenta.

SERVES 8

5 pounds beef chuck, cut into
   2- to 3-inch pieces
Salt, preferably kosher
Freshly ground black pepper
3 tablespoons all-purpose flour
6 tablespoons olive oil
1 large yellow onion, chopped
1 leek, white and light green parts
   only, split lengthwise, washed,
   and thinly sliced
1 large carrot, chopped
1 celery stalk, chopped

4 large garlic cloves, chopped
2 tablespoons tomato paste
$\frac{1}{2}$ bottle dry red wine, such as
   Cabernet Sauvignon, Zinfandel,
   or Barolo
4 cups chicken broth
$\frac{1}{2}$ teaspoon dried thyme
$\frac{3}{4}$ teaspoon dried rosemary, or 1
   large sprig fresh rosemary
1 bay leaf
5 tablespoons unsalted butter

1. Season the beef pieces with salt and pepper to taste. Sprinkle with the flour and toss to coat. Let stand for 5 minutes.

2. In a large sauté pan, heat 2 tablespoons of the olive oil over high heat. Add half the beef and sauté until browned on all sides, 8 to 12 minutes. Transfer the beef to a bowl. Deglaze the pan by adding 3 tablespoons water and scraping up the brown pieces. Pour this over the cooked beef.

3. Add another 2 tablespoons olive oil to the pan and repeat with the remaining beef. Deglaze the pan again.

4. In a large flameproof casserole, heat the remaining 2 tablespoons olive oil over medium-low heat. Add the onion, leek, carrot, and celery, and cook, stirring, until softened, about 10 minutes. Add the garlic and cook, stirring, for another 2 minutes. Add the tomato paste and wine, and simmer for 3 minutes. Add the chicken broth, thyme, rosemary, bay leaf, and the beef, and bring to a boil. Season with salt and pepper to taste. Reduce the heat to a simmer and cook until the meat is tender, about 1½ hours.

5. If the sauce is too thin, scoop out the beef, raise the heat, and reduce the sauce. Return the beef to the casserole and whisk in the butter, 1 tablespoon at a time.

WINE SUGGESTION: CANNONAU

There is nothing wrong with using tomato paste, except as the principal tomato flavoring in a dish. Tomato paste, called concentrato in Italian, is merely tomato that has been cooked down to drive out as much moisture as possible, thereby concentrating the intense, pure flavor. This flavor, which can certainly bolster a sauce or a stew, will not have the fresh, sunny taste of tomatoes themselves, however, and therefore should be used sparingly. Particularly handy are the toothpaste-like tubes of tomato paste that allow you to enrich a recipe with just a dab or two.

A postcard from Boston's Cafe Bova at 97 Arch Street at the early part of the 20th century typifies the decor of the period, Italian-American style, with a mural of what appears to be the Bay of Naples. On the tables breadsticks serve in the place of flowers.

CALVES' LIVER
WITH ONIONS
AND BALSAMIC VINEGAR

Calves' liver and onions is as readily found in England as it is in America, but cooked slowly in very thin slices, it is a particular specialty of Venice. As much as we like the Venetian-style liver and onions, we think the long cooking time robs the liver of its essential flavor, so we've shortened it to allow that flavor to stay bright under the mantle of sweet onions, which we do cook slowly until golden. The balsamic vinegar adds a lustrous note to the dish.

SERVES 4

½ cup plus 3 tablespoons olive oil
6 medium yellow onions, thinly
   sliced
Salt, preferably kosher
Freshly ground black pepper
1¼ to 1½ pounds calves' liver,
   thinly sliced diagonally

6 tablespoons balsamic vinegar
3 tablespoons chopped flat-leaf
   parsley
3 tablespoons unsalted butter

1. In a large sauté pan over medium heat, heat the ½ cup olive oil. Add the onions and cook, stirring, until they are browned and soft, about 10 minutes. Season with salt and pepper. Transfer to a platter.

2. Heat the same pan over high heat, and add the remaining 3 tablespoons olive oil. When it is very hot, add the liver and sauté to sear and brown it quickly. Cook until pink on the interior, 2 to 4 minutes; do not overcook.

3. Add the onions to the liver, reduce the heat to medium, toss, and season with salt and pepper to taste. Add the balsamic vinegar, scraping the bottom of the pan to loosen the brown bits. Stir in the parsley. Remove from the heat, stir in the butter, and serve immediately.

WINE SUGGESTION: CANNONAU

> If you want sautéed onions to be crisp and golden, do not salt them during the cooking process. Add salt afterward.

VEAL WITH
LEEKS AND LEMON

A really wonderful match-up of flavors, with the green sweetness of the leeks vying with the luxury of the veal and the sprightly tang of lemon. Serve with this rice.

SERVES 4

3 tablespoons olive oil
2 tablespoons unsalted butter
2 leeks, white and light green parts only, washed and cut into ¹/₂-inch-thick slices
1 yellow onion, cut into ¹/₂-inch-thick rings
1 carrot, cut into ¹/₂-inch-thick slices
¹/₂ celery stalk, chopped

Salt, preferably kosher,
Freshly ground black pepper
2 pounds boneless veal shoulder, cut into 2-inch pieces
¹/₂ cup dry white wine, such as Soave
2¹/₂ cups chicken broth
2 long strips lemon zest
1 large egg yolk
Juice of 1¹/₂ lemons

1. In a large flameproof casserole, heat the olive oil and the butter over medium-low heat. Add the leeks, onion, carrot, and celery. Toss and cook, stirring, until softened but not browned, about 8 minutes. Season with salt and pepper to taste.

2. Pat the veal pieces dry, and season them with salt and pepper. Add the veal to the casserole, mixing all the ingredients. Turn the heat to high and cook, tossing, until the veal turns white, 5 minutes. Add the wine, chicken broth, and lemon zest, and bring to a simmer. Cover, and cook until the veal is tender, 1 to 1¹/₄ hours.

3. Remove the veal from the casserole. Puree the sauce in a food processor or put it through a food mill, and return it to the casserole.

4. In a small bowl, mix the egg yolk and the lemon juice. Add 3 tablespoons of the sauce to the egg mixture, and stir together. Add another 3 tablespoons of the sauce and stir again. Return this mixture to the sauce, stirring well. Turn the heat to medium and heat the sauce just until it begins to bubble. Adjust the seasoning. Return the veal to the casserole, stir with the sauce, and serve.

WINE SUGGESTION: CABERNET FRANC

VEAL SCALOPPINE WITH LEMON

This is another of those clichés of Italian-American restaurants where the veal, often of inferior quality, comes out steamed and overcooked. But when made with finesse, this is a simple, delicious, and very easy dish that is ideal after rich antipasti and pastas.

SERVES 4

1¼ pounds veal scaloppine, thinly sliced and pounded flat
Salt, preferably kosher
Freshly ground black pepper
½ cup all-purpose flour
3 tablespoons olive oil

6 tablespoons (¾ stick) unsalted butter, softened
¼ cup chicken broth
3 tablespoons freshly squeezed lemon juice
3 tablespoons chopped flat-leaf parsley

1. Season the veal with salt and pepper. Spread the flour on a sheet of wax paper, and dredge the slices in the flour. Shake off the excess flour.

2. In a large skillet over medium-high heat, heat the olive oil and 3 tablespoons of the butter. Add half of the veal slices to the pan, being careful to not crowd the pieces, and sauté for 4 to 6 minutes. Remove the pieces to a warm platter. Sauté the remaining veal, and remove to the platter.

3. Add the chicken broth to the skillet and bring it to a simmer. Scrape up all the brown bits on the bottom of the pan, and cook until the broth is reduced to about 2 tablespoons, about 2 minutes. Add the lemon juice and parsley, and stir. Stir in the remaining 3 tablespoons butter. Add the veal, turning it to heat and coat with the sauce. Adjust the seasonings, and serve immediately.

WINE SUGGESTION: SOAVE

VEAL SCALOPPINE WITH MARSALA

A standard Italian-American item that is easy to make but also easy to turn into shoe leather. Be careful about the quality of the veal and the Marsala, watch the pan to make sure the veal is not overcooking, and don't ever let the meat become steamy.

SERVES 4

4 tablespoons (¹/2 stick)
  unsalted butter
6 tablespoons extra-virgin
  olive oil
8 ounces white mush-
  rooms, sliced
1¹/4 pounds veal scalop-
  pine, thinly sliced and
  pounded flat

Salt, preferably kosher
Freshly ground black
  pepper
¹/3 cup all-purpose flour
2 tablespoons chopped
  shallots
2 garlic cloves, minced
¹/3 cup chicken broth
¹/3 cup dry Marsala

1. In a large skillet over medium-high heat, heat 1 tablespoon of the butter and 2 tablespoons of the olive oil. Add the mushrooms and cook, tossing often, until lightly browned, 3 to 4 minutes. Remove to a platter and set aside.

2. Pat the veal dry, and season it with salt and pepper. Spread the flour on a sheet of wax paper, and dredge the slices in the flour. Shake off the excess flour.

3. In the same skillet, heat 1 tablespoon of the butter and 2 to 3 tablespoons of the olive oil over medium-high heat. Sauté the veal slices, in two batches if necessary to avoid crowding, until lightly browned, about 2 minutes on each side. Remove them to the platter with the mushrooms and keep warm.

4. In the same skillet, heat the remaining 1 tablespoon olive oil over medium heat. Add the shallots and garlic and cook, stirring, for 2 minutes.

5. Add the chicken broth and Marsala, bring to a gentle boil, then reduce the heat and simmer until slightly reduced, 2 to 3 minutes. Season with salt and pepper to taste.

6. Return the veal and mushrooms to the skillet, turning the veal slices to warm and coat them. Gently push the veal and mushrooms to one side, remove from the heat, and stir in the remaining 2 tablespoons butter, $^1/_2$ tablespoon at a time.

7. To serve, place the veal scaloppine in the middle of a heated platter and surround with the sauce and mushrooms.

WINE SUGGESTION: RUBESCO

VEAL SCALOPPINE WITH CREAM AND PEAS

This is a rich dish, but not a heavy one unless too much cream is used. It is based on a veal dish we had at Passetto, a charming garden restaurant in Rome, but the use of cream makes it more likely to be found on menus in this country.

SERVE 4

4 tablespoons ($^1/_2$ stick) unsalted
   butter
4 tablespoons olive oil
2 medium yellow onions, sliced
$1^1/_4$ pounds veal scaloppine, thinly
   sliced and pounded flat
Salt, preferably kosher
Freshly ground black pepper

$^1/_4$ teaspoon saffron threads,
   crushed in a mortar
1 cup chicken broth
1 cup dry white wine, such as
   Soave
$^1/_2$ cup heavy cream
1 cup frozen peas, thawed

1. In a large sauté pan over medium-low heat, heat 2 tablespoons of the butter and 2 tablespoons of the olive oil. Add the onions and cook, stirring, until softened, about 5 minutes. Transfer the onions to a plate.

2. Season the veal with salt and pepper.

3. In the same sauté pan, heat 1 tablespoon butter and 1 tablespoon olive oil over medium-high heat. When it is hot, add half of the veal

271

slices and sauté quickly, turning them once, until they are cooked and lightly browned, 2 to 3 minutes. Transfer to a platter and keep warm. Add the remaining 1 tablespoon butter and 1 tablespoon oil, and sauté the remaining veal. Transfer to the platter.

4. Return the onions to the sauté pan. Add the saffron (swirl a little of the chicken broth in the mortar to extract all the saffron), chicken broth, and wine, and bring to a boil. Cook until reduced by about a third, 2 to 4 minutes. Add the cream, and boil for another 2 minutes.

5. Return the veal slices to the pan, and add the peas. Simmer for 1 to 2 minutes, turning once. Adjust the seasoning, and serve immediately.

WINE SUGGESTION: BARBARESCO

SALTIMBOCCA

One of the classics of Roman cookery, saltimbocca (sahl-teem-BOH-kah) is too often sloppily and steamily prepared by non-Roman cooks who don't understand that this is a delicate dish as well as a hearty one. Careful cooking and veal that really tastes like veal (some unscrupulous restaurant cooks substitute cheaper pork for veal!) will give you a truly refined saltimbocca, which means "jump in the mouth."

SERVES 6

*1¹/4 pounds veal scaloppine, thinly
 sliced and pounded flat*
Salt, preferably kosher
Freshly ground black pepper
12 fresh sage leaves, cut in half
12 very thin slices prosciutto
All-purpose flour, for dredging

*6 tablespoons (³/4 stick) unsalted
 butter*
*³/4 cup dry white wine, such as
 Soave*
*¹/4 cup sweet Marsala or sweet
 vermouth*

1. Season the veal with salt and pepper. Place 2 pieces of sage on each slice, then a slice of prosciutto, and fold the slice in half. Secure with a toothpick. Season lightly with salt and pepper.

2. Pour about ¹/₂ cup flour onto a piece of wax paper, and dredge the veal pieces in the flour, shaking off any excess.

3. Heat 2 medium or large sauté pans over high heat, and add 2 tablespoons of the butter to each. When the butter is hot, add the veal pieces and sauté until browned, 2 to 3 minutes on each side. Remove to a platter.

4. Deglaze the pans by pouring half of the wine and half of the Marsala into each pan and scraping the brown bits off the bottom of the pans. Then pour the liquid from one pan into the other. Cook until reduced by about one third, 3 to 5 minutes. Reduce the heat, blend in the remaining 2 tablespoons butter, and return the veal slices to the pan. Turn them over to coat in the sauce, and serve immediately.

WINE SUGGESTION: EST! EST!! EST!!!

Mike Greco of Mike's Deli at the Arthur Avenue Market, who has been known to break into Italian arias while slicing the prosciutto and cutting the Parmigiano.

VEAL ROLLATINE

A standard item on Italian-American menus, Veal Rollatine ("veal rolls") is too often ruined by the addition of an unnecessary and un-Italian "brown sauce," which tends to make the meat steamy and the whole dish soupy. Our version keeps the flavors and textures intact.

SERVES 4

½ cup plain dry breadcrumbs
¼ cup diced mozzarella cheese
¼ cup diced salami
1 garlic clove, minced
2 tablespoons minced flat-leaf
    parsley
1 scallion, white and green parts,
    thinly sliced
2 tablespoons olive oil
Salt, preferably kosher

Freshly ground black pepper
1¼ pounds veal scallopine (about
    8 pieces), thinly sliced and
    pounded flat
6 tablespoons (¾ stick) unsalted
    butter
1 shallot, chopped
½ cup dry white wine, such as
    Soave

1. In a bowl, combine the breadcrumbs, mozzarella, salami, garlic, parsley, scallion, olive oil, and salt and pepper to taste. Mix well.

2. Season the veal pieces with salt and pepper, and spread about 2 tablespoons of the breadcrumb mixture on each piece. Roll the veal up to enclose the filling, forming a cylinder. Close the rolls by sticking a toothpick into the meat along the length of the roll, not straight through the middle.

3. In a large sauté pan, heat 4 tablespoons of the butter over medium-high heat. When it is hot, add the rollatine and cook, turning the pieces to brown them on all sides, about 5 minutes. Add the shallots and cook for 1 minute more. Then add the wine, scraping up the brown bits on the bottom of the pan. Cook over low heat until reduced by about one third, about 2 minutes. Blend in the remaining 2 tablespoons butter, and serve immediately.

WINE SUGGESTION: SASSELLA

The addition of a single anchovy to many sauces, stews, and braised dishes adds measurably to the final taste of the dish, even if that anchovy cannot be detected—which is just fine with those many people who say they can't stand the taste!

OSSO BUCO

Osso buco (OH-soh BOO-koh) is one of the great Lombardian dishes that has had many interpretations on this side of the Atlantic. One of the finest was at Amerigo's, an Italian-American restaurant in the Bronx, which opened in the 1930s as a pizzeria and became a full-fledged *ristorante* by the 1950s. The original owners, Amerigo Coppola and his wife, Millie, created all the recipes, and the next owners, Tony and Anna Cortese, maintained them impeccably until the restaurant closed in 1998. We're happy we were able to reclaim this terrific osso buco recipe—a representative of how an Italian-American version can sometimes surpass the original. Serve the veal shanks over rice or risotto.

SERVES 8

8 veal shanks (about 6 pounds in all), tightly tied
All-purpose flour, for dredging
1 cup corn oil
3 large yellow onions, chopped
3 anchovies, (rinsed if packed in salt), chopped
Freshly ground black pepper
7 carrots, finely chopped
9 celery stalks, finely chopped

^{1}/3 cup chopped flat-leaf parsley
^{1}/2 cup chopped fresh basil leaves
^{1}/2 cup dry white wine, such as Soave
1 cup chopped canned Italian-style tomatoes, with juices
8 tablespoons (1 stick) unsalted butter
One 48-ounce can chicken broth
Salt, preferably kosher

1. In a shallow bowl, dredge the veal shanks in flour. Shake off any excess.

2. In a large flameproof casserole, heat the corn oil over medium-high heat. When the oil is hot, add 4 of the veal shanks. Brown the veal shanks on both sides, 6 to 8 minutes, and transfer to a bowl. Repeat with the remaining veal shanks.

3. Keeping the oil hot, add the onions to the casserole and cook, stirring, over medium-high heat until browned, about 10 minutes. Add the anchovies and black pepper, and stir. Add the carrots, celery, and parsley, stir, and cook for 3 minutes. Add the basil, wine, tomatoes, butter, chicken broth, and the veal shanks. Turn the heat to high and bring to a boil. When it starts to boil, reduce the heat and simmer until the shanks are tender, 1 to 1^1/4 hours.

4. Transfer the veal shanks to a plate. Turn the heat up to medium-high and boil the sauce until it is reduced by about one fourth and is somewhat thick, 15 to 20 minutes.

5. Transfer 1¹/₂ cups of the sauce to a blender or food processor, and puree. Return the puree to the casserole, along with the veal shanks. Adjust the seasonings, adding salt if needed. Heat for 5 to 10 minutes, and serve.

WINE SUGGESTION: CANNONAU

VEAL CHOPS VALDOSTANA

I n the United States veal chops are pretty much a phenomenon of Italian-American meat markets and restaurants. Few Americans eat much veal to begin with, and a massive veal chop is not something they encounter in most markets. But for the Italian immigrant this represented the ultimate in meat eating, and veal chops seem to have gotten bigger and bigger over the past decade. In order to gild this lily still further, some enterprising Italian chef came up with the idea of enriching the meat with cheese and prosciutto, then treating it to a brown sauce. By using dried porcini mushrooms, that sauce achieves amazing levels of flavor that truly enhance this veal chop cooked, as the name suggests, in the style of the Val d'Aosta region.

SERVES 4

2 ounces dried porcini mushrooms
4 veal chops, 1¹/₂ inches thick
4 slices prosciutto, cut in half
8 thin slices mozzarella cheese
Freshly ground black pepper
All-purpose flour, for dredging
6 tablespoons (³/₄ stick) unsalted butter

4 tablespoons extra-virgin olive oil
8 ounces cremini mushrooms, thinly sliced
2 shallots, minced
¹/₂ cup dry Marsala
1 cup chicken broth
Salt, preferably kosher
¹/₄ cup chopped flat-leaf parsley

1. In a small bowl, cover the porcini with 1 cup hot water. Let soak for 20 minutes.

2. Meanwhile, cut the veal chops in half horizontally, slicing all the way to the bone but leaving them on the bone, to split them open. Open the 2 halves of the meat and pound with a meat pounder to flatten the two pieces. On one of the inside pieces, layer a slice of prosciutto, 2 slices mozzarella, and another slice of prosciutto. Season with pepper. Close the other piece of veal over the first to enclose the filling. Pound the edges together. Repeat with the other chops. Dredge them in flour, shaking off any excess.

3. In a sauté pan that is large enough to hold the 4 chops, heat 2 tablespoons of the butter and 2 tablespoons of the olive oil over medium-high heat. When it is hot, add the chops and sauté, turning them once, until they are almost done, about 5 minutes. Transfer to a platter and keep warm.

4. In the same sauté pan, heat 2 tablespoons of the butter and the remaining 2 tablespoons olive oil. Add the cremini mushrooms and cook over medium-high heat, tossing them often, until lightly browned, about 3 minutes.

5. While the cremini are cooking, squeeze the water out of the porcini, reserving the soaking water. Chop the porcini and add them to the cremini mushrooms, along with the shallots. Cook, stirring, for another 2 minutes.

6. Strain the porcini liquid through a cheesecloth-lined sieve into a small bowl.

7. Deglaze the pan with the Marsala, scraping up any brown bits on the bottom of the pan. Add the chicken broth and the strained porcini liquid. Season with a bit of salt and pepper, bring to a boil, and reduce the heat to medium. Cook until the sauce is reduced by half, 10 to 12 minutes.

8. Return the veal chops to the pan and heat for 1 to 2 minutes, turning them once. Transfer the chops to individual plates. Add the parsley to the sauce, and blend in the remaining 2 tablespoons butter, 1/2 tablespoon at a time. Adjust the seasoning and spoon over the veal chops.

WINE SUGGESTION:
BAROLO

RABBIT IN BAROLO WINE SAUCE

The Piedmontese cook with the noble Barolo all the time, though it is a fairly expensive wine. You could certainly substitute an American Zinfandel (which is very similar to the Italian *Primitivo*) or Cabernet Sauvignon. Serve this with steamed potatoes or polenta.

SERVES 4

6 tablespoons olive oil
2¹/₂ ounces pancetta, sliced ¹/₄ inch thick and cut into ¹/₄-inch cubes
1 large yellow onion, chopped
1 small leek, white and light green parts only, washed and chopped
1 small carrot, cubed
¹/₂ red bell pepper, cored and chopped
3 garlic cloves, minced

All-purpose flour, for dredging
1 rabbit, cut into 8 pieces (by a butcher)
Salt, preferably kosher
Freshly ground black pepper
2 cups Barolo, Zinfandel, or Cabernet Sauvignon
2 bay leaves
4 fresh sage leaves, sliced
1 cup canned Italian-style tomatoes, chopped, with juices

1. In a large flameproof casserole, heat 1 tablespoon of the olive oil over medium heat. Add the pancetta and cook, stirring, until browned, 3 to 5 minutes. Transfer to a bowl and set aside.

2. In the same casserole, heat 3 tablespoons of the olive oil over medium heat. Add the onion, leek, carrot, and bell pepper and cook, stirring occasionally, until softened, about 10 minutes. Add the garlic and cook, stirring, for another 2 minutes. Remove the vegetables and add them to the bowl with the pancetta.

3. Sprinkle some flour onto a piece of wax paper. Season the rabbit with salt and pepper to taste, and dredge the pieces in the flour, shaking off the excess.

4. Heat the same casserole over high heat, and add the remaining 2 tablespoons olive oil. Add half the rabbit pieces and sauté, turning to brown on all sides, 6 to 8 minutes. Transfer the pieces to the bowl with the vegetables and pancetta, and sauté the rest of the rabbit, adding more oil if needed.

5. Over low heat, add the Zinfandel to the casserole and deglaze the pan, scraping the brown bits off the bottom. Return the contents of the bowl to the casserole, and add the bay leaves, sage, tomatoes, and ¹/₂ cup water. Season with salt and pepper to taste. Bring to a boil, reduce the heat to medium-low, partially cover, and simmer for 45 minutes.

6. Serve the rabbit hot, with the sauce spooned over.

WINE SUGGESTION: BAROLO

NOTE: This can be made the day before.

EAST MEETS WEST OXTAIL STEW

Ming Tsai is perhaps the finest innovator of so-called East-West fusion cooking. He is chef-owner of Blue Ginger, a restaurant in Wellesley, Massachusetts, and star of his own TV show. We loved everything he served us when we visited his restaurant. This oxtail stew is a very good example of how non-Italian chefs—in this case an American born of Chinese parents—can take various ethnic ideas and turn them into something new and wholly American. In Italy dishes made with oxtail are called *alla vaccinara* (vah-chee-NAH-rah), "butcher style."

SERVES 6

³/₄ cup all-purpose flour
*2 tablespoons ancho chili powder
  (available in specialty markets
  and some supermarkets)*
Salt, preferably kosher
Freshly ground black pepper
2 oxtails, cut into pieces
¹/₂ cup olive oil
*2 cups dry red wine, such as
  Barbera or Merlot*
2 yellow onions, chopped
1 small fennel bulb, chopped
¹/₂ celery stalk, chopped

1 carrot, chopped
8 garlic cloves, chopped
1 tablespoon minced fresh ginger
*3 lemongrass stalks, white part
  only, pounded and minced, or
  the zest of 1 small lemon*
*1 cup chopped canned Italian-style
  tomatoes, with juices*
¹/₂ cup soy sauce
*3 sprigs fresh thyme, or ¹/₂ tea-
  spoon dried*
2 bay leaves

1. In a shallow bowl, mix the flour, chili powder, 1 tablespoon salt, and 1 tablespoon pepper. Add the oxtails, a few pieces at a time, and roll them in the flour mixture to coat. Shake off any excess flour. Set aside for 5 minutes.

2. In a large sauté pan, heat $^1/_4$ cup of the olive oil over medium-high heat. Add half the oxtail pieces and sear them on all sides until they have browned, 6 to 8 minutes. Transfer the pieces to a platter. Brown the remaining oxtail pieces, and remove them. Pour off any leftover oil and burned pieces. Deglaze the pan by adding the wine and cooking, scraping up the brown bits, for 3 minutes. Then remove from the heat.

3. In a large flameproof casserole, heat the remaining $^1/_4$ cup olive oil over medium heat. Add the onions, fennel, celery, carrot, garlic, ginger, and lemongrass. Season with salt and pepper to taste, and cook, stirring, until the vegetables are softened, about 10 minutes. Add the oxtails, the wine from the sauté pan, and the tomatoes, soy sauce, thyme, bay leaves, and 4 cups water. Bring to a boil. Reduce the heat to a simmer, partially cover, and cook until the oxtails are very tender, $2^1/_2$ to 3 hours. Remove the bay leaves and thyme sprigs.

> When cooking with wine, the wine you use should certainly not be an expensive bottling but neither should it be cheap jug wine, for while the former can vastly improve a dish, the latter will almost always ruin it. Our rule is never to cook with any wine you wouldn't truly enjoy drinking on its own, and that does not mean it has to be expensive—just good.

4. Transfer approximately half of the liquid in the casserole to a food processor or blender, and puree. Pour the puree back into the stew. Adjust the seasonings, and serve hot.

WINE SUGGESTION: NEBBIOLO

NOTE: This can be made the day before.

With their affinity for noodles, Italian and Chinese chefs have a good deal in common, and Ming Tsai, a Chinese-American, has successfully used ideas from both food cultures in his fusion cooking at his award-winning restaurant, Blue Ginger, in Wellesley, Massachusetts.

PORK CHOPS
WITH
VINEGARED PEPPERS

Very much an Italian-American preparation that shows off the big portions offered on this side of the Atlantic. It is key not to overcook the pork chops, which will turn them chewy and tasteless. Serve them with sautéed potatoes.

SERVES 4

4 thick pork chops
Salt, preferably kosher
Freshly ground black pepper
1/3 cup plus 1/4 cup olive oil
1 medium yellow onion, sliced
1 garlic clove, chopped

1/3 cup dry white wine, such as
   Soave
3/4 cup bottled marinated red
   peppers, chopped into 1/2-inch
   pieces, juice reserved
3 bottled pepperoncini peppers,
   finely chopped

1. Season the pork chops with salt and pepper.

2. In a large sauté pan, heat the 1/3 cup olive oil over medium-high heat. Add the pork chops and sauté until browned on both sides, 6 to 8 minutes. Remove the chops and set aside. Discard the oil.

3. In the same sauté pan, heat the remaining 1/4 cup olive oil over medium heat. Add the onion and cook, stirring, until lightly browned, about 3 minutes. Add the garlic and cook, stirring, another 2 minutes. Add the wine and 1/3 cup of the reserved red pepper juice. Simmer for 3 minutes. Add the red peppers, pepperoncini, and salt and pepper to taste. Return the pork chops to the pan. Simmer until the chops are done, turning them once, 3 to 5 minutes. Serve the pork chops with some of the sauce.

WINE SUGGESTION:
RECIOTO DELLA VALPOLICELLA AMARONE

"There were no restaurants in my neighborhood. We didn't go out to eat. We ate either at our house, or cousin Ronnie's, or Uncle Dom's, or whatever. My grandmother would start making her meat sauce at seven in the morning on Sunday and within five or six hours that smell would be all through the house, covering everything—clothing, furniture, appliances—and then it would go out the front door and into the streets, to mix with the aroma of neighboring meat sauces." — Jerry Della Femina, An Italian Grows in Brooklyn

PORK CHOPS
WITH QUINCE COMPOTE

The Italian term for "quince" is the mellifluous *mela cotogna* (MEH-lah koh-TOH-n'yah), which means "sweet apple." In Sicily and Apulia it is made into a sweet paste or jam, and sometimes molded and shaped in pans. In our recipe we do a variation of that with a quince compote and pork flavored with Riesling wine, which actually makes this closer to the kind of dish you'll find in Friuli.

SERVES 4

2 tablespoons sugar
1/2 cup Riesling wine
1 quince, peeled, pitted, and cut into small pieces
One 3-inch strip of lemon zest
1/4 cup dark raisins

1 bottled pepperoncini pepper, minced, with its seeds
Salt, preferably kosher
4 pork chops, 1 to 1 1/2 inches thick
Freshly ground black pepper
2 tablespoons olive oil

1. In a small saucepan, combine the sugar with 1/4 cup water and bring to a boil. Reduce the heat and simmer until the sugar has dissolved, about 1 minute. Add the wine, quince, and lemon zest. Cover, and simmer over low heat until the quince is soft, about 10 minutes.

2. Discard the lemon zest. With the back of a fork, mash the quince a bit. Add the raisins, pepperoncini, and 1/8 teaspoon salt. Cover, and continue to cook for another 3 minutes.

3. Season the pork chops with salt and pepper.

4. In a large sauté pan, heat the olive oil over medium-high heat. Add the pork chops (do not crowd them) and sauté, turning them once, until still slightly pink, 8 to 10 minutes. Serve the pork chops with some of the quince compote on the side.

WINE SUGGESTION:
RIESLING RENANO

ITALIAN SAUSAGE WITH SWEET POTATOES

Go to a good Italian butcher for good Italian sausage, which may be variously flavored with herbs or seeds like fennel, and will have different ratios of meat to fat and different textures owing to the individual grind. Find one you like, then make this dish, which we love for the way it uses a very American ingredient, the sweet potato, to give it a lovely undertone of sweetness.

SERVES 4

6 tablespoons olive oil
1 1/2 pounds sweet Italian sausage, cut into 3/4-inch-thick slices
2 medium sweet potatoes, peeled and cut into small cubes
1 green bell pepper, cut into squares
Salt, preferably kosher
Freshly ground black pepper
2 garlic cloves, minced
4 scallions, white and green parts, sliced
4 bottled pepperoncini peppers, finely chopped
1/4 cup balsamic vinegar

1. In a large sauté pan, heat 2 tablespoons of the olive oil over medium heat. Add the sausage and cook, stirring, until nicely browned and almost fully cooked, 8 to 10 minutes. Remove from the pan and set aside. Drain the fat and oil from the pan.

2. In the same sauté pan, heat the remaining 4 tablespoons olive oil over medium heat. Add the sweet potatoes and cook, tossing often, until lightly browned, about 3 minutes. Add the bell pepper and continue cooking until both the sweet potatoes and the peppers are browned and soft, about 10 minutes. Season with salt and pepper to taste. Scatter the garlic and scallions on the bottom of the pan and cook, stirring, for 2 minutes. Toss with the sweet potatoes and peppers.

3. Add the sausage and pepperoncini to the pan, toss, and heat for 3 minutes. Add the balsamic vinegar, stir to coat the vegetables and sausage, and cook for 2 minutes. Serve immediately.

WINE SUGGESTION: CANNONAU

SPICY ROASTED SAUSAGES AND GRAPES

Here's a great dish we adapted from *Cucina Simpatica* (HarperCollins), an aptly named book by two wonderful chefs, Johanne Killeen and George Germon of Al Forno restaurant in Providence, Rhode Island.

SERVES 6 TO 8

1½ pounds hot Italian sausage
1½ pounds sweet Italian sausage
4 tablespoons unsalted butter
7 cups (about 2½ pounds) green
    seedless grapes, stems removed

½ teaspoon crushed red pepper
Salt, preferably kosher
Freshly ground black pepper
¼ cup balsamic vinegar

1. Preheat the oven to 500°F.

2. In a large pot, combine 1½ quarts water and the sausages. Bring to a boil and simmer for 8 minutes, to eliminate the excess fat. Drain, and cut the sausages into 3- to 4-inch pieces.

3. Place a large roasting pan over two burners, add the butter, and quickly melt it. Add the grapes and red peppers, and toss with the butter to coat. Transfer the sausages to the roasting pan, pushing them down between the grapes. Season them with salt and pepper. Roast in the oven, turning the grapes and the sausages in order to brown them, for 20 to 25 minutes.

4. Transfer the sausages and the grapes to a heated platter, and set aside.

5. Place the roasting pan on top of the stove, turn the heat to medium-high, and add the balsamic vinegar. Stir, scraping any brown bits off the bottom of the pan. Cook until the sauce becomes syrupy, 2 to 3 minutes. Pour this reduction over the sausages and grapes, and serve.

WINE SUGGESTION: CANNONAU

> "Many immigrants had brought onboard balls of yarn, leaving one end of the line with someone on land. As the ship slowly cleared the dock, the balls unwound amid the farewell shouts of the women, the fluttering of the handkerchiefs, and the infants held high. After the yarn ran out, the long strips remained airborne, sustained by the wind, long after those on land and those at sea had lost sight of each other."
> —Luciano De Crescenzo, "The Ball of Yarn"

SAUSAGE AND PEPPERS

"Lusty" is the word that leaps to mind when describing this quintessential southern Italian dish, which ennobles pork and peppers in the most basic way.

SERVES 4

6 tablespoons olive oil
1¹/2 pounds sweet Italian sausage,
  cut into 6 pieces
2 green bell peppers, cored and cut
  into 1¹/2 x ¹/2-inch pieces
2 medium yellow onions, sliced
4 garlic cloves, chopped

Salt, preferably kosher
Freshly ground black pepper
¹/2 teaspoon dried oregano
2 cups canned Italian-style
  tomatoes, crushed, with juices
Pinch of sugar
¹/2 teaspoon red pepper flakes

1. In a large sauté pan, combine 3 tablespoons of the olive oil, the sausages, and ¹/3 cup water. Bring to a boil, then cover, reduce the heat to a simmer, and cook for 7 minutes. If any liquid is left, uncover the pan, increase the heat, and cook to evaporate it. Cut each sausage into 4 small pieces and return them to the pan.

2. Add the remaining 3 tablespoons olive oil to the sausages, along with the bell peppers and the onions, and turn the heat to medium-high. Cook, tossing often, until the meat and vegetables are nicely browned, about 10 minutes. Add the garlic and cook, stirring, for another 2 minutes.

3. Season with salt and pepper to taste. Add the oregano, tomatoes, and sugar, and stir to blend. Bring the mixture to a boil. Then reduce the heat to a simmer, cover, and cook for 10 minutes. Sprinkle with the red pepper flakes, and serve.

SUGGESTED WINE:
LACRIMA CHRISTI ROSSO

PORK ROAST
WITH PRUNES

P ork roast with prunes is found in many a French or even
American cookbook, but it is indeed a classic Italian pairing,
and using Marsala wine gives it even more of an Italian edge.

SERVES 6

12 ounces pitted prunes
3/4 cup dry Marsala
One 3- to 3 1/2-pound boneless
  pork roast
2 tablespoons olive oil
Salt, preferably kosher

Freshly ground black pepper
1 garlic clove, minced
3 tablespoons chopped shallots
1 cup chicken broth
4 tablespoons (1/2 stick) unsalted
  butter

1. In a small bowl, combine the prunes with the Marsala. Set aside.

2. Preheat the oven to 450°F.

3. In a large roasting pan, rub the pork roast with the olive oil and
season it with salt and pepper. Roast for 40 minutes, basting it every 10
to 15 minutes with the pan juices.

4. Drain the prunes, reserving the Marsala, and add the prunes to the
pan. Continue to roast for 20 minutes. The pork will be slightly pink
when done.

5. Remove the roast from the pan and let it rest for 5 to 10 minutes. In
the meantime, push the prunes to one side of the pan. If there is a lot
of fat in the pan, drain it, leaving about 2 tablespoons. Place the roasting pan on the stovetop. Add the garlic and shallots and cook, stirring,
over medium heat for 2 minutes. Add the reserved Marsala and the
chicken broth, and scrape up all the brown bits on the bottom of the
pan. Simmer for about 5 minutes. Season with salt and pepper to taste.

6. In a blender or food processor, combine about one third of the prunes
and 1/2 cup of the sauce, and puree. Pour the puree back into the roasting pan, and mix it with the rest of the sauce and prunes. Adjust the
seasoning. If the sauce is too thick, thin it with a little chicken broth.
Stir in the butter over low heat, 1 tablespoon at a time.

7. Cut the pork roast into thin slices, place them on a platter, and surround them with the prunes and sauce.

WINE SUGGESTION: SFURSAT

PORK ROAST WITH FENNEL

Make sure you let the garlic paste soak into the pork for several hours. It gives the meat a marvelous flavor.

SERVES 6

5 garlic cloves, minced
1¹/2 teaspoons salt, preferably kosher
³/4 teaspoon coarsely ground black pepper

1¹/2 teaspoons fennel seeds, crushed
2¹/2 tablespoons olive oil
One 3-pound boneless pork roast

1. In a mortar or a mini food processor, combine the garlic, salt, pepper, and fennel seeds. Mash together, adding the olive oil little by little to make a paste.

2. Using a sharp knife, score the meat by cutting ¹/8- to ¹/4-inch-deep diagonal slits, 1¹/2 inches apart, on all sides of the roast. Spread the paste over the pork roast, rubbing it well into the meat. Place the roast in a plastic bag, and refrigerate for 6 hours.

3. Preheat the oven to 425°F.

4. Place the pork in a roasting pan and roast for 1 to 1¹/4 hours, or until the meat is as done as you like. (We suggest that the meat is done when it is still slightly pink.) Let stand for 5 to 10 minutes before slicing.

WINE SUGGESTION: DOLCETTO

NOTE: If you're using a meat thermometer, an internal temperature of 150°F is recommended for pork. While it rests, the temperature will rise another 5 degrees. We like it a bit rarer, at 140°F (again, the temperature will rise 5 degrees while resting). Of course, if you're worried about trichinosis, you should cook the pork to a higher temperature.

All roasted meats require a setting time to rest after being removed from the oven. During ten to fifteen minutes' rest, the interior juices will be absorbed back into the meat cells. If you cut the meat too soon after its removal from the oven, those juices will run off onto the plate. Resting the meat also helps to keep it moist and tender.

SWEET AND SOUR PORK

Is pork the most versatile of meats? We're beginning to think so, and this recipe for pork *con agrumi* (with citrus) is evidence why. It is clearly a product of the Mediterranean food culture, a fabulous blend of the sweet and sour flavors that predominate in that region, especially in southern Italy and Sicily. The pork goes well with polenta.

SERVES 4

FOR THE MARINADE
Juice of 1 lemon
6 tablespoons extra-virgin olive oil
2 teaspoons coarsely ground black pepper
1 1/2 teaspoons salt, preferably kosher
2 garlic cloves, crushed in a garlic press or minced

2 pounds boneless pork loin, cut into 8 slices, 1/2 inch thick
5 tablespoons olive oil

2 medium yellow onions, thinly sliced
1 tablespoon sugar
5 tablespoons red wine vinegar
Juice of 2 juice oranges
Juice of 1 lemon
2 tablespoons dried currants
1 teaspoon salt, preferably kosher
1/2 teaspoon freshly ground black pepper
5 tablespoons chicken broth or water
2 tablespoons unsalted butter

1. Prepare the marinade: In a large bowl, combine the lemon juice, olive oil, pepper, salt, and garlic. Mix well.

2. Add the pork slices to the marinade, and turn to coat them well. Cover, and refrigerate for at least 4 hours, turning the pork slices every hour or two.

3. In a medium-size saucepan, heat 3 tablespoons of the olive oil over medium heat. Add the onions and cook, stirring, until they are lightly browned, about 10 minutes. Add the sugar and continue to cook until it caramelizes, 3 to 4 minutes. Add the vinegar and cook for about 1 minute, to reduce it slightly. Add the orange juice, lemon juice, currants, salt, and pepper. Simmer until reduced by about half, 6 to 8 minutes. Remove from the heat.

4. Heat a sauté pan that is large enough to hold all the pork slices without crowding them (or use 2 smaller pans) over medium-high heat.

Add the remaining 2 tablespoons olive oil and when it is very hot, add the pork slices and cook until slightly pink, 4 to 6 minutes. Transfer the pork to a platter.

5. Add the chicken broth to the pan, scraping up the brown bits on the bottom. Add this to the onion mixture, place it over low heat, and stir in the butter. Serve the pork slices and sauce immediately.

WINE SUGGESTION: SASSICAIA

A FEW WELL-NEEDED TRANSLATIONS OF ITALIAN CULINARY TERMS

in acqua pazza: *"crazy water"—term for dishes cooked in seawater*

barba di frate: *"monks' beard"—a thin, wild, slightly bitter grass*

batsoà: *"silk stockings"—pig's feet dipped in egg batter and fried*

binario di frolla: *"pastry railroad track"—ricotta-filled cheesecake topped with flat pastry strips resembling train tracks*

bruglione: *"big mess"—sauté of wild greens, mushrooms, and potatoes*

brutti ma buoni: *"ugly but good"—lumpy hazelnut cookies*

casu marzu: *"rotten cheese"—pungent Sardinina cheese containing little worms*

chiacchiere della nonna: *"grandma's chatter"—crunchy sweet fried pastries*

filu 'e ferru: *"iron wire"—Sardinian grappa*

formaggio all'argentiera: *"silversmith's cheese"—very rich caciocavallo fried in olive oil with red wine and oregano and served on bread*

gnudi: *"nakeds"—spinach and ricotta dumplings without a pasta casing*

mandilli de saêa: *"silk handkerchiefs"—Ligurian pasta sheets with pesto sauce*

minni di virgini: *"virgins' breasts"—pastry cream—filled semolina buns*

'ncip 'nciap : *"chop-chop"—Neapolitan mix of leftover chicken and eggs*

occhio di bue: *"eye of the ox"—a fried egg*

ombretta: *"shadow"—cocktail taken in the shade of the afternoon in Venice*

scamorza: *"dunce"—southern Italian cheese shaped like a dunce cap*

'sciue 'sciue: *"quick, quick"—quickly made spaghetti dish with garlic and peppers*

sfratti: *"eviction sticks"—stick-shaped cookies*

smacafam: *"push away hunger"—buckwheat*

TRIPE

Trippa (TREE-pah)—made from cow's stomach—is a poor man's dish beloved by Italians of every social class. In this country it made its way onto menus at the kind of Italian-American restaurant that had a few featured specials like this for those who craved them.

Make no mistake: Tripe is not for everyone. Its flavor is strong, its texture oddly gelatinous. It must be bought from a butcher who really knows how to clean and treat it. But cooked with plenty of spices and simmered till tender, tripe can be an example of Italian home cooking at its most authentic. If you like, parboil some potatoes and stir them into the dish.

SERVES 6

2 pounds tripe
1 medium yellow onion, slit into
  quarters but still connected at
  the base
1 teaspoon salt, preferably kosher
4 whole cloves
6 tablespoons olive oil
3 ounces pancetta, chopped
4 tablespoons (¹/2 stick) unsalted
  butter
2 large yellow onions, chopped

1 large leek, white and light green
  parts only, washed and sliced
2 carrots, chopped
1 celery stalk, chopped
1 cup dry white wine, such as
  Soave
1¹/2 cups beef broth
2 cups canned Italian-style
  tomatoes, crushed, with juices
Freshly ground black pepper
2 cups canned white beans,
  drained

1. In a large bowl, rinse the tripe in water, changing the water 3 times. Cut into 4 to 6 pieces.

2. In a large stockpot, cover the tripe, onion, salt, and cloves with 2 inches water. Bring to a boil. Reduce the heat to medium and simmer for 1 to 1¹/4 hours. Remove the tripe and let it cool a bit. Then cut it into 2 x ¹/4-inch strips. Set aside.

3. In a large flameproof casserole, heat the olive oil over medium heat. Add the pancetta and cook, stirring, until lightly browned, about 3 minutes. Add the butter, onions, leek, carrots, and celery, and stir to coat the vegetables with the oil. Reduce the heat to medium and cook the vegetables, stirring occasionally, until softened, about 10 minutes.

4. Add the tripe, wine, beef broth, tomatoes, and salt and pepper to taste, and bring to a boil. Reduce the heat and simmer for about 30 minutes to blend the flavors. Add the beans and cook for another 5 minutes.

WINE SUGGESTION: AGLIANICO DEL VULTURE

NOTE: The dish improves with time—make it a day or two before serving.

MOUNTAIN LAMB SCALOPPINE WITH FIGS AND HONEY

Todd English, who with his wife, Oliva, runs the small chain of Olives restaurants, is never at a loss for adapting a culinary idea, and this one is based on a dish he'd seen on a menu only once. This sumptuous dish, with its taste notes from the Middle East, might very well have found favor at the table of a wealthy Renaissance nobleman or Venetian trader.

In his cookbook *The Olives Table*, Todd insists that "it is important to buy very lean lamb, not the part with the sinews. Ask the butcher to cut it from the top round. And be sure not to overcook it—leave it medium-rare." This recipe is adapted from his book.

SERVES 4

FOR THE LAMB
2 tablespoons fennel seeds
1 1/2 tablespoons finely chopped
   fresh ginger
2 teaspoons salt, preferably kosher
2 teaspoons freshly ground black
   pepper
1/2 cup all-purpose flour
1 tablespoon olive oil
1 1/2 pounds lamb scaloppine,
   scored with 1/8-inch-deep diagonal slits every 1 1/2 inches and
   pounded to 1 1/4-inch thickness
   (see headnote)

FOR THE FIG SAUCE
1 cup dried figs, quartered
Juice of 2 oranges
1 tablespoon chopped fresh ginger
1/2 cup honey
1/3 cup balsamic vinegar
4 bay leaves
2 teaspoons chopped fresh thyme
1 teaspoon toasted sesame oil
2 teaspoons Dijon mustard
3 tablespoons butter

1. Place the fennel seeds, ginger, salt, and pepper in a blender and process until ground fine. Blend in the flour, and place the mixture on a large plate.

2. Place a large cast-iron sauté pan over medium-high heat, and when it is smoking hot, add the olive oil. Dredge the lamb in the fennel mixture and add it to the pan, one piece at a time, making sure that the pan is hot prior to each addition. Cook the lamb in batches if necessary. Sauté until the edges begin to color, 2 to 3 minutes on each side. Remove the lamb from the pan and set aside.

3. Prepare the sauce: Combine 1 1/4 cups water with the figs and orange juice in a saucepan. Bring to a boil over medium-high heat and cook until the figs have softened and are plump, about 10 minutes. Add the ginger, honey, vinegar, bay leaves, chopped thyme, and sesame oil, stirring well after each addition. Cook until the mixture is reduced and syrupy, about 10 minutes.

The cherished, if highly stereotypical, figure of the fat Italian-American mamma—in this case the matriarch of the Di Costanzo family, celebrating New Year's in 1942 in their restaurant on New York's Mulberry Street. Notice that the bottle of imported Brolio Chianti—unavailable during the war—is from a 1935 vintage.

4. Remove the bay leaves and add the mustard and the butter. Add the lamb to the pan, and cook until it is just heated through, about 1 minute. Serve immediately.

WINE SUGGESTION:
RECIOTO DELLA VALPOLICELLA AMARONE

SAUTÉED BABY LAMB CHOPS WITH PARMIGIANO-REGGIANO

Baby lamb chops grilled over an open fire are called *scottaditti* in Italian, which means "finger burners," because you pick them up by the bone to eat them and supposedly burn your fingers. The following recipe also uses baby lamb chops and comes from one of the best Italian restaurants in the Midwest—Tony's, in St. Louis, Missouri.

SERVES 4 TO 6

FOR THE LAMB
Twelve ¾-inch-thick rib lamb
  chops (about 3 pounds in all)
Salt, preferably kosher
½ cup freshly grated Parmigiano-
  Reggiano cheese
2 large eggs
1 cup plain dry breadcrumbs
Olive oil, for sautéing

FOR THE SAUCE
1 tablespoon olive oil
3 garlic cloves, minced
3 large tomatoes, peeled (see
  Note, page 89), seeded, and
  chopped
½ teaspoon freshly ground black
  pepper
3 tablespoons thin strips of fresh
  mint leaves

1. Sprinkle the lamb chops with 1 teaspoon salt and the Parmigiano-Reggiano.

2. In a shallow bowl, lightly beat the eggs. Next to the bowl, place a sheet of wax paper and pour the breadcrumbs onto it. Dip the lamb chops into the egg mixture and then into the breadcrumbs, coating both sides. Set aside for 10 minutes to set the breadcrumbs.

3. Prepare the sauce: In a small saucepan, heat the 1 tablespoon olive oil over low heat. Add the garlic and cook, stirring, for 2 minutes. Add the tomatoes, salt to taste, and the pepper. Stir, and cook over medium-low heat for 5 minutes. Set aside.

4. Heat 2 large sauté pans over medium-high heat, and add enough olive oil to coat the bottoms of the pans. When the oil is hot, add the lamb chops and sauté for 3 to 5 minutes on each side, or to the desired degree of doneness.

5. While the chops are sautéing, reheat the tomato sauce. Stir the mint into the sauce.

6. Serve the chops immediately, with the sauce spooned over them.

WINE SUGGESTION: BAROLO

NOTE: When sautéing either meat or vegetables, maintain space between the pieces so that any liquid can evaporate and the food can brown nicely. If crowded, food tends to steam and does not brown well.

LAMB CHOPS WITH LEMON AND OLIVE SAUCE

Succulence is the guiding principle behind this dish, which echoes the flavors of Sicily and its Greek settlements.

SERVES 4

8 loin lamb chops, 1 to 1$^{1}/_{2}$ inches thick
Salt, preferably kosher
Freshly ground black pepper
5 tablespoons unsalted butter
2 garlic cloves, chopped
8 capers (rinsed if packed in salt), chopped
6 Calamata olives, pitted and thinly sliced

1$^{1}/_{2}$ teaspoons freshly grated lemon zest
$^{1}/_{4}$ cup dry white wine, such as Soave
$^{1}/_{4}$ cup freshly squeezed lemon juice
2 tablespoons chopped flat-leaf parsley

1. Season the lamb chops with salt and pepper.

2. In a large sauté pan, heat 1 tablespoon of the butter over high heat. When it is hot, add the chops and sauté until medium-rare, turning them once, 6 to 8 minutes. Transfer to a platter and keep warm.

3. In the same pan, heat 1 tablespoon of the butter over low heat. Add the garlic and cook, stirring, for 2 minutes. Stir in the capers, olives, lemon zest, and wine, and scrape up the brown bits from the bottom of the pan. Cook over medium-low heat until the liquid is reduced by half, 1 to 2 minutes. Add the lemon juice and parsley, and simmer for 1 minute. Remove from the heat, and whisk in the remaining 3 tablespoons butter, $1/2$ tablespoon at a time. Season with a little salt (it may be salty enough because of the capers and the olives) and pepper. Add any meat juice that has accumulated around the lamb chops to the sauce.

4. Serve 2 lamb chops per person, topped with some sauce.

WINE SUGGESTION:
CORVO ROSSO

VENISON STEW

Come winter, Italians love to eat game, and the availability of excellent fresh game in the United States gives us the edge over those who must rely on bringing back the meat from the woods. (See "Sources for Italian Foods" to locate game suppliers.)

Venison has its own distinctive flavor, and although a wild deer can taste pretty gamey, the farm-raised venison in this country has a mild sweetness to the meat, which is also much leaner than beef or lamb. This stews keeps well—and gets better—for several days in the refrigerator.

SERVES 4

3 tablespoons olive oil
1 large yellow onion, chopped
1 small leek, white and light green parts only, washed, split lengthwise, and thinly sliced
2 small carrots, chopped
1/2 celery stalk, chopped
3 garlic cloves, chopped
1-inch piece of fresh ginger, minced
1/2 cup chopped cilantro
2 1/2 to 3 pounds boneless venison, cut into 2- to 2 1/2-inch pieces

Salt, preferably kosher
Freshly ground black pepper
2 tablespoons all-purpose flour
1/3 cup peanut oil
1 1/2 cups full-bodied red wine, such as Chianti
1/2 cup canned Italian-style tomatoes, chopped, with juices
1 cup beef broth
1 sprig fresh thyme, or 1/2 teaspoon dried
1 bay leaf

1. In a large flameproof casserole, heat the olive oil over medium-high heat. Add the onion and cook, stirring, until it starts to color, 8 to 10 minutes. Add the leek, carrots, celery, garlic, ginger, and cilantro. Reduce the heat to medium and cook, stirring, for about 7 minutes, or until the vegetables soften. Set aside.

2. Season the venison pieces with salt and pepper to taste. Sprinkle them with the flour and toss to coat.

3. In a large sauté pan, heat half the peanut oil over high heat. When it is very hot, add half the venison pieces and sauté, tossing them to brown on all sides, 7 to 10 minutes. Remove from the heat, and transfer the venison to the casserole with the vegetables. Deglaze the sauté pan with 3 tablespoons water, scraping all the brown bits off the bottom of the pan, and transfer this liquid to the casserole. Wipe the pan, heat it again, and repeat the process with the remaining peanut oil and the other half of the venison.

4. Add the wine, tomatoes, beef broth, thyme, bay leaf, and salt and pepper to taste to the casserole. Set it over high heat, and when the mixture comes to a boil, reduce the heat to low and simmer, partially covered, for about 1 1/4 hours or until the meat is tender.

5. Scoop out about 1 1/2 cups of the sauce and vegetables, and puree in a food processor or blender. Transfer the puree back to the casserole. Adjust the seasonings and serve.

WINE SUGGESTION: VENEGAZZÙ

NOTE: This dish tastes better if made the day before.

Rack of Venison with Pureed Apples and Quince

Y ou may have to special-order a rack of venison from your butcher, but once you've tasted it, you'll want to keep a steady supply coming in. This is a really great meal, and the combination with the sweet Port, quince, apple, and honey makes it one of the best dishes in our collection—ideal for a winter's dinner.

Serves 4

¼ cup sugar
⅓ cup Port
1 small quince, peeled and cut into
    small cubes
1 small apple (Cortland,
    McIntosh, or Greening), peeled,
    cored, and cut into small cubes

½ tablespoon honey
1 venison rack (6 to 7 ribs)
Salt, preferably kosher
Freshly ground black pepper
3 tablespoons corn oil

1. Preheat the oven to 450°F.

2. In a medium-size saucepan, combine the sugar with ½ cup water. Bring to a boil, then reduce the heat and simmer until the sugar is dissolved, 1 to 2 minutes. Add the Port, quince, and apple. When it comes to a boil, reduce the heat, cover, and cook until the fruit is tender, about 15 minutes.

3. Transfer the fruit to a food processor or blender, and puree. Return the puree to the saucepan, stir in the honey, and set aside.

4. Season the venison with salt and pepper.

5. Heat a large ovenproof frying pan over high heat. When it is very hot, add the corn oil, and swirl it around to cover the bottom of the pan. Add the venison and cook until browned, turning once, 6 to 8 minutes.

6. Transfer the frying pan to the oven and roast the venison for 12 to 15 minutes for rare, or to taste. (If using a meat thermometer, cook to

an internal temperature of 120°F for rare.) Remove the venison from the pan and let it rest for 5 minutes.

7. Quickly reheat the fruit puree just before serving it with the venison.

8. Cut the venison into 8 pieces, and serve with the fruit puree on the side.

WINE SUGGESTION:
BRUNELLO DI MONTALCINO

Mark Millitello was one of the founders of the "New Floridian Cuisine" back in the 1980s, as chef-owner of Mark's Place in North Miami. Now he owns Mark's in Las Olas. He has never forgotten the lessons he learned in his home kitchen.

"There was a great simplicity to my grandmother's cooking, an unparalleled freshness. I remember she had the smallest, most old-fashioned refrigerator I'd ever seen. It held just one day's worth of groceries. Grandma would walk across the street every day to the Italian market and shop for food for that day's meal. She never pulled food from the freezer, always bought it fresh, cooked it fresh, and enjoyed it fresh at that day's meal. If she was making a risotto, the stock was made from scratch. When she made pasta, it was hand-rolled with a dowel on the kitchen table. If a dish involved meat, it would be butchered and ground to order.

"I have fond memories of her cooking, though she didn't have a large repertoire. It revolved around the seasons. Growing up in New York State, we learned to appreciate the summer harvest after long, brutal winters: sweet corn, sun-ripened tomatoes, and bitter greens like dandelions, picked from the yard.

"Since then Italian food in this country has evolved for several reasons. The first is the flood of information we now have about Italian cooking, whether from cookbooks, television, or travel. In this day and age we have an understanding of techniques, products, and, most important, how they vary from region to region. Thanks to air freight, we can overnight buffalo mozzarella from Naples, radicchio from Treviso, and truffles from Piedmont. But I will always remember the simplicity of my grandmother's cooking and her understated elegance, a respect for flavor and the seasons. Today I may have a great palette to work from, but I still aim for those principles my grandmother taught me."

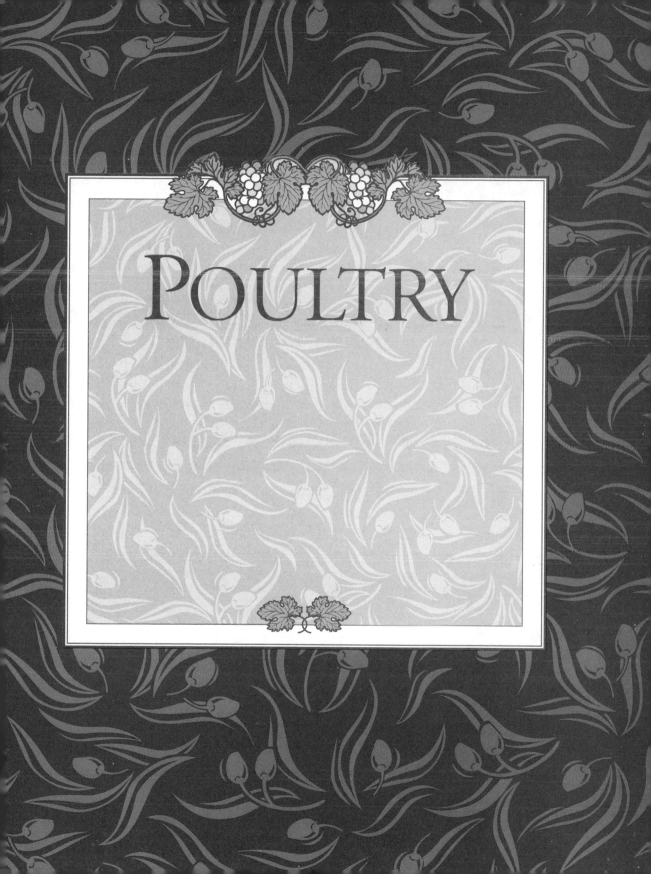

POULTRY

POULTRY

It's easy to assume that chicken—*pollo* (POH-loh)—has always been one of the most inexpensive, affordable, and readily available meats, but that was not the case at all until the American poultry industry revolutionized chicken production in the 1930s. Before then, the idea of "a chicken in every pot," first promulgated by the enlightened Henry IV of France back in 1589 and somewhat later used as a campaign slogan by Herbert Hoover in 1928, was something most people could only dream of. The tradition of Sunday chicken dinner was maintained only by those who could afford to do so.

A bright, modern, spanking-clean Italian-American grocery in St. Louis, Missouri, still carrying much the same kinds of food its antecedents did at the turn of the 20th century.

Before modern chicken production resulted in millions of birds being raised specifically for cooking, chickens were valued for their eggs, not their meat. Families, Italians and otherwise, did not kill the family chicken until it had outlived its usefulness as an egg layer, and by then it was a rather tough old bird fit only for the stewpot.

Today, however, there is a chicken in every pot, and on the grill, and in the oven, and in the sauté pan, several days a week, both here and abroad—though European chickens, still mostly free-range, are not produced in the quantities that American chickens are. Because of their diet, the Europeans birds tend to have less fat and more flavor.

Italian-American chicken recipes are, as you might expect, lavished with sauces, and in the case of the most famous Italian-American chicken dish—Chicken alla Parmigiana—with a crisp breading, a slice of mozzarella, and tomato sauce.

LEMON CHICKEN

This dish may share its name with the cloyingly sweet Chinese lemon chicken, but the Italian version is wonderfully piquant and can be either grilled or broiled. Make sure you slash the skin to allow the marinade to permeate the meat.

SERVES 4

FOR THE CHICKEN
One 3- to 3¹/2-pound chicken, cut in half
¹/3 cup olive oil
3 garlic cloves, minced
¹/4 cup freshly squeezed lemon juice
1 teaspoon freshly grated lemon zest
Salt, preferably kosher
Freshly ground black pepper

FOR THE LEMON SAUCE
¹/2 cup extra-virgin olive oil
¹/3 cup freshly squeezed lemon juice
2 garlic cloves, minced
1 teaspoon minced fresh oregano, or ¹/2 teaspoon dried
Salt, preferably kosher
Freshly ground black pepper
2 tablespoons chopped flat-leaf parsley

1. Using a sharp knife, cut ¹/8- to ¹/4-inch-deep diagonal slashes, 1 to 1¹/2 inches apart, through the skin and into the meat of the chicken.

2. In a large nonreactive bowl, combine the olive oil, garlic, lemon juice, lemon zest, salt, and plenty of pepper. Stir well and add the chicken. Coat the chicken well with the marinade. Cover the bowl, refrigerate, and let marinate for 4 to 6 hours.

3. Prepare the sauce: In a small bowl, combine the olive oil, lemon juice, garlic, oregano, and salt and pepper to taste. Mix well and set aside.

4. Prepare a barbecue grill or preheat the broiler.

When grilling chicken turn the pieces often, preferably every minute or two, in order to prevent scorching. Thick pieces like the legs should be cooked toward the center and then removed to the outer rim of the grill if they seem to be burning. Move the pieces around throughout the cooking process.

5. Remove the chicken from the bowl, reserving the marinade. Grill or broil the chicken, basting it occasionally with the reserved marinade, until done, 20 to 30 minutes (do not baste during the last 5 minutes of cooking). Cut the chicken into serving pieces.

6. In a small saucepan, heat the sauce until hot. Add the parsley and pour over the chicken pieces. Serve immediately.

WINE SUGGESTION: FRANCIACORTA ROSSO

CHICKEN ALLA FRANCESE

One of the real clichés of Italian-American cookery and unknown in most Italian kitchens, this can be a distressingly bland dish if it's not carefully tended while cooking. You want to avoid a steaminess in the texture and to achieve a lovely, light piquant flavor with a certain creaminess. We haven't a clue as to why it's called *"alla Francese"* (frahn-CHAY-seh), which means "French style."

SERVES 4

1 pound boneless, skinless chicken breast halves, each sliced into 3 thin diagonal slices
Salt, preferably kosher
Freshly ground black pepper
2 large eggs, beaten
3 tablespoons freshly grated Pecorino Romano cheese
1 tablespoon freshly grated Parmigiano-Reggiano cheese

All-purpose flour, for dredging
1/3 cup olive oil
1/3 cup dry white wine, such as Soave
1 cup chicken broth
1 small lemon, thinly sliced
3 tablespoons unsalted butter, softened

1. Place the chicken slices between 2 pieces of plastic wrap, and pound with a meat pounder to about 1/4-inch thickness. Season with salt and pepper.

2. In a shallow bowl, stir together the eggs, Pecorino, and Parmigiano. Next to the bowl, place a piece of wax paper and spread about 1/2 cup flour on it. Dip the chicken slices into the flour and then into the egg mixture, coating them thoroughly. Place the slices next to one another on a large piece of wax paper.

3. Heat the olive oil in a large sauté pan over medium-high heat. Add half of the chicken and sauté for about 2 minutes on each side, until golden brown. Remove to a platter and keep warm. Repeat with the remaining chicken, and add those slices to the first batch.

4. Drain the oil from the sauté pan, leaving any brown bits, and add the wine. Boil over medium heat for 1 minute. Then add the chicken broth and the lemon slices, and simmer over medium-high heat, scraping up the browned bits, until the liquid is reduced to about $^1/_3$ cup, 4 to 6 minutes. Remove the lemon slices, pressing out any liquid before throwing them out. Turn the heat to low, and gradually add the butter, incorporating it into the sauce. Adjust the seasoning. Add the chicken pieces, turn them in the sauce to coat them, and serve immediately.

WINE SUGGESTION: ORVIETO

CHICKEN PARMIGIANA

As with Eggplant Parmigiana (page 334), this is strictly an Italian-American concoction, and when made with care and the best ingredients, it is as welcome at the dinner table as it is in a hero sandwich.

SERVES 4

4 boneless, skinless chicken breast halves (1$^1/_2$ to 2 pounds total)
Salt, preferably kosher
Freshly ground black pepper
All-purpose flour, for dredging
1 cup plain dry breadcrumbs
2 large eggs, beaten with 1 table-spoon water

6 to 8 tablespoons olive oil
3 cups Galina's Meat Sauce or Marinara Sauce (page 126)
10 ounces mozzarella cheese, thinly sliced
$^1/_2$ cup freshly grated Parmigiano-Reggiano cheese

1. Preheat the oven to 350°F.

2. Separate the "tenderloins" from the larger, thicker muscles of the chicken breasts, and pound the larger pieces to flatten them a bit.

Season all the chicken pieces with salt and pepper. Dredge them in the flour, shaking off any excess. Place the breadcrumbs on a sheet of wax paper, and put the egg mixture in a shallow bowl. Coat the chicken pieces with the egg mixture and then with the breadcrumbs. Let them sit for 10 minutes, so the breadcrumbs will adhere well.

3. Heat a large sauté pan over medium-high heat, and add 3 tablespoons of the olive oil. When it is hot, add half of the chicken pieces and sauté until they are browned, 3 to 4 minutes. Turn them and sauté the other side for 3 to 4 minutes more, adding more oil if needed. Repeat with the rest of the chicken.

4. Spread ¹/₂ cup of the sauce over the bottom of an 8 x 12-inch baking dish, and arrange the chicken on top of the sauce. Cover with the rest of the sauce, then with the mozzarella slices. Sprinkle with the Parmigiano. Bake for 25 minutes, then finish for 2 to 3 minutes under the broiler to brown the top.

WINE SUGGESTION: VALPOLICELLA

Two generations of the Biancardi family that runs the meat market that bears their name on Arthur Avenue in the Bronx.

CHICKEN WITH PEPPERS AND BALSAMIC VINEGAR

Chicken is one of the most adaptable foods, but you don't want the natural flavor of the chicken to be masked by too many other flavors. This recipe is a perfect balance of tangy, sweet, and salty flavors with the crisp texture of the chicken itself. Browning the chicken well is the key to success here.

SERVES 4

6 tablespoons extra-virgin olive oil

1 large red bell pepper, cored and cut into 1 x ¼-inch strips

2 medium yellow onions, sliced

Salt, preferably kosher

Freshly ground black pepper

4 garlic cloves, minced

4 boneless, skinless chicken breast halves (1½ to 2 pounds total)

2 tablespoons dry white wine, such as Soave

6 tablespoons balsamic vinegar

1. In a large sauté pan, heat 3 tablespoons of the olive oil over medium-high heat. Add the bell pepper and onions, and cook, stirring several times, until softened and browned, about 10 minutes. Season with salt and pepper to taste, add the garlic, and cook, stirring, for another 2 minutes. Transfer the vegetables to a bowl and set aside.

2. Season the chicken breasts with salt and pepper. In the same sauté pan over medium heat, heat the remaining 3 tablespoons olive oil. When it is hot, add the chicken breasts and sauté until browned on both sides and cooked through, 5 to 8 minutes.

3. Add the vegetables to the chicken, and heat for 1 minute. Add the wine, scraping up the brown bits on the bottom of the pan. Adjust the seasonings. Add the balsamic vinegar, stir with the chicken, and cook for 1 minute. Serve immediately.

WINE SUGGESTION:
VALPOLICELLA

CHICKEN ALLA GIARDINIERA

With the introduction of radicchio to the United States, this presentation of chicken breasts topped with crisp salad greens has become typical of modern Italian-American cooking—whereas in Italy, the salad would be kept to the side, if served at all.

SERVES 4

FOR THE CHICKEN
4 boneless, skinless chicken breast
    halves (1½ to 2 pounds total)
Salt, preferably kosher
Freshly ground black pepper
2 large eggs, beaten with 1 table-
    spoon water
All-purpose flour, for dredging
1 cup plain dry breadcrumbs
4 tablespoons olive oil

FOR THE SALAD
½ sweet onion, such as Vidalia,
    cut in half, sliced, and sections
    separated into half-moons
2 tomatoes, cut into ¾-inch pieces
½ bunch arugula, leaves cut into
    thirds if large
1½ cups chopped radicchio
1 tablespoon red wine vinegar
1 tablespoon balsamic vinegar
3 tablespoons extra-virgin olive oil
Salt, preferably kosher
Freshly ground black pepper

1. Separate the "tenderloins" from the larger, thicker muscles of the chicken breasts, and slice the thicker pieces in half horizontally. Season the chicken pieces with salt and pepper. Dredge them in the flour, shaking off any excess. Place the breadcrumbs on a sheet of wax paper, and put the egg mixture in a shallow bowl. Coat the chicken pieces with the egg mixture and then with the breadcrumbs. Let the chicken sit for 10 minutes, so the breadcrumbs adhere well.

2. In a large sauté pan, heat 2 tablespoons of the olive oil over medium heat. Add the chicken (sauté in batches if necessary—do not crowd the pan) and sauté until browned, 3 to 4 minutes. Add the remaining 2 tablespoons olive oil, turn the chicken, and sauté on the other side for 3 to 4 minutes. Remove the chicken from the pan.

3. While the chicken is sautéing, prepare the salad: In a medium-size bowl, combine the onion, tomatoes, arugula, and radicchio. In a small bowl, stir together the red wine vinegar, balsamic vinegar, olive oil, salt, and a generous amount of pepper. Pour the dressing over the salad, and toss to mix.

4. Place some chicken on each plate, top with the salad, and serve immediately

WINE SUGGESTION: CIRÒ ROSSO

CHICKEN ALLA SCARPARIELLO

Another fancifully named dish—*alla scarpariello* (skahr-pah-ree-EH-loh) means "shoemaker's style." This should be a forceful, gutsy dish, with as much garlic as you desire to give it a real heftiness.

SERVES 4

One 3- to 3¹/2-pound chicken, cut
   into 8 pieces
Salt, preferably kosher
Freshly ground black pepper
¹/4 cup olive oil
1 medium yellow onion, sliced
4 ounces white mushrooms, sliced

6 garlic cloves, chopped
2 tablespoons dry white wine, such
   as Soave
3 tablespoons red wine vinegar
3 tablespoons chopped flat-leaf
   parsley

1. Pat the chicken dry and season the pieces with salt and pepper.

2. In a large sauté pan, heat the olive oil over medium-high heat. When it is hot, add the chicken pieces, skin side down. Sauté for 10 minutes, turning the pieces often. Then reduce the heat to medium and continue to cook until just done, another 5 to 8 minutes. Transfer the chicken to a platter.

3. Add the onion to the same sauté pan and cook over medium-high heat, stirring, until softened, about 3 minutes. Push the onion to the side a bit, and add the mushrooms. Cook, stirring, for 3 minutes. Then add the garlic and cook, tossing all the vegetables together, for 2 minutes.

4. Return the chicken to the pan and add the wine, scraping up the brown bits on the bottom of the pan. Finally, add the red wine vinegar and the parsley, and cook, stirring, for 1 to 2 minutes. Add more salt and plenty of pepper, and serve at once.

WINE SUGGESTION: CANNONAU

CHICKEN WITH OLIVES AND BASIL

This is as fragrant and savory a chicken dish as you'll find in southern Italy, with its saline and zesty notes of olive and lemon married to the bright greenness of the basil. Try always to use the freshest, youngest shoots of basil, avoiding any limp leaves.

SERVES 4

3 tablespoons olive oil
4 boneless, skinless chicken breast
    halves (1¹/2 to 2 pounds total),
    each cut into 3 pieces
Salt, preferably kosher
Freshly ground black pepper
1 garlic clove, minced
1 shallot, finely chopped
¹/2 cup dry white wine, such as
    Soave

¹/2 cup chicken broth
¹/2 cup chopped canned Italian-
    style tomatoes, drained
¹/4 cup sliced pitted Calamata
    olives
1 teaspoon freshly grated lemon
    zest
3 tablespoons unsalted butter
¹/4 cup thinly sliced fresh basil
    leaves

1. In a large sauté pan, heat the olive oil over medium heat. Season the chicken with salt and pepper, and sauté, turning the pieces to brown on all sides, until almost cooked through, 6 to 8 minutes. Transfer the pieces to a dish and set aside.

2. In the same pan, cook the garlic and shallot, over low heat, stirring, for 2 minutes. Add the wine, chicken broth, and tomatoes, and bring to a boil. Reduce the heat and simmer for 5 minutes. Add the olives, lemon zest, pepper to taste, and the chicken pieces. Simmer for about 2 minutes, or until the sauce has thickened. Depending on the saltiness of the olives, add salt after tasting the sauce.

3. Just before serving, stir in the butter and the basil.

WINE SUGGESTION: NEBBIOLO D'ALBA

CHICKEN BREASTS WITH MUSHROOM SAUCE

What makes this dish more than just chicken with mushrooms is the *mixture* of mushrooms—few of which would have been available in the local market even ten years ago.

SERVES 4

1 ounce dried porcini mushrooms
4 boneless, skinless chicken breast
* halves (1¹/2 to 2 pounds total)*
Salt, preferably kosher
Freshly ground black pepper
5 tablespoons unsalted butter
2 tablespoons olive oil

12 ounces mixed mushrooms
* (white, cremini, shiitake, or*
* others), sliced*
2 shallots, chopped
²/3 cup dry white wine, such as
* Soave*
²/3 cup chicken broth
¹/2 cup heavy cream

1. In a small bowl, combine the porcini mushrooms with ²/3 cup hot water. Set aside to soak for 20 minutes. Then squeeze the liquid from the porcini, reserving the liquid, and chop the porcini. Strain the liquid through a cheesecloth-lined sieve. Set the porcini and the strained liquid aside.

2. Season the chicken pieces with salt and pepper.

3. Heat a large sauté pan over medium heat, and add 2 tablespoons of the butter and 1 tablespoon of the olive oil. When it is hot, add the chicken breasts and sauté until almost done, 4 to 6 minutes. Transfer them to a platter and keep warm.

4. Heat the same pan over medium-high heat, and add the remaining 3 tablespoons butter and 1 tablespoon olive oil. When it is hot, add the fresh mushrooms and cook, tossing often, until lightly browned, about 5 minutes. Season with salt and pepper to taste.

5. Add the shallots and the porcini to the sauté pan and cook, stirring, for another 2 minutes. Add the wine, chicken broth, and the strained porcini liquid. Bring to a boil, scraping up any brown bits on the bottom of the pan. Reduce the heat to medium and simmer until the liquid is reduced by about a third, 3 to 5 minutes.

6. Add the cream and simmer until slightly reduced and thickened, about 2 minutes. Return the chicken breasts and any accumulated liquid to the pan, and simmer for 2 minutes. Adjust the seasonings, and serve.

WINE SUGGESTION: ORVIETO

ROAST CHICKEN
WITH AL'S STUFFING

My father, Al Mariani, used to make this stuffing only once a year, for the Thanksgiving turkey—a delightful marriage of American traditions with Italian flavorings. But it is just as good year-round as stuffing for a chicken.

SERVES 4

1 cup Italian bread cubes (¹/4-inch pieces)
5 tablespoons olive oil
1 medium yellow onion, chopped
4 ounces sweet Italian sausage, casing removed, meat cut up
¹/4 cup chopped salami
³/4 cup chopped mozzarella cheese
2 tablespoons chopped flat-leaf parsley

¹/4 teaspoon red pepper flakes, or to taste
Salt, preferably kosher
Freshly ground black pepper
1 large egg, beaten
2 tablespoons unsalted butter
One 3¹/2- to 4-pound chicken, rinsed and patted dry

1. Preheat an oven to 325°F.

2. Place the bread cubes on a baking sheet and bake for 8 to 10 minutes, until lightly toasted. Set aside.

3. In a medium-size sauté pan, heat 3 tablespoons of the olive oil over medium heat. Add the onion and cook, stirring occasionally, until softened, about 5 minutes. Add the sausage and cook, breaking it up, for 8 minutes. Transfer the mixture to a large bowl and let cool.

4. When the onion-sausage mixture is cool, add the bread cubes, salami, mozzarella, parsley, red pepper flakes, and salt and pepper to taste. Mix well. Add the egg and mix well.

5. Preheat the oven to 425°F.

6. Fill the chicken with the stuffing, and close the cavity by overlapping the skin at the opening and securing it with 2 or 3 toothpicks.

7. In a roasting pan, heat the remaining 2 tablespoons olive oil and the butter over medium heat. Place the chicken in the pan, breast side down, and brush it with the hot fat. Place in the oven and roast for 20 minutes, basting every 10 minutes. Then carefully turn the chicken over onto its back, baste, and continue roasting and occasionally basting for another 40 minutes, or until the juices from the thigh run clear. Remove from the oven, let rest for 10 minutes, and then cut up and serve.

WINE SUGGESTION: NEBBIOLO

In roasting poultry, the pan should generally be only slightly larger than the bird itself. This allows the bird to cook more evenly and concentrates the juices. A large roasting pan is in order, though, in the case of a big bird like a goose, which throws off a tremendous volume of fat that must be drained off once or twice during the cooking process.

CHICKEN TETRAZZINI

Here is another of those Italian-American dishes created to honor a famous Italian, in this case Luisa Tetrazzini (1871–1940), a coloratura soprano who toured widely and with immense success in the United States. The dish is first mentioned in print in 1931 and may have originated in San Francisco. In her autobiography, *My Life in Song*, the rotund singer wrote of her own eating habits: "I eat the plainest of food always, and, naturally, being Italian, I prefer the foods of my native land. . . . I allow the tempting pastry, the rich and over-spiced patty to pass untouched, consoling myself with fruit and fresh vegetables." Perhaps so, but it's difficult to imagine the diva passing up a dish as scrumptious as this—which, incidentally, is often made with turkey.

SERVES 6

8 tablespoons (1 stick) unsalted
  butter
1 medium yellow onion, chopped
1/4 cup finely chopped celery
1/4 cup all-purpose flour
1 1/2 cups heavy cream
1/2 cup milk
1 1/3 cups chicken broth
Salt, preferably kosher

Freshly ground black pepper
1 cup freshly grated Parmigiano-
  Reggiano cheese
3 boneless, skinless chicken breast
  halves (about 1 1/2 pounds total),
  cut into 3/4-inch cubes
1 pound spaghetti
1/2 cup plain dry breadcrumbs

1. Preheat the oven to 400°F.

2. In a large saucepan, heat 2 tablespoons of the butter over low heat. Add the onion and celery and cook, stirring, until softened but not browned, about 8 minutes.

3. Add 3 more tablespoons butter to the pan, and heat. Then add the flour and cook, stirring, for about 3 minutes to thoroughly cook the flour. Add the cream and the milk all at once, increase the heat to medium, and stir constantly until the sauce thickens and starts to simmer. Reduce the heat and simmer for 3 minutes. Add the chicken broth and bring to a boil. Season with salt and pepper to taste, and stir in 1/3 cup of the Parmigiano. Set aside.

4. In a large sauté pan, heat 1 tablespoon of the butter over medium

heat. Season the chicken pieces with salt and pepper, and add them to the pan. Sauté, stirring occasionally, until the pieces turn white and are almost cooked through but not browned, 4 to 5 minutes.

5. In a large stockpot, bring 5 quarts water to a boil. Add 2 teaspoons salt and the spaghetti and cook until the pasta is just al dente. Drain, and toss with the remaining 2 tablespoons butter.

6. Spread the spaghetti out in a 9 x 13 x 2-inch baking pan. Arrange the chicken pieces evenly over the spaghetti, and pour the sauce over the top.

7. In a small bowl, mix the remaining ²/₃ cup Parmigiano with the breadcrumbs. Spread this evenly over the chicken and spaghetti. Bake for 15 minutes. Finish for 2 to 3 minutes under the broiler to brown the top.

WINE SUGGESTION: TOCAI FRIULANO

CHICAGO-STYLE CHICKEN VESUVIO

As *Chicago* magazine has noted, "by legend, chicken Vesuvio is a Chicago invention—though the details are hard to nail down." The dish has been around since the 1940s, and there's a recipe for it in *The Italian Cookbook*, published by the Culinary Arts Institute of Chicago in 1954, but the creator of the dish has never been satisfactorily identified. The name of the dish obviously refers to Mount Vesuvius near Naples, and speculation has it that the smoke that rises in the air while cooking the dish is the reason for the name. Others say that the arrangement of the potatoes at the rim of the casserole gives it the look of a volcano. Whatever, it is a simple dish to make—as long as you don't mind too much smoke in the kitchen.

Chicago magazine also lists its favorite local places to find the dish, including Giannotti's Steak House and Harry Caray's in town, and the Erie cafe in Skokie.

SERVES 4

¹/4 cup peanut oil
One 3-pound chicken, cut into 8
    pieces, rinsed, and patted dry
Salt, preferably kosher
Freshly ground black pepper
¹/4 cup olive oil
4 medium all-purpose potatoes,
    cut into 1¹/2-inch pieces

4 garlic cloves, chopped
¹/2 cup dry white wine, such as
    Soave
1¹/4 cups chicken broth
¹/2 rounded teaspoon dried oregano
1 cup frozen peas, thawed
2 tablespoons unsalted butter

My mother, Renee Mariani, who was second-generation, always prided herself as being raised an American first, with Italy far in her background. This caused a bit of a problem when it came to marrying my father.

"When Al asked me to marry him he made it clear that it was only with the approval of his mother, Rosa. She was an intimidating woman. She refused to learn English and asked Al, 'Why do I have to learn English? Why doesn't she learn Italian?' She was very stern. Before meeting her I really had been quite spoiled and never cooked much of anything. But she told me that I'd better learn to cook Italian food for her son or the marriage was off. So after a period of trial and error I learned how to make marinara sauce, polenta, baccalà, and all the favorite dishes his mother served him. She blessed the marriage as soon as she was sure I could cook."

J.M.

1. Preheat the oven to 450°F.

2. In a large ovenproof skillet, heat the peanut oil over medium-high heat. Season the chicken with salt and pepper. When the oil is hot, add the chicken pieces and brown them well on both sides, about 8 minutes. Remove the chicken from the pan and set aside.

3. In a large sauté pan, heat the olive oil over medium-high heat. Add the potatoes and cook until browned on all sides, about 10 minutes. Set aside.

4. Drain most of the oil from the skillet you used for the chicken. Add the garlic and cook over low heat, stirring, for about 2 minutes. Add the wine, chicken broth, and oregano, and bring to a boil, scraping up all the brown bits on the bottom of the pan. Remove from the heat.

5. Arrange the chicken and potatoes in a 9 x 13-inch roasting pan. Pour the flavored broth over, and roast in the oven for 20 minutes, or until done.

6. Place the chicken on a platter, surround it with the potatoes, and keep warm. Add the peas to the roasting pan and simmer in the pan juices for 3 to 4 minutes. Adjust the seasonings, stir in the butter, and pour over the chicken.

WINE SUGGESTION:
MONTEPULCIANO D'ABRUZZO

ROCK CORNISH GAME HENS WITH FIGS

This dish could certainly be made with chicken, but we find that Rock Cornish game hens get better and better in this country—plump, succulent, and possessed of their own flavor. By the way, the Rock Cornish game hen is, despite its English-sounding name and the fact that America had no indigenous chickens, an American breed originally developed from a Plymouth Rock and a Cornish game cock, and was at first called "Indian game fowl."

SERVES 4

2 Rock Cornish game hens (about 3¹/₂ pounds total), cut in half, backbone removed
4 tablespoons olive oil
Salt, preferably kosher
Freshly ground black pepper
¹/₄ cup chopped pancetta
¹/₂ cup chopped shallots
8 fresh sage leaves, chopped

1¹/₂ teaspoons chopped fresh rosemary, or ¹/₂ teaspoon dried
7 dried figs, cut into ¹/₄-inch pieces
¹/₂ cup Marsala
1 cup chicken broth
3 tablespoons chopped flat-leaf parsley
2 tablespoons butter

1. Preheat the oven to 400°F.

2. Pat the Cornish hens dry, rub them with 1 tablespoon of the olive oil, and season them with salt and pepper.

3. In a large sauté pan, heat 1 tablespoon of the oil over medium-high heat. Sauté the Cornish hens, skin side down, until nicely browned, 4 to 6 minutes. Then turn them over and brown on the other side, 4 to 6 minutes. Transfer them to a large roasting pan and roast in the oven for 30 minutes.

4. Meanwhile, heat the remaining 2 tablespoons olive oil in a medium-size sauté pan over medium heat. Add the pancetta and sauté until lightly browned, 2 to 3 minutes. Add the shallots and cook, stirring, for another 2 minutes. Add the sage, rosemary, figs, and Marsala. Bring to a boil, and season with salt and pepper to taste. Add the chicken

broth and simmer over medium-low heat until the sauce has reduced a bit, about 10 minutes. Keep warm.

5. When the Cornish hens are done, transfer them to a platter. Set the roasting pan over medium heat, add 2 tablespoons water, and scrape up all the brown bits on the bottom of the pan. Add this to the pancetta-fig mixture. Stir in the parsley. Add the butter, ¹/2 tablespoon at a time, stirring after each addition. Adjust the seasonings, and serve the sauce with the Cornish hens.

WINE SUGGESTION:
RECIOTO DELLA VALPOLICELLA AMARONE

ROAST CHICKEN
WITH SAUSAGE STUFFING

More ink has been spent on the subject of roasting chicken than any food we can think of, yet it's very easy to accomplish a burnished, crispy skin and a moist bird, as this recipe shows.

The stuffing adds to the appeal of this dish, and with the balsamic vinegar–laced sauce, this roast chicken becomes something quite special, suitable for even the most lavish dinner.

SERVES 4

FOR THE CHICKEN
3 tablespoons olive oil
3 tablespoons unsalted butter, softened
1 small yellow onion, chopped
6 ounces sweet Italian sausage, removed from its casing and cut up
¹/2 cup plain fresh breadcrumbs (see Note, page 239)
¹/4 cup chopped dried apricots (¹/4-inch pieces)
¹/4 cup chopped flat-leaf parsley

¹/4 teaspoon dried oregano
Salt, preferably kosher
Freshly ground black pepper
¹/3 cup chicken broth
One 3¹/2- to 4-pound chicken, preferably free-range

FOR THE SAUCE
1 tablespoon balsamic vinegar
¹/3 cup chicken broth
Salt, preferably kosher
Freshly ground black pepper
2 tablespoons unsalted butter

1. Preheat the oven to 450°F.

2. In a medium-size sauté pan, heat 1 tablespoon of the olive oil and 1 tablespoon of the butter over medium heat. Add the onion and cook, stirring, until soft, about 5 minutes. Transfer the onion to a medium-size bowl.

3. In the same sauté pan, heat 1 tablespoon olive oil. Add the sausage and sauté, tossing and breaking the sausage into smaller pieces, until browned and cooked through, about 8 minutes. Transfer the sausage to the bowl with the onions.

4. Add the breadcrumbs, apricots, parsley, oregano, salt and pepper to taste, and the chicken broth to the sausage mixture, and stir to blend. Let the stuffing cool.

5. Season the chicken cavity with salt and pepper, and fill it with the stuffing. Close the cavity by overlapping the skin and securing it with 2 toothpicks.

6. Place the chicken in a large roasting pan, and rub the remaining 2 tablespoons butter and the remaining 1 tablespoon olive oil over it. Season it with salt and pepper, and roast in the oven for 1 hour, basting the chicken with the pan drippings every 15 minutes.

7. Remove the chicken from the roasting pan and place it on a large cutting board.

8. While the chicken is resting, prepare the sauce: Add the balsamic vinegar and chicken broth to the roasting pan, and set over medium heat. Heat the sauce, scraping up all the brown bits on the bottom of the pan. Season with salt and pepper. Remove from the heat, and stir in the butter.

9. Cut the chicken into 8 pieces, and place them on a platter with the stuffing off to one side. Strain the sauce over the chicken pieces, and serve.

WINE SUGGESTION:
BONARDA

CHICKEN LIVERS
AND SCRAMBLED EGGS

This is the kind of breakfast dish that would send my great-grandfather off to work in the morning, and my mother would make it for me on occasional weekends. With a salad on the side, it also works as a fine lunch dish—or it can even be a first course at dinner.

—J.M.

SERVES 4

1/4 cup olive oil
1 yellow onion, minced
12 ounces chicken livers, cut into
  small morsels

1 tablespoon unsalted butter
6 large eggs, well beaten
Salt, preferably kosher
Freshly ground black pepper

JEWISH FOOD, ITALIAN-STYLE

Some of the finest contemporary writers on Italian food are Jews—including Arthur Schwartz, Faith Willinger, Fred Plotkin, and Carol Field, a fifth-generation San Franciscan of Jewish-Italian heritage whose book Celebrating Italy (1990) is one of the most outstanding volumes on food culture ever written. In it she includes details of a seder of the kind held in Rome (where Jews were confined to a ghetto until 1848), whose menu included Roman dishes like the air-dried beef called bresaola, fried artichokes, risotti with peas or other vegetables, the fruit-and-nut mixture called haroset, and a Sephardic dish called scacchi (SKAH-kee), a form of vegetable lasagna made with matzo instead of pasta—a dish she still enjoys at her annual seders in San Francisco.

Another Italian-Jew, Edda Servi Machlin, whose family can be traced back 2,000 years in Italy, wrote the lovely, authoritative Classic Cuisine of the Italian Jews (1981), in which she quotes an old Italian adage, "Vesta da Turco e mangia da Ebreo," which means "Dress like a Turk and eat like a Jew." She explains: "We are thus exhorted by the Italians—who created a cuisine that is the delight of gourmets the world over—to become acquainted with the cuisine of the Italian Jews if we really would like to eat well." As Machlin notes, the food of the Italian Jews differed considerably from that of Eastern European Jews, so that the Italian Jews who emigrated to the United States would have been wholly unfamiliar with the traditional foods consumed by the majority of Jews who settled in New York's Lower East Side.

1. In a medium-size skillet, heat the olive oil over medium heat. When it is hot, add the onion and cook, stirring, until it begins to turn golden, about 10 minutes.

2. Add the chicken livers and sauté until they are lightly browned and are almost cooked to the desired degree of doneness, about 3 minutes.

3. Add the butter to the skillet, and then add the eggs, combining them with the liver and onion. Add salt and pepper to taste, and cook until the eggs are scrambled to the desired degree of doneness. Serve immediately.

WINE SUGGESTION: PINOT GRIGIO

BUFFALO CHICKEN WINGS

If ever there was an unexpected food phenomenon, it's Buffalo chicken wings. The wholly documented story goes like this: On the night of October 4, 1964, at the Anchor Bar in Buffalo, New York, owner Teressa Bellissimo was asked by her son, Dominic, and his friends for something to nibble on. Having received an oversupply of chicken wings, Teressa deep-fried some, dipped them in margarine, then concocted a hot sauce and put blue cheese dressing on the side. This being Friday night and the boys being Catholics, they had to wait until midnight to dive in. The dish became an immediate sensation locally, and the City of Buffalo declared July 29, 1977, "Chicken Wing Day" to honor the Bellissimos' contribution to Italian-American snack food.

SERVES 4

FOR THE BLUE CHEESE
DRESSING
3/4 cup mayonnaise
1/4 cup sour cream
1 garlic clove, minced
1 1/2 tablespoons freshly squeezed
   lemon juice
1/2 teaspoon sugar
Freshly ground black pepper
1/3 cup crumbled blue cheese

FOR THE WINGS
24 chicken wings
6 cups corn oil, for frying
Salt, preferably kosher
4 tablespoons (1/2 stick) unsalted
   butter
2 to 3 tablespoons Louisiana-style
   hot sauce
1 1/2 tablespoons cider vinegar
2 celery stalks, cut in half and
   then sliced lengthwise into sticks

1. To make the dressing; Combine the mayonnaise, sour cream, garlic, lemon juice, sugar, and pepper in a medium-size bowl, and mix well. Add the cheese and mix it in gently.

2. Rinse the chicken wings and pat them dry. Cut off and discard the tips. Cut the wing at the joint into 2 pieces.

3. Pour the oil into a heavy 10-inch skillet; it should be about 2¹/₂ inches deep. Heat it to 380°F (use a deep-frying thermometer, or test the heat by dipping the tip of a wing into the oil—if it sizzles immediately, the oil is hot enough). Add half of the chicken wings and fry until they are golden and crispy, 5 to 8 minutes. (If necessary, cook a smaller batch—if you crowd the wings in the pan, they will not brown well.) Using a slotted spoon, remove the wings from the oil. Set them on paper towels to drain, and keep warm. Repeat with the remaining wings. Season the wings with a little salt.

4. In a small saucepan, heat the butter and hot sauce over medium heat. Remove from the heat, and add the cider vinegar. Pour this sauce over the chicken wings, and toss to coat well. Serve with the celery sticks and blue cheese dressing on the side.

WINE SUGGESTION: BRUSCO DEI BARBI

NOTE: Use salt sparingly. If the blue cheese is salty enough, you may not need any salt on the wings.

CHICKEN ROLLATINE WITH SAUSAGE

Rollatine (roh-lah-TEE-neh) refers to any ingredient—meat, chicken, seafood, or vegetable—that has been rolled up and secured tightly. Usually it is stuffed with other ingredients or herbs. Our recipe is very full flavored, very satisfying, and goes a long way. Serve polenta alongside. The chicken tastes even better the next day.

SERVES 4

4 boneless, skinless chicken breast
   halves (1½ to 2 pounds total)
6 tablespoons olive oil
1 medium yellow onion, finely
   chopped
8 ounces sweet Italian sausage,
   removed from its casing and cut
   into pieces
1 large garlic clove, minced
1 tablespoon capers (rinsed if
   packed in salt), chopped
1 anchovy (rinsed if packed in
   salt), minced

2 tablespoons dried currants
2 tablespoons minced flat-leaf
   parsley
Salt, preferably kosher
Freshly ground black pepper
6 tablespoons freshly grated
   Pecorino Romano cheese
4 tablespoons (½ stick) unsalted
   butter
½ cup dry white wine, such as
   Soave

1. Slice each chicken breast in half horizontally. Place each piece between 2 pieces of plastic wrap and pound with a flat pounder until it has thinned out. Set the chicken aside.

2. In a medium-size sauté pan, heat 4 tablespoons of the olive oil over medium-high heat. Add the onion and cook, stirring, for 2 minutes. Add the sausage and cook, cutting it up with a fork or spatula as it cooks, until browned, about 5 minutes. Add the garlic, capers, and anchovy, and cook, stirring, for another 2 minutes. Stir in the currants and parsley. Add 2 tablespoons water, and scrape up any brown bits on the bottom of the pan. Season the mixture with salt and pepper, transfer to a bowl, and let cool for 10 minutes.

3. When the sausage mixture has cooled, mix in the Pecorino. Divide the filling among the 8 chicken slices. Roll each one up, securing it with 2 toothpicks. Season with salt and pepper.

4. In a large sauté pan, heat the remaining 2 tablespoons olive oil and 2 tablespoons of the butter over medium-high heat. Add the chicken *rollatine* and sauté, turning them to brown on all sides, 5 to 8 minutes. Add the wine and scrape up all the brown bits on the bottom of the pan. Reduce the heat to medium and simmer until slightly reduced, about 2 minutes. Stir in the remaining 2 tablespoons butter, ½ tablespoon at a time. Serve with the sauce spooned over.

WINE SUGGESTION: SALICE SALENTINO

CORNISH HENS
ALLA DIAVOLO

In America, the term *fra diavolo* (FRAH dee-AH-voh-loh), which means "brother Devil," came to be associated with spicy hot pepper sauces in which seafood was cooked (see page 233). But back in Italy, *alla diavolo* ("Devil's style") refers to a dish heavily seasoned with coarsely ground black pepper, as here. This is a great dish to make on the grill outdoors.

SERVES 2 TO 4

2 Rock Cornish game hens, rinsed and patted dry
2 tablespoons extra-virgin olive oil
2 teaspoons salt, preferably kosher
1 tablespoon freshly ground black pepper

3 tablespoons chopped flat-leaf parsley
Juice of 1 lemon
1 lemon, cut into 4 wedges
3 tablespoons extra-virgin olive oil

1. Cut each Cornish hen in half from neck to tail and remove the backbone. Press down on the halves to flatten them a bit.

2. Place the Cornish hens in a shallow bowl, and toss them with the olive oil. Season with the salt and pepper, and sprinkle with the parsley and lemon juice. Cover the bowl with plastic wrap, and refrigerate for 4 to 6 hours.

3. Preheat the broiler.

4. Remove the Cornish hen halves from the marinade (reserve the marinade), and place them, skin side up, in a large roasting pan. Broil 6 inches from the the heat for 10 minutes, brushing occasionally with the marinade during the first 5 minutes. Turn the hens over, brush once with the marinade, and broil for another 5 minutes.

5. Turn off the broiler and set the oven heat to 425°F. Turn the Cornish hens skin side up, and roast for about 8 minutes, or until done.

6. Arrange the hens on a platter, and drizzle the 3 tablespoons olive oil over them. Place the lemon wedges alongside, and serve.

WINE SUGGESTION: MONTEPULCIANO D'ABRUZZO

QUAIL WITH APPLE-FIG COMPOTE

Perfect for autumn and early winter, the quail's delicate flavor is enhanced by the sweetness of the fruit in this dish.

SERVES 4

6 tablespoons (³/4 stick) unsalted butter
2 Greening or Granny Smith apples, peeled, cored, and each cut into 6 slices
³/4 teaspoon Szechuan peppercorns, roasted and crushed (see Note)
3 dried figs, chopped

¹/3 cup dry red wine, such as Chianti
¹/4 cup balsamic vinegar
²/3 cup chicken broth
Salt, preferably kosher
8 quail
Freshly ground black pepper
2 tablespoons olive oil

1. In a medium-size sauté pan, heat 2 tablespoons of the butter over medium-high heat. Add the apples and sauté until the slices are browned on both sides, 8 to 10 minutes. Add the figs, wine, balsamic vinegar, and chicken broth. Bring to a boil, then reduce the heat to medium and simmer until the liquid is reduced by half, 6 to 8 minutes. Season with a little salt. Remove from the heat.

2. Rinse the quail under cold water and pat dry. Cut them down the spine and butterfly them open, cutting down a little at the breast so they stay open. Season with salt and pepper to taste.

3. In a sauté pan that is large enough to hold the quail without crowding them (or 2 sauté pans), heat 2 tablespoons of the butter and the olive oil over medium-high heat. When it is very hot, add the quail, skin side down, and sauté until nicely browned and crisp, about 4 minutes. Then turn them over and sauté for another 4 minutes. They should be just done—do not overcook. The total cooking time will be 8 to 10 minutes.

4. Just before serving, reheat the fruit compote briefly. Then remove it from the heat and stir in the remaining 2 tablespoons of butter, ¹/2 tablespoon at a time. Serve 2 quail per person, with some compote on the side.

WINE SUGGESTION: SAN GIORGIO

325

NOTE: To roast Szechuan peppercorns, put them in a small preheated saucepan over medium-high heat and roast, shaking the pan often, until they release their aroma, 3 to 4 minutes. Then place them in a mortar and crush with a pestle, or place them on a board and crush them with the side of a wide knife.

Former New York Governor Mario Cuomo's parents immigrated from Salerno. Andrea and Immaculata Cuomo arrived in the late 1920s with a "burning desire to climb out of poverty on the strength of their labor. At first, my father went to work in Jersey City, New Jersey, as a ditchdigger. After Momma and Poppa had three children, Poppa realized he needed to earn more money to support his growing family. So he opened a small Italian-American grocery store in South Jamaica, in the New York City borough of Queens.

"By the time I was born in 1932, the store was open 24 hours a day, and it seemed as if Momma and Poppa were working there all the time. I can still see them waiting on customers and stocking shelves. And I can still smell and see and almost taste the food that brought in the customers: the provolone, the Genoa salami, the prosciutto, the fresh bread, the fruits and vegetables. Our store gave our neighbors a delicious taste of Italy in New York." —From Mario M. Cuomo's introduction to Dorothy and Thomas Hoobler, The Italian-American Family Album

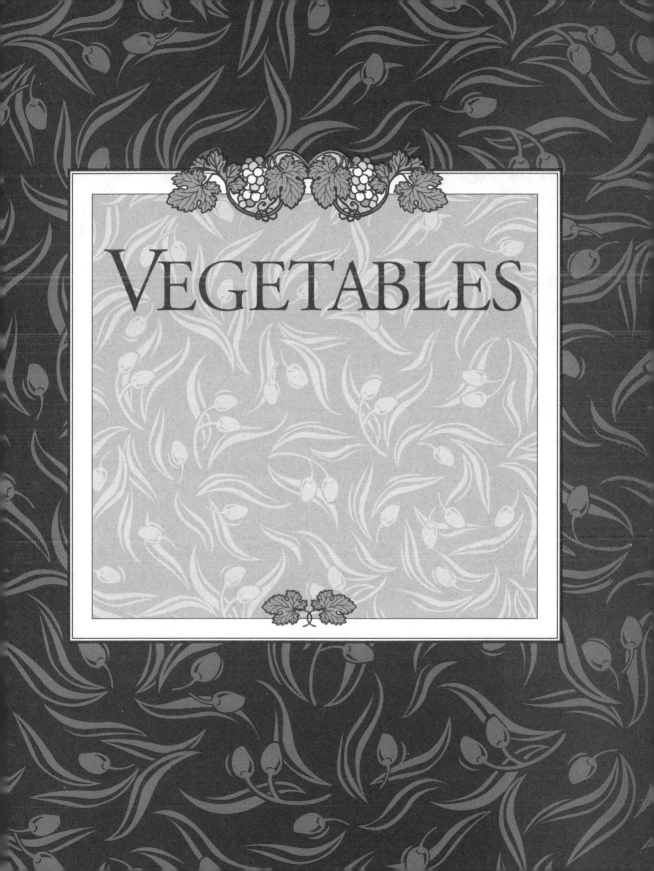

VEGETABLES

VEGETABLES

Vegetarianism is most certainly not among Italians' favorite philosophies, yet for much of Italian history most Italians were forced to subsist principally on a vegetable and grain diet—even the Roman legions, for whom meat and fish were a rarity as they fought their way through Europe building an empire.

For millennia poverty and scarcity made vegetables, fruits, and grains the primary part of the Italian diet. Meats like beef, veal, and lamb were almost unknown to most Italians prior to the twentieth century. Chickens were kept for their eggs, not their flesh, and few peasants had more than a single hog, if any. Italians therefore had to be very resourceful in making a vegetable diet palatable day after day, and the results, from north to south, are wondrous.

Vegetable cookery is at the heart of all Italian cuisine, for the vegetables buoy up so many of their finest dishes.

Italians eat vegetables at the beginning of the meal, as antipasti, and in pastas and soups. Side orders of vegetables, served with the main course, don't go much beyond roast potatoes or perhaps a little spinach with lemon.

Americans, on the other hand, treat vegetables more as a side dish than as a principal course or as a salad. For this reason Italian-American restaurants long ago started offering the options of having either a potato croquette, some escarole or broccoli, or a portion of spaghetti alongside a main course, and often served a salad before the pasta course.

These days such traditions have been blurred, and Italians, Italian-Americans, and Americans in general have greater access to a wider range of good-quality vegetables—including once rare varieties like radicchio and fava beans—so the inclination to serve them as a main dish or side dish has grown measurably in our health-conscious age.

SPINACH WITH PIGNOLI

I n Italy this might well be served as a room-temperature antipasto, and it is quite delicious that way. But we've found that it makes a superior side vegetable to just about any simply grilled meat, poultry, or seafood.

SERVES 4

6 tablespoons extra-virgin olive oil
2 garlic cloves, minced
1¹/2 to 2 pounds fresh spinach, rinsed, spin-dried, and very coarsely chopped
5 tablespoons dark raisins

Salt, preferably kosher
Pinch of sugar
¹/2 teaspoon red pepper flakes
2 tablespoons unsalted butter
¹/4 cup toasted pignoli (pine nuts)

1. In a pot that is large enough to hold the spinach, heat the olive oil over low heat. Add the garlic and cook, stirring, for 2 minutes. Add the spinach, raisins, salt to taste, sugar, and red pepper. Toss, cover, and cook over medium heat until the spinach is wilted, 3 to 4 minutes.

2. Add the butter, in pieces, and the pignoli, stir to mix, and serve.

WINE SUGGESTION: TOCAI

OVEN-ROASTED TOMATOES

For reasons that escape us, so-called sun-dried tomatoes became very trendy in America in the 1980s, although they were never particularly venerated in Italy. The problem is that they are far too dry and chewy and therefore lose any flavor or appeal they might otherwise possess. This is a better alternative to sun-dried tomatoes purchased in stores. Here the cook makes the decision about the degree of dryness, the color remains vivid red, and the flavor is fresh and very intense.

MAKES 24 HALVES

*12 plum tomatoes, cut in half
 vertically*
1¹/₂ tablespoons olive oil

Salt, preferably kosher
Freshly ground black pepper

1. Preheat the oven to 200°F.

2. Place the tomatoes, cut side up, on a baking pan. Brush them with the olive oil, and sprinkle with salt and pepper to taste. Place them in the oven and bake for 8 to 10 hours, depending on the degree of moistness or dryness desired. Remove from the oven and use immediately, or store in a plastic container in the refrigerator for up to 5 days.

ROASTED RED PEPPERS

You can buy roasted red peppers in a jar, and they are quite good. But they are much better when made fresh, with a brightness of flavor you don't get from those in a bottle. Since they are so wonderful as an antipasto and as a condiment or ingredient in so many recipes, it's a good idea to make extra and keep them in the refrigerator.

Red bell peppers, all of similar size

1. Preheat the broiler.

2. Line a roasting pan with a piece of aluminum foil that overlaps the edges by a few inches. Put the peppers in the pan and place it under the broiler, 2 to 3 inches from the heat source, and let them char. Turn them and char the other side. Keep turning until all sides are fairly evenly charred, about 12 to 15 minutes total.

3. Remove the pan from the oven, push all the peppers to the center of the aluminum foil, and fold the edges together, sealing the sides carefully. Then put this sealed foil container into a paper bag, close it tightly, and set aside to steam for 1 hour or more, until the skin slips off easily.

4. Remove the peppers, one at a time, from the foil and peel off the skins (they will come off very easily). Scoop out the seeds, but save the tasty juices. Store the peppers and their juice in a plastic container in the refrigerator for up to 5 days.

THE MISUNDERSTOOD FRUIT

While the tomato may well be one of the most identifiable foods of both Italian and Italian-American cooking, few appreciated the wholesome goodness of the fruit (the tomato is not actually a vegetable) when it was introduced to Europe in the sixteenth century. In 1544 Italian botanist Pierandrea Mattioli first called it by the charming name mala aurea ("golden apple"), but he later took the fruit down several notches, calling it mala insana ("unhealthy apple"). Toward the end of the century Pietro Antonio Michiel warned, "If I should eat this fruit, cut in slices in a pan with butter and oil, it would be injurious and harmful to me." Both these fellows can be forgiven in the sense that, taxonomically, the tomato is a member of the Deadly Nightshade family, Solanaceae, which also includes the potato and eggplant along with more troublesome plants like belladonna and black henbane. And if they did eat the tomato's leaves instead of its fruit, they might well have become sick. But once the Neapolitans discovered which end to eat, southern Italian culinary history was in for a monumental change.

EGGPLANT PARMIGIANA

Eggplant Parmigiana is one of those Italian-American items you'll not find in the Old Country, but it is ubiquitous in restaurants here. Often, however, the dish is compromised by the use of poor ingredients and by precooking, which turns it steamy and listless. Made fresh, this is as fine an Italian-American dish as any in the repertoire.

SERVES 6

2 eggplants (about 2¹/2 pounds
    total), cut into ¹/2-inch-thick
    lengthwise slices
Salt, preferably kosher
²/3 cup olive oil
3 cups Galina's Meat Sauce (page
    126) or Marinara Sauce (page
    126)

³/4 cup coarsely chopped fresh basil
    leaves
10 ounces mozzarella cheese,
    thinly sliced
1 cup freshly grated Parmigiano-
    Reggiano cheese
Freshly ground black pepper

If you are planning to reuse frying oil, make sure you strain it twice or more through fine cheesecloth to rid it of burnt particles of food. Also, if you have cooked seafood in the oil, it is highly likely that the oil will have acquired a slight fishy taste, so do not attempt to fry other foods in it.

1. Sprinkle both sides of the eggplant slices with 2 tablespoons salt, stand them up in a colander, and set the colander in a large bowl or in the sink. Let the eggplant sweat for 1 hour. Then pat the slices dry with paper towels.

2. Preheat the oven to 350°F.

3. In a sauté pan, heat about ¹/4 cup of the olive oil over medium-high heat. Sauté the eggplant slices in batches, adding more olive oil as needed, until they are browned on both sides, 6 to 8 minutes. Drain the eggplant on paper towels.

4. Spread ¹/2 cup of the sauce over the bottom of an 8 x 12-inch baking dish. Layer half of the eggplant, half of the basil, half of the remaining sauce, half of the mozzarella slices, and half of the Parmigiano, in that order, over the sauce. Sprinkle with a little salt and pepper. Repeat with the rest of the eggplant, basil, sauce, mozzarella, and Parmigiano.

5. Bake in the oven for 30 minutes. Then put under the broiler for 2 minutes to brown the top. Let sit for 10 minutes, and serve.

WINE SUGGESTION: SPANNA

POTATO CROQUETTES

I n Italian-American restaurants it used to be expected that you'd be given a choice of three items to go with your main course: spaghetti cooked hours in advance, escarole cooked hours in advance, or potato croquettes that were probably just heated up in the oven before serving and came out rather leaden. But when made well, potato croquettes are irresistible. In fact, you'd better make more than you figured on to sate the appetite of those who taste this remarkably light rendition for the first time.

SERVES 4 TO 6

Salt, preferably kosher
1¹/2 pounds all-purpose potatoes,
    peeled and cut into 2-inch pieces
1 tablespoon olive oil
1 small yellow onion, finely
    chopped
¹/2 cup freshly grated Pecorino
    Romano cheese
¹/2 cup finely cubed mozzarella
    cheese
1 ounce soppressata, salami, or
    other similar sausage, finely
    chopped

2 tablespoons chopped flat-leaf
    parsley
¹/8 teaspoon freshly grated nutmeg
Freshly ground black pepper
3 large egg yolks
All-purpose flour, for dredging
1 large egg, beaten with 2 table-
    spoons water
³/4 cup plain dry breadcrumbs
Vegetable oil, for deep-frying

1. Bring 1¹/2 to 2 quarts water to a boil in a medium-size saucepan. Add 1 teaspoon salt and the potatoes, and boil until potatoes are cooked, 8 to 10 minutes. Drain, and let the potatoes cool to room temperature. Puree them with a food mill or electric mixer.

2. In a small sauté pan, heat the olive oil over medium-low heat. Add the onion and cook, stirring, until softened, about 6 minutes. Remove from the heat.

3. In a large mixing bowl, combine the potatoes, onion, Pecorino, mozzarella, soppressata, parsley, nutmeg, and salt and pepper to taste. Mix well. Add the egg yolks and mix well. Form the mixture into approximately 12 logs, each measuring 3 to 4 inches long and 1¹/2 inches in diameter.

4. Place some flour in a shallow bowl. Put the egg mixture in another shallow bowl. Spread the breadcrumbs on a piece of wax paper. Roll each log in the flour, and shake off any excess; then coat it in the egg wash and finally in the breadcrumbs. Set aside.

5. Pour enough oil into a large saucepan to deep-fry the croquettes. Heat the oil to 365°F (use a deep-frying thermometer). Carefully lower a few croquettes into the oil (do not crowd them) and fry for 2 minutes. Remove, and drain on paper towels. Repeat with the rest. Serve immediately.

WINE SUGGESTION: PINOT GRIGIO

SCALLOPED GORGONZOLA POTATOES

This is a rendition of a very rich and extremely satisfying dish made at Tony's, in St. Louis. You'll say you only intend to eat a little, but everyone goes back for seconds.

SERVES 6

2 tablespoons unsalted butter
1 small yellow onion, finely
   chopped
1 garlic clove, minced
1/2 cup dry white wine, such as
   Soave
2 sprigs fresh thyme, or 1/2 teaspoon dried
1 tablespoon all-purpose flour
1 1/3 cups whole milk

2/3 cup heavy cream
Salt, preferably kosher
Freshly ground black pepper
2/3 cup freshly grated Parmigiano-
   Reggiano cheese
4 baking potatoes, peeled,
   quartered lengthwise, then
   thinly sliced
4 ounces Gorgonzola cheese

1. Preheat the oven to 350°F.

2. In a medium-size saucepan, heat the butter over medium-low heat. Add the onion and cook, stirring, until translucent, about 5 minutes. Add the garlic and cook, stirring, for another 2 minutes. Add the wine and thyme, and simmer until reduced by half, about 5 minutes.

3. Meanwhile, in a small bowl, combine the flour and 2 tablespoons of the milk, and stir to mix well. Stirring, add the remaining milk and the cream.

4. Add the milk mixture to the onions, turn the heat to medium, and stir continuously until the mixture begins to bubble. Cook for 2 minutes. Then remove from the heat and season with salt and pepper to taste. Stir in the Parmigiano.

5. Spread the potato slices out in a 2-quart ovenproof baking dish or casserole. Cover with the onion mixture, and dot with the Gorgonzola. Bake in the oven for about 1½ hours, or until the potatoes are tender and the top is brown.

WINE SUGGESTION: BAROLO

BRAISED POTATOES AND CARROTS

An ideal accompaniment to a stew or braised meat dish.

SERVES 4

5 tablespoons olive oil
1¼ pounds large red pota-
toes, cut into 1½-inch
pieces
3 carrots, cut into 1½-inch
pieces
1 medium yellow onion,
sliced
3 garlic cloves, chopped
8 fresh sage leaves, sliced

1½ to 2 teaspoons fresh
rosemary leaves, or ¾
teaspoon dried
Two 4-inch sprigs fresh
thyme, or ½ teaspoon
dried
Salt, preferably kosher
Freshly ground black pepper
½ cup dry white wine, such
as Soave

1. In a large sauté pan, heat 4 tablespoons of the olive oil over medium-high heat. Add the potatoes and carrots and cook, stirring, until browned, about 10 minutes. Add the onion and cook, stirring, until all the vegetables are

Italians don't put much thought into the varieties of potatoes they cook, and until recently, most Americans didn't think much beyond whether to use a so-called Idaho (actually a russet) or a smaller all-purpose, or Eastern, potato. Italians do insist on a starchy potato without much moisture for making gnocchi, and baking a russet potato is a good way to drive out moisture. Now, however, new American varieties like fingerlings and Yukon Gold have made the choice of potato variety much more tantalizing, and we think such American varieties beat anything you'll find in Italy today.

nicely browned, 3 to 5 minutes. Add the garlic and the remaining 1 tablespoon olive oil, and cook, stirring, for 2 minutes. If the vegetables brown too rapidly, reduce the heat to medium.

2. Add the sage, rosemary, and thyme, and season with salt and pepper to taste. Add the wine and ³/4 cup water. Bring to a boil, reduce the heat to medium, cover, and cook for 6 to 8 minutes. Uncover and continue cooking until the potatoes are tender and the liquid has thickened so it is just thick enough to coat the vegetables, 3 to 4 minutes. (If necessary, add a little more water to coat the vegtables.)

WINE SUGGESTION: ROSSO DI MONTALCINO

CAULIFLOWER WITH PEPPERONCINI AND RAISINS

Avery southern Italian dish, with its hot peppers (which originally came from the Americas) and sweet Mediterranean raisins.

SERVES 4

Salt, preferably kosher
¹/2 large cauliflower head, broken into large florets
5 tablespoons extra-virgin olive oil
1 large garlic clove, cut in half lengthwise
1¹/2 tablespoons white vinegar

1¹/2 teaspoons sugar
¹/4 teaspoon freshly ground black pepper
5 bottled pepperoncini peppers, seeded, cut into thin strips
¹/4 cup dark raisins

1. In a large pot, bring 2 quarts water to a boil. Add 1 teaspoon salt and the cauliflower, and cook until al dente, 3 to 5 minutes. Drain, plunge into cold water to stop the cooking, and drain again.

2. In a small saucepan, heat 3 tablespoons of the olive oil over low heat. Add the garlic and cook until lightly browned, 3 to 5 minutes. Press the oil out of the garlic, and then discard the garlic.

3. In a large bowl, combine the garlic oil, vinegar, sugar, ¹/2 teaspoon salt, the pepper, and the remaining 2 tablespoons olive oil. Mix well.

Add the pepperoncini, raisins, and cauliflower, and toss. Let marinate at room temperature for 3 hours (or longer, refrigerated). Serve at room temperature.

WINE SUGGESTION: TAURASI

BROCCOLI RABE WITH PEAS

The green bitterness of the broccoli rabe and the green sweetness of the peas make this a delectable marriage of vegetables. It goes beautifully as a side dish to chicken, veal, beef, and full-flavored fish.

SERVES 4

1 pound broccoli rabe
1/4 cup extra-virgin olive oil
4 garlic cloves, smashed
Salt, preferably kosher

Freshly ground black pepper
4 ounces fresh peas, shelled (about
  1/2 cup)

1. Cut the stems off the broccoli and cut them in half; if the stems are thick, peel them a bit by pulling off some of the outer skin with a knife. Wash the broccoli stems and heads in a bowl of water and drain. Set aside.

2. In a large saucepan, heat the oil over low heat. Add the garlic and cook slowly, stirring, until it is lightly colored, 2 to 3 minutes. Add all the broccoli rabe, and sprinkle with salt and pepper to taste. Toss to coat with the oil. Add a scant 1/4 cup water, cover, and cook for 4 minutes. Add the peas, toss, and cook for another 3 minutes. Adjust the salt and pepper, and serve.

WINE SUGGESTION:
BARBERA D'ASTI

QUICK FIX FOR LESS-THAN-PERFECT VEGETABLES

If, as so often happens, the peas or green beans you bring home from the supermarket have very little flavor, set them in an inch or two of chicken broth and simmer them slowly until the broth is absorbed into the vegetables. Then add a dab of salted butter.

ARUGULA MASHED POTATOES

W e've read—devoured—books entirely about potatoes, but we've never seen a potato dish containing arugula, and we wonder why it's taken us so long to put the two ingredients together.

SERVES 4

Salt, preferably kosher
1 pound red potatoes, cut into 2-
inch pieces
4 tablespoons (¹/2 stick) unsalted
butter

4 garlic cloves, minced
¹/2 cup heavy cream
¹/4 to ¹/3 cup whole milk
Freshly ground black pepper
2 cups chopped arugula

1. Bring 2 quarts water to a boil in a medium-size saucepan. Add 2 teaspoons salt and the potatoes, and boil until the potatoes are tender, 8 to 10 minutes. Drain, and mash with a fork or a potato masher.

2. While the potatoes are boiling, heat 1 tablespoon of the butter in a small saucepan over low heat. Add the garlic and cook, stirring, until softened but not colored, 2 to 3 minutes. Add the cream and ¹/4 cup of the milk, and heat. Season with salt and pepper to taste, add the arugula, and stir for 30 seconds to slightly wilt the greens.

3. Add the arugula mixture to the potatoes, and stir. If the potatoes are too thick, add a little more milk. Adjust the seasonings, and serve.

WINE SUGGESTION: FRANCIACORTA ROSSO

E uropeans generally prefer potatoes and other root vegetables pureed rather than just mashed and lumpy. There are several kitchen utensils that can accomplish a puree—food mills and ricers are the most readily available—but an electric hand beater will give you the texture you desire, as long as you add the milk and fats very gradually so that they become absorbed slowly. Otherwise you may put too much in and have a paste rather than a puree.

BASIL MASHED POTATOES

C uriously, one finds basil-flecked mashed potatoes more on this side of the Atlantic than in Italy, which has picked up on the trendiness of the idea. It's particularly good with steak.

SERVES 4

Salt, preferably kosher
1 pound all-purpose potatoes, cut
   into 2-inch pieces
1 cup fresh basil leaves
2 small garlic cloves, chopped

3 tablespoons extra-virgin olive oil
2/3 cup whole milk, warmed
4 tablespoons (1/2 stick) unsalted
   butter, softened
Freshly ground black pepper

1. Bring 1 1/2 to 2 quarts water to a boil in a medium-size saucepan. Add 2 teaspoons salt and the potatoes, and boil until tender, 8 to 10 minutes. Drain, and puree in a food mill or with a mixer.

2. In a mini food processor, combine the basil and garlic, and process by pulsing a few times. Add the olive oil and process again.

3. Add the basil mixture, milk, butter, and salt and pepper to taste to the potatoes. Mix well. If too thick, add a little more milk.

WINE SUGGESTION: CHIANTI CLASSICO

ESCAROLE WITH PEAS

Too often escarole is steamed—or worse, boiled—hours in advance and reheated. But when it is freshly made, or prepared and allowed to cool to room temperature, escarole is one of the most flavorful of bitter-salty vegetables. The addition of the peas and onions here gives it a delightful sweet undertone. Escarole goes extremely well with poultry.

SERVES 4 TO 6

1 to 1 1/4 pounds escarole, well
   rinsed, cut across into 2-inch-
   wide slices
3 tablespoons olive oil
2 medium yellow onions, chopped
2 garlic cloves, chopped

5 ounces (1 1/4 cups) fresh peas or
   thawed frozen peas
Salt, preferably kosher
Freshly ground black pepper
3 tablespoons extra-
   virgin olive oil

1. Bring 3 quarts of water to a boil in a stockpot. Add the escarole and simmer for 5 minutes. Reserving 1/2 cup of the cooking liquid, drain and set aside.

Long before there were food processors there was the mandoline, as useful today as ever. The blade can be varied for slicing and dicing, shredding and making a julienne. If you buy one, make sure it is constructed of sturdy metal.

2. Meanwhile, in a large saucepan, heat the olive oil over medium heat. Add the onions and cook, stirring, until softened, about 7 minutes. Add the garlic and cook, stirring, for another 2 minutes.

3. Add the escarole and peas to the onions, season with salt and pepper to taste, and mix. Add ¼ cup of the reserved escarole liquid. Heat, and simmer for 5 minutes. If the liquid evaporates, add a little more. Stir in the extra-virgin olive oil before serving.

WINE SUGGESTION: MERLOT

GRILLED VEGETABLE LASAGNA

Here's a perfect example of the exceptional savoriness of Italian vegetable cookery. If you substitute a tomato sauce for the meat sauce, this luscious pasta-less lasagna becomes a vegetarian dish that everyone will love.

SERVES 6 TO 8

1 eggplant (about 1 pound), cut into ¼- to ³/8-inch-thick lengthwise slices
Salt, preferably kosher
2 zucchinis, cut lengthwise into ¼- to ³/8-inch-thick slices
1 large red bell pepper, cored and cut lengthwise into 8 to 10 slices
1 sweet, such as Vidalia, or Spanish onion, cut into ¼-inch-thick rings

²/3 cup extra-virgin olive oil
Freshly ground black pepper
2 cups Galina's Meat Sauce (page 126)
²/3 cup ricotta cheese
8 ounces mozzarella cheese, cut into ¼ x 1 x 2-inch slices
1 cup freshly grated Parmigiano-Reggiano cheese

1. Place the eggplant in a large colander and sprinkle both sides with salt. Set the colander in a large bowl or in the sink, and let the slices sweat for 30 minutes. Then wipe them dry with paper towels and set aside.

2. Preheat the oven to 375°F.

3. Brush all the vegetables with the extra-virgin olive oil, and season with salt and pepper to taste.

4. Heat a stovetop grill (or an outdoor barbecue) to medium-high heat.

5. Grill the vegetables on both sides until nicely browned and tender but not soft. Set aside.

6. Spread 2 to 3 tablespoons of the meat sauce on the bottom of a 9 x 13 x 2-inch baking dish. Layer half of the eggplant, half of the zucchini, half of the onions, half of the bell peppers in the dish, and cover with half of the remaining sauce. Top with dollops of the ricotta (using it all), then half the mozzarella slices and half the Parmigiano. Repeat the layers with the remaining ingredients, ending with the mozzarella and then the Parmigiano.

7. Bake for 20 minutes. Finish under the broiler for about 2 minutes to brown the top. Let the lasagna rest for 5 minutes before serving.

WINE SUGGESTION: BARBARESCO

By the 1930s, most New York hotel restaurants—like the Waldorf-Astoria, pictured here—had kitchen and dining room staffs over-whelmingly com-posed of Italian-Americans. Managers, chefs, and other personnel had to speak a bit of Italian to survive.

GRILLED ASPARAGUS AND ONIONS

This dish is just as easy to make on a stovetop grill or griddle as it is on an outdoor grill.

SERVES 4

2 tablespoons olive oil
10 ounces asparagus, hard bottoms cut off, bottom half peeled
1 medium sweet, such as Vidalia, or Spanish onion, cut into ¼-inch-thick rounds

Salt, preferably kosher
Freshly ground black pepper
1 tablespoon extra-virgin olive oil
1 tablespoon balsamic vinegar

1. Brush the olive oil over the asparagus and the onion rounds, trying to keep the onion rings together. Season with salt and pepper.

2. Heat a stovetop or outdoor grill or a griddle to medium-high heat.

3. Place the asparagus on one side and the onions on the other, and cook, turning the asparagus and the onions until they are done but still firm, 5 to 8 minutes. Place the vegetables on a platter, sprinkle with the extra-virgin olive oil and vinegar, toss gently, and serve hot or at room temperature.

WINE SUGGESTION: CERASUOLO

ONION AND PARMIGIANO GRATINATA

Hot from the oven, warm and luscious to the palate, this wonderfully wintry dish is a big favorite. It can be served as a side dish to just about any meat or poultry dish you decide to make.

SERVES 4

2 tablespoons extra-virgin olive oil
2 tablespoons unsalted butter
2 pounds yellow onions, sliced
3 sprigs fresh thyme, or ¹/₂
    teaspoon dried
Salt, preferably kosher

Freshly ground black pepper
2 large egg yolks
¹/₄ cup heavy cream
1 cup freshly grated Parmigiano-
    Reggiano cheese

1. In a large skillet, heat the olive oil and butter over medium heat. Add the onions and thyme and cook, stirring, until browned and soft, about 20 minutes. Season with salt and pepper to taste.

2. Meanwhile, in a small bowl, combine the egg yolks, cream, and ²/₃ cup of the Parmigiano. Mix well.

3. Preheat the broiler.

4. Spread the hot onion mixture out evenly in a 1¹/₂-quart ovenproof dish, and pour the egg mixture over the top. Sprinkle the remaining ¹/₃ cup Parmigiano over the onions. Finish under the broiler for about 2 minutes, or until golden brown. Serve immediately.

WINE SUGGESTION: VINO NOBILE DI MONTEPULCIANO

ROASTED VEGETABLES

The rich, sweet, caramelized subtlety you get from roasting vegetables makes them ideal to serve with just about any main course. And if you happen to be a vegetarian, these make a great main course in themselves.

SERVES 4 TO 6

1¹/₂ pounds all-purpose potatoes,
    peeled and cut into 1¹/₂-inch
    pieces
3 carrots, cut into 3-inch pieces
    (top sliced in half if thick)
1 fennel bulb, cut into 6 to 8 slices

4 tablespoons olive oil
1 large red onion, cut into 6 to 8
    wedges
Salt, referably kosher
Freshly ground black pepper

1. Preheat the oven to 400°F.

2. In a large roasting pan, combine the potatoes, carrots, and fennel. Toss well with 3 tablespoons of the olive oil. Bake for 30 minutes, tossing the vegetables every 10 minutes. If the vegetables are crowded, they will not brown well.

3. In a small bowl, toss the red onion with the remaining 1 tablespoon olive oil, and add it to the vegetables. Continue to roast for another 10 to 15 minutes, or until all the vegetables are done and nicely browned. Season well with salt and pepper, and serve.

WINE SUGGESTION: MERLOT

*P*otatoes should always be stored in a cool, dry place. They are best kept in a plastic bag with holes in it to allow for the circulation of air. Once a potato has developed roots and "eyes," it is certainly not at its peak.

BAKED CABBAGE, POTATO, AND SAUSAGE

*W*hile cabbage is certainly used throughout Italy, it is most closely associated with the north, in the regions near the Austrian border. But this dish, with its sweet sausage and two kinds of cheeses, is very clearly in the Italian repertoire.

SERVES 6

Salt, preferably kosher
2 to 2¹/₂ pounds cabbage, cored and cut into 1-inch-wide pieces
2 large leeks, white and light green parts only, split in half and washed
3 all-purpose potatoes, unpeeled
1¹/₄ pounds sweet Italian sausage, cut into 4- to 5-inch pieces

FOR THE BESCIAMELLA
6 tablespoons (³/₄ stick) unsalted butter
2¹/₂ tablespoons all-purpose flour
2 cups whole milk
Pinch of freshly grated nutmeg
6 ounces Fontina cheese, grated
³/₄ cup freshly grated Parmigiano-Reggiano cheese

1. Bring 6 quarts water to a boil in a stockpot. Add 2 tablespoons salt, the cabbage, and the leeks, and cook until slightly softened, about 5 minutes. Drain. When cool enough, slice the leeks into ³/₄-inch pieces.

2. Meanwhile, in a medium-size saucepan, cover the potatoes with 1 inch water. Bring to a boil, and cook until the potatoes are tender, 8 to 10 minutes. Drain, and let cool a bit. Then peel, cut into quarters, and cut each piece into ¹/₄-inch-thick slices. Set aside.

3. Preheat oven to 400°F.

4. Prepare the *besciamella* (béchamel) sauce: Heat a medium-size saucepan over medium heat, and melt 3 tablespoons of the butter. Add the flour and cook over medium heat, stirring, for 2 minutes. Add the milk all at once, ½ teaspoon salt, and the nutmeg. Cook, stirring, until the sauce thickens and starts to bubble. Simmer for 2 minutes, then remove from the heat and set aside.

5. In a medium-size saucepan, cover the sausage with water. Bring to a boil, and simmer over medium heat for 6 minutes. Drain, and cut the sausage into ¼-inch-thick slices.

6. In a sauté pan, melt 1 tablespoon of the butter over medium heat. Add the sausage and cook, stirring, until lightly browned, about 5 minutes.

7. Spread 2 to 3 tablespoons of the *besciamella* in a 9 x 13 x 2-inch baking dish. Layer the ingredients as follows. First layer: one third of the cabbage, half of the leeks, one third of the *besciamella*, half of the sausage, one third of the Fontina, and one third of the Parmigiano. Repeat for the second layer. Third layer: the remaining cabbage, Fontina, *besciamella*, and Parmigiano. Top with the remaining 2 tablespoons butter, broken up into bits.

8. Bake for 20 minutes. Let the dish rest for 5 minutes before serving.

WINE SUGGESTION: PINOT NERO

"My family grew up together on Tenth Avenue, between Thirtieth and Thirty-First Streets, part of the area called Hells Kitchen. . . . I never came home to an empty house; there was always the smell of supper cooking. My mother was always there to greet me, sometimes with a policeman's club in her hand (nobody ever knew how she acquired it). . . . During the Great Depression of the 1930s, though we were the poorest of the poor, I never remember not dining well. Many years later as a guest of a millionaire's club, I realized that our poor family on home relief ate better than some of the richest people in America.

"My mother would never dream of using anything but the best imported olive oil, the best Italian cheeses. My father had access to the fruits coming off the ships and the produce from the railroad cars, all before it went through the stale process of middlemen; and my mother, like most Italian women, was a fine cook in the peasant style." —Mario Puzo, The Fortunate Pilgrim

ROASTED GARLIC BUTTER

Asavory condiment that is as good on a slice of bread as it is mixed into a sauce.

3 heads garlic *3 tablespoons olive oil*

1. Preheat the oven to 350°F, or preheat a covered grill.

2. Remove the papery skin from the outside of the garlic heads, exposing the cloves (still attached).

3. Slice across the top of the heads, about ¼ inch down, exposing the tips of the garlic cloves.

4. Place the heads of garlic on a sheet of aluminum foil, then drizzle the olive oil over them. Wrap them loosely in the foil, then bake in the oven or on the grill for 45 minutes to 1 hour.

5. Carefully remove the foil from the garlic, and, wearing insulated kitchen gloves, squeeze out the soft garlic from the cloves. It may be used in this form, or mashed into a puree with salt and pepper to taste.

SEVEN GREAT REASONS TO EAT GARLIC

❖ *When eaten raw, it acts as an antibiotic.*

❖ *It can prevent gangrene.*

❖ *It lowers the bad (LDL) cholesterol in the blood and raises the good (HDL).*

❖ *It lowers triglyceride levels and cuts the chances of heart attack and stroke.*

❖ *It can help clear sinuses and cold symptoms.*

❖ *It is said to soothe dog bites and scorpion stings.*

❖ *It keeps witches and vampires away.*

ITALIAN FRENCH FRIES

The flavor of olive oil and the generosity of the cut make these potatoes a perfect accompaniment for simply grilled seafood or veal. Come to think of it, they go with just about anything.

SERVES 4

3 long russet potatoes *Salt, preferably kosher*
Olive oil *Freshly ground black pepper*

1. Peel the potatoes and cut them into fat sticks, about ³/4 inch wide and ¹/2 inch thick. Place them in ice water for an hour or so. Then remove from the water and pat dry with paper towels.

2. Pour about ¹/2 inch olive oil into a 12-inch skillet. Heat the oil to 375°F. Add the potatoes, keeping them separate from one another, and cook, turning occasionally, until golden brown and cooked through, 10 to 12 minutes. Remove with a slotted spoon, and drain on paper towels. Season with salt and pepper to taste.

WINE SUGGESTION:
VERNACCIA DI SAN GIMIGNANO

ROSE MIGLUCCI'S SPICY CARROTS

R ose Miglucci carries on as *materfamilias* of her family, now fourth-generation restaurateurs at Mario's in the Bronx (see page 260), and she has a few of her own treats that she doles out to regulars—or, for that matter, to anyone who asks for them.

SERVES 4

2/3 cup white vinegar
4 large carrots, cut into 2¹/2-inch pieces and julienned
3 garlic cloves, sliced
1 teaspoon red pepper flakes
3/4 teaspoon dried oregano
1/3 cup extra-virgin olive oil

2 tablespoons chopped flat-leaf parsley
5 large fresh basil leaves, sliced
Salt, preferably kosher
Freshly ground black pepper

1. In a medium-size saucepan, bring 1¹/3 cups water and the vinegar to a boil. Add the carrots, bring back to a boil, and cook until al dente, 7 to 10 minutes. Strain the carrots, reserving the liquid. Let the carrots cool.

2. In a glass jar or bowl, combine the reserved hot carrot liquid with the garlic, red pepper flakes, and oregano. Let cool.

The most famous of American cookbooks, Irma S. Rombauer's The Joy of Cooking, has gone through many editions, always increasing the number of ethnic dishes in each succeeding volume. But in the original, published in 1931, Italian food is given very short shrift. There's a recipe for "Italian Rice," and Rombauer gives directions on cooking a "new addition to the vegetable list" called "Italian squash" (zucchini), but not much else. Her instructions to cook spaghetti "until it is tender"—about twenty minutes!—would cause any Italian chef to go into a rage at the sins Americans commit against pasta. The newest edition of Joy, however, treats Italian dishes in considerable depth, reflecting their popularity in the United States, and recommends cooking times of between four and eight minutes.

3. When the liquid has cooled, add the olive oil, parsley, basil, salt and pepper to taste, and the carrots. Swirl to mix. Refrigerate and let marinate for at least a day before eating. Serve at room temperature.

WINE SUGGESTION:
MONTEPULCIANO D'ABRUZZO

NOTE: The taste of the carrots improves over several days. They can be stored in the refrigerator for up to 2 weeks.

Three-fourths of the cranberry pickers in Burlington County, New Jersey, during the Depression were children, like this Italian immigrant girl.

POTATO TORTA

The potato, which came to Europe from South America, was once thought of as a poisonous plant. But eventually Europeans found hundreds of ways to treat this everyday food, and the Italians love it as a *torta di patate* (TOHR-tah dee pah-TAH-teh), enriched with mortadella and Parmigiano.

SERVES 6

2½ pounds small Idaho potatoes
Unsalted butter, for the pan
4 ounces mortadella, sliced and minced
1 cup freshly grated Parmigiano-Reggiano cheese
2 large eggs, lightly beaten
3 tablespoons whole milk

3 tablespoons finely chopped flat-leaf parsley
Pinch of freshly grated nutmeg
Salt, preferably kosher
Freshly ground black pepper
3 tablespoons plain dry breadcrumbs
3 tablespoons unsalted butter

1. In a large pot, cover the potatoes with 1 inch water. Bring to a boil, and cook until tender when pierced with a sharp knife, 10 to 15 minutes. Drain, and let sit until cool enough to handle. Then peel the potatoes and pass them through a food mill or mash with a potato masher.

2. Preheat the oven to 400°F.

3. Generously butter a 10-inch springform pan or ovenproof sauté pan. Line the pan with parchment paper, and generously butter the paper.

4. In a large bowl, combine the potatoes, mortadella, Parmigiano, eggs, milk, parsley, nutmeg, and salt and pepper to taste (not too much salt because there is salt in the mortadella and the Parmigiano). Mix well. Spoon the mixture into the mold, and smooth the top. Sprinkle with the breadcrumbs, dot with the butter, and bake in the oven for 30 to 35 minutes. Remove from the oven and let rest for 5 minutes. Unmold, and cut into wedges to serve.

WINE SUGGESTION: DOLCETTO

> "While he approves of home canning, the Italian [immigrant] believes that the commercial method [of canning] removes all the goodness from food and a minimum of processes should intervene between harvesting and consumption." —Wage Earners' Budget: A Study of Standards and Costs of Living in New York City (1907).

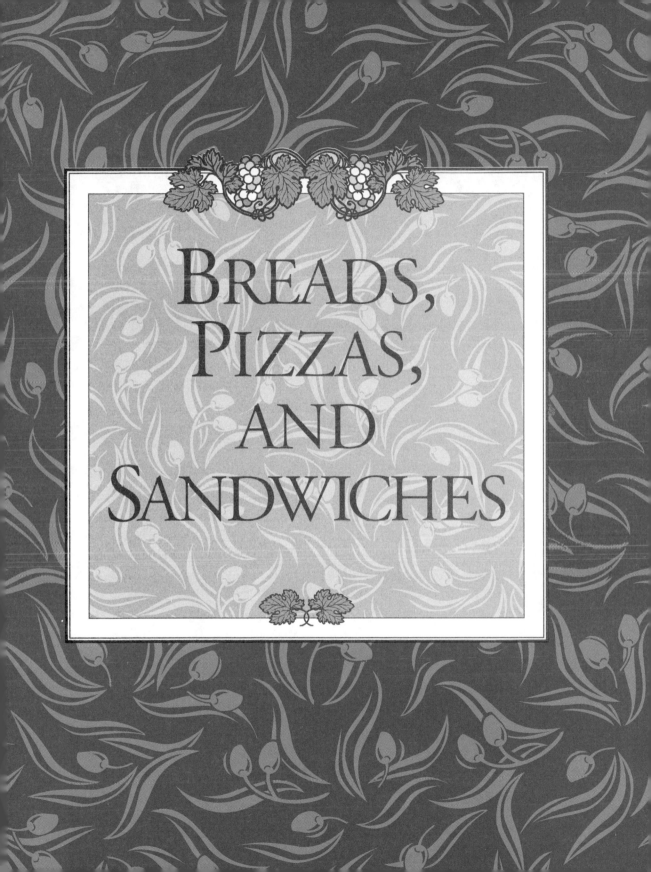

BREADS, PIZZAS, AND SANDWICHES

BREADS, PIZZAS, AND SANDWICHES

Bread is the staff of life in Italy, where each region, city, town, and village has its own particular breads. Carol Field's comprehensive *The Italian Baker* (1985) has hundreds of recipes for bread, and notes that there are 35,000 bakers in Italy, many of whom are now reviving the artisanal traditions of regional bread-making. As a result, few Italians bother to make bread at home, and with the availability of better and better Italian-style breads now sold in the American market, we see little reason to venture into this vast subject, except to give recipes for breads that are better made at home, like focaccia and bruschetta.

So, too, pizzas have gained some ground in home kitchens, though those who choose to make their own seem to tend to become fanatical about it. (We've included one such recipe from a friend who is *very* fanatical on the subject.) Going out for pizza is as much an American tradition as it is an Italian one at this point, so we've offered only a few recipes that we think work especially well.

The pizza, of course, was created in Naples, but it was popularized in the United States long before it became ubiquitous in Italy. In many cases, we deplore what American pizza-makers—especially the big chains—have done to the original Neapolitan idea of pizza, with its dimpled crust, simple ingredients, and smoky aroma. Most American pizzas are too thick or too thin. America has given the world white clam pizzas, and grilled pizzas, pioneered in this country by Johanne Killeen and George Germon of Al Forno restaurant in Providence, Rhode Island. The latter are quick, easy, and irresistible.

Italians adapted the sandwich from American models, especially the Italian-American hero or sub—but in Italy they tend to be much, much smaller, set on slices of bread from skinny cylindrical loaves. These sandwiches are called *panini* ("little breads") and may serve as a quick lunch, but more often make for a late-afternoon snack.

Amighetti's Bakery in St. Louis, Missouri, shows off its crusty Italian loaves just out of the oven in a photo from 1967. The bakery was started by Marge Amighetti on "The Hill"—the city's Little Italy section—and grew into a sandwich shop selling stuffed heroes full of cheese, meat, and peppers.

PIZZA FRITTA

If you have any pizza dough left after making the pies themselves, cut the dough into balls and roll them or flatten them into strips about the size of a hot dog. Fry them in a little olive oil that you have flavored with a clove of garlic (then removed). Serve them plain, with salt, or with a little marinara sauce on the side. We guarantee you'll start to make more pizza dough than you need to make pizza.

FOCACCIA

This dimpled, puffy bread, similar to a thick pizza crust, became very popular in Italian restaurants here in the 1990s, serving as an alternative to the usual seeded loaf of Italian bread. *Focaccia* (foh-KAH-chah) lends itself to all sorts of toppings. The version here is basic and wonderfully aromatic, but feel free to add anything from oven-dried tomatoes and onions to Gorgonzola and dried fruit.

SERVES 6 TO 8

1¹/₂ packages (1¹/₂ tablespoons)
  active dry yeast
1¹/₂ tablespoons sugar
3¹/₃ cups all-purpose flour
3 teaspoons salt, preferably kosher

5 tablespoons olive oil
1 medium yellow onion, thinly
  sliced
2 teaspoons fresh rosemary leaves

1. In a small bowl, combine the yeast, ¹/₂ cup warm water, and the sugar. Stir, and let stand for 10 minutes to dissolve the yeast.

2. In a food processor fitted with the dough blade, combine the flour, 1¹/₂ teaspoons of the salt, 2 tablespoons of the olive oil, the yeast mixture, and ¹/₂ cup warm water. Process. Slowly add up to ³/₄ cup more warm water, as needed, to make a rather soft, slightly sticky dough. (You can also mix the ingredients in a bowl with a wooden spoon, and then knead by hand.)

3. Transfer the dough to a lightly floured board and knead for 5 minutes. Then place it in a large oiled bowl, cover with a kitchen towel, and put it in a warm spot. Let it rise for 1 to 2 hours, or until it has doubled in size.

4. Take the dough out of the bowl, fold it onto itself a few times, and then stretch it to fill an oiled 8 x 12-inch baking pan. Brush 1 tablespoon of the olive oil on the top, cover with the towel, and let the dough rise for 30 minutes.

5. Meanwhile, preheat the oven to 400°F.

6. In a bowl, separate the onion slices and toss them with the remaining 2 tablespoons olive oil.

7. Gently scatter the onions and the rosemary on top of the focaccia, and sprinkle with the remaining 1¹/₂ teaspoons salt. Bake for 20 to 25 minutes, or until nicely browned.

8. Transfer the focaccia from the pan to a rack, and serve warm or at room temperature, the same day.

WINE SUGGESTION: CHIANTI CLASSICO

PANINI WITH HAM AND FETA

The term *panini* (pah-NEE-nee), which means "little breads," was apparently coined at Milan's Paninoteca Bar Quadronno, which makes a wide variety of them. They are a smaller version of the Italian-American hero, more like the New Orleans po' boy sandwich.

SERVES 4

1 tablespoon balsamic vinegar
4 tablespoons extra-virgin olive oil
1 small garlic clove, minced
Salt, preferably kosher
¹/₂ Focaccia (page 358), cut into
* 4 pieces*

8 ounces boiled ham, thinly sliced
²/₃ cup crumbled feta cheese
10 halves Oven-Roasted Tomatoes
* (page 332), sliced lengthwise*
¹/₂ bunch arugula
Coarsely ground black pepper

1. Preheat an outdoor or stovetop grill to medium heat.

2. In a small bowl, combine the balsamic vinegar, 2 tablespoons of the olive oil, the garlic, and salt to taste. Whisk to blend.

3. Cut the focaccia pieces in half horizontally, and open them up. On the bottom sides, spread some of the dressing. Evenly divide the ham, feta, tomatoes, and arugula among the 4 pieces. Drizzle the rest of the dressing on the 4 sandwiches, add a generous amount of pepper, and cover with the tops.

4. Turn the sandwiches upside-down and brush the bottoms with the remaining 2 tablespoons olive oil. Place them, oiled side down, on the

grill. Place a heavy sauté pan over the sandwiches to press them down, and grill for 2 to 3 minutes to crisp the bottoms. Serve immediately.

WINE SUGGESTION: LAMBRUSCO

PANINI WITH ROAST BEEF, PEPPERS, AND ONIONS

Very American to use roast beef, very Italian to add peppers, very delicious any way you slice it.

SERVES 4

2 tablespoons olive oil
1 small red bell pepper, cored and cut into 8 slices
1 large sweet, such as Vidalia, or Spanish onion, cut into ¼-inch-thick slices
Salt, preferably kosher
Freshly ground black pepper
⅓ cup mayonnaise
1 garlic clove, minced

½ Focaccia (page 358), cut into 4 squares
8 ounces roast beef, thinly sliced
4 slices provolone cheese
½ cup sliced Parmigiano-Reggiano cheese (slice with a vegetable peeler)
1 teaspoon coarsely ground black pepper

1. Preheat a stovetop grill to medium heat.

2. Brush about 1½ tablespoons of the olive oil over the bell pepper and onion slices, and grill until browned and slightly softened, 8 to 10 minutes. Remove to a bowl, and season with salt and pepper to taste.

3. In a small bowl, combine the mayonnaise, garlic, and a little salt. Mix well.

4. Cut the focaccia pieces in half horizontally, and open them up. Spread the mayonnaise mixture on all 8 pieces. Evenly divide the roast beef, provolone, peppers and onions, and the sliced Parmigiano among the bottom

GRISSINI

Italians do not serve bread with pasta or risotto because it would be adding one starch on top of another. Breadsticks (grissini, grih-SEE-nee), which are crisp and light, are preferred with antipasti, while bread is best with soups, stews, and cheeses.

halves of the focaccia. Sprinkle generously with pepper, cover with the tops, and turn them upside-down. Brush the bottoms with the remaining olive oil.

4. Place the 4 sandwiches, oiled side down, on the grill. Place a heavy sauté pan over the sandwiches to press them down, and grill for 2 to 3 minutes to crisp the bottoms. Serve immediately.

WINE SUGGESTION: BARBERA D'ALBA

BRUSCHETTA STICKS WITH GORGONZOLA SAUCE

Curiously enough, we got this idea from chef David Waltuck of Michael Jordan's Steakhouse (yes, *that* Michael Jordan) in New York's Grand Central Terminal. It's very rich, so don't plan to follow it with anything too heavy.

SERVES 2 TO 4

FOR THE SAUCE
1¹/2 tablespoons unsalted butter
1 large garlic clove, minced
¹/3 cup heavy cream
3 ounces Gorgonzola cheese,
   coarsely chopped
Freshly ground black pepper

2¹/2 tablespoons extra-virgin olive
   oil
8 fresh sage leaves
8 pieces crusty Italian bread,
   crusts removed, cut into
   4 x 1 x 1-inch pieces

1. Prepare the sauce: In a small saucepan, melt the butter over low heat. Add the garlic and cook for 2 minutes. Add the cream, Gorgonzola, and pepper, and heat over medium-low heat until it starts to boil. Set the sauce aside.

2. In another small saucepan, heat the olive oil over low heat. Add the sage leaves and sauté for 3 minutes. Remove from the heat.

3. Brush the sage oil all over the bread, and grill on a stovetop grill or in a cast-iron skillet over medium-high heat, turning the bread to brown on all sides, 6 to 8 minutes.

4. To serve, pour the sauce into a serving dish and place 2 of the bread sticks in the sauce. Place 2 more across the first 2, and repeat with the others in a Lincoln Log pattern. Serve immediately. (You can eat these with a knife and fork—or, more casually, with your fingers, dipping the bruschetta into the sauce.)

WINE SUGGESTION: MERLOT

BRUSCHETTA WITH WHITE BEANS AND PROSCIUTTO

The toppings for bruschetta are not endless—one must have a certain respect for what does and does not go well on this toasty Italian bread. We do know that this combination of garlic, prosciutto, and white beans, with the spark of red pepper flakes, works very well indeed.

SERVES 4

10 tablespoons extra-virgin olive oil
4 ounces prosciutto, chopped
2 garlic cloves, minced
10 fresh sage leaves, shredded
1/4 teaspoon red pepper flakes
2 cups cooked cannellini beans (or canned beans, drained and rinsed)

Salt, preferably kosher
Freshly ground black pepper
8 pieces crusty Italian bread, cut into 1/2-inch-thick pieces
1 garlic clove, peeled

1. In a medium-size sauté pan, heat 1 tablespoon of the olive oil over medium heat. Add the prosciutto and sauté until browned, 2 to 3 minutes. Push the prosciutto to the side of the pan, add 4 tablespoons of the olive oil, and then add the minced garlic, sage, and red pepper flakes. Cook, stirring, for about 1 minute. Add the beans and stir, mashing about one third of the beans. If mixture is too dry, add 1 to 2 tablespoons water. Season with salt and pepper to taste, and cook over medium-low heat for 3 minutes. Set aside.

2. Heat a large sauté pan over medium-high heat. Brush the remaining 5 tablespoons olive oil over the bread, and when the pan is hot, add the bread and sauté until golden brown on both sides, 4 to 6 minutes. Transfer the bruschetta to a platter, rub one side of each piece with the whole garlic clove, and spread the bean mixture on that side. Serve immediately.

WINE SUGGESTION: ORVIETO

PHILADELPHIA CHEESE STEAK

A variety of the hero sandwich, the Philadelphia cheese steak was invented during the Depression, around 1932, by Pat Olivieri, a hot dog–stand vendor who got tired of eating his own wares. The story goes that while frying some beef and onions on his griddle, he attracted a passing taxi driver who said he'd pay ten cents for the sandwich. Olivieri knew a good thing when he saw it, and soon the sandwich was popular all over Philadelphia. Competition grew rapidly, so that today you can get into a heated argument as to who serves the best cheese steak in town. (The cheese was not added by Olivieri until the 1940s.) Legend has it that Frank Sinatra was a big fan of the sandwich. Olivieri proclaimed himself "Prince of Steaks" and eventually, with his grandson, franchised his operation. The main shop is in the wonderful Reading Terminal Market. By the way, a Philly cheese steak at Olivieri's now sells for $4.05.

SERVES 4

1 pound boneless beef chuck
2 tablespoons peanut oil
2 yellow onions, thinly sliced
4 Italian-style soft rolls

8 ounces mozzarella or provolone
cheese, cut into 8 slices, or 8
ounces American cheese spread

1. Place the beef, wrapped, in the freezer to make it firm enough to slice very thin, about 3 hours (at Olivieri's the beef is held at 38°F for 17 hours).

2. Slice the beef into 1/8-inch-thick slices.

3. In a large sauté pan or griddle, heat the peanut oil over low heat. Add the onions and cook until they just start to turn golden, 12 to 15 minutes. Remove the onions from the pan. Turn the heat to medium high.

4. Stack the beef slices on top of one another to make four 1/4-pound portions. Place the stacks in the sauté pan and sear on both sides, sprinkling with a little water to keep the meat from sticking, 4 to 6 minutes total. When the meat is just cooked through, remove the stacks from the pan (do not separate the slices, it would dry them out).

5. Split the rolls and warm them briefly in the sauté pan. Place each portion of meat on a roll, add the onions, and then place 2 slices of cheese or a layer of cheese spread on the meat. Close the roll, and let the heat of the sandwich melt the cheese.

WINE SUGGESTION: VALPOLICELLA

MUFFULETTA FROM CENTRAL GROCERY

The Italian immigrants in New Orleans are largely of Sicilian origin, and the muffuletta has become their version of the po' boy sandwich, which is itself a form of hero. The name comes from the Sicilian term for a certain shape of bread, which forms the basis of this generously endowed sandwich. The sandwich was created in 1906 by Salvatore Lupo and is still served at the Central Grocery in New Orleans, across from the French Market in that Creole city.

SERVES 4

Two 7-inch muffuletta rolls, or 1
    round Italian bread with sesame
    seeds
4 teaspoons extra-virgin olive oil
4 ounces domestic ham, thinly
    sliced
4 ounces Genoa salami, thinly
    sliced

4 ounces provolone cheese, thinly
    sliced
4 ounces mortadella, thinly sliced
4 to 6 tablespoons prepared olive
    salad (see Note), coarsely
    chopped if needed

Slice the rolls or bread in half horizontally. Brush both sides with
the olive oil. Layer the sliced fillings on the bottom pieces, top with the
olive salad, and cover with the top pieces of the bread. Cut each sandwich into 2 or 4 pieces.

WINE SUGGESTION: CORVO ROSSO

NOTE: "Olive salad" is a mixture of olives and pickled vegetables
(peppers, celery, cauliflower).

The Madonia
bakery on Arthur
Avenue in the
Bronx shows the
range of Italian
breads and rolls
available. Inside
the cases are
crammed with
Italian cookies
and pastries.

MOZZARELLA IN CARROZZA

As a snack, as a sandwich, as an antipasto or first course, this fried combination of bread and mozzarella—a staple of Italian-American restaurants—is easy to make at home. Mozzarella *in carrozza* (een kah-ROH-t'zah) is a simpler version of *spiedino* (spee-eh-DEE-noh), in which the bread slices are cut into smaller squares, layered with mozzarella, skewered, then fried—a process that makes a pretty loaf but that also has the problem of absorbing too much oil if not carefully tended.

SERVES 2 TO 4

*4 slices sandwich bread, crusts
    removed*
*3 to 4 ounces mozzarella cheese,
    cut into ¹/4-inch-thick slices*
¹/4 cup all-purpose flour
¹/2 cup plain dry breadcrumbs
1 large egg, beaten

*2 tablespoons freshly grated
    Pecorino Romano cheese*
3 tablespoons whole milk
Salt, preferably kosher
Freshly ground black pepper
Vegetable oil, for frying
1 cup Marinara Sauce (page 126)

1. Cover 2 slices of the bread with the mozzarella slices, and top with the other 2 slices of bread. Carefully slice the sandwiches in half diagonally.

2. On a large piece of wax paper, place the flour on one side and the breadcrumbs on the other.

3. In a shallow bowl, mix together the egg, Pecorino, milk, and salt and pepper to taste.

4. Dredge the sandwich triangles in the flour, and shake off any excess. Then dip them into the egg mixture, making sure that the sides are dampened also. Then coat them in the breadcrumbs, coating the sides as well. Let the triangles rest for 5 to 10 minutes, to let the breadcrumbs adhere well.

5. Heat a medium-size frying pan (large enough to hold all the triangles) over medium-high heat. Add oil to a depth of ¹/4 to ¹/2 inch. When the oil is hot (test by putting a corner of one of the triangles into the oil—it should sizzle immediately), add the triangles and fry until the bread has browned, 1 to 1¹/2 minutes. Turn to the other side and fry for another 1 to 1½ minutes. Transfer to paper towels to drain. Serve immediately, with marinara sauce.

WINE SUGGESTION: BIANCO DI CUSTOZA

THE NO-LIFE
PIZZA DOUGH

We did not agonize for long over how many pizza recipes this book should include. For one thing, we don't believe many people in America or in Italy make their own pizzas at home. Second, once you've found the perfect pizza dough, there's really nothing much else to say, except "Use your imagination with toppings."

This pizza dough was perfected by a rather manic friend of ours named Bill Pepe, who for years has spent every weekend analyzing every aspect and detail of pizza-making. He uses different measurements of different flours; he puts in a little red wine or maybe some white wine; he lets it rise for one, two, three risings over five, six, ten hours; he kneads it by machine, he kneads it by hand; he stretches it one way, he stretches it another; he cooks it in an electric oven, he cooks it in a gas oven. Finally, a few years ago, he came up with the perfect pizza dough—thin, puffy, bubbly, crisp but chewy, with a flavor all its own. And it takes him all day to make it.

Which is why we call this "The No-Life Pizza Dough": If you are willing to spend your entire day tending, coaxing, and waiting for this dough, you will have something you can be proud of. If, on the other hand, you have any intention of doing something like going to work, picking up the kids, seeing a movie, or shoveling snow—just forget about it!

MAKES 3 PIZZAS

WHICH IS WHY THEY TASTE THE WAY THEY DO

It seems ironic that all the major pizza chains in the U.S. were created by non-Italians in midwestern or western cities with negligible Italian-American communities:

❖ Pizza Hut, Wichita, Kansas (1958), by Frank and Daniel Carney.

❖ Domino's Pizza, Ypsilanti, Michigan (1960), by Jim and Tom Monaghan (who once said, "God meant me to be a pizza man").

❖ Godfather's Pizza, Omaha, Nebraska (1973).

❖ Little Caesars, Farmington Hills, Michigan (1959).

❖ Shakey's Pizza Parlors, Burlingame, California (1954)—complete with banjo players.

1 tablespoon honey
1 package active dry yeast
5 to 5¹/4 cups bread flour
³/4 cup slightly sweet white wine,
   such as Riesling or white
   Zinfandel

1 tablespoon salt, preferably
   kosher
1 tablespoon extra-virgin olive oil
1 to 2 tablespoons olive oil, for
   oiling the bowl
Cornmeal, for the pizza peel

1. In a large bowl, combine 1¹/3 cups warm water with the honey and yeast. Stir, and set aside for 5 minutes to let the yeast dissolve. Then add 1¹/2 cups of the flour, stir with a whisk, and cover with a piece of plastic wrap. Set in a warm, draft-free place to rise for 1¹/2 hours.

2. Add 1 cup of the flour to the dough, and stir to mix with a wooden spoon. Cover again with plastic wrap and set aside in a warm place until risen, another 1¹/2 to 2 hours.

3. Add the wine, a little at a time, and mix into the dough. Add another 1 cup of flour, mixing with the wooden spoon. (The dough does not have to be completely lump-free.) Cover with plastic wrap and set in a warm place until risen, 1¹/2 to 2 hours.

4. Place the dough in the bowl of a standing mixer fitted with the dough hook, and start mixing the dough at medium-low speed. Sprinkle in the salt and then the extra-virgin olive oil, and mix. Gradually add the rest of the flour, checking the dough after you have incorporated a total of 4¹/2 cups. The dough should be slightly sticky to the touch, but not gooey nor too dry. Be careful not to put in too much flour. Once the dough has been mixed well in the machine, remove it to a wooden board and knead by hand for 3 to 5 minutes, adding a little flour if needed, and form a ball.

5. Use the 1 to 2 tablespoons olive oil to oil a large clean bowl. Roll the dough in the bowl to coat it with the oil. Cover with a piece of plastic wrap, and set the bowl in a warm place for 1¹/2 hours.

6. Turn the dough out onto a wooden board and cut it into 3 equal pieces. Form each one into a ball, and if you will be using all the dough, put each piece in a separate bowl. Cover with a piece of plastic wrap and set to rise in a warm place for 1¹/2 to 2 hours, until doubled in size. (If you are not using all the dough, put the remainder in a bowl, cover with plastic wrap, and refrigerate for up to 3 days. Let it come to room temperature before using.)

7. While the dough is rising the last time, place a pizza stone on the bottom rack of the oven and turn the oven to 500°F. Let it heat for 1 to 1½ hours.

8. Sprinkle a pizza peel with cornmeal and set it aside. Remove the plastic wrap from the bowl. Push the dough gently with your fingers to make it collapse. Remove the dough from the bowl by inverting it onto your hand with the fingers spread apart. Place the dough on the back of your two hands, and start turning and stretching it out to form a 12-inch-diameter pizza with a thicker ridge around the edges. Place the pizza on the peel, adjust the shape if necessary, and slip it off onto the heated pizza stone. Bake in the oven for 4 minutes.

9. Using the peel, remove the pizza dough. Add the toppings of your choice (tomato sauce, mozzarella, sausage, onions, Gorgonzola, olive oil. . .) and slip the pizza back onto the stone for 2 minutes. After 2 minutes, quickly transfer the stone to the top third of the oven, and continue to bake for another 2 to 2¾ minutes to brown the top. Remove with the peel, and serve immediately.

WINE SUGGESTION:
CHIANTI CLASSICO

NOTE: Only trial and error with your own oven will give you the perfect results. Every oven differs from the next, and moving, elevating, or cooking the pizza longer may be necessary.

The explosion in the popularity of pizza after World War II—made, with typical Italian-American exuberance, much bigger than the pizza in Naples, its city of origin— led to its being as identifiable as hamburgers, hot dogs, and French fries as an all-American fast food. Pizza eventually became a major food export to Europe, Asia, and Central and South America.

PIZZA AMERICAN-STYLE

Even in Naples, where the pizza originated, you'll find more than the traditional toppings of mozzarella, tomato, and basil. But American pizzerias have taken the item into whole other realms of creativity, some good, some weird. Here are a few American pizzerias that display just about every aspect of pizza-making possible.

JOHN'S PIZZERIA
278 Bleecker Street, New York, New York; 212-243-1680

For more than seven decades John's has reigned as the paradigm of Neapolitan pizza, New York–style. Its crust is on the thin side, crisp but inundated with craters and bubbles beneath the golden-brown, beautifully blistered classic topping of mozzarella and tomato. The oven is coal-fired, as at many of New York's best old-fashioned bakeries, and this adds that smoky luster to the pie. Its nine topping options are simple—some excellent sausage, perhaps some nice sliced mushrooms, although the veggie pizza, with mushrooms, onions, peppers, and black olives, is gaining on the popularity of the classic pizza alla Margherita made with cheese, tomato, and basil.

This Greenwich Village pizzeria is the original John's (there are three others in Manhattan, including one set in a former church), and it hasn't changed much since 1929. It's still got wooden benches and scruffy walls, it's still in the same family (John Sasso himself passed away thirty years ago), and there's still a line out the door every day, from 11:30 in the morning until midnight, a line that might well include celebs like Woody Allen, Johnny Depp, Danny DeVito, and any number of New York Rangers.

PEPE'S PIZZERIA NAPOLETANA
157 Wooster Street, New Haven, Connecticut; 203-865-5762

Pepe's has made some wild claims over the years—like the one that they brought pizza to America (which they didn't), but you will forgive them anything, even the brusque waitresses and the long waits, for one of their superlative pies. Once you savor a Pepe's pizza, you'll understand the long wait for a table and the long wait for a pie, which is cooked slowly in a vast brick oven that takes up an entire wall of one of the two dining rooms. The long-handled pizza peels go into the fiery ovens, and you can watch the artful movements of the pizza-makers in shuffling the pies around to cook evenly in the pockets of swirling superheated air. When the pizzas hit your table, they are still sizzling and bubbling.

On parents' weekend and after football games at Yale, the enormous number of local regulars are cheek-to-cheek with visitors who have heard about the extraordinary white clam pizza here (which maybe, just maybe, Pepe's did invent). This is made on the regulation crisp, splotchily blackened crust with freshly shucked clams and plenty of garlic and grated Romano cheese, all drizzled with olive oil. The result is sheer pizza heaven, and the clams even give it a little New England tang.

AL FORNO
577 Main Street, Providence, Rhode Island; 401-273-9760

Johanne Killeen and George Germon had no idea they would create a fad when they started grilling pizzas at their Mediterranean-style restaurant in this lovely New England city. They had seen the technique in a restaurant in Italy and adapted it back home, giving their thin, crisp, oddly shaped crust a pliancy and brittleness that has been copied all over the United States.

TACONELLI'S
2604 East Somerset Street, Philadelphia, Pennsylvania;
215-425-4983

Philly is a very good pizza town, with a lot of Italians who know what's good for them. And Taconelli's more often than not wins hands-down as the city's best pizzeria. Philadelphia Magazine has installed it in its Hall of Fame of notable city institutions.

Taconelli's is a fourth-generation family operation. It was opened in 1948 by Giovanni Taconelli; his great-grandson Vincent and Vincent's wife, Doris, now run it. Five days a week Taconelli's fires up the old brick oven, then turns it off just before service, maintaining a constant even temperature that gives their crusts an unreplicable flavor. The most popular topping is a white pizza (without tomato sauce but with slices of tomato, spinach, and plenty of garlic). Five days a week regulars call up throughout the day to "reserve their dough" for a certain number of pizzas that will be made upon their arrival, and after 4:30 there's a good chance you won't be able to claim one of the hundred seats at Taconelli's no *matter long you're willing to wait. After Taconelli's uses up the day's dough, about 160 pies' worth, that's it for the evening. So call far in advance and say a Hail Mary.*

FIGLIO
1369 Grandview Avenue, Columbus, Ohio; 614-481-0745

The Columbus Dispatch's "Grumpy Gourmet" (Doral Chenoweth) has for several years now rated Figlio among the top ten restaurants in Columbus, and much of its renown is due to the unorthodox pizzas that make up about 40 percent of the business at this nine-year-old hot spot. They recently opened a nearby branch to take the overflow.

The postwar interest in pizza among non-Italians is depicted in this 1957 photo from the Boston Herald-Traveler, which identified Italian chef Angelo Viglione and four of the consumers—Boston Irish girls through and through: Patricia Riley, Nancy Brennan, Betty Fitzpatrick, and Elaine Tutela.

Owners Peter and Laurie Danis left careers as lawyers to follow "our passion for food and people." The only thing they knew about running a restaurant was to buy the best. "We import our feta cheese from Greece and FedEx in special sun-dried tomatoes from California," says Peter, "and we are the only pizza restaurant in town with white tablecloths, napkins, and silverware." Nevertheless, Figlio has a casual bistro atmosphere, and customers love nothing better than to walk by the open kitchen and chat with the cooks about the special ingredients displayed before them.

The fifteen pizzas available—baked in just two minutes in a hardwood fire oven at 900°F—range from a topping of seared fresh salmon brushed with olive oil, Roma tomatoes, feta, and red onions to a teriyaki pizza made with chicken in a Japanese marinade and assembled with pineapple, red and yellow peppers, red onions, and Fontina cheese. "The pizza crust is the palette," explains Peter, "and we can get pretty creative with our pizzas." For dessert go with the spice cake with maple-butternut cream.

SIDNEY'S PIZZA CAFE
2120 Hennepin Avenue, Minneapolis, Minnesota; 612-870-7000

The eight-year-old Sidney's, now with several branches in Minnesota (and one in Montana), would be out of the ordinary for its unusual pizza toppings, which range from Buffalo chicken and asparagus with Brie cheese, to peanut butter and jelly, to Asian pizza (with grilled chicken, onions, and peanut sauce), as well as for its pizza dough wraps enclosing wild mushrooms, sun-dried tomatoes, and cheese. Its decor is unusual, too: a comfortable family-style log cabin setting, complete with fireplace. And the dedication to using organic products and freshly made mozzarella is unstinting, all baked carefully in a wood-burning oven on heated stones. But how many places can claim to serve a "brunch pizza" on Saturdays and Sundays? The pizza crust is topped with fried eggs, bacon, and potatoes—and when you come to think of it, it makes not only perfect but delicious sense. When the Vikings and Timberwolves are off, you'll find the big guys hovering over a pizza at Sidney's.

PIZZERIA BIANCO
623 East Adams Street, Phoenix, Arizona; 602-258-8300

Chris Bianco is only thirty-seven but he's been a student of pizza all his life, and there's little he doesn't know about how to make it better. That's why his little three-year-old, forty-seat pizzeria in Phoenix—not exactly a hotbed of Italian food culture—is always jammed. Chris and partner Susan Pool refuse to compromise on any aspect of pizza-making, from the handmade (not machine-made) dough to the three types of extra-virgin olive oil, fresh mozzarella (made twice a day), organic vegetables and herbs, expensive prosciutto di Parma, and sea salt.

Chris grew up in the Bronx and knew all of New York's great pizzerias, like Mario's in the Bronx, John's in Manhattan, and Totonno's in Brooklyn, and he studied the art of making a great pie in Italy. He makes only one size pizza, and he swears that despite numerous offers to bankroll him, "I will never open another pizzeria. I may not get rich, but I know that I can make great pizza in this one place. I'm here for every shift, six days a week, and I want to be in on making every pie. If I had another place I couldn't be in both at once, so here I stay."

PAULINE'S PIZZA
260 Valencia Street, San Francisco, California; 415-552-2050

It's always a good sign when credit is given where it's due, and Sidney Weinstein and Randall Nathan admirably named their two-story, yellow-and-green, fifteen-year-old pizzeria after the original dough-maker's grandmother, who provided the recipe. The dough is the heart and soul of Pauline's Pizza, which produces a thin, crisp crust with its own wonderful flavor. To this they add toppings sparingly, with a basic tomato sauce, herbs from their own garden in Berkeley, and tomatoes, peppers, and eggplant from their ranch in Calaveras County. Some signature pizzas here include linguiça sausage and capers, fresh asparagus and winter savory, and pesto pizza. Customers are invited to make up their own toppings if they prefer.

The owners refuse to serve any pasta or other food besides pizza, salads, and desserts like mango sorbet and pecan meringue tarts, because all their energies are put into doing pizza the way they believe it should be done. For that reason Pauline's has become something of a shrine to pizza, a place pizza pilgrims head to watch their favorite food being made before their eyes in an open kitchen. Wine-lovers also go to Pauline's because it has one of San Francisco's best-selected wine lists. Even art-lovers hie here for exhibitions of some of the city's best-known artists.

ORIGINAL CHICAGO DEEP-DISH PIZZA

Chicago-style pizza, cooked in a black iron skillet, was the creation of Ike Sewell and Ric Riccardo in 1943, at their Pizzeria Uno in the Windy City. Frankly, we think the whole idea is rather odd: It takes one of the classics of Neapolitan foods and inflates it to midwestern American size, and in so doing compromises everything that makes a good pizza so delightful. In addition, the outrageous toppings plopped onto a Chicago-style pizza seem completely wrongheaded. Nevertheless, we've come up with what we think is a pretty good Chicago-style pie, thick crust and all.

SERVES 4 TO 6

FOR THE CRUST
1 package active dry yeast
1 teaspoon sugar
2³/4 cups all-purpose flour
¹/2 cup yellow cornmeal
1 teaspoon salt, preferably kosher
¹/4 cup olive oil

FOR THE TOPPING
1 pound Italian sausage
One 28-ounce can Italian-style tomatoes, crushed and drained well
2 teaspoons dried oregano
8 ounces mozzarella cheese, sliced
¹/4 cup freshly grated Parmigiano-Reggiano cheese

1. Prepare the crust: In a small bowl, combine the yeast and the sugar with 1 cup tepid water (110°F—no hotter). Stir, and set aside for about 10 minutes for the yeast to dissolve.

2. In a food processor fitted with the dough blade, combine the flour, cornmeal, salt, olive oil, and the yeast mixture. Process. (You can also mix the ingredients in a bowl with a wooden spoon.) If the dough is too dry, add more water, little by little, while the machine is running. Turn the dough out onto a lightly floured board, and knead for 5 minutes. Form the dough into a ball and place it in an oiled bowl. Cover with a dish towel, place in a warm, draft-free spot, and let rise until doubled in size, 1¹/2 to 2 hours.

3. Oil a 12-inch ovenproof skillet. Punch the dough down, fold it over itself, and form a ball. Flatten it and stretch it out to fit the skillet,

pushing the dough out to form a lip against the skillet's edges. Cover, and let rise for 30 minutes.

4. To cook the sausage, first remove the casing and cut the meat into ¹/₂-inch pieces. Heat 1 tablespoon olive oil in a medium-size skillet over medium-high heat, add the sausage, and cook, stirring often, until browned, 6 to 8 minutes.

5. Preheat the oven to 500°F.

6. To assemble the pizza, layer the tomatoes, oregano, mozzarella, and sausage over the dough, and top with the Parmigiano. Bake for 12 minutes. Then lower the heat to 375°F and bake for another 15 to 20 minutes. The pizza is done when the bottom is lightly browned. Serve from the pan.

WINE SUGGESTION: GRIGNOLINO

NOTES: If the water is too hot when mixed with the yeast, the heat will kill the yeast and the dough will not rise.

TRUFFLE-OIL PIZZA

Stephen Kalt is a superbly creative chef—a non-Italian who is passionately committed to reproducing or refining those dishes and flavors he has tasted in Italy. His New York restaurants, Spartina in TriBeCa and Spazzia on the Upper West Side, are paragons of what the new Italian-American cooking is all about, and this is one of his best offerings.

SERVES 4 TO 8

FOR THE CRUST
2¹/₂ teaspoons active dry yeast
¹/₄ teaspoon sugar
¹/₄ cup johnnycake meal or finely ground white cornmeal
3 tablespoons whole-wheat flour
3 to 3¹/₂ cups all-purpose flour
2¹/₄ teaspoons salt, preferably kosher
1 tablespoon extra-virgin olive oil

FOR THE TOPPING
2 tablespoons olive oil
8 ounces Fontina cheese, shredded
6 ounces fresh ricotta cheese
4 ounces Parmigiano-Reggiano cheese, freshly grated
3 to 4 tablespoons white truffle oil

1. Prepare the crust: In a small bowl, dissolve the yeast in 1 cup warm water. Add the sugar, stir, and set aside in a warm place for 10 minutes.

2. In a food processor fitted with the dough blade, combine the johnny-cake meal, whole-wheat flour, all-purpose flour, salt, the yeast mixture, and the olive oil. Process for 1 to 2 minutes. The dough should be soft, not too dry or firm. If it is too thick, add more water, little by little. (The dough can also be made in a bowl and mixed together with a wooden spoon.) Transfer the dough to a lightly floured board, knead for 2 minutes, and form a ball. Transfer the dough to an oiled bowl, cover it with a dish towel, and set it in a warm draft-free place for $1^1/2$ to 2 hours, or until doubled in size.

3. Punch the dough down, and let it rise again for about 40 minutes.

4. Preheat an outdoor grill.

5. Punch the dough down again, and divide it into 4 pieces. Sprinkle some flour on a board, and roll out or stretch 1 piece to form a 10-inch free-style round. Brush the top with some of the olive oil and grill it, oiled side down, until it puffs up and the underside turns light brown. Remove from the grill.

6. With the grilled side up, scatter one quarter of the Fontina and one quarter of the ricotta in small dollops evenly over the dough. Then sprinkle with one quarter of the Parmigiano. Carefully put the pizza back on the grill, and cook for about 3 minutes, or until the cheeses have melted and the underside is brown. Drizzle one quarter of the white truffle oil over the top. Cut into slices and serve. Repeat with the remaining dough and topping.

WINE SUGGESTION: ORNELLAIA

Truffle oil can be a wonderfully aromatic addition to a table, but be aware that you are not buying oil chock-full of truffles, which would make it ridiculously expensive. It is usually made with the tiny pieces and shards left over from grating or slicing white truffles. And one must be careful to buy it fresh; otherwise it may go rancid.

WOLFGANG PUCK'S JEWISH PIZZA

I took an Austrian chef in Los Angeles to give the humble pizza the glamour it now enjoys: Wolfgang Puck, classically trained in French cuisine, opened what he thought was going to be a casual grill and pizzeria in Hollywood, called Spago (which means "string" in Italian). From the first night he attracted a show-business clientele that came for the crisp, bubbly, thin pizzas, one of which Puck made especially famous by topping it with smoked salmon, sour cream, and caviar. You may also add chopped red onion.

SERVES 4

1 recipe dough for Truffle-Oil
  Pizza (page 376), prepared
  through Step 3
4 tablespoons minced fresh dill
1/4 cup extra-virgin olive oil

1/3 cup sour cream
4 ounces smoked salmon, thinly
  sliced
4 teaspoons golden caviar
1 teaspoon black caviar

1. Preheat the oven to 500°F, and heat a pizza stone in it for 30 minutes.

The mere appearance of Italian-American singers Dean Martin (left) and Frank Sinatra (right) at a restaurant like that owned by "Prince" Mike Romanoff (center) in Los Angeles seemed to give the imprimatur that the cooking was as good as the glamour. Dean made pizza famous throughout the U.S. with his song "That's Amore," which has the classic refrain "When the moon hits your eye like a big pizza pie ..."

2. Knead 2 tablespoons of the dill into the pizza dough, and form the dough into four 8-inch circles. Brush the tops of the pizzas with the olive oil.

3. Slide the pizzas onto the baking stone, and bake for 8 to 10 minutes, until golden brown. Transfer to serving plates.

4. Spread sour cream over each pizza, then arrange the smoked salmon decoratively on top. Spoon the two caviars onto the center of the pizzas. Sprinkle with the remaining 2 tablespoons dill.

WINE SUGGESTION: PROSECCO

Edward Brivio is an Italian-American food and wine writer whose memories of feast-day dinners in America are as vivid as those of his best meals in Paris and Rome.

"It's hard to believe, but back in the 1950s when I was growing up, and Thanksgiving and Christmas came around, my mother had to drive from one end of Queens to the other to find the foodstuffs essential to our holiday feasts. In Corona, the Italian neighborhood, we'd go to one of the two Italian delis for the cold cuts used to make up our antipasto—prosciutto, Genoa salami (there was no other kind of Italian salami available), mortadella, et cetera.

"There was one store that sold homemade ravioli—we always used meat ravioli back then—which we only had maybe four or five times a year at holidays. Tortellini didn't exist, as far as we knew, and forget about anything as exotic as squid ink fettuccine, pumpkin ravioli, or sun-dried tomatoes. Even the Italian vegetables for our feasts, like fennel and artichokes, could only be found in greengrocers in Italian-American neighborhoods. Is it just adult nostalgia, or did the finocchio [fennel]—available then only from just before Thanksgiving until the New Year—have much more intense flavor? Torrone, or Italian nougat, was also a treasure that we got only at the Christmas holidays. I can remember how amazed we kids were that you could actually eat the 'paper' that was its top layer.

"There were, also, only two choices for pasta sauce: the meat sauce that my parents, whose parents came from northern Italy, always used, or marinara sauce, which my uncle Joe, whose forebears came from the south of Italy, preferred.

"My father worked long hours as a waiter, even on Thanksgiving, and I can remember waiting with anticipation, and staring hungrily at the trays of cold cuts, until he finally arrived home and we could start eating. Back then we always ate so much antipasto, and the big helpings of ravioli, drenched in a rich meat sauce—we never called it 'ragù' or, God forbid, gravy—that the turkey, when it finally arrived, was hardly touched at all."

PIZZA WITH POTATO AND HAM

One of the most welcome sights—and smells—in Italy is a pizzeria that has its wares set out in large square pans, a display now being seen more often in the United States. While we almost always find it difficult to choose among the various pizzas of the day in such places—and *still* think the pizza alla Margherita is the best of all—here's one we'd have difficulty turning down. It makes an especially good lunch dish to serve with a salad.

SERVES 4 TO 8

1 recipe dough for Truffle-Oil Pizza (page 376), prepared through Step 3
2 tablespoons olive oil
8 ounces Virginia ham, thinly sliced

12 small red potatoes, boiled until tender and cut into 1/4-inch-thick slices
8 ounces Fontina cheese, shredded
2 tablespoons white truffle oil

1. Preheat an outdoor grill.

2. Punch the dough down, and divide it into 4 pieces. Sprinkle some flour on a board and roll or stretch each piece out to form a 10-inch free-style pizza.

3. Brush the top of one of the dough pieces with some of the olive oil and grill it, oiled side down, until it puffs up and the underside is lightly browned, 2 minutes. Remove the pizza from the grill.

4. With the grilled side up, arrange one quarter of the ham on top. Scatter one quarter of the potatoes over the ham. Then, sprinkle with one quarter of the Fontina. Carefully put the pizza back on the grill. Cook until the underside is brown and the cheese has melted, 2 minutes. Remove, drizzle 1/2 tablespoon white truffle oil over the pizza, and slice it. Repeat with the remaining dough and topping.

WINE SUGGESTION:
CORVO BIANCO

WHITE CLAM PIZZA

Whether or not the white clam pizza actually was created at Pepe's Pizzeria Napoletana in New Haven, Connecticut, has never been decided once and for all, but it is the signature dish of this New England pizza parlor and is typical of the way the pie was transformed once it got to these shores.

SERVES 4 TO 6

3 garlic cloves, minced
3 tablespoons olive oil
1 recipe dough for Truffle-Oil
  Pizza (page 376), prepared
  through Step 3

12 small clams, such as littlenecks
1 teaspoon dried oregano
2 tablespoons freshly grated
  Parmigiano-Reggiano cheese

1. Preheat the oven to 450°F, and heat a pizza stone in it for at least 30 minutes.

2. To prepare the clams, combine them with 1/4 cup water in a small saucepan, cover, and bring to a boil. Steam the clams for 3 to 5 minutes, or until they open. (Discard any that don't open.) Pull the clams out of the shells, reserving any clam juice in a separate bowl. Coarsely chop the clams.

3. Punch the dough down and divide it in half. Place 1 portion on a lightly floured surface. Using a rolling pin, roll it out to form a 12-inch round. With your fingers, make a slightly thicker edge. Repeat with the other portion.

4. In a heavy bowl, mash the garlic in the olive oil. Spread the oil mixture over the 2 pizza dough rounds, leaving a 1/2-inch border around the edges.

5. Arrange the clams evenly on the pizzas, and sprinkle with a little of the reserved clam juice. Sprinkle the oregano and cheese evenly over the pizzas.

6. Place one of the pizzas on the pizza stone, and bake for about 15 minutes, until the crust is browned and cooked through and the cheese has browned. Repeat with the second pizza.

WINE SUGGESTION: SOAVE

BASIL PITA CRISPS

You could use baked pizza dough for this savory snack or canapé, but the pita bread is just as easy and has a nice crispiness.

SERVES 4

$^1/_2$ cup packed fresh basil leaves
$1^1/_2$ tablespoons pignoli (pine nuts)
1 large garlic clove, coarsely
  chopped
$^1/_2$ teaspoon salt, preferably kosher
$^1/_4$ teaspoon freshly ground black
  pepper

3 tablespoons butter, softened
3 tablespoons extra-virgin olive oil
2 pita pocket breads, split in half
$^1/_3$ cup freshly grated Parmigiano-
  Reggiano cheese

1. Preheat the oven to 400°F.

2. In a small food processor, combine the basil, pignoli, garlic, salt, and pepper, and grind quickly. Do not grind it too fine.

3. In a small bowl, combine the basil mixture, butter, and olive oil, and mix. Spread the mixture on the rough (inside) side of the 4 pieces of pita. Sprinkle with the Parmigiano, and bake in the oven for 5 to 7 minutes. (Keep an eye on them toward the end of the baking time, because they can burn quickly.) Cut each round into 6 wedges, and serve immediately.

WINE SUGGESTION: PINOT GRIGIO

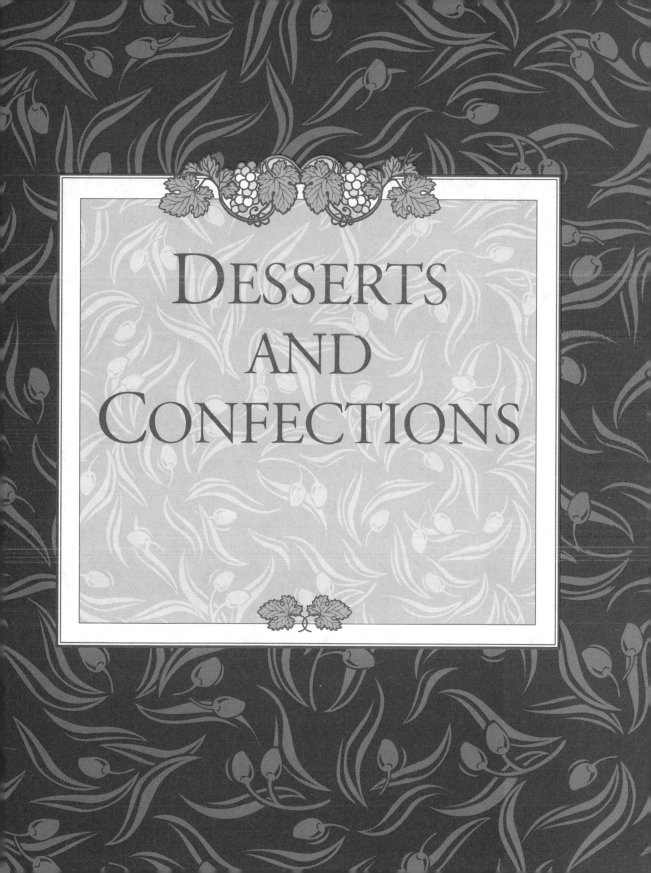

DESSERTS AND CONFECTIONS

DESSERTS AND CONFECTIONS

Italians are not big dessert eaters at dinner, though they may well have a gelato or a little pastry in the afternoon. Still, it's traditional to bring a box of pastries or a cake to someone's house, and on weekends or on feast days, desserts are most certainly enjoyed with great gusto. But for the most part, Italians have a piece or two of fruit after their meal.

Fruit was certainly one of the rewards after a good meal in Italian-Americans homes, too, but affluence and the availability of store-bought sweets created an appetite for desserts, pastries, and cookies. Indeed, the Old Country tortas and cheesecakes became bigger, taller, and richer in America, with cheesecakes becoming the very symbol of Italian largesse at the end of a big meal at home or in a restaurant. For decades cheesecake, cannoli, biscuit tortoni, and spumoni were the staples of Italian-American restaurants, and pastry shops offered counters full of Italian-style cookies. One might find zabaglione in one of the fancier Italian-American restaurants, but such a luxury would be a rarity at home.

It really was not until the 1970s and '80s that those old-fashioned desserts were supplanted, primarily by one single lavish finale—*tiramisù*—which became a requisite, not only on Italian-American menus but in restaurants of every stripe. Little by little, semifreddos and panna cottas were found on menus, biscotti gained popularity right along with the boom in upscale coffeehouses, and many American companies began producing Italian ices and gelati. Today, both here and in Italy, pastry-making has become as serious as it has traditionally been in France and Austria.

Were we writing this cookbook ten years ago, we might have had a much smaller dessert chapter. And ten years from now we might well consider an entire book on Italian and Italian-American desserts!

BISCOTTI WITH PECANS

I t's puzzling that these crunchy twice-baked cookies (the word *biscotti*—bee-SKOH-tee—means "twice baked") took so long to catch on in America. In Tuscany they are often made with toasted almonds, but we think American pecans give them an even richer, nuttier flavor.

SERVES 4 TO 6

1 cup pecans, very coarsely chopped	6 tablespoons (³/4 stick) unsalted butter, softened
1³/4 cups all-purpose flour	³/4 cup sugar
1¹/2 teaspoons baking powder	1¹/2 teaspoons vanilla extract
	2 large eggs

1. Preheat the oven to 325°F.

2. Place the pecans in a shallow baking pan and toast them in the oven until they have browned a bit, 8 to 12 minutes. Keep a watchful eye out, as they burn quickly. Remove the pecans from the oven and increase the temperature to 400°F.

3. In a small bowl, mix the flour with the baking powder. Set aside.

4. In a mixing bowl, beat the butter with an electric mixer. With the mixer on high speed, gradually add the sugar, beating until the mixture is light and fluffy. Add the vanilla. On low speed, add the eggs, one at

One of the earliest entrepreneurs to grasp the power of graphics and advertising was Domingo Ghirardelli, Jr., whose family, immigrants from Rapallo, Italy, began making chocolates and candies under their own name in San Francisco in 1850.

a time, beating until incorporated. Then add the flour in 3 batches, mixing until just blended. Stir in the pecans with a wooden spoon.

5. Line a cookie sheet with aluminum foil. Spoon the batter in 2 strips, about 12 inches long and 2 inches wide, on the cookie sheet. Leave plenty of room between the strips for spreading. Even the thickness of the strips with the back of a spoon.

6. Bake the strips until they are golden and the tops spring back when lightly touched, 15 minutes. Remove them from the oven and reduce the temperature to 300°F.

7. Transfer the strips to a cutting board and let them cool for 10 minutes. Then cut them into ³/4-inch-wide slices, slightly on the diagonal, and return them to the baking sheet, leaving space between them. Bake for 25 minutes.

8. Open the oven door slightly, turn the oven off, and let the biscotti dry out for 10 minutes. Then transfer them to racks to cool completely. These can be stored in an airtight container for up to 2 weeks.

WINE SUGGESTION: VIN SANTO

BABAS AU RHUM
WITH FRUIT

Though long associated with Naples, *baba* has Polish origins, supposedly when Stanislas Leczinsky, the deposed king of Poland who resettled in Lorraine in 1737, poured rum on his traditional Gugelhopf cake to moisten it and made the confection popular. He thereupon named the cake after Ali Baba, hero of *The Thousand and One Nights*. Other less romantic stories about the cake's origins suggest the name may simply come from the Polish *baba*, for "old woman." In any case, it has long been popular among Italians and Italian-Americans, and we think the addition of fruit makes this an even more regal dessert.

SERVES 8

FOR THE DOUGH
1 package active dry yeast
2 tablespoons sugar
¹/4 cup whole milk, room
    temperature
3 large eggs, room temperature
1¹/2 cups all-purpose flour
7 tablespoons unsalted butter,
    softened
¹/4 teaspoon salt, preferably kosher

FOR THE SYRUP
³/4 cup sugar
¹/2 vanilla bean, slit in half, or
    1¹/2 teaspoons vanilla extract

¹/4 cup plus 2 tablespoons dark
    rum
3 tablespoons Triple Sec
¹/4 cup freshly squeezed lemon
    juice

FOR THE FRUIT
4 very ripe peaches, peeled, pitted,
    and sliced
2 cups blueberries
2 tablespoons freshly squeezed
    lemon juice
2 tablespoons sugar

1. Prepare the dough: In a medium-size bowl, combine the yeast, ¹/2 tablespoon of the sugar, and 3 tablespoons water. Stir, and set aside for 10 minutes.

2. Add the remaining 1¹/2 tablespoons sugar, the milk, and the eggs, one at a time, mixing well after each addition. Stir until smooth. Add the flour, ¹/2 cup at a time, beating until smooth. Set the bowl aside in a warm area, cover it with a dish towel, and let the dough rise until it has doubled in size, 1¹/2 to 2 hours.

3. Add the butter and salt to the dough, and mix vigorously to completely incorporate. Cover again with a dish towel and set aside until doubled in size, about 1¹/2 hours.

4. Butter 10 muffin cups or 8 small soufflé dishes, and fill them two-thirds full with the dough. (The dough will be sticky; the tops will smooth out as they rise.) Cover them with a dish towel, but do not let the towel touch the dough. Let rise until doubled in size, 1 to 1¹/2 hours.

5. Meanwhile, preheat the oven to 350°F.

6. Bake the babas in the oven until they are light brown, 15 to 20 minutes. Let them rest for 5 minutes. Then remove them from the molds, place them on a rack, and let them cool to room temperature.

7. While the babas are cooling, prepare the syrup: In a small saucepan, combine the sugar, 1¹/2 cups water, and the vanilla bean. Bring to a simmer and cook for 5 minutes. Let cool to room temperature.

8. Remove the vanilla bean and scrape the seeds into the syrup; discard the pod. Add the rum, Triple Sec, and lemon juice to the syrup.

9. Place the babas upside-down in a nonreactive baking dish that is large enough to hold them in a single layer, and spoon the syrup over them. Keep on spooning the syrup until all or most of it has been absorbed.

10. Prepare the fruit: In a medium-size bowl, combine the peaches, blueberries, lemon juice, and sugar. Mix gently and set aside for 10 to 15 minutes, or until the sugar has dissolved.

11. To serve, cut each baba into quarters, slicing almost all the way down, and open it like a flower. Spoon some fruit into the middle, and serve.

WINE SUGGESTION: MOSCATO D'ASTI

PLUM CAKE

The beauty of this cake is that the sweetness comes from the ripe plums, not from a lot of sugar.

SERVES 8

FOR THE DOUGH
10 tablespoons (1¹/4 sticks)
  unsalted butter
1 cup sugar
2 large eggs
1¹/2 teaspoons vanilla extract
1¹/4 cups all-purpose flour
1¹/4 teaspoons baking powder
¹/2 teaspoon cinnamon

¹/8 teaspoon salt, preferably kosher
10 to 12 small Italian plums,
  pitted and halved

FOR THE TOPPING
¹/2 tablespoon unsalted butter,
  melted
2 teaspoons sugar
¹/4 teaspoon ground cinnamon

1. Preheat the oven to 350°F.

2. Prepare the dough: In a mixing bowl, beat the butter with an electric mixer on high speed until fluffy. Gradually add the sugar and beat for 2 to 3 minutes, until light and fluffy. Add the eggs, one at a time, beating after each addition. Blend in the vanilla extract.

3. In a small bowl, combine the flour, baking powder, cinnamon, and salt and mix.

4. On low speed, in two additions, add the flour to the butter mixture, being careful not to overmix the dough.

5. Butter a 10-inch springform pan. Spread the dough evenly in the pan. Place the plum halves, skin side up, on top of the dough.

6. Prepare the topping: Brush the plums with the melted butter. In a small bowl, stir the sugar and cinnamon together and sprinkle over the cake.

7. Bake the cake for 45 to 50 minutes, or when cake tester comes out clean. Cool on a rack, and serve.

WINE SUGGESTION: ASTI SPUMANTE

TIRAMISÙ

What cheesecake was to the first ninety years of Italian-American desserts, *tiramisù* (tee-rah-mee-SOO) has been for the past ten. It is now ubiquitous on Italian-American menus and, ironically, has become so in Italy as a result. There are many stories as to where *tiramisù* originated, though the claim that the dessert in its current form originated at El Toulà restaurant in Treviso is as close to the truth as we're likely to get. Starting in the 1980s, *tiramisù* was popularized in Italian-American restaurants as a more sophisticated alternative to cheesecake, and that popularity has been transferred to restaurants all over Italy by now, so that it is as likely that you'll find it on a dessert menu in Venice as you would in Palermo. The name, which means "pick me up," is a good one for a rich and delectable sweet that is even more appealing in the late afternoon with a cup of espresso.

     The recipe is ridiculously easy—there's no cooking involved. The only trick is to avoid soaking the ladyfingers too long in the espresso. If you use *savoiardi* (ladyfingers) purchased from a pastry shop, they are better if they are a day old. Otherwise, the commercially packaged *savoiardi* work very well.

SERVES 10

One 17.5 ounce container
  mascarpone cheese
2 tablespoons orange liqueur, such
  as Triple Sec or Cointreau
1 tablespoon dark rum
3 tablespoons sugar

1 teaspoon vanilla extract
1 cup heavy cream
24 ladyfingers
1¹/2 cups brewed espresso
6 ounces semisweet or bittersweet
  chocolate, finely chopped

1. In a large bowl, combine the mascarpone, orange liqueur, and rum. Then gradually blend in the sugar.

2. In a chilled bowl, combine the vanilla extract and the cream, and whip until it forms soft peaks. Fold this into the mascarpone mixture.

3. Place half of the ladyfingers in a flat baking dish, and pour half of the espresso over them. Let the ladyfingers moisten for about 10 seconds, turning them often. Carefully lift them out of the pan and arrange them in a single layer in a 12 x 6-inch baking pan.

4. Spread half the mascarpone mixture over the ladyfingers, and sprinkle with half the chocolate. Repeat the process with the remaining ingredients, creating 2 layers of ladyfingers.

5. Cover and refrigerate for at least 1 hour. Serve on individual plates.

WINE SUGGESTION: ASTI SPUMANTE

MARY PICKFORD

MOTION PICTURE STAR
IN EVERY PACKAGE OF
GHIRARDELLI'S
MILK CHOCOLATE

The Ghirardelli company was the first to package trading cards of silent movie stars with the candy they sold at movie theaters. Today Ghirardelli Square is a major tourist attraction in San Franscisco.

TORRONE SEMIFREDDO

Asemifreddo (seh-mee-FREH-doh), sometimes referred to as
a *dolce al cucchiaio* (a sweet to be eaten with a spoon), is a
custard or a chilled mousse. *Torrone* is a hazelnut nougat
candy available at specialty and Italian markets.

SERVES 8

2 large eggs
¹/4 cup sugar
1 cup heavy cream
1 tablespoon Triple Sec
1 teaspoon vanilla extract

4 ounces torrone (Italian nougat
  candy), finely chopped
2 ounces semisweet chocolate,
  finely chopped

1. Bring a saucepan of water to a simmer. Line a 9 x 5 x 3-inch loaf
pan with plastic wrap, leaving a 3-inch overlap at the ends.

2. In a small bowl, beat the eggs with the sugar until light and fluffy. Put
the bowl into the pan of simmering water and continue to beat until
the eggs begin to hold peaks. Remove the bowl from the hot water and
place it in a bowl of ice water. Let cool, stirring often.

3. In a medium-size bowl, beat the cream with the Triple Sec and
vanilla until the mixture holds peaks. Gently fold the cooled eggs into
the whipped cream. Fold in the *torrone* and the chocolate, and transfer to the loaf pan. Even out the top, fold the plastic wrap over the top,
and refrigerate for about 9 hours or overnight.

4. Unmold the *semifreddo* and slice as desired.

WINE SUGGESTION: TORCOLATO

ALMOND TORTONI

Not too long ago, every Italian-American restaurant served
biscuit *tortoni* in little pleated paper cups. It was a very rich
vanilla ice cream topped with crumbled sugared almonds—
usually a dessert for the kids while the parents scarfed up cheesecake or zabaglione. Rarely was it made on the premises.

Our version is very easy to make and has a far better consistency than the rock-hard, frozen-solid biscuit tortoni served in the old days.

SERVES 10

2/3 cup sugar
3 large egg yolks
Pinch of salt
2 tablespoons Amaretto
2 cups heavy cream

3 tablespoons confectioners' sugar
1 teaspoon vanilla extract
1/2 teaspoon almond extract
1/2 cup slivered blanched almonds,
   toasted (see Note)

1. In a small saucepan, combine the sugar with 1/3 cup water and heat until the syrup reaches 236°F (use a candy thermometer).

2. In a mixing bowl, beat the egg yolks with the salt until light. Add the sugar syrup in a stream, beating on high speed until light. Stir in the Amaretto, and refrigerate.

3. Meanwhile, in a medium bowl, beat the cream until it starts to thicken. Add the confectioners' sugar, vanilla, and almond extract, and continue beating until the whipped cream is firm.

4. Fold the almonds into the egg mixture, and then fold the mixture into the whipped cream. Divide among 10 ramekins, cover with plastic wrap, and refrigerate.

WINE SUGGESTION: MOSCATO D'ASTI

NOTE: To toast the almonds, place them on a small baking pan and bake in a preheated 325°F oven for 8 to 10 minutes, or until lightly colored. Let cool.

TIRAMISÙ LOAF CAKE

We were intrigued by something called "tiramisù pound cake" that we saw in a bakery in Chicago, but the item turned out to be heavy, bland, and nothing to get excited about. However, we loved the idea of making a kind of pound cake using the flavors of *tiramisù*—espresso, chocolate, and mascarpone—and so worked out a delightful version of our own that is terrific as a breakfast or afternoon cake. We've used cream cheese instead of mascarpone, but you may use either.

SERVES 8

FOR THE BATTER
3/4 cup all-purpose flour
1 1/4 teaspoons baking powder
1/2 teaspoon salt
10 tablespoons (1 1/4 sticks) unsalted butter
1 cup sugar
1 large egg
2 large egg yolks
2 teaspoons vanilla extract
1 tablespoon instant coffee granules, mixed with 1 teaspoon hot water
3/4 cup sour cream

6 ounces semisweet chocolate, coarsely chopped

FOR THE COFFEE CREAM CHEESE SPREAD
1 teaspoon instant coffee granules
2 tablespoons strong brewed espresso, cooled
8 ounces cream cheese
3/4 cup confectioners' sugar, sifted

1. Preheat the oven to 350°F. Butter a 9 x 5 x 3-inch loaf pan, and set it aside.

2. Prepare the batter: In a bowl, mix the flour, baking powder, and salt. Set aside.

3. In a mixing bowl, whip the butter with an electric mixer until it is light and fluffy. Keep beating while gradually adding the sugar. Continue beating until the mixture is light and fluffy. On medium speed, add the egg and egg yolks, one at a time, beating well after each addition. Add the vanilla extract and the coffee.

4. Lower the mixer speed and alternately add the flour mixture and the sour cream, ending with the flour. Add the chocolate pieces, and mix just to blend them into the batter. Pour the batter into the prepared loaf pan, evening the level of the batter.

5. Bake in the oven for 1 hour to 1 hour 10 minutes, or until a skewer inserted into the middle comes out

Joseph Scelsa, a professor of Italian studies in New York, was surprised when he was growing up to find that few Americans ate as well as he did.

"My people arrived here in 1900 from Caccamo. My grandmother, Francesca Givenco, was the Sicilian matriarch of the family and she'd mount these extravagant Sunday dinners. I thought, growing up, that everybody ate the way I ate. We'd sit down for a three- or four-hour dinner. That was normal. We felt wrapped around the family table, and everything was wonderfully orchestrated around a delicious meal— cicarone soup with little chicken meatballs—she'd grind the chicken, make the pasta with the volcano in the flour, everything. I'd ask for a piece as she was making it fresh while it was drying. Oh, and the cassata she made! My grandfather was a barber who could shave the hair off a peach to show how finely he worked. He'd cut up the candied fruit and place them in a pattern on the cassata. She made her own fresh cannoli. I'd have to scour the neighborhood for bamboo poles they wrapped carpets around. My grandfather would cut them as molds for shells for the cannoli."

clean. (If, after 45 to 50 minutes, the cake starts getting dark, cover it loosely with a piece of aluminum foil.) Place the loaf on a wire rack and let it cool for 20 minutes. Then carefully invert the cake, remove it from the pan, and cool completely on the wire rack.

6. While the cake is cooling, make the Coffee Cream Cheese Spread: In a small bowl, stir the instant coffee into the espresso. In a mixing bowl, beat the cream cheese until soft. Add the confectioners' sugar and the coffee mixture, and beat for 2 to 3 minutes. Refrigerate until ready to use.

7. To serve, slice a piece of the cake and serve with a dollop of the Coffee Cream Cheese Spread.

WINE SUGGESTION: PICOLIT

PANNA COTTA

This eggless custard—*panna cotta* (PAH-nah KOH-tah) means "cooked cream"—has a simple, pure flavor that lends itself to fruit sauces.

SERVES 6

2 cups whole milk, chilled
1 package unflavored gelatin
1 cup heavy cream

1 1/2 teaspoons vanilla extract
5 tablespoons sugar
Pear Puree (page 411) for serving

1. Pour 1/2 cup of the milk into a small saucepan, sprinkle the gelatin over the milk, and stir. Let the gelatin soften for about 7 minutes.

2. Place the saucepan over low heat and stir for 5 minutes. Add the remaining 1 1/2 cups milk, the cream, and the vanilla. Heat, stirring frequently, over medium heat until small bubbles appear around the edges. Remove from the heat, stir in the sugar until dissolved, and let cool for 10 minutes.

3. Pour the mixture into 6 ramekins. Cover with aluminum foil and refrigerate until set, 2 to 3 hours.

4. To unmold, dip the ramekins into hot water for 20 to 30 seconds and invert onto a plate. Spoon some Pear Puree around each unmolded *panna cotta*, and serve.

WINE SUGGESTION: ASTI SPUMANTE

FIGS WITH RICOTTA AND HONEY

Serve this as either a cheese course or as dessert. The light creaminess of the ricotta blends wonderfully with the sweet figs and honey, tinged with the lemon zest.

SERVES 4

1 1/4 cups ricotta cheese
1/2 teaspoon freshly grated lemon
  zest
2 tablespoons sugar

12 fresh figs, sliced into quarters
  but still attached at the bottom
4 tablespoons good-quality honey
3 tablespoons pignoli (pine nuts),
  toasted (optional; page 248)

1. In a small bowl, combine the ricotta, lemon zest, and sugar and mix well.

2. Divide the ricotta mixture among 4 plates. Place 3 figs on each portion of ricotta, with the sections fanned out. Drizzle 1 tablespoon of the honey over each fig, sprinkle with the pignoli, if you are using them, and serve.

WINE SUGGESTION: PINOT BIANCO

RICE PUDDING
WITH
ORANGE AND SAFFRON

The flavors of this rice pudding evoke the eastern part of the Mediterranean, which had a great influence on the sweets of the Middle Ages and Renaissance. Saffron would be affordable only to very affluent families, and rice was not cultivated in Italy until the fifteenth century. We've found that American long-grain rice works best with this kind of dessert.

SERVES 6 TO 8

4¹/2 cups whole milk
¹/2 cup long-grain rice
²/3 cup sugar
¹/8 teaspoon salt, preferably kosher
¹/4 teaspoon saffron threads
3 large eggs

²/3 cup heavy cream
1 tablespoon Cointreau or other
    orange-flavored liqueur
1 teaspoon freshly grated orange
    zest

1. In a large, heavy saucepan, bring the milk just to a boil to scald it. Reduce the heat, add the rice, sugar, and salt, and simmer gently for 30 to 35 minutes, stirring often so the milk doesn't scorch. The rice should be cooked but firm. Remove from the heat.

2. While the rice is cooking, put the saffron in a small saucepan and heat the pan over medium heat to toast the saffron, about 1 minute. As soon as the saffron becomes slightly darker in color, transfer it to a mortar and grind it with the pestle. Add about ¹/4 cup of the hot milk mixture to the mortar, mix it with the saffron, and pour it back into the milk mixture. Repeat the process with another ¹/4 cup of milk to get all of the saffron out of the mortar.

3. In a mixing bowl, beat the eggs. Add the cream and blend. Add ¹/2 cup of the hot rice mixture and stir (this tempers the eggs so they will not cook). Repeat with another ¹/2 cup rice mixture. Slowly add the egg mixture, stirring constantly, to the rice mixture. Add the Cointreau and orange zest, and place over low heat. Stir constantly until the mixture thickens enough to coat the back of the spoon, 2 to 4 minutes. Be careful not to overcook or the eggs will start curdling. Transfer the rice pudding to a serving bowl, and let it cool to room temperature. Serve at room temperature (our preference) or cold.

WINE SUGGESTION: ASTI SPUMANTE

DRIED FIGS
WITH
WALNUTS AND CHOCOLATE

This is a typical Old World confection that was superseded in the New by sweeter cheap candies. But old-timers still love these delightfully chewy, crunchy, chocolatey morsels, and once you taste them, you may become addicted too.

MAKES 20 PIECES

20 dried figs
20 walnut halves
Candied orange peel

4 ounces good-quality bittersweet chocolate, such as Tobler, Suchard, Valrhona, or Callebaut
1 tablespoon unsalted butter

1. Remove the remnants of the stems from the tops of the figs, then slit the figs open vertically, but do not cut all the way through. Place a walnut half and a piece or two of candied orange peel inside, and press the fig closed with your fingers.

2. In a saucepan, melt the chocolate and butter over very low heat until smooth. Remove from the heat.

3. Dip the figs into the chocolate to coat them, and then place them on a rack or wax paper until the chocolate hardens. Store, wrapped in wax paper in a box, for up to 1 week.

WINE SUGGESTIONS: SWEET MARSALA

ESPRESSO FLAN

T he eggs make this a form of custard—as opposed to *panna cotta*, which does not contain eggs. And that makes for a rich dessert. A little goes a long way.

SERVES 8

1 cup sugar
1 1/2 cups whole milk
1 1/2 cups heavy cream
1/3 cup finely ground espresso beans

1 ounce bittersweet or semisweet chocolate, coarsely chopped
5 large egg yolks
1 teaspoons vanilla extract

1. Preheat the oven to 350°F.

2. In a small saucepan, heat 2/3 cup of the sugar over medium heat, stirring occasionally, until it melts and turns golden brown, 5 to 8 minutes. Immediately pour the caramel into 8 ramekins, swirl it around to coat the inside of the ramekins, and set aside.

3. In a large saucepan, heat the milk and cream over medium heat until little bubbles start to appear on the sides of the pan, 4 to 8 minutes. Remove from the heat, add the espresso grinds, and stir. Let stand for 10 minutes. Then add the chocolate and stir to melt.

4. In a medium-size bowl, combine the egg yolks, the remaining 1/3 cup sugar, and the vanilla extract, and stir to mix. Slowly, stirring constantly, strain the hot espresso mixture through a fine-mesh sieve into the egg mixture. Add the espresso mixture slowly at first, to mix well and temper the eggs so they will not cook, then pour it in a stream.

5. Divide the mixture among the caramel-lined ramekins. Place them in a roasting pan, and pour hot water into the pan so it reaches two-thirds of the way up the ramekins' sides. Cover with a piece of aluminum foil, and bake in the oven for about 35 minutes, or until a sharp knife inserted in the custard comes out clean. Remove the ramekins from the pan, and let them cool on a rack. Then refrigerate for about 6 hours.

6. To serve, dip each ramekin in a bowl of hot water for a few seconds, and then invert the flan onto a plate.

WINE SUGGESTION: SWEET MARSALA

NOTES: Do not overbrown the caramel. When it becomes too brown, it turns bitter.

If a fine-mesh strainer is not available, use a regular strainer lined with several layers of cheesecloth to catch the grinds.

STRAWBERRIES GRATINATA

I t's impossible to imagine anyone not drooling over this dish of sweetened strawberries with a browned top. You might substitute raspberries, but just make sure that whatever fruit you're using, it's at its seasonal best.

SERVES 4

1 large egg
3 large egg yolks
$1/2$ cup sugar
$1/2$ teaspoon vanilla extract
3 tablespoons Cointreau or
   Triple Sec

1 pint strawberries, each hulled
   and cut into 4 pieces
1 container (6 ounces) raspberries
   or blueberries

1. Preheat the broiler.

2. In the top of a double boiler, combine the egg, egg yolks, and sugar. Beat with a whisk or a portable beater until light and fluffy. Place the pan over simmering water and continue to beat until the mixture is fluffy and holds a soft peak. Then add the vanilla and the Cointreau and beat for another 30 seconds. Remove the double-boiler top from the heat.

3. Place the strawberries and raspberries in a 10 x 8 x 2-inch baking pan, and pour the egg mixture evenly over the berries. Place under the broiler for 1 to 2 minutes, until lightly browned. The *gratinata* browns very quickly, so keep an eye on it. Serve immediately.

WINE SUGGESTION: MOSCATO D'ASTI

NOTE: If you don't have a double boiler, beat the eggs in a heatproof bowl and then place it in a saucepan of simmering water.

ALMOND CAKE
WITH RASPBERRY JAM

T ypical of northern Italy, this is good after a meal, for breakfast, or for an afternoon snack with a cup of espresso.

SERVES 6 TO 8

1³/4 cups blanched almonds
1 cup sugar
¹/2 cup all-purpose flour
¹/4 teaspoon baking powder
Pinch of salt
5 tablespoons unsalted butter,
   softened

4 large eggs, room temperature
2 teaspoons vanilla extract
¹/2 cup seedless raspberry jam
Whipped cream (optional)

1. Preheat the oven to 325°F. Butter an 8-inch round cake pan, and fit
it with an 8-inch circle of wax paper. Butter the paper. Sprinkle with
flour and shake off the excess. Set aside.

2. Place the almonds in a shallow pan and bake for 12 to 14 minutes,
or until slightly colored. Remove and let cool. Keep the oven on. Slice
enough almonds to make ¹/4 cup, and set aside. Set the whole almonds
aside as well.

3. In a food processor, combine the toasted whole almonds with ¹/4
cup of the sugar and process until the almonds are finely ground. Add
the flour, baking powder, and salt, and pulse just to blend.

4. In a large mixing bowl, beat the butter with an electric mixer on
high speed for 1 to 2 minutes, until fluffy. Gradually add the remaining ³/4 cup sugar, beating until light and fluffy. On a lower speed, beat
in the eggs, one at a time, until incorporated. Add the vanilla. On the
lowest speed, fold in the flour mixture, being careful not to overmix.

5. Pour the batter into the prepared pan, and sprinkle with the reserved
¹/4 cup sliced almonds. Bake in the oven for 40 to 45 minutes, or until
an inserted toothpick comes out clean. Let cool for about 15 minutes,
and then remove from the pan and cool further on a rack.

6. When the cake is cool, carefully slice it in half horizontally. Spread the jam over the bottom half, and replace the top. Serve with whipped cream if desired.

WINE SUGGESTION: PICOLIT

COCOA COOKIES
WITH HAZELNUTS

Italians adore hazelnuts and chocolate, perhaps in that order, so the combination, as in the famous Perugina Baci chocolate candies, is irresistible. With the bittersweet taste of cocoa and the crunch of hazelnuts, this cookie is as good an example of an afternoon treat or after-dinner nibble as we can think of.

MAKES 50 COOKIES

2 cups all-purpose flour
3/4 cup unsweetened cocoa
   powder, preferably Dutch
   process
1/8 teaspoon salt
1 1/2 teaspoons baking powder

1 cup (2 sticks) unsalted butter,
   softened
1 1/3 cups sugar
1 large egg
2 teaspoons vanilla extract
3/4 cup hazelnuts, toasted and
   coarsely chopped

1. In a large bowl, sift together the flour, cocoa powder, salt, and baking powder. Set aside.

2. In a mixing bowl, beat the butter with an electric mixer on high speed until light. Gradually add the sugar, beating until light and fluffy. Add the egg and vanilla, and beat until incorporated. Mix in the hazelnuts. On a lower speed, add the dry ingredients and mix, scraping the sides of the bowl, until just blended.

3. Place an 18-inch-long piece of wax paper on a work surface, and turn the dough out onto it. Shape the dough into an even rectangle 15 inches long, 1 1/2 inches thick, and 3 inches wide (I do this by folding the wax paper over

Italians usually serve fruit at the end of the meal, placing the various whole fruits in a bowl of cold water, which gives them a slight bath and a refreshing temperature on the skin without chilling the flesh, which would diminish its flavor.

it and tapping it gently on all sides on a board). Wrap the rectangle in the wax paper and refrigerate for 3 hours, or put in the freezer for about 30 minutes.

4. Meanwhile, preheat the oven to 400°F.

5. Using a sharp knife, slice the chilled dough into ¼-inch-thick slices. Place on a cookie sheet, 1 inch apart. Bake for 8 to 10 minutes. Let cool on the cookie sheet for 2 minutes and then, using a spatula, transfer to a rack. Let cool completely. Store in airtight tins.

WINE SUGGESTION: VIN SANTO

ZABAGLIONE

Zabaglione (zah-bahl-YOH-neh) is the big show dish of Italian-American restaurants. The tuxedoed headwaiter comes to the table and with great flourish proceeds to whisk the ingredients together over a can of Sterno, then ceremoniously ladles it into dessert dishes, usually with the addition of fresh fruit like strawberries or raspberries. This luxurious and Lucullan dessert is amazingly easy to make.

Its egg yolk content may seem decadent, but it really comes down to just about one egg per serving. The crucial ingredient here is the sweet Marsala. We recommend either of two readily available brands—Florio or Rallo. Anything less, and your zabaglione will taste bitter and alcoholic.

SERVES 4

5 large egg yolks
5 tablespoons sugar

5 tablespoons good-quality sweet Marsala
½ teaspoon vanilla extract

In the top of a double boiler, combine the egg yolks, sugar, Marsala, and vanilla. Place the pan over barely simmering water, and whisk or beat with an electric mixer until the mixture is pale and fluffy and holds its shape, about 5 minutes.

Serve immediately, preferably with berries or mixed fresh fruits.

WINE SUGGESTION: SWEET MARSALA

*Horse-drawn bread
delivery by the
A. Gonnella Bakery
on Sangamon Street
in Chicago, circa
1900.*

LEMON GRANITA

On a hot summer's day a granita is the most refreshing thing
in the world. Light, briskly flavored, with a texture between
a sorbet and a slush drink, granitas are extremely easy to
make, provided you stay around to stir the ice crystals every once in
a while. You don't need an ice cream machine—a tablespoon does
all the handwork necessary.

SERVES 4

¹/2 cup sugar
*Peel of 1 lemon (without the white
  pith), in strips*

*¹/2 cup freshly squeezed lemon
  juice (2 to 3 lemons)*

1. In a small saucepan, combine the sugar with 1 cup water. Bring to a boil, then reduce the heat and simmer for 2 minutes, until the sugar melts.

2. Twist the lemon strips to release the oils, and add to the hot sugar syrup. Pour the syrup into a small metal bowl and let it cool completely.

3. When the syrup has cooled, remove the lemon strips, stir in the lemon juice, and place in the freezer. Stir the granita every 30 minutes, scraping off any frozen crystals that are stuck to the side of the bowl. Break up any clumps with a spoon. The granita is ready when it is spoonable but not hard and crumbly, 3 to 4 hours. Serve immediately. (This cannot be made ahead of time.)

COFFEE GRANITA

As tangy as lemon granita is, coffee-flavored granita is another refreshing pick-me-up. Its bittersweet qualities make it a delightful alternative to a cup of espresso in summer, or a fine dessert after a rich meal.

SERVES 4 TO 6

2 to 3 tablespoons sugar
2 cups hot, strong, freshly brewed
  espresso

Whipped cream, for serving

1. Stir the sugar into the hot espresso until completely dissolved. Allow to cool.

2. Pour the espresso mixture into a shallow bowl, and place it in the freezer. About every 30 minutes, stir to break up the ice crystals as they form. Eventually the mixture will become slushy. Scrape off any frozen crystals that are stuck to the side of the bowl, and break up any clmups with a spoon. Allow the granita to firm up slightly, but not as much as a sorbet, 3 to 4 hours total.

3. Serve in individual dishes, topped with whipped cream.

RENEE MARIANI'S CHEESECAKE

My mother, Renee Sofia Mariani, was forever apologizing that whatever she made didn't turn out the way she wanted or the way we might have remembered it, but to us it always came out the same, which was pretty close to perfect. As Italian cheesecakes go, this is a superb example, even with the typically American addition of the graham-cracker crust.

If you wish to add the traditional candied fruit to the cheese mixture, go right ahead, but most people I know have never much cared for it.

—J.M.

SERVES 8

FOR THE CRUST
1³/4 cups graham cracker crumbs
8 tablespoons (1 stick) unsalted
   butter, melted
¹/4 cup sugar

FOR THE FILLING
2 pounds whole-milk ricotta cheese
6 large eggs, separated
1¹/4 cups sugar
Grated zest of 2 lemons
1 teaspoon vanilla extract
1 tablespoon all-purpose flour
Pinch of salt

1. Preheat the oven to 350°F.

2. Prepare the crust: In a medium-size bowl, combine the graham cracker crumbs, melted butter, and sugar. Mix well.

3. Transfer the crust mixture to a 10-inch springform pan, and press it down so it covers the bottom and makes a 2¹/2-inch-high edge.

4. Prepare the filling: In a food processor, process the ricotta for 30 seconds.

5. In a large mixing bowl, beat the egg yolks. Then gradually beat in the sugar until the mixture is light. Mix in the lemon zest and the vanilla.

6. In a clean, grease-free mixing bowl, beat the egg whites until they barely hold their shape and are still very soft.

7. Combine the flour with the pinch of salt. Add the ricotta and the flour to the egg yolk mixture, and mix. Thoroughly fold in the egg whites.

8. Pour the filling into the crust-lined pan, and place in the middle of the oven. Bake for 40 to 50 minutes, or until an inserted toothpick comes out clean. (If the cake browns too quickly, place a piece of aluminum foil loosely over the top.) Remove the cheesecake from the oven, let it cool, and then remove the sides of the springform pan. Refrigerate.

9. Do not serve the cheesecake ice-cold—let it stand at room temperature for 1 hour before serving.

WINE SUGGESTION: PICOLIT

> *Always heat your espresso or cappuccino cups before filling them with the coffee.*

PEACH TART

The sour cream in the crust makes a big difference in the taste and texture of this summery tart.

SERVES 6

FOR THE PASTRY CRUST
1 cup all-purpose flour
1/8 teaspoon salt, preferably kosher
1 1/2 teaspoons sugar
1/4 teaspoon baking powder
4 1/2 tablespoons unsalted butter, chilled, cut into 10 pieces
3 1/2 tablespoons sour cream

FOR THE FILLING
1/3 cup dark raisins
1 1/2 pounds peaches, peeled, pitted, and each cut into 8 to 10 wedges

1 tablespoon freshly squeezed lemon juice
2 teaspoons Cointreau
1 teaspoon vanilla extract
1/2 teaspoon ground cinnamon
1/4 cup vanilla-flavored sugar (see Note, page 411) or regular sugar
2 tablespoons all-purpose flour
2 tablespoons sugar
1 tablespoon unsalted butter

1. Prepare the pastry crust: In a food processor, combine the flour, salt, sugar, and baking powder, and pulse quickly to mix. Add the butter and pulse briefly until the mixture resembles coarse meal. Add the sour cream and pulse again for 3 to 5 seconds. Check to see if the mixture holds together when it is pressed together. If not, add 1 to 2 tablespoons water and process quickly. Press the dough into a ball, flatten it out a bit, cover with plastic wrap, and refrigerate for about 1 hour.

2. Meanwhile, preheat the oven to 400°F.

3. Prepare the filling: In a small saucepan, cover the raisins with water, and bring to a boil. Remove from the heat and let soak for about 10 minutes. Drain, and pat the raisins dry with paper towels.

4. In a medium-size bowl, combine the raisins, peaches, lemon juice, Cointreau, vanilla extract, cinnamon, and vanilla-flavored sugar. Stir carefully so as not to damage the peaches.

5. Lightly flour a work surface. Unwrap the dough and roll it out to form a 14-inch circle. Transfer the pastry to a baking sheet. Mix the flour with 1 tablespoon of the sugar, and sprinkle this over the dough, leaving a 1½-inch border. Arrange the peach mixture on the dough, leaving a 2-inch edge. Fold the 2-inch edge up over the peaches, all around the circle. Sprinkle the remaining 1 tablespoon sugar over the peaches, and dot with the butter.

6. Bake in the middle of the oven for 35 to 40 minutes. After 25 minutes, if the tart is browning too fast, cover it loosely with a piece of aluminum foil. Remove from the oven and serve warm or at room temperature.

WINE SUGGESTION: SWEET MARSALA

PEAR CUSTARD

This is another example of what Italians call a *dolce al cucchiaio* (DOHL-cheh al koo-k'YEYE-oh), meaning a "dessert you eat with a spoon." Made with pears in season, it is a great and not all that rich ending to a fine meal. It might also be made with apples.

SERVES 6

FOR THE PEARS
1/4 cup sugar
2 ripe pears, Comice if available,
  peeled, cored, and cut into 1/2-
  inch cubes

FOR THE CUSTARD
1 1/2 cups half-and-half
1/2 vanilla bean, split lengthwise
  (see Note)
1/8 teaspoon salt, preferably kosher
1/2 teaspoon vanilla extract
1/3 cup sugar
3 large eggs, lightly beaten

1. In a medium-size saucepan, combine the sugar with 1/2 cup water. Bring to a boil and boil until the sugar is dissolved, about 1 minute. Add the pears and cook until soft, about 5 minutes. Transfer the mixture to a food processor, and puree (or use a hand blender). Set aside.

2. Preheat the oven to 325°F.

3. In a medium-size saucepan, heat the half-and-half with the vanilla bean just to the boiling point. Then remove from the heat. Scrape the seeds out of the vanilla bean and mix them into the half-and-half. Discard the vanilla pod. Add the salt, vanilla extract, and sugar, and stir until the sugar has dissolved.

4. In a medium-size mixing bowl, combine the eggs and about 1/2 cup of the half-and-half mixture, stirring constantly, to temper the eggs so they will not cook. Then, stirring continuously, slowly add the rest of the half-and-half mixture. Stir in the pear puree. Pour the custard mixture into 6 ramekins.

5. Place the ramekins in a roasting pan, and add hot water to the pan, stopping about 1/2 inch from the top of the ramekins. Place the pan in the oven and bake for 35 to 40 minutes, or until a sharp knife inserted into the custard comes out clean. Remove the ramekins from the hot water and let cool on a rack. When they are cool, refrigerate for at least 2 hours before serving.

WINE SUGGESTION:
SWEET MARSALA

NOTE: If a vanilla bean is not available, simply increase the quantity of vanilla extract to 1 1/2 teaspoons.

PEAR PUREE

A great dessert with fresh fruit flavor. Serve this plain or with whipped cream, with a simple cake, or on ice cream. Note that the pears must be ripe and aromatic—otherwise the puree will not be flavorful.

SERVES 4 TO 6

½ cup sugar
1 vanilla bean, split lengthwise
3 ripe pears, peeled, cored, and
  cubed

1 McIntosh apple, peeled, cored,
  and cubed

1. In a medium-size saucepan, combine the sugar with 1½ cups water and the vanilla bean. Bring to a boil, cover, and simmer over low heat for 5 minutes.

2. Add the pears and apple to the saucepan and simmer until tender, 5 to 7 minutes. Remove the vanilla bean and scrape the seeds into the pears; discard the pod. In a food processor or with a hand blender, puree the mixture. Refrigerate to chill.

NOTE: The vanilla bean can be rinsed off, dried, and placed in a jar with sugar to flavor the sugar; let it remain in the sugar for at least 2 weeks.

PEARS IN RED WINE

An Italian is much more likely to end his meal with some cheese and fruit—but if he has a sweet tooth, this lustrous dessert, at its best served slightly warm, will make him very happy. The key is to use a good, not expensive, red wine, such as a Chianti, Montepulciano d'Abruzzo, or Lacrima Christi.

SERVES 4

½ cup sugar
1 cup full-bodied red wine
½ vanilla bean (optional), split
  lengthwise
One 2- to 3-inch cinnamon stick

3 whole cloves
4 ripe pears, such as Bartlett or
  Comice
Vanilla ice cream (optional), for
  serving

1. Preheat the oven to 425°F.

2. In a small baking dish, combine the sugar, wine, vanilla bean if using, cinnamon stick, and cloves.

3. Cut a small, thin slice off the bottom of the pears so that they will stand up in the baking dish without toppling over. Place the pears in the baking dish. Bake, basting the pears every 10 to 15 minutes, for 45 to 60 minutes or until the pears are tender when pierced with a sharp knife. Remove from the oven, let cool, and serve, with vanilla ice cream if desired.

WINE SUGGESTION: PROSECCO

Sirio Maccioni is owner of what has been called the most famous and most celebrated restaurant in the world, Le Cirque 2000 in New York, which, despite its French name and menu, is very much an expression of Maccioni's Tuscan heritage. It was Maccioni who created one of the most trend-setting dishes of the 1970s and 1980s—pasta alla primavera.

Born poor in the town of Montecatini, orphaned in the war, and determined to make his way into the restaurant world, Maccioni worked in Europe, then emigrated to America, where, in 1960, the tall handsome Italian—who looked like an Italian John Wayne—obtained a job as captain at Le Cirque's most celebrated predecessor, the Colony.

"I knew I was in trouble on my first day on the job," he recalls. "Frank Sinatra, Aristotle Onassis, the Duke and Duchess of Windsor, and Cary Grant all called for their regular table. It was my first shift and I took the calls. I asked my boss [owner Gene Cavallero] which tables they liked, and he pointed to one single table in the corner. I started to shake. When I asked, 'What should I do?' Mr. Cavallero just grinned and said, 'Ah, so being a maître d' is not just kissing hands and being suave, eh? Do what you think is best.'"

It was similar advice to what Maccioni's father imparted on the day he died: "Always tell the truth." And so Maccioni did. "Cary Grant was the gentleman you'd expect him to be about the inconvenience," he recalls, "but Onassis accused me of giving the table to Sinatra because he was 'a paisan.' The Windsors were not amused.

"I had to win these people over or lose my job. So I served the Duke and Duchess a little salad, with my compliments, dressed with my own Tuscan virgin olive oil. They loved it so much they forgave me and always asked for me afterwards to make them their salad."

STRUFFOLI

At Christmastime every family in Naples makes or buys *struffoli* (STROO-foh-lee)—little fried honeyed balls of dough that are formed into a wreath or cone shape and sometimes showered with colored candy sprinkles. They can be leaden and heavy if cooked too long in oil that is not hot enough, but when fried with care, they come out light and crispy, even under the mantle of honey. It is essential to use a good-quality honey, which will impart most of the flavor to these little morsels.

SERVES 4 TO 6

1 to 1¼ cups all-purpose flour
¼ teaspoon salt, preferably kosher
1 teaspoon freshly grated lemon
 zest
2 large eggs, room temperature

Corn oil or peanut oil, for frying
1 cup good-quality honey (orange-
 blossom if available)
1 teaspoon vanilla extract

1. Place 1 cup of the flour, the salt, and the lemon zest on a work surface, and mix. Mash the lemon zest into the flour with a fork.

2. Scoop the flour mixture together to form a mound, and make a well in the middle. Add the eggs to the well and start beating them with the fork, incorporating the flour little by little until a stiff dough forms. If it is too sticky, add some of the remaining ¼ cup flour.

3. Knead the dough for 8 to 10 minutes, until smooth. Wrap it in plastic wrap and let it rest for 20 minutes.

4. Unwrap the dough, flatten it to a thickness of ½ inch, and cut it into ½-inch-wide strips. With your hands, roll each strip on the board until it is about ¼ inch in diameter. Repeat with the rest of the dough. Cut each strip into ¼-inch pieces.

5. In a medium-size skillet, pour the oil to a depth of about ½ inch, and heat it to 375°F. (To check that the oil is hot enough, dip a piece of dough into the oil—it should sizzle immediately.) Add about a quarter of the dough pieces to the oil and fry until they are doubled in size and nicely browned, about 2 minutes. Do not crowd the *struffoli* or they will not cook properly. Transfer with a slotted spoon to drain on paper towels. Repeat with the rest of the dough.

6. In a large saucepan, heat the honey and vanilla over medium-low heat; do not boil. Remove the pan from the heat. Add the cooked *struffoli* to the honey and stir with a wooden spoon to coat all the pieces. Stir gently every 2 minutes as the honey cools, until it has thickened and coats the *struffoli*, 10 to 15 minutes.

7. Spoon the *struffoli* onto a plate in a mound or in a donut shape. Cool, and serve.

WINE SUGGESTION: ASTI SPUMANTE

ZEPPOLE

Zeppole (ZEH-poh-lee)—"zeppelins," after their fat, elongated shape—are a ubiquitous street food, especially during Italian-American fairs like the Feast of San Gennaro, which closes the streets of New York's Little Italy while roulette wheels vie with parades of religious statues for attention from the crowds. You smell the sausage and onions sizzling on the grill, the vinegar peppers being stuffed into hero loaves, and the sweet *zeppole* cooking in the deep-fryers.

Frankly, many of the *zeppole* we've had at such festivals have been oily and heavy. Our recipe makes a crispy, light *zeppole*, not unlike a popover—which makes it much easier to eat half a dozen at a pop.

MAKES ABOUT 18 ZEPPOLE

5 tablespoons unsalted butter
Pinch of salt
2 tablespoons sugar
1 cup all-purpose flour

4 large eggs
Vegetable oil, for frying
1/2 cup confectioners' sugar
1/4 teaspoon ground cinnamon

1. In a medium-size saucepan, combine the butter, salt, and sugar with 1 cup water, and bring to a boil. Remove from the heat, and add all the flour at once. Stir vigorously to blend well. The mixture will form a dough. Return the pan to the burner, turn the heat to medium, and stir the dough for another minute. Remove from the heat.

2. Add the eggs, one at a time, to the flour mixture, beating well with a hand-held mixer until incorporated.

3. In a medium-size saucepan or skillet, pour the oil to a depth of 1 inch, and heat it to 375°F. Take two teaspoons and dip them into the hot oil to coat. Then, with one spoon, scoop out a walnut-size piece of dough and carefully drop it into the hot oil, helping to scrape it off with the other spoon. Quickly repeat, dropping in more scoops of dough. Do not crowd the pan, because the dough pieces will double or triple in size as they cook. Fry for about 6 minutes, until the *zeppole* have grown in size, cracked a bit, and are nicely browned. Drain on paper towels. Repeat with the remaining dough, keeping the oil at 375°F.

4. Mix the confectioners' sugar and cinnamon together and place in a sifter. Sift the cinnamon sugar over the *zeppole*. Serve them hot or warm. They cannot be made in advance.

WINE SUGGESTION: SWEET MARSALA

> *If you want to get the best out of an Italian restaurant in America, ask where the owner and the chef are from. If he or she is from the south, the dishes from regions like Calabria, Campania, Puglia, Abruzzo, and Sicily are likely to be among the best on the menu. If the owner is from Liguria or Venice, go with the seafood items. And if he or she is from Tuscany, the kitchen probably grills well.*

DRINKS

DRINKS

Italians do not drink much in the way of cocktails like martinis, Scotch and soda, and margaritas, but they do enjoy *aperitivi* based on their own bittersweet liquors, such as Campari, vermouth, Cynar, and Ramazzotti. Indeed, just about every region has its own range of such mixtures of spices, herbs, and roots—many created centuries ago at monasteries or in apothecaries—which are served over ice before the meal or after the meal as a digestive.

Before World War I, bars of the kind known throughout the United States were uncommon in Italy. But when Prohibition began in 1920, Europeans began to open "American bars" to accommodate the drinking habits of Americans abroad. "Harry's New York Bar" in Paris—where the Bloody Mary (under its original name, Bucket of Blood) and the sidecar were created—and the (unrelated) Harry's Bar in Venice were as much a part of Americans' grand tour of Europe as were the Arc de Triomphe and the Bridge of Sighs, and the bars were famously inserted into the works of F. Scott Fitzgerald

and Ernest Hemingway. Later on, Italian vermouth and anise-flavored liqueurs such as Sambuca, Galliano, and Strega found their way into faddish cocktails. In the 1980s the fashion for all things Italian made the Bellini, created at Harry's Bar, the most sophisticated cocktail in the world for more than a decade.

At Harry's Bar and in many of the best Italian restaurants in the United States, the spirits are often chilled in the refrigerator so as to keep the drinks cold, and in some cases, a whole batch may be made ahead and kept cold until time to pour them.

Adding a little sex appeal to the annual grape stomping in St. Louis's Italian neighborhood known as "The Hill" are local girls Viki Parente and Barbara Frame, pictured in October 1971.

HARVEY WALLBANGER

This once very popular drink was supposedly created at Pancho's Bar in Manhattan Beach, California, and named after a late-1960s surfer named Harvey, who, after the loss of a tournament, consoled himself with several of these cocktails, causing him to bang into the wall at the bar.

MAKES 1 DRINK

2 ounces vodka

1/2 ounce Galliano, plus extra for serving

4 ounces orange juice

1/2 teaspoon sugar

In a cocktail shaker, combine the ingredients with crushed ice and shake until very cold. Then pour into a cocktail glass, floating some extra Galliano on the top.

My father, Eligio "Al" Mariani, used to tell me how one of the most indelible memories of his childhood was having to go get wine for his father during Prohibition. "The wine was made by some guy way down in Brooklyn," he recalled, "and we lived in the Bronx. I was only about twelve, maybe thirteen years old, but I had to get on the subway and go down to this horrible place and follow this scary man down into his dark cellar, where he made the wine. He'd pour it out of a huge barrel into two jugs, then put it into a cardboard box, and I'd pay him, I don't know, fifty cents, and I'd have to lug it back on the subway, all the time thinking I was going to get arrested or mugged, or that I would drop it on the floor of the subway car.

"I did this once a month or so, always scared to death. But after a while I started to wonder what this red wine tasted like, so when I got home one night early I had a glass of it. I immediately got so sick, I threw up on the rug in the living room. Believe me, when my father got home, he gave me a lesson that put me off wine for many years after that."

J.M.

BELLINI

One of the most popular cocktails in the world right now, the Bellini was created at Harry's Bar in Venice in the 1930s. It was not given its name until 1948, when an exposition in honor of the Renaissance artist Giovanni Bellini was held in that city.

According to Arrigo Cipriani, the son of Harry's original owner, the peach puree must be made by using a food mill to produce pulp, which is then pushed through a fine-mesh sieve. White peaches are certainly not easy to find in America, and at Harry's they used to make the drink only when the sweetest white peaches were in season. Nowadays, the Cipriani family packages the puree and ships it around the world to their many restaurants and hotels.

Prosecco, which is a light sparkling wine made in Friuli, is widely available in the United States and is cheaper and more authentic in this drink than California sparkling wine or French Champagne.

MAKES 1 DRINK

*1 ounce white peach puree, well
chilled*

2 ounces Prosecco

Scoop the puree into a tall chilled glass, add the Prosecco, and stir.

TIZIANO

After the white peach season ended in Venice, Harry's Bar stops making Bellinis and switches to Tizianos, which are made with the fresh grape juice of the fall harvest and named after the Renaissance painter Titian, who was famous for his use of a particular purplish-red that this drink's color should approximate.

MAKES 1 DRINK

*1 ounce fresh red grape juice, well
chilled*

2 ounces Prosecco

Pour the grape juice into a tall glass, add the Prosecco, and stir to blend.

ROMA

MAKES 1 DRINK

1 ounce grappa
1 ounce gin
1/2 ounce Sambuca

1/2 ounce dry vermouth
1 cocktail olive, for garnish

In a cocktail shaker, combine the liquid ingredients with crushed ice, strain into a chilled cocktail glass, and garnish with the olive.

NEGRONI

The Negroni is said to be named after Count Emilio Negroni, who concocted the cocktail back in 1935 at the Hotel Casoni in Florence. It's an excellent summer drink.

MAKES 1 DRINK

2 ounces gin
1 ounce Campari
1/2 ounce sweet vermouth

1 strip orange zest

In a cocktail shaker, combine the liquid ingredients with crushed ice and shake until very cold. Strain into a chilled cocktail glass, twist the strip of orange zest over the drink, and add it as a garnish.
If served on the rocks, use a tall cylindrical glass.

A GOOD TIME AND PLACE
TO BE ITALIAN

To be an Italian in the Bronx in the early 1950s seemed the greatest thing in the world. The Yankees dominated baseball, and the Yankees were dominated by players with names like DiMaggio, Rizzuto, and Berra. No one rode a horse faster than Eddie Arcaro. The heavyweight champ of the world was Rocky Marciano, a pug who resembled former New York City mayor Fiorello LaGuardia, was built like Mount Vesuvius, and had a fearsome right hand that he used to pummel his opponents to the canvas. Jake LaMotta, the lightweight champ who could take a vicious beating, sap a guy's strength, then put him through the ropes, lived among us, in a brick house over on Pelham Parkway, and we'd see him out in the front yard with his gorgeous young blond wife, waving at us as we drove by and honked our horn. If we were lucky, he'd do a little mock shuffle, like he'd hit us if we got out of the car.

We even had an Italian mayor—the first since LaGuardia—although Vincent "the Imp" Impelletteri was no more than a political hack, better at attending clambakes than running the city. He was a Tammany appointee, after the former Tammany mayor, an Irishman named Bill O'Dwyer, took an appointment as ambassador to Mexico rather than face corruption charges in New York. Anyway, the Imp was beaten badly in the next election by Bob Wagner.

We had better, truer heroes to look up to, to emulate and to flaunt in the faces of people who thought we were just ditch diggers and spaghetti eaters. What of Arturo Toscanini, the impossibly demanding perfectionist whose work on television, starting in 1948, made him the most famous conductor in the world? He was a master interpreter of Debussy, Strauss, and Beethoven, and he had heroically refused to play under the Nazi and Fascist regimes in the 1930s, moving to New York where the NBC orchestra was created just for him in 1937. People who had never seen a conductor in action, except in Hollywood movies, watched this intense little Italian with the white hair and mustache on television, and it was an image you'd never forget. He was nearsighted and couldn't read the score from the rostrum, so he'd memorize every note and conduct entirely from memory.

Toscanini was a particular hero in our house, not only for his supreme virtuosity but for the unalloyed passion and emotion he brought to the music of Italian and non-Italian composers alike. My father used to love to tell the story of how Toscanini, frustrated by a famous Wagnerian soprano who kept missing her cues, rushed to the music stand, grabbed her by her enormous bosoms, and screamed, "If these were only brains!"

My mother even bought my father a baton so that he could stand in the middle of our living room and conduct Puccini's Turandot or Beethoven's Third, imitating Toscanini's every thrust, calming the brass, bringing the violins to a feverish pitch, and holding the orchestra in his arms as he brought them through the finale.

Then there was Ezio Pinza, the handsome, patrician baritone who took Broadway audiences by storm with his performance in Rodgers and Hammerstein's South Pacific in 1950. My parents saw the show five times, and my father, who loved to be told he looked a bit like Pinza, would conduct the music at parties as his dentist friend Bill Verlin sang "Some Enchanted Evening" at the top of his lungs.

A younger, even more handsome Italian was Alfred Arnold Cocozza, a Philadelphia kid who took the stage under the name Mario Lanza and became a Hollywood tenor, even playing Caruso himself on screen in 1951.

The Hit Parade was full of Italian voices—Sinatra, Como, LaRosa, Damone, and a few who had anglicized their names, like Bennett (born Tony DeBenedetto) and Martin (Dino Martino). Julie LaRosa had a enormous hit with an old Neapolitan gimmick song called "Eh Cumpari," sung in dialect and incomprehensible to just about everyone. Tony Bennett's big hit "Rags to Riches" became an Italian-American immigrant's anthem, and Dean Martin's "That's Amore" was a joyous expression of everything that was good and beautiful about being an Italian.

With his perfectly cut black hair slicked back over his ears and curls tumbling down his forehead, his thick eyebrows and dark eyes, a nose like a Roman boxer's, his dark Sicilian complexion, full mouth, and gleaming white teeth, Dean Martin played off the Jewish-American schlemiel comedy of his partner Jerry Lewis, and when Dean started to sing in a voice that was deep, husky, smooth, seductive, and gay, American women went crazy, the way they had over Sinatra a decade before.

Other Italian singers milked "That's Amore" for its sentimentality and made it sappy. They exaggerated the Italian words, blubbered through the lyrics, swayed back and forth like gorillas, and played the dumb dago to the hilt.

But Dean Martin knew how to inflect the song with just enough lilt, throwing in a few extra vowels, playing with the song's lyrics but putting them over with exuberance and brio so that it made people listening to him wish they were Italian.

In the candy stores, factories, and living rooms, the radios blared pop music—girl ballads like Jo Stafford's "You Belong to Me," Gogi Grant's "The Wayward Wind," and Patti Page's "The Tennessee Waltz." A cute Irish girl named Rosemary Clooney had major hits doing mock-Italian songs with names like "Botch-a-Me" and "Come On-a My House," whose lyrics held out the sweet, salacious promise of "figs and things" and "everything."

Every Italian could sing and did sing, and street corners in the Bronx were stages for what later came to be called "doo-wop" groups, trios and quartets whose intricate wailing a cappella renditions of old standards and new music formed the basis of what was to become urban rock-and-roll.

Many of these groups became famous, and one of the most famous of them all came from the Belmont section of the Bronx, after which they took their name—Dion & The Belmonts. Their biggest hits drew on puberty's quivering plaints like "Why Must I Be A Teenager in Love?" The doo-wop groups competed with each other for the sweetest sound, the most soulful lament, and the most intricate scat line, like the Belmonts' dazzlingly baroque "Wop! Wop! Wop-bop-a-looma-awop-bang-bang" on "I Wonder Why."

There was always music in the air around Belmont, which was largely Neapolitan, isolated to this day from the blight that began to encroach on Fordham in the 1950s. From the windows came the strains of old Neapolitan folk songs like "O sole mio!" and "Torna a Surriento" played on old phonographs and wooden radios. Most of these songs were unrelievedly melancholy, many of them expressing a despair at never seeing Naples again. Others were tied to great moments in Neapolitan history, like "Funiculi, Funicula," which commemorated the opening of a railway up the side of Mount Vesuvius.

All of these were known and sung by the vendors along Arthur Avenue, which, crisscrossed by 187th Street, formed the heart of Belmont. This was where all the food stores were—the pasta shops, the cheese shops, the pizzerias, meat and seafood markets, fruit and vegetable stands. Every vendor sang as he worked, plopping lemons into a paper bag to the waltz time of "Santa Lucia." Another would croon the lilting refrain of "Oj Mari" while slicing prosciutto on a machine—back and forth, as he looked across the counter at a pretty girl. He would gently take a thin slice and place it daintily in her hand, shaking his head back and forth and singing.

All along Arthur Avenue the air smelled like garlic and tomato, fresh basil, the aroma of pizza from Mario's, where all the Yankees came to eat, and the inebriating smell of breads baking in the ovens of Addeo & Sons and Madonia Brothers.

There was also the stench of the live poultry market, where children goaded each other to enter, hold their noses, and force themselves to watch the slaughter of the screeching chickens and rabbits. The owner would tie their legs with a string, slit the neck, and cut down through the chest and stomach as the rabbit's high-pitched squeal rang through the stinking room. You could see the steam come out of the innards and the guts glistening with clean, warm blood.

Although my family lived several miles from Arthur Avenue, my father would go there almost every Thursday afternoon, when he finished his office hours early. For him it was a return to his old neighborhood, for he'd grown up on Cambrelling Avenue, just off Arthur Avenue, and though his people had come from the province of Abruzzi on the Adriatic, he understood and enjoyed hearing the Neapolitan melodies as he shopped among the vendors. He'd double park the Chevy, signal the most proximate vendor where he'd be in case anyone had to get out, then go into the salumeria to buy some prosciutto, which he demanded be sliced thin enough so he "could read Il Progresso through it." Then next door to Madonia Brothers for an enormous round loaf of crusty Italian bread straight out of the oven.

While the girl wrapped the bread in white paper and tied it with a string, he'd point to the light, wafer-like biscuits called savoiardi and say he'd take a dozen.

Last stop was the cheese shop to buy a fresh mozzarella in water. Heavy, creamy, and glistening, with the heft and shape of a woman's breast, the mozz were kept in salted water to keep them fresh. My father would specify which one he wanted, and the woman would ladle it out onto a piece of wax paper, then place it in a paper carton.

By the time my father arrived home, I'd already had lunch. If it was during the school year, the bread, prosciutto, and mozzarella would be my snack at three o'clock. But in summer, I waited for my father to arrive back at our apartment at around two o'clock, and I'd always ask, "Did you bring some mozz home?" and he'd kid around, scrunch up his face like he was going to say he'd forgotten, then bring out the bag from behind his back.

He'd take off his jacket and had and lay them on the living room couch. Then he'd turn on the Victrola and put a 78 rpm record on the turntable. It would be Toscanini conducting *Capriccio Italienne* or Carmen Cavallaro playing the *Toselli Serenade* on the piano. My father would then unwrap the mozzarella carefully, and with the same surgical precision and gentleness he used in treating his patients, he'd slice the bread thin enough to absorb the flavors of the meat and cheese but thick enough not to turn soggy. He'd unwrap the rosy, salty slices of prosciutto that had been laid out in impeccably neat layers between sheets of paper, and with a fork he would then deftly curl back a single slice of prosciutto. The light would shine through it. Then he cut into the yellow-white mozzarella that oozed milk and was still a little warm when you bit into it. The flavors were the same week after week.

My father would sit there in his shirt and tie, drinking a beer with his meal. I ate slowly, stretching out the time, and we talked about nothing in particular. But I always felt closer to him on those days than at any other time in my life. He would sit at the kitchen table, bite off a morsel of his sandwich, take a sip of beer, then close his eyes and raise his hand. "Listen," he said very softly, as Toscanini lulled the orchestra into a slow, sad movement. "That's very . . . very Italian."

—J.M.

MONTGOMERY

Another Harry's Bar drink, this is basically just a martini made with fifteen parts gin to one part dry vermouth, the ratio enjoyed by Ernest Hemingway, who said that it was the same ratio of British troops to the enemy that Field Marshall Montgomery liked to have when facing the Germans in battle.

MAKES ABOUT 6 DRINKS

15 ounces gin
1 ounce dry vermouth

Lemon zest, for garnish

In a large pitcher, combine the gin and vermouth over ice cubes and shake until cold. Strain into another pitcher and place in the coldest part of the refrigerator until ready to serve. Garnish each drink with a twist of lemon zest.

MILANO A ROMA

The name of this drink supposedly derives from its being a specialty of the bar car trains that ran from Rome to Milan. It is really nothing more than a Campari and soda, but the storage of the Campari in the freezer gives it a remarkable liqueur-ish consistency.

MAKES 1 DRINK

2 ounces Campari
Sparkling water

Lemon zest, for garnish

Place the bottle of Campari in the freezer and chill until it develops a thick, liqueur-like consistency, at least 2 hours. Pour the Campari into a cocktail glass, add a dash of sparkling water, stir briefly, and garnish with a twist of lemon zest.

LITTLE ITALY

MAKES 1 DRINK

2 ounces Amaretto
5 ounces orange juice

1 orange slice, for garnish

In a highball glass, pour the Amaretto and orange juice over ice cubes.
Stir, and garnish with an orange slice.

DI NUOVO

The term means "something new," and the drink was created at Yellowfinger's, one of the first singles' hangouts on New York's Upper East Side in the 1960s and '70s. It was one of those deceptively innocent cream-based drinks popular in those less-than-innocent decades.

MAKES 1 DRINK

1 ounce black raspberry liqueur
³/4 ounce Fra Angelico
¹/4 cup pureed raspberries

¹/2 cup heavy cream
Chopped hazelnuts, for garnish
Fresh berries, for garnish

In a blender, combine the raspberry liqueur, Fra Angelico, raspberries, and cream, add 1 cup crushed ice, and blend until smooth. Pour into an 8-ounce glass, and garnish with the hazelnuts and berries.

Many Italian-Americans got into the manufacture and delivery of bottled beverages, as shown in this photo of a factory and truck in western Pennsylvania in the 1930s.

CAFFÈ AMARETTO

MAKES 1 DRINK

1 cup hot brewed coffee
1 ounce Amaretto
1 ounce coffee liqueur

1 tablespoon whipped cream
1 coffee bean, for garnish

Into the cup of hot coffee pour the Amaretto and coffee liqueur. Top with the whipped cream, and garnish with a single coffee bean.

AMERICANO

This drink dates back to 1880, when someone named Domenico Marenco (whose name may have eventually been corrupted into "Americano" for this drink) created it in Cuneo. The name of the drink may also refer to its popularity among Americans who began visiting Italy after the turn of the century.

MAKES 1 DRINK

1 ounce Campari
2 ounces sweet vermouth

Sparkling water
1 orange slice, for garnish

In a cocktail shaker, combine the Campari and vermouth with crushed ice, and shake until very cold. Pour over ice cubes into a cocktail glass, add a splash of sparkling water, and garnish with an orange slice.

AMARETTO STINGER

MAKES 1 DRINK

2 ounces Amaretto   1 sprig fresh mint, for garnish
1 ounce white crème de menthe

In a cocktail shaker, combine the Amaretto and crème de menthe with
ice cubes, and shake until very cold. Strain into an old-fashion glass,
and garnish with a sprig of mint.

My aunt, Marilyn Sofia, has always been the most dramatic member of our family,
which fitted her career as an operatic soprano. And while she never considered
herself a great cook, she remembers stories of her grandmother's kitchen.

"I only knew my grandmother and grandfather when they were older, but my
mother, who was born in America, told me about how they had one foot in the old
country and one in the new. Each morning my grandmother would make my grandfather a good-sized veal chop and give him a glass of whiskey, which would fortify
him for the tough workday ahead. He was a plasterer—he even worked on the Metropolitan Opera House—and when he came home he was so tired. The moment he'd
come through the door, she'd sit him down and she'd pour him another whiskey; then
dinner. And, because of the way she'd been raised, she would never, ever bring up
any problems of the day while he ate. Maybe after he ate a little and drank his
whiskey, she'd ease into something, but for her the man had to relax without any
further stress put on him as he ate.

"And they ate well. My mother said they ate a lot of cabbage, and my grandfather would always complain that it was 'not shiny enough,' so his wife would put
more lard into it. But on weekends even Grandpa started to become a bit more
American. He would announce on Sunday morning that the family would have those
hard rolls and they must have butter! Absolutely! No lard, but American butter!"

J.M.

SOURCES FOR ITALIAN FOODS

While even the small-town supermarket now carries a wide array of Italian products, some Italian ingredients are available only at the better food stores in major American cities. Mail order is another source, and many purveyors now have web sites. Here's a list of those we recommend.

CALIFORNIA

AIDELLS SAUSAGE COMPANY
1625 Alvarado Street
San Leandro, California 94577
877-AIDELLS
www.aidells.com
Myriad varieties of sausage from one of the most knowledgeable companies in the field.

THE CHEESE STORE
419 North Beverly Drive
Beverly Hills, California 90210
800-547-1515
310-278-2855
www.cheesestorebh.com
Thirty years old and still offering an extraordinary array of cheeses—more than five hundred—along with wine and other delicacies.

CORTI BROTHERS
5810 Folsom Boulevard
Sacramento, California 75819
800-509-3663
One of the great emporiums for wine and very special, rare food products from Italy. Ask to receive their newsletter.

DOMINGO'S ITALIAN GROCERY
17548 Ventura Boulevard
Encino, California 91316
818-981-4466
Good selection of cheeses and sausages, with some Sicilian specialties.

FUSANO CALIFORNIA VALLEY
SPECIALTY OLIVE COMPANY
P.O. Box 11576
Piedmont, California 94611
800-916-5483
510-530-3516
All kinds of olives and homemade extra-virgin olive oil, all packaged with beautiful labels.

MOLINARI & SONS
1401 Yosemite Avenue
San Francisco, California 94124
415-822-5555
www.molinarisalame.com
Since 1896 one of the premier purveyors of every kind of Italian sausage and salami.

VIVANDE, INC.
2125 Fillmore Street
San Francisco, California 95115
415-346-4430
Carlo Middone's reverie of great Italian and other foods. The prepared foods are first-rate and quite special.

DISTRICT OF COLUMBIA

LITTERI'S
517-519 Morse Street, Northeast
Washington, DC 20002
202-544-0184
*Opened in the 1930s, Litteri's is
hidden away but always jammed with
people coming for the terrific pastas
and cheeses.*

ILLINOIS

GEPPERTH'S MEAT MARKET
1964 North Halsted Street
Chicago, Illinois 60614
773-549-3883
*Sawdust on the floor and a friendly
welcome at the counter. Gepperth's
brings in excellent free-range chicken,
sells Provimi veal, and makes its own
sausages.*

MICHIGAN

ZINGERMAN'S
422 Detroit Street
Ann Arbor, Michigan 48104
888-636-8162
www.zingermans.com
*Fine olive oils, balsamic vinegars, and
imported pastas.*

NEW JERSEY

CENTO FINE FOODS
100 Cento Boulevard
Thorofare, New Jersey 08086
732-651-7600
www.cento.com
*Strictly mail order, not a store, this im-
porting company carries great Italian
pastas from small producers.*

D'ARTAGNAN
280 Wilson Avenue
Newark, New Jersey 07105
800-DARTAGNAN
www.dartagnan.com
*For its foie gras alone, both domestic
and imported, this is nirvana. But it is
also one of the best sources for game
meats.*

NEW YORK

AGATA E VALENTINA
1505 First Avenue
New York, New York 10021
212-452-0690
*A great and beautiful all-around
Italian grocery, specializing in Sicilian
foods.*

BALDUCCI'S
424 Sixth Avenue
New York, New York 10011
800-225-3822
www.balducci.com
*Very famous for everything from its
cheeses and meats to prepared foods
ready for shipping. They send out a
very extensive catalog.*

BIANCARDI'S
2350 Arthur Avenue
Bronx, New York 10458
718-733-4058
*This bright butcher's shop is where
many of New York's greatest chefs buy
their meat. They can order anything
for you with a few days' notice.*

CITARELLA
2135 Broadway
New York, New York 10023
212-874-0383
Once known as a leading seafood store,

Citarella now produces its own pre-pared food, great pastas, and sausages.

IDEAL CHEESE SHOP
942 First Avenue
New York, New York 10022
800-382-0109
212-688-7579
www.idealcheese.com
One of the widest selections anywhere of the world's best cheeses.

DEAN & DELUCA
560 Broadway
New York, New York 10012
800-221-7714
www.deandeluca.com
Balducci's biggest competitor, now with several branches around the eastern U.S. An extraordinary array of unusual foods.

MANGANARO'S
488 Ninth Avenue
New York, New York 10018
800-4-SALAMI
212-563-5331
www.manganaros.com
For a century now, this has been the best Italian grocer in New York's Midtown, beloved for its array of everything from olive oils to antipasti.

MIKE'S DELI
2344 Arthur Avenue
Bronx, New York 10458
718-295-5033
www.arthuravenue.com
Our all-time favorite salumeria for sausage, cheese, olives, and many prepared foods. A grandly ebullient place to shop.

OREGON

DUNDEE ORCHARDS
P.O. Box 327
Dundee, Oregon 97115
503-538-8105
Good source for the finest American hazelnuts, including roasted and skinned varieties.

PENNSYLVANIA

JAMISON FARM
171 Jamison Lane
Latrobe, Pennsylvania 15650
800-237-5262
www.jamisonfarm.com
Many of America's finest restaurants buy their spring and baby lamb from Jamison's.

RHODE ISLAND

KENYON'S CORNMEAL COMPANY
Box 221, Usquepaugh
West Kingston, Rhode Island 02892
401-783-4054
www.kenyansgristmill.com
Real stone-ground cornmeal, rye, and whole-wheat flours.

TEXAS

THE MOZZARELLA COMPANY
2944 Elm Street
Dallas, TX 75226
800-798-2954
214-741-4072
www.mozzco.com
A pioneer in fresh Italian cheeses since 1982. Always shipped in impeccable condition.

Although the pasta may not have been "al dente" and the sauce was unlike any made in an Italian-American kitchen, Chef Boy-Ar-Dee canned and boxed spaghetti dinners were one of the most successful mass-market products featuring Italian-American food.

VERMONT

VERMONT BUTTER AND CHEESE
COMPANY
Pitman Road, P.O. Box 95
Websterville, Vermont 05678
800-884-6287
www.vtbutterandcheeseco.com
Excellent source for good butter and mascarpone cheese.

VIRGINIA

SUMMERFIELD FARM
10044 James Monroe Highway
Culpeper, Virginia 22701
800-898-3276
540-547-9600
Some of the finest veal in the world comes from this farm, where all the veal is milk-fed.

Magic for meatless menus... real Italian-style
CHEF BOY-AR-DEE® Spaghetti Dinner

This 12-minute dinner features a mushroom sauce prepared just as in the Italian Lake Country—plus quick-cooking spaghetti and tasty cheese. Makes 3 hearty, delectable servings for about 15¢ each. Treat your family this week!

Complete in one box

Now available in Canada

IMAGE ACKNOWLEDGEMENTS

The images in this book were provided with the permission and courtesy of the following:

American Advertising Museum: 155, 436
Archive Photos: 130
Barbetta Restaurant: 251
Beech-Nut: 155
Bettmann/CORBIS: 32, 199, 249, 378
Charles O'Rear/CORBIS: (Robert Mondavi photo) 216
Biancardi's: 306
Boston Public Library, Print Department: 103, 231, 266, 369, 372
The Bostonian Society/Old State House: 49
Fior d'Italia Restaurant: 92
Ghirardelli Chocolate Company: 387, 392
Library and Archives Division, Historical Society of Western Pennsylvania, Pittsburgh, PA: 430
International Home Foods, Inc. (Chef Boy-ar-dee): 436
Italian-American Collection, Special Collections, The University Library, The University of Illinois at Chicago: 60, 167, 222, 305
Library of Congress: 55, 68, 77, 98, 108, 175, 292, 330, 350
Mamma Leone's: 14
Galina Mariani: 260, 273, 365
Ming Tsai: 280
Minnesota Historical Society: 86
Globe–Democrat Archives, St. Louis Mercantile Library at the University of Missouri – St. Louis: 302, 357, 420
The Waldorf-Astoria: 343
The Walt Disney Company: 13

INDEX

C

E

F

G

N, O

P